Stories of Philosophy

Stories of Philosophy

An Introduction Through
Original Fiction and Discussion

THOMAS D. DAVIS

Oxford   New York
OXFORD UNIVERSITY PRESS

Oxford University Press is a department of the University of Oxford. It
furthers the University's objective of excellence in research, scholarship,
and education by publishing worldwide. Oxford is a registered trade mark of
Oxford University Press in the UK and certain other countries.

Published in the United States of America by Oxford University Press
198 Madison Avenue, New York, NY 10016, United States of America.

For titles covered by Section 112 of the US Higher Education
Opportunity Act, please visit www.oup.com/us/he for the
latest information about pricing and alternate formats.

Library of Congress Cataloging-in-Publication Data
Names: Davis, Thomas D., 1941-, author.
Title: Stories of philosophy : an introduction through original fiction and
    discussion / Thomas D. Davis.
Description: 1 [edition]. | New York : Oxford University Press, 2019. |
    Includes bibliographical references.
Identifiers: LCCN 2019006430 (print) | LCCN 2018041099 (ebook) |
    ISBN 9780190903695 (pbk.) | ISBN 9780190903718 (eBook)
Subjects: LCSH: Philosophy—Study and teaching. | Philosophy in literature. |
    Ethics in literature. | Fiction—History and criticism.
Classification: LCC B52 .D38 2019 (ebook) | LCC B52 (print) | DDC 100—dc23
LC record available at https://lccn.loc.gov/2019006430

9 8 7 6 5 4 3 2 1
LSC Communications, United States of America

To Diane,
again and as always,
with love and thanks

CONTENTS

4. Freedom and Responsibility   169

5. God and Suffering   223

The Evolution of this Text and How It Works

I n an episode called "The Lonely" from the classic TV series *Twilight Zone*, a prisoner is exiled on a deserted asteroid. For company he is given a sophisticated robot who looks and feels and behaves just like a real woman. As time goes by, the robot and the prisoner become lovers and friends. Then one day an official arrives, telling the prisoner he has been reprieved. But there is no room in the shuttle for the robot, and the prisoner refuses to leave her—in spite of the official's arguments that she is "just a machine." To illustrate his argument, the official shoots the female, who falls down, wires springing out of her chest, crying "no" in a voice that winds down like a broken tape recorder. "See?" says the official triumphantly, but the prisoner just stares down at the robot, not sure how to react. We viewers are not sure how to react either. Does the fact of the wires make ridiculous every feeling that the prisoner felt for the robot? Do the wires mean she had no moral right to exist? Is she supposed to be "just a machine" because she had no real feelings? But how could we be certain of that, since feelings can be experienced only by the creature having them?

In *Brave New World*, after a terrible period of war and famine and social upheaval, the world is altered through embryo engineering, early conditioning, and drugs to be a stable, happy world in which such things as art, inquiry, and individuality no longer fit. John, the "Savage," a holdover from the old world, is appalled by this new world. "I want God, I want poetry, I want real danger, I want freedom, I want . . . the right to be unhappy." Mustapha Mond, the "Controller," says he doesn't much like this new world either but thinks it's the right one from a moral standpoint. He had the choice of giving people misery and its compensations or happiness and stability. Most people, Mond claims, would prefer happiness and stability, and that's what the new world gives them. Who's right, Mond or the Savage? On the one hand, it seems wrong of Mond to take away people's free will. On the other hand, how much suffering is free will really worth? Are we so sure people have free will in the first place? It also seems wrong of Mond to pick a world with no art or individuality. And yet, don't most people avoid art like the plague? Aren't most people trying desperately to be just like everybody else? Isn't happiness what most people really care about?

It was dramatized questions such as these that got me interested in philosophy and led me to take my first philosophy course. It was a course I almost flunked, in part because it went against my temperament at the time. I wanted to throw around great (and mostly fuzzy) ideas; my instructor wanted me to define my terms and present careful arguments. I wanted to read philosophical fiction; my instructor wanted me to struggle through the aged exposition of such thinkers as Plato and Descartes.

I could have thrown up my hands and said philosophy is boring and gone on to something else. But I still had those questions I wanted answered, and I saw that I couldn't pretend to any seriousness in my answers unless I was willing to do some hard thinking. I realized that exposure to some of the best minds in philosophy could help me with that kind of thinking.

Eventually I went to graduate school, where I had my first teaching experiences as an assistant in another instructor's course. We'd try to discuss Descartes's question as to whether or not we can be sure we're not now dreaming, and the students would shake their heads as if that was the most insane question they'd ever heard. Then outside the class I'd hear one of those same students say, "Hey, man, did you see that great *Star Trek* last night where the guy was dreaming his whole life?" and I realized some crucial connection was being missed. When I started doing my own teaching, I'd preface each topic with some piece of dramatic literature, and that helped to make the connection, but in most of the pieces I could find there wasn't enough philosophy to get us deeply into the topic. Having done some writing myself, I decided to create my own stories. Hence the evolution of this textbook.

The tough stuff is here—the analysis and arguments and careful thinking. But the point of this text is to start you off with the wonder, the drama, and the fun of philosophy, which is what will sustain you through the harder material. It has worked for a lot of students; I hope it works for you.

The text consists of six chapters: Logic; Appearance and Reality; the Nature of the Mind; Freedom and Responsibility; God and Suffering; and Morality. In each chapter, there are two stories that dramatize aspects of the topic, followed by a discussion of the topic that refers back to details in the stories. For instance, the story, "Philosophy Is Murder: A Nebuchadnezzar Hulk Mystery," requires you to learn some bits of symbolic logic in order to work out the solution to the mystery; the discussion of deductive and inductive reasoning that follows uses examples of reasoning used by the detective. In "The Land of Certus," a medieval character who stumbles on a land where good and evil are marked by lights must decide what to do when his feelings and the lights disagree. The discussion uses this dilemma to explore questions about how we're to decide what's right and wrong and what roles reason and emotion play in this process.

Each story starts with a *Preview* to give you some idea of what to look for as you read; then the story is followed by questions. The discussion sections start with a list of things you should learn from the chapter. Within the discussions are frequent *Let's Review* questions to help you make sure you're clear about certain essential elements of the discussion to that point. The most important concepts in the discussion are in bold print; the concepts are defined at the end of the chapter in the order in which they appeared in the discussion. Definitions, Questions, Notes, and Further Materials follow.

What Is Philosophy?

What is **philosophy**, this subject we'll be studying? The *Oxford Living Dictionary* defines philosophy as follows:

> The study of the fundamental nature of knowledge, reality, and existence, especially when considered as an academic discipline; a particular system of philosophical thought ([e.g.,] "the philosophies of Plato and Aristotle"); and the study of the theoretical basis of a particular branch of knowledge or experience ([e.g.,] "the philosophy of science").

Philosophy, mingled with religion, starts out as the broadest area of thought there is, covering virtually everything, asking questions such as: Why do crops grow? Why does rain come? Why do we get sick? Who are the beings in charge of things? What do they want of us, and how can we please them so that they will help rather than hurt us? What is the world of dreams in which ancestors appear but also we see demons? What happens to us after we die?

Gradually, sciences appear, first in rudimentary, then more sophisticated, forms, sciences with their special methodologies and growing bodies of systematic knowledge. In a way, philosophical questions are the "leftovers," those that haven't found the right framework within which to develop an appropriate science that can produce generally accepted answers based on reason and evidence. If someone says that philosophy never gives answers, you can respond that it has given us all sorts of answers— in the form of physics, biology, psychology, and the other sciences that were generated out of what was once called "natural philosophy." There are legitimate questions about whether or not the leftover questions of philosophy will ever be answered. Some of them are pretty profound, dealing with the nature of morality and the ultimate nature of reality (metaphysics rather than physics). However, we won't know if they can be answered unless we try, and anyway most of them are questions we ask ourselves. Also, asking those questions can generate some weird and exciting ideas, such as whether or not we might be living in a computer simulation run by a much more advanced civilization.

Another way of saying that philosophers study the "theoretical basis" of other branches of knowledge is to say that they are like the proverbial backseat drivers, looking over the shoulders of others to see what they're doing and offering critiques. (The ancient Greek philosopher Socrates likened philosophers with their constant questioning to "gadflies," flies that bite and annoy.) Thus, in the philosophy of psychology or biology or physics, we get philosophers asking, "What are your basic assumptions?"; "How is that one justified?" (Note that philosophy also tries to be *self-reflective*, asking about the justifiability of its own methods.)

It wasn't only sciences that got spun off from the earliest questions humans asked. Various religions emerged that codified a set of basic answers to life's questions and went on to develop certain institutions and practices based on their creeds. Philosophers are likely to poke and prod at those creeds, saying such things as, "Those arguments of yours date back 400 or 1400 years: Are you sure they still work in the light of modern logic and science?"

Four of the major areas of philosophy are metaphysics, epistemology, value theory (including ethics), and logic or reasoning. Let's discuss them one at a time.

Metaphysics is the study of reality. It asks questions such as: What is the ultimate nature of reality? Is it one or many? Is it mental or physical, or both? What is the mind, and how is it related to the body? Is there a soul? Is there life after death? Is there a God? Do I have free will, or are my thoughts and actions determined? (The word ***ontology***, sometimes used in connection with metaphysics, has to do with the fundamental types of things one thinks exist. For instance, a materialist's ontology would consist only of material things.)

Epistemology is the theory of knowledge. For any claim put forward by metaphysics, epistemology would ask, "How do we know that?" In fact, "Do we really know that at all?" More generally, it asks: "What is involved in the claim that I know this or that? What is knowledge? What might be legitimate paths to knowledge? Reasoning? Sense perception? Faith?"

Value theory (sometimes called **axiology**) deals with values as they appear in everyday decisions about what is and is not worthwhile, as well as in ethics, political philosophy, and aesthetics. Philosophical ethics is divided between normative ethics and metaethics. **Normative ethics** asks questions about what is right or wrong and what our obligations are to ourselves and others; it also covers general normative theories that try to answer such questions. **Metaethics** deals with questions and theories about the fundamental nature of normative ethics. Are some ethical judgments true? If so, how can we know which ones are true? If not, is ethics completely subjective, or does rationality still have a place in our ethical reasoning?

Logic is the study of reasoning, attempting to distinguish good reasoning from bad and to systematize the results. It deals with formal and informal logic, with deductive and inductive logic, and with general guidelines to reasoning well and avoiding logical fallacies.

Definitions

1. *Philosophy*: The study of the fundamental nature of knowledge, reality, and existence.
2. *Metaphysics*: The study of reality.

3. *Ontology*: A branch of metaphysics dealing with the fundamental kinds of things that exist.
4. *Epistemology*: The theory of knowledge.
5. *Value theory (axiology)*: The theory that deals with values as they appear in everyday decisions and in such disciplines as ethics and aesthetics.
6. *Normative ethics*: The branch of philosophy that asks questions about what is right or wrong, formulating general theories that try to answer such questions.
7. *Metaethics*: The branch of ethics that deals with questions about the fundamental nature of normative ethics, such as: Are some ethical judgments true? If so, how can we know which ones are true?
8. *Logic*: The study of reasoning that attempts to distinguish good reasoning from bad.

Acknowledgments

For their support and good advice, I would like to thank Robert Miller, Sydney Keen, Anna Deen, Claudia Dukeshire, and the following reviewers:

Mark Alfano, *Delft University of Technology*
Guy Axtell, *Radford University*
Stephen Daniel, *Texas A&M University*
Debby Hutchins, *South Texas College*
Chris Kramer, *Rock Valley College*
Karl Stocker, *Eastern Connecticut State University*
Ted Stolze, *Cerritos College*

About the Author

THOMAS D. DAVIS received his PhD in philosophy from the University of Michigan. He has taught at Grinnell College, the University of Redlands and De Anza college. He has published three novels, a short comic play about Jean Paul Sartre, called "Dear Jean," and an ethics text, *Contemporary Moral and Social Issues: An Introduction Through Original Fiction, Discussion and Readings*.

Stories of Philosophy

CHAPTER 1

Logic
Fiction

READING 1: Philosophy Is Murder: A Nebuchadnezzar Hulk Mystery

PREVIEW

In this story, the detective solves the murder of a logician by deciphering a clue written in logical symbolism on the victim's desk pad.

* Reason your way to the solution of the mystery while you learn a little symbolic logic.

I've pulled plenty of stunts on Nebuchadnezzar Hulk over the years. You might say that's one of my jobs. Hulk is a genius, but he's as lazy and contrary as he is smart. Someone has to make sure that he keeps working. After all, Hulk is the sole support of a four-story house filled with hundreds of expensive orchids, a plant nurse who feeds the orchids, a French chef who feeds Hulk, and an assistant detective—me—who is no genius but is ingenious, particularly at pulling stunts that get Hulk working.

I must say I hesitated this time. To admit to Hulk's office, unannounced, a gaudily dressed six-foot blonde carrying a poodle, a nightclub dancer wanting help for her underpaid philosophy-professor husband—that seemed to be going a bit far. But I decided Hulk needed a real shocker. A week before, with our bank balance below six figures, Hulk had returned a $50,000 retainer because the twelve directors of the Global Corporation had had the audacity to insist that he come to their offices rather than

1

the other way around. I don't begrudge Hulk his idiosyncrasies, like never leaving the house on business and never missing his four hours a day in the plant rooms. But he's made exceptions to his rules in the past, and he should have made an exception for the Global Corporation. Now I would let him know quite vividly what he could expect in the way of cases if he continued to be so stubborn.

Hulk was sitting at his desk, reading *Principia Mathematica*, when I ushered the dancer into the office.

"Sir, allow me to introduce Miss Gloria Lovely. That's 'L-O-V-E-L-Y.' Actually, that's her stage name. She is a nightclub dancer currently working at the Starlight Lounge. She is married to Heinrich Bergmann, an existentialist, who is suspected of murder, and she is here to engage your services on his behalf. I told her we didn't have a case at the moment, and you'd probably be happy to have the work."

Mrs. Bergmann couldn't have done better if I'd coached her. She shifted the poodle to her left arm, extended her right hand to the man who avoids shaking hands with anyone, and murmured:

"It's a pleasure to meet you, Mr. Hulk. Or may I call you Nebuchadnezzar?"

I thought for a moment Hulk's jaw was going to drop, but he managed to stop it. He stared at Mrs. Bergmann for a moment, keeping his hands on his book, and then slowly lifted his seventh of a ton out of his chair.

"Madame. My assistant, Mr. Crocker, has been known to dabble in the inane before but never in the occult. Allow me to say that you are an extraordinary creature. Now, if you will excuse me. Arnie, be sure this woman is not paid from office funds for her acting here today. As you are so cleverly reminding me, they are not up to the challenge."

He was halfway to the door when her fist struck the desk. "Mr. Hulk!" Hulk turned around, his eyebrows raised in surprise.

"Obviously, you and Mr. Crocker regard me as a joke," she went on angrily, "but this certified check for $10,000 is no joke. Nor is my husband's situation. He is in serious trouble and needs your help!"

"Indeed," said Hulk. "If this is a performance, Mrs. Bergmann, it is most certainly a commanding one. But don't you think the existentialist touch strains credulity?"

Her voice softened a bit now that she had his attention.

"My husband, Mr. Hulk, is a professor at Fountain College. His specialty is existentialism, and he has published several articles on Sartre's early work. He has maintained to his colleagues that his marrying me was Gide's *acte gratuit*, a gratuitous act demonstrating his complete freedom of choice. It is a conceit of his to which I don't object, since we have a good marriage in any case. My husband's interests in life are not purely intellectual. And it helps that I am not as devoid of intelligence as you seem to think I am. I have a degree in philosophy from Fountain, but I happen to find what I do much more enjoyable, not to say lucrative, than teaching. It goes without saying that my tastes are not terribly conventional."

"You say that your husband is suspected of murder. Whose murder?"

"Professor William Lanchaster, chairman of the philosophy department at Fountain, was shot to death in his study at his home last Thursday evening."

Hulk looked at Mrs. Bergmann, then at me, then back at her. He nodded slightly and started back to his desk.

"Arnie, please find a place for that dog other than this office and the kitchen. Mrs. Bergmann, please take a seat. What may I offer you to drink?"

Obviously, my joke had backfired, but it had us moving in the right direction. After all, the point had been to get Hulk working, and now he was working. We had a murder case, and we had a $10,000 retainer. So I was feeling rather pleased with myself as I returned to the office, without the poodle, and sat behind my desk. I reached for my notebook, signaling Hulk I was ready.

"Now then, Mrs. Bergmann," said Hulk, "suppose you tell me about the events related to the murder in what seems to you the most logical order."

Mrs. Bergmann took a sip of her drink and began:

"Fountain College, Mr. Hulk, has, or had, a five-person philosophy department: Heinrich Bergmann, my husband; William Lanchaster, the deceased, who taught logic; Herbert Lord, history of ancient philosophy; Beatrice Trilling, history of modern philosophy; and Reggie Stout, contemporary American and British philosophy.

"Fountain, like many small private colleges, is having financial difficulties, and the trustees have undertaken a considerable reduction of faculty positions. Every faculty member is theoretically vulnerable: Fountain is an experimental college and has never had a tenure or seniority system.

"A couple of months ago, the trustees affirmed Lanchaster's position and directed him to eliminate one member of the philosophy department. Since that time, there has been a great deal of nasty politicking among the philosophers. Eventually, Lord, Trilling, and Stout banded together to try to eliminate my husband. They have even gone so far as sending willing students to Lanchaster to complain about my husband. He's particularly vulnerable because he's an unorthodox personality, even for Fountain, and because existentialism is viewed with some contempt by most professional American philosophers.

"Professor Lanchaster was to announce his decision to the members of the department, individually, at his home, on Thursday evening. He asked Lord to come at 7:00, Stout at 7:30, my husband at 8:00, and Trilling at 8:30. This schedule has been confirmed by the department secretary.

"Lord says he arrived at 7:00 and left at 7:30. He claims that Lanchaster told him that he, Lord, would be retained and that my husband was to be fired. Of course, Lord maintains that Lanchaster was alive when he left. There was no one else in the house to confirm this or to tell of any arrivals or departures. Professor Lanchaster's children are grown, and his wife had been out of town for several weeks visiting a sick sister. The only other visitor that we know of was Lanchaster's niece, Lisa Williams, who stopped by the house at 7:25, with a friend, to pick up some books. Her friend, apparently, can confirm her presence at the library for the rest of the evening. When Lisa arrived, Lord answered the door at Professor Lanchaster's request, he says, and gave her a bundle of books that was on the table in the hallway.

"Stout says that he did not come to the house at 7:30. He arrived instead at 8:30 and found Beatrice Trilling outside the door. Stout has produced a typewritten note that he claims was put in his mailbox at the college that day asking him to come at 8:30 rather than 7:30. The note had apparently been typed on a departmental typewriter and was unsigned. Stout says he assumed that one of the secretaries had typed it at Lanchaster's direction.

"Stout and Trilling say that they rang the bell for several minutes and then entered the house. They say the door was slightly ajar. They found Lanchaster's body and called the police. After the police arrived, Trilling told them she had passed my husband in Lanchaster's neighborhood as she was going to her appointment.

"My husband, I regret to say, has acted stupidly. He now claims that he got back late from an out-of-town lecture, arrived at the Lanchaster house at 8:15, discovered the body, but left without reporting the murder. He has an elaborate rationale for leaving the scene, but the plain fact is that he panicked. When the police questioned him, he first denied being in the Lanchaster neighborhood, then denied being in the house, before telling the police what he now says is the truth.

"The police asked my husband how he thought he could get away with denying his presence at the house, since his appointment was part of a schedule known to the whole department. My husband said that he knew of no schedule. Apparently, Lanchaster did not make a point of telling each person that he was seeing the others. Stout, Trilling, and Lord knew about the schedule because they had talked with one another. My husband was not in on their conversations.

"Unfortunately, my husband's admission makes plausible the assumption that he went to Lanchaster's house with a gun, killed him, and then left, all with a reasonable expectation that no one would ever know he had done it.

"The police have not arrested my husband. They are obviously aware of the other possibilities. The medical examiner places the time of death between 7:45 and 8:15. Trilling or Lord could have faked the note to Stout and killed Lanchaster during Stout's appointment time. Or Stout could have kept his appointment and typed the note himself.

"But my husband is the prime suspect. The police are suggesting that Lanchaster might have typed the note to Stout so that Lanchaster would have an hour with my husband to discuss his dismissal. Lord says Lanchaster told him that my husband was to be fired, and Stout and Trilling say that they had hints of this.

"I don't like the situation at all. The police are obviously antagonistic toward my husband, as are the other professors in the department. And one of those others is the murderer. If some piece of planted evidence should show up—well, it would certainly be all over for my husband. I want you to clear him by finding the murderer for us."

Mrs. Bergmann had moved forward in her chair during this recital. Now she let out a breath and leaned back. After a pause, Hulk began to speak. He was scowling.

"I must admit, Madame, that I can't help sharing the negative attitude of the police. Whether or not we assume your husband is the killer, his ineptitude is amazing. Is he an utter idiot? This is a man who has been employed to teach reason to the young. I find myself astounded."

Mrs. Bergmann stared at Hulk for a moment, and then, much to my surprise, she laughed.

"Mr. Hulk, you may have heard the story of how Thales, the Greek philosopher, fell into a ditch while gazing at the stars. My husband is like that. He can develop very impressive arguments concerning the existence of God, free will, and the nature of the unobservable world. But ask him which foot fits his left shoe, and he is lost. It is part of his charm for me, but I must admit that I'm less than charmed with him at the moment. However, I'm not asking you to like him. I'm asking you to prove him innocent."

"Are you so sure of his innocence?" said Hulk. "Obviously, you don't have any evidence in his favor that the police will accept."

"True. But I know my husband. He is not a violent man. And, quite frankly, he wouldn't have the courage."

"Mrs. Bergmann, you should know that I do not shield murderers. I do not, in the end, hide evidence from the police. If I go after a murderer, I find him, and if it turns out to be your husband, the police shall know about it. Nor will I return your retainer. Are you sure you want to engage me on those terms?"

"I'm quite certain."

"Satisfactory. Tell me, what do the police know about the murder weapon?"

"Lanchaster did not own a gun, and none of the suspects is known to have owned one. The weapon was a handgun—the police can tell you the type. As far as I know, the police have not found the gun."

"You said that the three other suspects disliked your husband. How did the deceased feel about him?"

"They weren't close, but I think Professor Lanchaster was quite fond of him. A case of opposites attracting, perhaps. Lanchaster was a very precise, proper person, but not dogmatic. I think he enjoyed my husband's flamboyance. Of course, there was no question of competition. My husband posed no threat to Lanchaster's position at the college."

"And Mrs. Lanchaster? How does she feel about you and your husband?"

"Mrs. Lanchaster has always been very kind to both my husband and me."

"Do you think you could persuade her to admit Mr. Crocker to the house?"

"To the house, yes. But I'm afraid questioning Mrs. Lanchaster would be unadvisable. The doctor has ordered her to rest. Lisa Williams, the niece, who is a friend of ours, is staying with her. She could show Mr. Crocker around. Professor Lanchaster was quite a fan of yours, as a matter of fact. He used some of your cases as exercises in his introductory classes. He referred to you as a fellow logician doing battle outside the ivory tower.

That's how I happened to think of your name. Yes, I'm quite sure that Mrs. Lanchaster would admit a representative of yours."

Hulk glanced at the clock and noticed that it was time to do battle in the plant rooms. He rose from his chair.

"Very well. Please arrange it, and call Mr. Crocker. If you will excuse me now, I have an appointment. But please stay a few more minutes. Mr. Crocker will need some more information from you."

*****

LET'S REVIEW

There are four suspects: Bergmann, Trilling, Stout, and Lord.

* *Match each with an appointment time (7:00, 7:30, 8:00, 8:30).*
* *What does each one say happened at his/her appointment time?*
* *What happened at 7:25?*
* *What was the estimated time of death?*

Mrs. Bergmann arranged to have me visit the Lanchaster house the next afternoon. Before visiting the house, I made inquiries at police headquarters and at the philosophy department of Fountain College.

Inspector Shultz wasn't very philosophical about my visit. He loses any composure he has at the sound of Hulk's name or at the sight of me. I suppose I can't blame him. It never makes him look good when Hulk solves a case that Shultz can't. Shultz let me cool my heels for an hour outside his office before letting me know the only thing he was planning to show me was the door.

Reggie Stout, who was now acting chairman of the department, showed me into his office immediately—once he realized I was questioning a secretary about a certain note. He was soon joined by Professors Herbert Lord and Beatrice Trilling. Stout looked like a radical who had lost his causes but had managed to hang on to his faded jeans. Lord looked like the professors you see in cartoons: balding head, glasses, sport coat with patches on the sleeves, a slightly confused look on his face. Trilling was razor thin with an intense gaze.

Even though you know it does no good, you never get out of the habit of looking into eyes, trying to find the guilt there. Stout looked cynical, Lord nervous, and Trilling alert, but no one looked guiltier than the others.

I told them what I'd found, but, when it became apparent that they intended to ask all the questions, I left. One thing was clear to me: They were all happy to have Bergmann on the hot spot and weren't about to help him.

My next stop was the Lanchaster house. Lisa Williams opened the door seconds after my first ring. She was a pleasant young woman, about eighteen. She greeted me with a finger to her lips and signaled me to follow her to the study, which was at the back of the house. Once we were inside the room, she shut the door carefully.

"Betty—Mrs. Lanchaster—is sleeping. You are Mr. Crocker, aren't you?"

"That's right. I appreciate this."

"Gloria and Heinrich are my friends."

I looked around the study. It was mostly old mahogany and old books. There was a large desk on the far side of the room, facing the door, with a chair behind it, and two other chairs to the side and front of it.

"Your uncle was sitting in the desk chair when he was shot?"

"Yes. The police say he was shot by someone standing there, in front of the desk."

I walked over to the desk and found the bullet hole in the padded back of the desk chair. I looked quickly at the papers and books scattered on the desk.

"Is the room the same as it was that evening? Did the police take anything?"

"As far as I know, everything is here."

I inspected the area around the desk and noticed that the cord of the desk phone had been cut. I held up a cut length of cord.

"Was this done on the evening of the murder?"

"Yes. At least, this phone was working that afternoon when I called my uncle. I know he was on this line because he was looking for the books I wanted while holding the phone."

"It was this phone rather than his cell?"

"He always preferred using the desk phone." Lisa laughed. "He had this out-of-date Nokia which he hated to use and was always misplacing."

"Do you know if he had the cell phone on him at the time he was killed?"

"I believe the police said they found it on a table in the hall."

"Where is his computer?"

"I heard someone say he'd left it in his office at school."

"So you came by to get books that evening? Why don't you tell me about that."

"There's nothing much to tell," she said. "I needed some books for a paper I'm writing. My uncle said he'd be busy and wouldn't be able to see me, but he would put the books on the hall table and leave the front door unlocked. He must have forgotten to unlock the door. So I rang the bell. Lord answered the door and handed me the books. Then I left. I was with a friend all evening at the library, as I told the police."

"Did Lord say anything when he gave you the books?"

"No. He just met me at the door and handed the books to me before I could say a thing. He obviously knew I was coming for them."

"Did you think it strange that Lord should answer the door?"

"No. My uncle was lame and often asked people to do little things for him so that he wouldn't have to move around too much. And Lord was always anxious to please him."

"How did Lord seem to you?"

"The same as always."

I looked more closely at the items on the desk. There were some books on logic, including one written by Lanchaster, some journal reprints, a draft of a paper on some logical controversy, and notes on a logic exam he'd been preparing. I also went through the desk drawers. There was nothing among the papers that seemed to bear on the murder.

"I assume the police found nothing that indicated which professor was to be fired?"

"No."

"Professor Lanchaster didn't tell his wife?"

"No. The police asked her that."

"All right," I said, pulling out my phone. "I need to call Hulk in case he has any instructions."

When I reached Hulk, he didn't want a report on my entire day, just on what I had found in the house. That took only a few minutes.

"I'm heading back now, unless you want me to do something else here," I told him.

There was a long pause.

"Photographs," he said finally. "I want photos of every paper, of all writing on or in that desk. Then get back here and print them out for me."

"Will do," I said, wondering what Hulk could be after.

*****

LET'S REVIEW

* What does Lisa Williams say happened when she arrived at the house?
* What do we know about the phone in the study?
* Were there any wireless devices in the study?
* Does this information give us any useful information about the murder?

They were all in place in the office by 4:00, when Hulk came down from the plant rooms: Stout, Lord, and Trilling seated together on Hulk's right, Lisa Williams in the center, Heinrich and Gloria Bergmann on Hulk's left, and Inspector Shultz and Sergeant Joe Kurz in the back row. I'd never seen an existentialist before, but had I imagined one, he would have looked just like Heinrich Bergmann. His long hair and beard, jeans, and shirt were all black. The only contrasts were the brown eyes and the nicotine-colored skin at the center of all that hair.

"All right, Hulk, they're all here," said Inspector Shultz. "They've been told you have no official standing, and they're not legally obligated to answer any of your questions. However, we have asked for their cooperation. What do you have?"

"I don't have any questions," said Hulk. "What I have is something to show all of you. Arnie, if you please."

I gave each person in the room a copy of the sheet of paper shown here

$$D \supset B$$
$$D \supset (B \supset W)$$
$$B \supset (W \supset S) / \therefore D \supset S$$

$$M \equiv N / \therefore {\sim}N \vee M$$

$$A \supset B$$
$$C \supset D$$
$$(B \vee D) \supset E$$
$${\sim}E / \therefore {\sim}(A \vee C)$$

$${\sim}R \vee {\sim}S$$
$$A \supset (R \cdot S) / \therefore {\sim}A$$

$${\sim}(M \cdot N)$$
$$(O \cdot T) \vee (M \cdot N)$$
$$(M \cdot N) \vee (R \cdot L)$$
$$O \supset (I \cdot D)$$
$$D \equiv S / \therefore$$

Ont·Arg.

"The reason I have no need to ask questions," said Hulk, "is that Professor Lanchaster has given us the answer we are looking for."

Puzzled exclamations burst out all over the room.

"What kind of nonsense is this?" said Shultz. "What are all these scribbles?"

"This is a reproduction of a page from Professor Lanchaster's desk pad," said Hulk. "And it is not nonsense. Quite the opposite. Apparently, Lanchaster had been jotting down logical exercises on his desk pad. Before he died, he managed to add one exercise that gives us all we need to solve his murder."

Switching parodies, in mid-mystery, from Rex Stout to Ellery Queen, I interrupt the story to issue:

A CHALLENGE TO THE READER

You now have all the clues necessary to solve the mystery. A little deduction will indicate "whodunit." Some additional reflection should enable you to give a full explanation of the crime. (For instance, when and why was the phone cord cut?) For those readers who have had no courses in logic, the following information should suffice (and *don't panic, this isn't difficult—just take it a step at a time*):

The relevant logic problem is the one at the *lower right-hand side* of the paper, the one without a solution filled in after the "/∴" sign, which means "therefore":

$$\sim (M \cdot N)$$
$$(O \cdot T) \vee (M \cdot N)$$
$$(M \cdot N) \vee (R \cdot L)$$
$$O \supset (I \cdot D)$$
$$D \equiv S / \therefore$$

A, B, C, and so on, stand for distinct statements. But you could not know which, if any, specific statements these letters symbolize. Therefore, you have to concern yourself with the letters themselves. The conclusion you want is a conjunction of all the letters that can be deduced from the premises, without any letter being repeated.

The other symbols should drop out. The conclusion should have the following form: A and B and C, and so on. The letters you can deduce from these premises can be rearranged to form a message.

Here are the meanings of the various symbols:

"~ A" means "not A" (~ is called the "curl")
"A • B" means "A and B" (• is called the "dot")
"A v B" means "A or B" (v is called the "wedge")
"A ⊃ B" means "If A, then B" (⊃ is called the "horseshoe")
"A ≡ B" means "If A, then B, and if B, then A" (≡ is called the "triple bar")
"/∴" means "therefore" (having the same meaning as a line drawn under the premises)

The parentheses group symbols together, acting as a kind of punctuation. For instance:

"(A • B) v (C • D)" means "either both A and B or both C and D"

If we translate the symbols other than the letters themselves into their English-language meanings, our logic problem reads like this:

> Not (M and N)
> Either (O and T) or (M and N)
> (M and N) or (R and L)
> If O, then (I and D)
> If D, then S and vice versa
> Therefore: ??

Start by deducing what letters you can; put those in the conclusion. Then use those letters to deduce others; add those to the conclusion.

Symbolic logic simply formalizes the logic we use every day, and you can do the logic informally. For instance, from both A and B, you can get A and you can get B. Another example:

> A and B
> If (A and B) then (C and D)
> _____
> A and B and C and D

REASONING: The first premise gives us both A and B; these can be put in the conclusion. The second premise says that, if we have both

A and B, we can get both C and D. Since we have A and B, we also get C and D. These are added to the conclusion.

Another example:

$$\begin{array}{c} \text{Not A} \\ \underline{\text{Either A or B}} \\ \text{B} \end{array}$$

REASONING: The first premise says not A; therefore, A cannot be put in the conclusion. But the first premise is helpful in conjunction with the second premise, which says either A or B. Since it's not A, it's B.

Also: "Ont. Arg." = "Ontological Argument" = famous proof for the existence of God. (Summary in story.)

The people in the room began to study the paper intently. No one came up with the answer. Shultz was the first to speak.

"We're not here to play games, Hulk. If you've got an answer, let's have it."

"What's written at the bottom of the page?" asked Lisa. "'Ont. Arg.'"

"Ontological argument," said Stout.

"Is that some kind of clue?" asked Mrs. Bergmann.

"Indeed it is," said Hulk. "Ladies and gentlemen, consider the taxing, not to mention frightening, predicament of a man who knows he is going to die and wants to leave a clue as to the name of his murderer. If it is too obvious, the murderer will remove it. If it is too obscure, no one will notice it. Professor Lanchaster got his clue past the murderer but almost erred on the side of subtlety. I have been told that Professor Lanchaster admired my work, and I flatter myself with the supposition that he took a chance that someone, perhaps his wife, would bring me into the case. In any event, it is fortunate that I did get involved. Had the situation been left to the police, the clue would have gone undetected."

"All I've gotten so far is talk," said Shultz.

"You will also get a murderer, Inspector. A man wants to leave a clue as to the identity of his murderer. He would hardly write out the name. So what would he do instead? He'd devise some word association perhaps.

Here the abbreviation 'Ont. Arg.' stands out on a sheet otherwise devoted to logic exercises. As Professor Stout has noted, this abbreviation stands for 'ontological argument.' None of the books and papers on Lanchaster's desk had any connection with the ontological argument. Perhaps a clue lay there.

"What is the ontological argument? The four professors here can tell you better than I, but, briefly, it is an argument that claims that the actual existence of God is necessarily implied by the mere definition of God. It is a proof concerning God. God . . . why not Lord? A good association. I thought: Lord is the killer."

"Hulk, you're an idiot," said Professor Trilling.

"How so, Professor?"

"The proof you refer to is Anselm's ontological proof, also used by Descartes. But it is not the only ontological proof. Sartre has another, a proof for the existence of Being, independent of consciousness. In fact, Bergmann has written an article on it. Perhaps Lanchaster was indicating Bergmann."

"More likely it is only a random scribble," said Stout. "If it isn't, it might as well be. No, Hulk, that gets you nowhere."

"I doubt very much that it was random," said Hulk. "I believe it was written intentionally as a clue. But it was invented in haste, and Lanchaster saw the ambiguity. So he came up with something else, a clue hidden among the logic exercises on his desk pad. Fortunately, that clue is not ambiguous.

"The philosophers here know how introductory logic courses proceed. Students learn to translate normal sentences into symbols that express their logical form. Look." Hulk lifted up a large sheet of paper on which he had printed the symbols and pointed to them as he explained. "Letters like A and M, replace basic sentences. Other symbols stand for the logical connectives: $\sim$ means 'not'; • means 'and'; v means 'either . . . or'; ⊃ means 'if—then'; and ≡ means 'if either, then the other.' For example, 'If Bob gets paid, then Bob buys groceries' can be symbolized as A ⊃ B. Or 'Either Bob goes to work, or he does not go to work' can be symbolized as M v $\sim$ M.

"Having learned such symbolization, the students are then taught a series of valid argument forms. A valid argument is an argument such that, if the premises are true, then the conclusion must be true. For example, ' A ⊃ B; A; therefore, (/∴) B' is a valid argument form, and any argument having that form is valid. 'If the sun shines, then the grass will grow;

the sun shines; therefore, the grass will grow' is a valid argument having that form.

"Students then analyze more complex arguments. If the conclusion of an argument can be derived from the premises by employing a series of valid argument forms, then that more complex argument is valid. If not, then there are definite procedures for showing the argument to be invalid.

"Consider the example at the center of Lanchaster's desk pad:

$$A \supset B$$
$$C \supset D$$
$$(B \lor D) \supset E$$
$$\sim E \; / \therefore \sim (A \lor C)$$

This is a typical example of a logic exercise at a point in the course where the ability of the student to translate from English to logical symbolism is assumed. Only the symbolized argument is given. The conclusion, marked by "/∴" of the argument is given. The student is asked to determine whether the argument is valid.

"Now consider the example at the lower right-hand side of the desk pad.

$$\sim (M \cdot N)$$
$$(O \cdot T) \lor (M \cdot N)$$
$$(M \cdot N) \lor (R \cdot L)$$
$$O \supset (I \cdot D)$$
$$D \equiv S / \therefore$$

No conclusion is given after the therefore (/∴), as if one were being invited to draw a conclusion. Of course, it could be that Lanchaster was simply interrupted there, but a little work shows that such was not the case. The solution to the murder is there.

"Of course, in a sense, there is no single answer to any logic problem. '$\sim (M \cdot N)$,' for example, can be deduced from the premises and would be a 'solution.' Also, since any letter can be deduced from itself, any letters in the conclusion could be repeated indefinitely. But, presumably, a message would be a conjunction of all the individual letters that could be deduced from the premises, with no repetition of any letters. Such, indeed, is the case.

"The second premise says, 'Either both O and T or both M and N.' The third premise says, 'Either both M and N or both R and L.' Since the first premise says 'not M and N,' we can deduce the other pairs of letters. That gives us O and T and R and L. The fourth premise says, 'If O, then both I and D.' Since we have O, we can deduce I and D. The last premise says that whenever we have D, we have S, and vice versa. Since we have D, we can deduce S. The conclusion, then, is O and T and R and L and I and D and S.

"Appropriately, Lanchaster, professor of logic, used his own tools to name his murderer. He gave us a problem whose solution is an anagram, giving us his statement: ITS LORD."

Lord was staring at Hulk without speaking, his fingers playing at his lips. Everyone else was staring at Lord. Shultz motioned Sergeant Kurz to move in Lord's direction and then turned to Hulk.

"I don't get it, Hulk. Lanchaster died instantly and obviously didn't write his message after the killer left. Do you mean to tell me that Lord was stupid enough to sit there while Lanchaster jotted down notes that would convict him?"

"Inspector, it would not be the first time that one of this group of supposedly educated people has exhibited blatant stupidity. But, no, Lord wasn't that stupid.

"Presumably, Lord had some early hint from Lanchaster that he would be dropped from the department, and Lord planned to kill Lanchaster should that be the decision. He was taking an awful chance, killing him when he did. But he did not want to act before the final decision had been confirmed. Had he waited longer, others would have learned of his dismissal.

"Of course, the time of his appointment was known to the others, so he had to commit the crime in such a way that another would be blamed or, at the very least, that others would be suspected. He sent a note to Stout and perhaps even verified that Stout would be coming late. Would you care to comment, Professor Stout?"

Stout glanced quickly at Lord. "Yes," he said. "He knew I had gotten the note. We discussed it."

"Thank you," said Hulk. "Lord had also decided to kill fairly close to 8:00. That way, both Stout and Bergmann would be suspects. He did not know, of course, that Professor Bergmann would be so helpful with his panic and his bumbling stories.

"Lord arrived at 7:00, learned that he was to be fired, pulled a gun on Lanchaster, and waited. But then a problem arose. The doorbell rang. It was Lisa Williams, who had come to pick up her books. No doubt Lord had locked the door upon entering the house. But he did not dare let the doorbell go unanswered. Miss Williams knew Lanchaster would be there, the lights in the house were on, and the car was in the driveway. For his part, Lanchaster had to cooperate or jeopardize the life of his niece. He told Lord that she had come for the books and told him where they were.

"Lord did not dare let Lanchaster go to the door: he might pass a message to his niece. He saw only one danger in leaving a lame man alone in the room—the desk phone. Lord saw that Lanchaster didn't have his computer with him and either grabbed Lanchaster's cell phone or realized it wasn't there. So the only danger was the desk phone, and he cut that cord. It was the cut cord that first made me suspect that there might be a message among the things on the desk.

"Perhaps Lord quickly searched for a message when he returned to the room. Perhaps he didn't think of that possibility. In any case, Lanchaster had hidden his message well. It would not have been spotted by someone afraid and in haste, even a colleague who knew his symbolic logic.

"Lord then waited in the study with Lanchaster for another 15 or 20 minutes before killing him. All of you know the rest. I am certain that a jury will find the accusation, 'ITS LORD,' in the deceased's own handwriting, evidence of Lord's guilt, given the cogency of the hypothesis I have outlined. Also, I have no doubt that now that the police know where to focus their resources, it won't be long before they find—if not the murder weapon itself—evidence that Lord recently purchased a similar weapon. Would you care to comment, Professor Lord?"

"No," said Lord, still rubbing his lips.

"Rest assured, sir, that you will be convicted and sent to prison for the rest of your life. Perhaps the prison authorities will let you teach Plato and Aristotle in prison. If so, I hope that the inmates enjoy your courses. I suspect, from Professor Lanchaster's decision, that your students at Fountain did not. But in prison, at least, you will have tenure."

"Damn you, Hulk, damn you!"

Many men have tried to get at Hulk in that office and none has succeeded yet. Lord certainly didn't, though he made quite a try for a man of his size. I intercepted him, wrestled him to the floor, and held him while Sergeant Kurz put on the cuffs.

*****

Hulk refuses to talk business at dinner, so I waited until we were drinking coffee in the office to tell him.

"While you were in the plant rooms, a messenger arrived with a package from Mrs. Bergmann. It was the second check for $10,000 we expected. It has been put in the safe and will be deposited tomorrow. Mrs. Bergmann also sent you a present. It's a copy of an article by her husband on Sartre's ontological proof. The major question seems to be: Is the phenomenon of Being itself the Being of the phenomena, or is it merely a phenomenal representation, nonidentical with, but indicating the nature of, the Being of the phenomena? I haven't quite made up my mind. Perhaps we could discuss the matter after you've read the article."

"Rubbish. They should fire the whole department at Fountain and hire four logicians. At least that is a sensible subject."

"You're just prejudiced because you're a fellow logician, even if you are doing battle outside the ivory tower. But that reminds me, sir. There is one point about the case that hasn't been cleared up to my satisfaction— something you said when you were disclosing the murderer."

"Yes? What was that?"

"You said, 'If Bob gets paid, then Bob buys groceries.' What I want to know is: Did Bob get paid?"

"Pfui. Go amuse yourself elsewhere."

It is a shame to be living with a genius and yet have to do without intellectual conversation. Fortunately, my interests are not purely intellectual. I grabbed my hat and headed for the Starlight Lounge.

Questions

1. Regarding "Philosophy Is Murder," trace the steps in Hulk's reasoning from his first search for evidence to his proposed solution to the crime.

2. Is it implausible to suppose that the exercise yielding the message "ITS LORD" was written prior to Lord's appearance in the study? Explain. If one assumes that it was, what account might one give of the crime?

3. Compare your preliminary solution with those of Hulk and of the other students. (Don't simply assume that Hulk's explanation must be correct.) Are these various explanations equally reasonable? Discuss.

4. Do you think the evidence against Lord would be enough to convict him? If not, what other evidence might be needed, and how might Hulk or the police go about getting it?

5. Do the following logic exercise as you did the exercise in the mystery story. Here you will need to derive some negative statements in the course of your reasoning (for example, ~ O), and you may find it convenient to put these in the conclusion as you proceed. But when you have completed your reasoning, cross out any negative statements in the conclusion. The remaining conjunction of letters can be arranged to form a one-word admonition. As before, there should be no double letters in the conclusion. In reasoning out logic problems, one does not usually follow the written order of the premises. In this case, it would be a mistake to begin with the first one. Look over the premises, and choose a reasonable starting point.

Here's a reminder of the translation of the symbols:

"~ A" means "not A"; "A • B" means "A and B"; "A v B" means "A or B"; "A ⊃ B" means "If A, then B."

The parentheses group symbols together, acting as a kind of punctuation. For instance: "H v (B • L)" means "either H or both B and L."

$$(K • I) ⊃ ~ O$$
$$~ O ⊃ T$$
$$I • ~ A$$
$$(K • N) v A$$
$$H v (B • L)$$
$$\underline{~ (B • L)}$$
$$?$$

READING 2: Another Pilgrim's Progress

PREVIEW

In this story, Pilgrim and her brothers find the road to the Heavenly City, beset with logical fallacies as well as spiritual dangers.

* *Try to identify each instance of bad reasoning in the story.*
* *Explain why the reasoning in each case is bad.*

Conditions in the town of Status Quo were rapidly deteriorating. First had come the drought, parching the crops; next the winds, filling the air with dust; then the fires, destroying the dwellings in twos and threes. Within the last month, many of the townspeople had departed, driven away by fear and drawn elsewhere by hope. Rumors spread of a Heavenly City somewhere to the north—a city, so it was said, where there was never drought, wind, fire, or famine. Pilgrim had been inclined to leave Status Quo long ago. She was an optimistic soul and had never doubted that there was a Heavenly City. But she was also a kindly soul, her brothers' keeper. She had twin brothers, Skeptic and Caution, who thus far had refused to leave. There was no hope of convincing Skeptic: He could never be convinced of anything. However, he wouldn't offer much resistance if simply pushed down the road. It was Caution who must be convinced.

That day, as on most others, Pilgrim and her brothers were sitting in the tavern. There was no longer any work to be done, and even if there had been, the fierce, choking winds would have made it impossible. The only sensible thing to do was to seek shelter, and the tavern was the only shelter left with space and refreshment enough for a large gathering. The talk, as on other days, concerned the wisdom of leaving the town.

"My family has lived here for generations," Provincial was saying. "This has always been my home. How can any other place be better?"

Caution looked up. He had heard this particular speech too many times.

"What nonsense, Provincial! The crops are destroyed. The rich soil is gone. Most of our town has burned or is burning. The air is so filled with dirt and heat that one can scarcely breathe. Our provisions are dwindling, and soon we may starve. How can you maintain that this is the best place on earth?"

"I didn't say it was perfect," said Provincial. "Anyway, it's always easy to be critical."

"Yes. And it's getting easier all the time!"

Provincial crossed the room to Caution's table.

"Speaking man to man, Caution, you've got no right to criticize. I've lived here all my life and you've lived here only five years."

"That's true," said Caution. "But what has that to do with what I say?"

"Why should we listen to you, anyway?" said Provincial. "You're the one who says he doesn't believe in anything."

"Provincial," said Pilgrim, "you're mixing up my brothers again. Skeptic's the one who doesn't believe in anything."

"Yea, well, Caution will end up like Skeptic if he keeps questioning things."

"I don't know what all this quarreling is about," said the tavern keeper. "The whole thing is no dilemma to me. As I see it, either you go out there in the dust and die, or you stay in here and drink my fine ale. That doesn't take much thought, does it?"

"But then again," said Caution, "if we leave here, we might find the Heavenly City. Or, if we stay, you might run out of ale, and we would die of thirst."

"You know, Caution," said the tavern keeper, "I'm beginning to lose patience with you myself. Careful you don't get me angry, or I'll toss you out there in that dust and make the choice for you. How would you like that?"

LET'S REVIEW

* *Say what's wrong with the following two arguments:*

1. "My family has lived here for generations," Provincial was saying. "This has always been my home. How can any other place be better?"

2. "I don't know what all this quarreling is about," said the tavern keeper. "The whole thing is no dilemma to me. As I see it, either you go out there in the dust and die, or you stay in here and drink my fine ale. That doesn't take much thought, does it?"

* *Can you find any other instances of bad reasoning so far?*

As the tavern keeper walked away, Pilgrim leaned toward Caution.

"The Heavenly City is there, Caution. I'm sure of it. Won't you make up your mind to go?"

"I'm considering it, Pilgrim. Give me time."

"You, Skeptic. Please come with me."

"But Pilgrim," said Skeptic, "I don't *know* that there's a Heavenly City out there. And I don't *know* that things here are as bad as they seem."

"But you don't know that there isn't a Heavenly City," said Pilgrim. "And you don't know that things here aren't as bad as they seem. If you don't know anything, what difference can it make to you whether you stay or go?"

Skeptic looked thoughtful.

"I don't know much," he said. "But I think I know that it seems to be more trouble to seem to walk than to seem to sit still."

So they talked until late that night, when it was time for the tavern to close. As was his custom, the tavern keeper did not try to convince Skeptic that it was time to leave; that would have been a hopeless task. Instead, he pulled Skeptic to his feet, guided him out the door, and pushed him in the direction of his home. Like a billiard ball, Skeptic would never move until pushed, but, once pushed, he would continue in a straight line until someone or something stopped or turned him. His sister and brother followed behind him. In former days, Pilgrim would have stayed by Skeptic's side, ready to pull him out of the way of wagons coming down the road. But there had been no traffic on that road for some days. And tonight Pilgrim was intent on trying to convince Caution that they should leave. So it was that Skeptic walked some distance ahead of them. They noticed this only when a loud, cracking sound caught their attention. They looked ahead and saw a huge oak tree beginning to topple toward the road. Skeptic was moving toward the spot where the tree would fall.

"Skeptic, stop!" cried Pilgrim. "The tree is falling!"

"How do you know that?" said Skeptic.

"Don't be stupid!" said Caution. "Look overhead."

Skeptic did look up, but he did not alter his stride.

"I will grant you that the tree seems to be falling on me. But appearances can be deceiving."

Pilgrim and Caution began to run as the tree came crashing down on their brother. They found Skeptic lying under the huge tree; only his feet and head protruded from beneath the trunk.

"You know," groaned Skeptic, "it may be that you were right. It seems to be the case that a tree has fallen upon me. It seems to be the case that my body is broken and that I am dying. Perhaps I am jumping to conclusions, but it certainly seems to me that I hurt a great deal."

And with that, Skeptic died.

"Oh, my brother," moaned Pilgrim.

"The poor fool," said Caution.

"At least he died honorably," said Pilgrim. "Whether or not one agrees with him, one must admit that he stood up for what he believed . . . or what he thought he believed . . . .or what he thought he didn't believe."

"Well, he's not standing now," said Caution. "Pilgrim, I may be careful, but I'm not a fool. Tomorrow we shall get some friends to help us bury our brother. After we have mourned him, we shall leave this place. I doubt that we shall find any Heavenly City. But whatever becomes of us, it cannot be worse than this."

LET'S REVIEW

* Do you think Skeptic was reasoning badly?
* Do you think the tree proved him wrong?

And so it was that two days afterward, carrying on their backs what provisions they had been able to obtain, Pilgrim and Caution left Status Quo on the road north. The morning's walk was difficult, but the weather began to clear. Pilgrim took this as a promising sign. Caution refused to be optimistic. Perhaps this was but a brief respite from the bad weather. Or perhaps the weather was now clearing all over the land, and they had been fools to leave their town. As they talked, they came upon a fork in the road. In front of them was a sign, done in a crude hand.

THIS ROAD IS HEAVENLY ⸺⸺⸺⸺>
<⸺⸺⸺⸺ THIS ROAD IS HELLISH

Automatically, they took the right fork as they continued to talk. Then Caution stopped.

"I'd like another look at that sign."

"Why?" said Pilgrim. "It was quite plain."

"Perhaps," said Caution, walking back to the sign.

Reluctantly, Pilgrim followed him. Together they read the smaller lettering, which they hadn't noticed before, at the bottom of the sign.

The heavenly road, which is the scenic route, leads to the Great Pitfall; the hellish road, which is in disrepair, leads to the Heavenly City.

As they took the left fork, Pilgrim said:

"I must admit you were right that time. Perhaps I am not always careful enough."

The road was hellish indeed: pitted, cut by gullies, overgrown with brush. But Pilgrim was quite cheerful about this inconvenience. No longer were they simply guided by rumor. They had now seen a sign that proved that there was a Heavenly City and that this was the road to it. Caution was not so optimistic. After all, he argued, no one, as far as was known, had ever seen the Heavenly City and returned to verify its existence and location. So what if they had seen a sign? The sign, which had been done in a rough hand, might have been placed there by some fool who was merely guessing about the way.

"Now you are being ridiculous," said Pilgrim.

Sometime later they came upon a ragged figure seated by the side of the road. They recognized her at once as Circles, a beggar who had left their town a few days before. Caution, knowing that Pilgrim would want to give the beggar something and fearing that they might not have enough for themselves, tried to dissuade Pilgrim from charity. But Pilgrim would not hear of it.

"We must help our friends, Caution. Anyway, we are on the road to the Heavenly City, and certainly we shall reach it soon enough. Hello there, Circles! We don't have much, but we can give you a little."

Circles took the coin and the piece of bread Pilgrim offered and thanked her warmly.

"Bless you, Pilgrim, bless you. I may be a beggar now, but I shall not be one for long. They say there is plenty for everyone in the Heavenly City. "

"If there is a Heavenly City," grumbled Caution. "And if this is the right road."

"But this is the right road," said Circles. "I know it."

"How do you know that?" said Caution.

"Didn't you see the sign back there?" said Circles.

"Yes, yes. But how do we know that the sign is correct?"

That's easy," said Circles. "I know that the sign is correct because this is the right road."

"Very helpful," said Caution, with disgust.

"But Caution, I have more evidence," said Circles, anxious to please her benefactors.

"Not more of the same, I hope."

"No," said Circles. "Here, look at this."

Circles pulled a crumpled piece of paper out of her pocket and unfolded it on the ground before them. It was a sizable sheet, apparently torn from a larger one, scribbled with lines and letters. Pilgrim and Caution peered at it.

"A map?" said Pilgrim.

"Indeed," said Circles. "It is a map of the way to the Heavenly City."

"Oh happy day!" exclaimed Pilgrim. "Caution, let us memorize the map so that we shall know the way."

"I'm afraid it won't help you there," said Circles. "It has been torn off at just this spot. Apparently, the owner discarded the portion that wasn't needed any more."

"What a shame," said Pilgrim.

"Still, it's important," said Circles. "It tell
in the right direction. See here: There is Stat
ing north. There is the fork in the road, with
toward the Great Pitfall and the hellish road
City. Here we are, right at the edge of the map wh
Caution was worried that we might be on the wrong road.
feel better now."

But Caution did not feel better.

"This map looks even less official than the sign we saw back there. How do we know this is not merely some travelers' guesswork, based on where they've been and where they think they're going? How do we know this map is correct?"

"That's easy," said Circles. "Read what it says at the bottom."

Pilgrim bent over first and read the statement aloud:

"'This is a true map of the way to the Heavenly City.'"

"There, you see?" said Circles.

"Come on, Pilgrim," said Caution. "I've had quite enough of this."

Pilgrim protested as Caution dragged her away, but Caution was insistent.

"Really, Caution, this is a bit too much," said Pilgrim. "That was awfully rude, you know. And I don't know what you are making such a fuss about. I swear, sometimes you seem exactly like our poor dead brother, Skeptic. When we walk through the gates of the Heavenly City, will you still be doubtful?"

"No, Pilgrim. If I see it with my own eyes, I'll believe it."

"Well, that's something. In any case, I feel much relieved. We got a lot of valuable information from Circles. You certainly can't say we didn't get our money's worth."

"On the contrary," said Caution. "It seems to me that Circles has taken our money and made beggars of our questions."

LET'S REVIEW

* What is confusing about the this-road-is-heavenly/this-road-is-hellish sign?
* What is Caution's complaint about the reasoning of Circles the Beggar?

night fell, they made camp by the side of the road, ate a modest d, exhausted by the day's walk, fell asleep at once. At the first light , they continued on their way. After they had walked for two hours, tion came to an abrupt stop and groaned. Ahead the road ended, form- g a T with another road.

"Not another junction!"

"I'm sure the way is marked," said Pilgrim. "In any case, there are some people standing about. If there is any doubt as to the way, I'm sure they can advise us."

At the end of the road, the travelers were faced with another crudely lettered sign:

HEAVENLY CITY TO THE RIGHT ⟶
⟵ HEAVENLY CITY TO THE LEFT

"Well, that is certainly clear enough," said Pilgrim, starting to the right.

"Pilgrim, wait a minute. Why are you going that way?"

"The sign says 'Heavenly City to the right.'"

"It also says 'Heavenly City to the left.'"

"So?"

"Pilgrim, you don't suppose there are two Heavenly Cities, do you?"

"I wouldn't suppose so," said Pilgrim. "I've always heard there was only one."

"Do you imagine that one city could be way off in that direction and, at the same time, way off in that other direction?"

"I don't know."

"Pilgrim, you're hopeless."

"On the contrary, I'm full of hope."

"Pilgrim! We do not know which way to go. That sign is no help at all."

"Well, if you really think we are lost, why don't you ask those people for advice?"

Standing next to the sign were three people. One was a heavy-set man who was talking animatedly. Another was a thin woman who kept fidget-ing about, apparently impatient with the conversation. The third was a young boy, who seemed quite amused by something and who was trying, unsuccessfully, to keep from laughing. Caution politely greeted the three strangers, introduced himself, and asked them if they were lost.

"Not lost, son," said the heavy-set man. "Just resting."

"Then you know the way to the Heavenly City?" asked Caution.

"Of course," said the heavy man.

"But the sign. . . . "

"Oh that," said the man. "The work of some trickster, I would imagine."

"Then how. . .?"

"When you run across a problem, son, you've got to look around. You've got to use your eyes, use your head. It didn't take me long to figure it out."

Caution smiled and said: "It certainly is a relief to meet a man like you. A man who uses his head is a man after my own heart."

The heavy-set man chuckled.

"I like you, son. Call me 'Pop.' All my friends do."

"How did you figure out the way to go?" asked Caution.

"Really, it was easy," said Pop. "Look at the road to the right. See all those footprints? Now look at the left road. Hardly any footprints at all. The road to the right is the road that most of the people took. That's got to be the way to go."

Caution frowned.

"Unless they all made a mistake."

"Unlikely," said Pop.

"Perhaps they were all together and just had to take a guess," said Caution. "Or perhaps the first ones took a guess, and the rest just followed the crowd."

The woman interrupted.

"I thought of that. Didn't I say that, Pop? But look here, Caution. The footprints all go one way. Surely, if this were the wrong road, there would be some footprints coming back."

"Unless they haven't discovered their mistake yet," said Caution. "Or unless they all encountered some great pitfall and couldn't return."

"Thought of that, too," said the woman. "But you can see that some of these footprints are very old and that the others have been made over a span of many days. If this were the wrong road, you'd think that someone would have returned by now. Even if there is a Great Pitfall up ahead, you'd think that someone toward the rear would have gotten some warning."

"Good point," said Caution. "But let's not be hasty."

"But I am Hasty."

"I know. But I'm saying. . . ."

"Her name's Hasty, son," said Pop. "She can't help her name."

"Well, Hasty," said Caution, "what about the other road? Are there any footprints coming back from that direction?"

"I don't know," said Hasty, glancing toward the other road. "No, I guess not."

"It seems to me," said Pop, "that anybody who's fool enough to take the wrong road would be fool enough not to come back."

All the while they were talking, the boy continued to snicker. Caution was beginning to get annoyed.

"What is he laughing about?" said Caution.

"He's always like that," said Pop. "He just enjoys himself. His name is Suppressed."

"Because he tries to hold back his laughter? Why does he do that?"

"He's shy," said Pop.

Caution studied the boy for a moment and then caught a glimpse of something over the boy's shoulder. Caution pushed the boy aside and discovered a small sign.

THESE ROADS ARE ONE-WAY.
NO TURNING BACK.
THIS ORDINANCE STRICTLY ENFORCED.

"So much for your argument, Hasty," said Caution. "Those people were forbidden to return no matter what. As for you, Suppressed, I'm going to give you such a . . ."

"Stop it, Caution!" said Pilgrim. "Don't hurt him. This isn't like you at all."

"But he was trying to trick us," said Caution.

Suppressed was no longer snickering; he was whining.

"Didn't mean anything by it. It was just a joke. Don't hurt me."

"I still don't know what all this fuss is about," said Pop. "If that's the road that most people took, then. . . . "

LET'S REVIEW

* *Pop points to evidence and offers reasoning based on the evidence. Caution accepts the evidence but has an objection to the reasoning. What is Caution's objection?*
* *Hasty offers more evidence and reasoning. Caution is sympathetic but still has some questions. What are those questions?*
* *How does the sign hidden by the boy affect the reasoning they've all been using?*

"Really, I didn't mean anything by it," said Suppressed. "I'll make it up to you. I have an idea. If you're lost, why don't you appeal to the authorities?"

"The authorities?" said Caution. "What authorities?"

"Over there. That little house. The man in charge of the junction is inside."

There was indeed a small building by the side of the road. Caution had noticed it before, but it was so rundown that it hardly looked habitable, let alone official. Still, perhaps it had suffered much damage in the recent storms. Pilgrim was already heading for the hut and Caution followed. Pilgrim called inside, and in a moment an official appeared, wearing an impressive uniform.

"Are you in charge here?" asked Pilgrim.

"I sure am."

"Which way to the Heavenly City?"

"Take the road to the right," said the official.

"See, Caution?" said Pilgrim. "That was the direction I was going to go in the first place. That was the road those men told you to take. You are always making such a fuss about nothing."

Caution didn't reply but turned to go. However, Pilgrim had another question.

"Sir, how long ago did the last people come through here? Perhaps some of our friends are among them. Perhaps we could still catch up with them."

"I don't know," said the official. "I just got here an hour ago. I'm working for my brother. He's ill."

"Oh," said Pilgrim.

"But you've worked here before?" said Caution.

"No," said the official. "My brother's never been ill before."

"But he did leave you instructions?" said Caution.

"He sure did."

"Well, that's a relief," said Caution.

"And I'm sure I'll find them just as soon as I get that mess in there cleaned up."

"But he did tell you the correct road to take, didn't he?" said Pilgrim.

"No," said the official. "He doesn't talk much about his work."

"This is absurd," said Caution, throwing up his hands. "You're no authority."

"What do you mean, I'm no authority? You see this badge? It says, 'Authority.' See it?"

"Just because you wear a badge. . . ."

"You're a troublemaker," said the official. "I heard you arguing with those people over there. That was one thing. But when you start to argue with an authority . . . then you're the one in trouble."

"But why should we take your word?"

"That does it," said the official. "You like to argue, don't you? Well, here's an argument that should appeal to the likes of you."

With that the official grabbed Pilgrim and Caution by their collars, turned them around, and marched them to the road that led to the right. He pushed Pilgrim ahead and then gave Caution a kick in the pants that sent him sprawling in the dust.

"There. That'll fix you. You keep going now, and don't let me see you again. That road is strictly one-way, and if you try coming back, you'll get more of the same."

Caution got slowly to his feet, and Pilgrim helped him brush the dust off his clothes.

"Come on, Caution," said Pilgrim. "I think we'd better do what he says."

They walked along in silence for a while. Then Pilgrim spoke again.

"Caution, please don't be so glum. I'm sure everything will be all right."

"Pilgrim, you're hopeless."

"On the contrary, I'm. . ."

"Never mind!"

"I'll admit that there has been some confusion," said Pilgrim. "And it certainly was unfortunate that that official should have abused us so—you especially. But you must admit that there have been many indications that we are on the right road."

"There have been none," said Caution. "Or almost none. Let us suppose that the first sign, the map, and even the rumors do count for something. Still, we gained nothing useful at that junction."

"On the contrary," said Pilgrim. "The sign pointed this way, and so did the footprints. And those men at the junction told us this was the way. And that official did seem quite sure of himself. Perhaps he was really doing us a favor by forcing us to take the correct road."

"Pilgrim, you're . . . incorrigible. Can't you see that none of that means a thing?"

"But Caution, we don't know this isn't the right road. That ought to count for something."

LET'S REVIEW

* *Why is Caution so frustrated with the official at the junction?*
* *Why does the official think Caution should follow his directions?*

As they were talking, they came upon two other travelers. There was a tall man who moved very mechanically and slowly, never turning his head, as if he had to concentrate all his attention on the simple act of walking. Holding his arm was a woman who glanced at her companion constantly, as if with concern. As Pilgrim came alongside the other travelers, she bid them good day. The tall man did not respond, but the woman returned the greeting in a most pleasant manner. She introduced herself as Faith and asked about their welfare. Pilgrim decided that, under the circumstances, an offer of help would not be amiss.

"I don't mean to intrude," said Pilgrim. "But could you use some help? Is your friend all right?"

"All right?" said Faith. "He's wonderful!"

"I'm certainly happy to hear that," said Pilgrim. "It appeared to me that you were guiding your friend, and I thought perhaps he might be ill."

"I guiding him?" said Faith, laughing. "It's quite the opposite. He's guiding me."

"Well," said Pilgrim, "as my poor departed brother used to say, 'Appearances can be deceiving.'"

"My friend here knows the way to the Heavenly City."

"He does? Do you hear that, Caution? This may be our lucky day. Faith, would you mind if we accompanied you? We are not sure of the way."

"Please do."

"Just a minute," said Caution to Faith. "This friend of yours—has he been to the Heavenly City before?"

"Many times."

"That's a relief," said Caution.

"There now, Caution," said Pilgrim. "I hope you are satisfied for once."

What satisfaction Caution did feel soon gave way to irritation. No matter how slowly he and Pilgrim tried to walk, they kept getting ahead of Faith and the guide. They were moving at a snail's pace.

"Can't we go a little faster?" said Caution.

"Don't be rude to our friends," said Pilgrim. "You are certainly in no position to complain about someone who takes great care. It is quite obvious that our guide is going slowly so that he will make no mistake."

At that, Faith laughed.

"You are a charitable soul, Pilgrim, but I'm afraid that in this case your charity is misplaced. My friend knows the way to the Heavenly City as well as I know the streets of my town. He has no need to take care."

"Then why is he moving so slowly?" said Pilgrim.

"It's just his habit," said Faith. "And no doubt he is being considerate of me. I'm quite a clumsy person, likely to trip over things or go wandering off in the wrong direction. He wants to make certain that I can keep up."

"I must say that your friend is wonderful indeed," said Pilgrim. "It would certainly be unfair to complain about him, wouldn't it, Caution?"

Caution just mumbled, and Pilgrim paid him no attention. Instead, Pilgrim began to daydream about the Heavenly City; however she found her images vague.

"Faith," she said, "do you suppose that your friend might describe the wonders of the Heavenly City to us as we walk? That would certainly be a delightful way to pass the time, and it would encourage us on our journey."

"I'm sure that my friend would be more than happy to do that," said Faith. "Unfortunately, he cannot speak at all. He is mute."

"Oh, I'm so sorry," said Pilgrim, blushing, lowering her voice to a whisper.

"Why are you whispering?" said Faith, and then she laughed. "Oh, don't worry about embarrassing my friend. It's quite all right. He's deaf."

"Is he blind, too?" said Caution.

"Of course not," said Faith. "How could he be guiding me if he were blind?"

"Well, that's something," said Caution.

"Perhaps, Faith," said Pilgrim, "you could communicate with your friend in whatever way you do and then translate for us. I'd love to hear his stories. He must have many."

"I'm sorry," said Faith. "We have no way of communicating. I'm afraid we will just have to wait until we get to the Heavenly City to find out what it's like."

"What a shame," said Pilgrim, but then she brightened. "Oh, well. We shall be there soon enough. I suppose our delight will be all the greater for the surprise of it."

"Hold it!"

Caution had moved out in front of them and now turned to face Faith and the guide. Caution put out his hands to stop them but then realized they were moving so slowly that there was hardly any point. Caution walked backward as he spoke.

"Just a minute, Faith. First you tell us that your friend has been to the Heavenly City and knows the way quite well. Then you tell us that he's mute . . . and deaf. Now you tell us that you cannot communicate with him in any way. Just how do you know that he knows the way?"

"Stop it, Caution," said Pilgrim. "It is quite obvious that our guide had some credentials, or that he and Faith were introduced through some mutual acquaintance who knew our guide's abilities quite well."

"No," said Faith. "My friend carries no credentials. Nor were we introduced. When he came walking through my town one day, walking just as he is now, I had never seen him before, nor had I heard of him."

"What made you follow him?" asked Pilgrim.

Faith thought for a moment.

"I think . . . I think it was his eyes. They had that special look about them. Yes, his eyes convinced me."

"Ah!" said Pilgrim. "You had seen that look before."

"Are you joking?" said Faith. "How could it be special if I had seen it before? And would I follow a man on an exceptional journey like this one if he looked like any other person?"

"I've had enough of this," said Caution. "You say that your wonderful friend knows many wonderful things. But for all I know, his head may be as empty as yours.

Come on, Pilgrim, we're going."

LET'S REVIEW

Faith is convinced that her wonderful friend has been to the Heavenly City before and can guide Faith and the others there.

* *Why is Faith convinced of this? What are her reasons?*
* *Why is Caution so frustrated with what Faith has to say?*

"But, Caution," said Pilgrim. "You don't know he doesn't know the way."

Caution shook his head with disgust and hurried away. Pilgrim hesitated. Then she said to Faith:

"I'm sorry. I would like to accompany you. But I should stay with my brother. He may need me."

"I understand," said Faith. "It's quite all right. In any case, if you get confused, just stop and wait for us. We'll be along eventually."

Pilgrim hurried after her brother but could not see him as he rounded the next bend, nor the one after that. Pilgrim had almost decided that some misfortune had befallen Caution when she came upon him at last. Caution was standing midway down a path that sloped toward the plains, holding his hand to his forehead, shaking his head slowly. Pilgrim was perplexed until she also saw. Then she clapped her hands in delight. At the base of the hill, their road met another road that stretched from the other side of the hill; the roads joined and headed straight across the plains. At the junction of the roads was a sign that was visible from where they stood: Heavenly City Straight Ahead.

"I'm sorry, Caution, if I must laugh at you," said Pilgrim. "But surely you must laugh at yourself as well. After all your fussing! After all your talk about how one city couldn't be in two different directions! It is quite obvious now that the sign was no trick. Both roads were leading to the Heavenly City. Though they seemed to go in entirely different directions, it turns out that each curved northward around a different side of the hill, and here they meet."

Caution grumbled, "A competent sign maker would have said, 'Both roads lead to the Heavenly City.' Then there would have been no confusion."

"Caution, must you always quibble? In any case, we're on the right road. Be happy for that."

"I will admit that I'm a bit relieved," said Caution. "But as for being happy, I shall wait awhile for that. We may be on the right road. That's all I know at the moment."

"Caution, *you* are hopeless."

"There's some truth in that," said Caution. "But what reason have I to be hopeful? We do not really know that there's a Heavenly City or, if there is one, that this is the right road to it. If we do find the Heavenly City, it will be mere luck."

"Suppose it is luck," said Pilgrim. "Does that matter, as long as our luck is good?"

That night, sister and brother made camp on the plains. In the morning, they were awakened not by the light but by a terrible wind that roared in their ears and threw dust in their eyes. Far in the distance, a whirlwind could be seen. They gathered the lightest of their belongings and hurried along the road.

"Pilgrim," said Caution, "let us hope that the luck you speak of finds us a Heavenly City very soon. We shall certainly not survive if that whirlwind comes upon us while we are unsheltered."

For two hours, they stumbled along the road, buffeted by the wind and nearly blinded by the dust. Then they both stopped abruptly. Pilgrim had noticed a sign; Caution had noticed what lay ahead of them.

"Caution, the sign says, 'Heavenly City One League Ahead Through the Valley.' We shall surely make it."

"But look at the valley, Pilgrim! Look and listen. Even smell."

Before them the road dipped sharply into fog and darkness. Threatening forms moved about in the fog, and there were howls like those of wild beasts. The stench was that of a swamp.

"It does look quite fearsome," said Pilgrim. "But the sign would not be here if we could not pass through unharmed."

"What I see before me convinces me more than any sign," said Caution. "Go if you will. I shall not."

Pilgrim pleaded, but Caution sat down by the side of the road and refused to move. Sitting down next to him, Pilgrim was determined to stay until Caution changed his mind. There they stayed for the rest of the morning and part of the afternoon. Pop and Hasty and Suppressed passed by, and Circles the beggar, and Faith and her wonderful friend, and others as well. All urged Caution and Pilgrim to come with them, but Caution refused and Pilgrim remained with him. Through the day, the dust and wind became more and more terrible.

"By now, Caution," said Pilgrim, "all those people are safe and happy in the Heavenly City."

"Or they are dead, devoured by the swamp."

"I doubt it," said Pilgrim. "But if we stay here much longer, we shall surely die. I can barely breathe now. And that whirlwind should be upon us at any moment."

"All right, Pilgrim," said Caution. "I don't know if there is a Heavenly City. I certainly don't believe that we shall get through that terrible valley in any case. But it is clear now that there is little to gain by staying here. Were I alone, I believe I would prefer to die out here in the wind. But I will not have you die believing that I kept you from the Heavenly City. For your sake, we shall go."

They got to their feet and approached the edge of the dark valley. Pilgrim was cheerful.

"In a little while, Caution, we shall be in the Heavenly City, and I shall enjoy seeing you happy for the very first time."

"Good-bye, Pilgrim."

"Don't be so pessimistic, Caution. Here goes."

"Here goes nothing," said Caution.

And into the valley they went.

Questions

1. Explain, in context, the reasoning of the following characters in "Another Pilgrim's Progress."
   a. Provincial
   b. the tavern keeper
   c. Circles the beggar
   d. Pop
   e. Hasty
   f. Suppressed
   g. the official at the junction
2. What, if anything, is wrong with the reasoning of each of these characters in 1?
3. What is confusing about the sign regarding the roads being heavenly or hellish?
4. What bothers Caution about Faith's claims? Do you feel that Caution's attitude is justified in terms of what's portrayed in the story? Explain.
5. Explain the differences in outlook among Skeptic, Caution, and Pilgrim. Do you feel that one outlook is better than the others?

Discussion

PREVIEW

At the end of this discussion, you should be familiar with:

* *what an argument is;*
* *the differences between deductive and inductive arguments;*
* *the differences between valid and invalid deductive arguments;*
* *the logical symbols introduced in "Philosophy Is Murder" and repeated here;*
* *the specific examples of valid and invalid arguments given;*
* *three types of inductive arguments;*
* *the 15 informal fallacies discussed;*
* *what skepticism is;*
* *the meaning of terms listed in "Definitions" (which are also marked in bold in the discussion).*

Arguments

In "Another Pilgrim's Progress," Caution and the tavern keeper engage in the following argument:

> "I don't know what all this quarreling is about," said the tavern keeper. "The whole thing is no dilemma to me. As I see it, either you go out there in the dust and die, or you stay in here and drink my fine ale. That doesn't take much thought, does it?"
>
> "But then again," said Caution, "if we leave here, we might find the Heavenly City. Or, if we stay, you might run out of ale, and we would die of thirst."
>
> "You know, Caution," said the tavern keeper, "I'm beginning to lose patience with you myself. Careful you don't get me angry, or I'll toss you out there in that dust...."

This is an argument in at least three senses of the term:

1. A heated dispute (involving two or more people).
2. An attempt to persuade (someone of something).
3. Giving reasons in support of the truth of some statement.

These three types of argument can occur together, but they need not. "It's time for bed"/"No, it's not!"/"Yes, it is" would be an example of a heated dispute with no reasons given (at least not yet). If a salesperson gets you to buy a product by making you feel sorry for her, that's persuasion without a heated dispute and without giving reasons why the product is the best one for you. If I'm considering reasons (related, say, to price, gas mileage, and reliability ratings) in support of the conclusion that a certain model of car would be my most economical choice, I could be having a heated debate with a car dealer, or trying to persuade my partner to agree to the purchase, or simply making a decision on my own.

In the course of studying philosophy, we will be primarily concerned with arguments in the third sense of the term—giving reasons in support of the truth of some statement. Of course, we may be persuading ourselves or others of the truth of some conclusion, but the emphasis is on truth rather than persuasion. Some familiar logical fallacies we'll discuss later involve ways people try to persuade others with bad arguments.

The word "**argument**" in this text will refer to reasons (the **premises**) in support of the truth of some claim (the **conclusion**). We will be judging arguments as good or bad in terms of whether, and to what degree, they establish the truth of the conclusion. As we're using the term, an argument can be bad even if it succeeds in persuading someone of something.

If we look for premises and a conclusion in what the tavern keeper is saying, they might go something like this:

Either the best choice is to stay in here and drink fine ale, or
  the best choice is to go out in the dust and die.
It's not the best choice to go out in the dust and die (obviously).

It's the best choice to stay in here and drink fine ale.

With any argument we need to consider at least two questions:

Do the premises properly support the conclusion?
Are the premises true?

The tavern keeper's argument has a familiar **logical form** that we saw in "Philosophy Is Murder." To determine its form, we follow the procedure outlined in "Philosophy Is Murder" with one change. There for the sake of the mystery we used letters like A and B. We will now adopt the more standard practice of using p and q.

> p, q, and so on, stand for distinct statements. (Note that a letter can stand for only one statement in an argument and must stand for that same statement throughout the argument.)
> "~ p" means "not p" (~ is called the "curl")
> "p • q" means "p and q" (• is called the "dot")
> "p v q" means "p or q" (v is called the "wedge")
> "p ⊃ q" means "If p, then q" (⊃ is called the "horseshoe")
> "p ≡ q" means "If p, then q, and if q, then p" (≡ is called the "triple bar")
> "/∴" after the last premise or a line drawn under the premises means "therefore"

If we substitute "p" for "the best choice is to stay in here and drink ale" and "q" for "the best choice is to go out in the dust and die," we get this:

Either p or q
Not q
_____
p

If we now substitute the wedge (v) for "either . . . or" and the curl (~) for "not," we get:

p v q
~ q
_____
p

If you're getting nervous about using symbols, don't be. You won't need to use them in discussing the other topics in this text. Logical symbols are being used here partly to acquaint you with such symbols, but mostly to help you understand argument forms. We will be using some of those argument forms throughout the text, but we will do so informally, in English, not formally, with symbols. You already use these forms of argument in your everyday conversation: We just want to make them explicit.

"p v q; ~ q; /∴ p" (or "p v q; ~ p; /∴ q") is a valid deductive argument form. To say that this is a **valid deductive argument** form is to say that every argument of that form is such that *if the premises are true, the conclusion must be true*. Saying this says nothing about whether or not the premises are true—that's a separate matter. Saying an argument is deductively valid is saying that you don't need to worry about the connection between the premises and the conclusion since true premises would guarantee a true conclusion. Worry only about whether the premises are true. (More on this in the next section.)

If Caution had told the tavern keeper that his conclusion didn't follow from his premises, he would have been incorrect. What Caution does instead is to attack the first premise of the tavern keeper's argument. The first premise of the tavern keeper's argument is a case of what we'll discuss later as the **fallacy of false dilemma**: claiming that there are only two relevant possibilities when in fact there are more. Caution challenges the first premise by pointing out those other possibilities: "But then again, if we leave here, we might find the Heavenly City. Or, if we stay, you might run out of ale, and we would die of thirst." If there are more than two possibilities, then eliminating one doesn't show which of the remaining possibilities is correct.

In terms of its form, the argument given by the tavern keeper is deductively *valid*. It has a form such that *if the premises are true, the conclusion must be true. A valid argument with true premises is called a* **sound deductive argument**. Caution concludes that this argument is not sound.

LET'S REVIEW
* *What are the two questions we should ask with any argument?*
* *What is the definition of a valid deductive argument?*
* *If you know you have a valid deductive argument, do you know the premises are true? Do you know the conclusion is true?*
* *What makes a deductive argument sound?*

Now let's consider a different sort of reasoning that Caution engages in with Pop, Hasty, and Suppressed. Pop, Hasty, and Suppressed all represent informal fallacies, but we will discuss those fallacies later. For the moment, let's view the exchange as a matter of reasoning from certain pieces of evidence as to which road is most likely to lead to the Heavenly City.

Pop reasons that there are many footprints on the road to the right and few footprints on the road to the left, so the road to the right probably leads to the Heavenly City.

Caution isn't satisfied. "Perhaps they were all together and just had to take a guess. Or perhaps the first ones took a guess, and the rest just followed the crowd." Hasty then points out an additional fact and reasons from it as follows: "The footprints all go one way. Surely, if this were the wrong road, there would be some footprints coming back." But then comes another piece of evidence that seems to undermine Hasty's reasoning: The roads are one-way; no one would have had the opportunity to come back. What I want you to note is how natural it is to use words such as "likely" and "probable" in the context of such reasoning. Whatever evidence is gathered, it will not *guarantee* that this or that road *must* lead to the Heavenly City. At best, the evidence will show that the Heavenly City is more likely to be down this road than that.

When our reasoning involves us in probabilities, we are dealing with an inductive argument rather than a deductive argument. True premises in a valid deductive argument guarantee the truth of the conclusion. True premises in a **strong inductive argument** give good support to the conclusion but don't guarantee its truth. What accounts for this difference? With valid deductive arguments, the truth of the premises guarantees the truth of the conclusion because the conclusion contains no information that is not contained, at least implicitly, in the premises. In a sense, the conclusion of a valid deductive argument is merely a repetition of some information already in the premises. Thus, the conclusion could not possibly be false if the premises are true. This does not mean that it is easy to see whether or not the information in the conclusion is contained in the premises. (Note the word "implicitly.") Figuring out if a deductive argument is valid can be a complicated business—as is shown by the discussion of symbolic logic in "Philosophy Is Murder."

On the other hand, the conclusion of an inductive argument does contain information not contained in the premises. Thus, it is conceivable that the premises of such an argument could be true and the conclusion false. In the discussion with Pop, Hasty, and Suppressed, no evidence to be found at that junction would guarantee which is the correct road: At best it would show that one of the roads is *probably* the correct one. This apparent weakness of induction is intrinsic to its crucial importance: Induction gives us new information about the world rather than simply telling us what is implicit in the information we already have. Since an inductive argument will always have more information in the conclusion than in the premises, the premises can at best support the conclusion with a degree of probability.

Once again, with any argument you need to answer the following two questions:

Do the premises properly support the conclusion?
Are the premises true?

Deductive arguments are either valid or invalid. If their form is such that the truth of the premises would guarantee the truth of the conclusion, they are valid; otherwise they are invalid. Valid deductive arguments with true premises are called "sound."

With inductive arguments we don't use the words "valid" and "sound": These terms have an either-or quality that doesn't fit with induction with its degrees of probability. However, we're looking for something parallel with inductive arguments. We want to know whether or not the premises offer strong support for the conclusion (and if so, how strong this support is); and we want to know whether or not the premises are true.

Consider the following four arguments:

1. If it is *(fill in the current year)*, then it is the twenty-first century.
   It is *(fill in the current year)*.
   _____
   It is the twenty-first century.
2. If this is 2094, then it is the twenty-first century.
   It is 2094.
   _____
   It is the twenty-first century.
3. All human beings observed thus far have lived less than 175 years.
   _____
   The next human being observed will live less than 175 years.
4. All human beings observed thus far have lived less than 20 years.
   _____
   The next human being observed will live less than 20 years.

Arguments 1 and 2 are valid deductive arguments. You already know their form: If p, then q; p; therefore q. However only valid argument 1 has true premises, and only valid argument 1 is sound. Argument 2 is valid but not sound.

Arguments 3 and 4 are inductive arguments: Notice how information in the conclusion (re "the next human being observed") goes beyond the information in the premises (re "all human beings observed thus far"). In each case, the premise offers strong support for the conclusion, so that *if* the premise is true, then the conclusion is probably true. (Arguments 3 and 4 are the inductive analogue of valid.) However, the premise of argument 3 is obviously true; the premise of 4 is obviously false. (Argument 3 is the inductive analogue of sound.) We can answer both of our questions positively in the case of argument 3. Yes, the premise properly supports the conclusion. Yes, the premise is probably true.

LET'S REVIEW

* What's the difference between a sound deductive argument and a strong inductive argument with true premises? What accounts for this difference?
* Analyze argument 3 above using whichever of the following terms are relevant: deductive/inductive; valid/invalid; strong/weak; premises true/premises false.

Many of you will have heard the definitions of deduction as going from the general to the particular and induction as going from the particular to the general. These definitions are incorrect. In arguments 3 and 4, we have examples of inductive arguments going from the general to the particular. A valid deductive argument going from the particular to the particular would be, "Bob is human; therefore Bob is human" (p; therefore p).

Let's take a closer look first at deductive arguments, then at inductive arguments.

Deductive Arguments

In assessing deductive arguments, one examines argument forms. The following arguments have the same form:

It is raining.	It is snowing.
It is cool.	It is warm.
———————————	———————————
It is raining and it is cool.	It is snowing and it is warm.

The form of these arguments is:

$$p$$
$$q$$
$$\overline{}$$
$$p \cdot q$$

(Or, "r; s; /∴ r • s" Remember that the letters are merely place markers.)

Every argument of this form is valid. How do we know that this is a valid argument form? Our knowledge of validity is based on our knowledge of the meanings of the logical connectives. The word "and" *means* that the statement "p and q" will be true if, and only if, "p" is true and "q" is true. Given this definition, it is impossible for "p and q" to be false if "p" is true and "q" is true.

Such definitions given in terms of truth and falsity are set out in what are called "truth tables." Truth tables are used to develop a series of inference rules and replacement rules that can then be used to prove arguments valid. That's something we'll leave to logic texts. However it is important that you be acquainted with a few standard valid argument forms so that you'll be able to recognize them when they come up informally. (We'll start doing the logical connectives in English to make things a bit easier.)

Modus Ponens	Modus Tollens	Hypothetical Syllogism	Disjunctive Syllogism
If p, then q	If p, then q	If p, then q	Either p or q
p	Not q	If q, then r	Not p
q	Not p	If p, then r	q

Consider the following arguments:

(i) If we have free will, then our choices aren't caused. If our choices aren't caused, then they happen by chance. So if we have free will, then our choices happen by chance.

(ii) If the mind and the brain are identical, then the mind and brain have all the same characteristics. But the mind and brain don't have all the same characteristics. Therefore it's not the case that the mind and the brain are identical.

(iii) Moral questions are like either scientific questions or questions of taste. But moral questions aren't like scientific questions, so they must be like questions of taste.

These are parts of larger arguments that would be supported by further arguments and then (presumably) attacked with counterarguments. We'll get to that later. The point here is that you should (eventually) be able to see that each of these arguments is deductively valid. The first (*i*) is an example of a hypothetical syllogism (If p, then q; if q, then r; therefore, if p, then r):

> If we have free will, then our choices aren't caused.
> If our choices aren't caused, then our choices happen by chance.
> _____
> If we have free will, then our choices happen by chance.

ii is an example of modus tollens (If p, then q; not q; therefore, not p):

> If the mind and brain are identical, then the mind and brain have all the same characteristics.
> It's not the case that the mind and brain have all the same characteristics.
> _____
> It's not the case that the mind and brain are identical.

iii is an example of disjunctive syllogism (Either p or q; not p; therefore, q):

> Either moral questions are like scientific questions or they're like questions of taste.
> It's not the case that moral questions are like scientific questions.
> _____
> Moral questions are like questions of taste.

It may take a little practice to see basic argument forms under the looser informal wordings of arguments, but you'll get there. You won't have to deal with many of these valid argument forms.

Again, to say that these arguments are deductively valid is *not* to say that they are sound—that the premises are true—that the conclusion ought to be accepted. It is only to say that *if* the premises are true, then the conclusion must be true. Are the premises true? At the very least, all three arguments are incomplete. For instance, regarding *ii*, I'd want to know what is meant by "identical" and I'd need information about what the differences are supposed to be between the brain and the mind.

We will see all three arguments in later chapters. When we do, we'll discuss supplementary arguments as well as counterarguments. Here we are simply considering them as examples of particular argument forms.

There are also invalid argument forms, and some of these are particularly tricky because they resemble familiar valid argument forms. Below are two invalid deductive arguments. ("**Antecedent**" is the name for what comes before "then" in an if-then statement, and "**consequent**" is the name for what comes after "then" in an if-then statement.)

Fallacy of denying the antecedent	Fallacy of affirming the consequent
If p, then q	If p, then q
Not p	q
Not q	p

How do we know these arguments aren't valid? There are technical methods for proving invalidity that we won't get into. But there's a way to show that such simple deductive fallacies are in fact fallacies. Consider the following argument which is being made up to show the fallacy of denying the antecedent.

If this is 2050, then this is the twenty-first century.	(If p, then q)
This is not 2050.	(not p)
This is not the twenty-first century.	(not q)

Ask yourself: Are the premises true? Remember that the first premise isn't saying that this is 2050 but only what is true if it is 2050. Is the second premise true? Is the conclusion true? (Think a minute.) Here we have a deductive argument with true premises and a false conclusion. Is that possible with a valid deductive argument? No. Therefore, we can see that the argument above is invalid.

With a valid argument form, it is impossible for any argument of that form to have true premises and a false conclusion. Here the premises are obviously true and the conclusion is obviously false. Hence, the argument form—if p, then q; not p; therefore, not q—must be invalid.

LET'S REVIEW

* *Familiarize yourself with the valid deductive argument forms modus ponens, modus tollens, hypothetical syllogism, and disjunctive syllogism.*
* *Using English statements, make up some everyday arguments that exemplify these argument forms.*

Inductive Arguments

As we've discussed, when our reasoning involves us in probabilities, we are dealing with inductive rather than deductive arguments. True premises in a strong inductive argument give good support to the conclusion but don't guarantee its truth. This is because the conclusion of an inductive argument contains information not contained in the premises.

Induction is the method we use to learn from experience, to gain new information about the world, and to develop theories and make predictions. It is the method humans used to learn to avoid poison oak, make cakes that don't fall, throw a curve ball, make a combustion engine, predict rain, and build airplanes; where we don't use it ourselves, we learn from others who have—in which case deciding where to get the most reliable information is also a matter of induction.

There are different types of inductive arguments. Some of these types are quite specific; others are more vague. Some yield numerical probability; some only support an hypothesis as being more likely than the alternatives.

Logicians debate how many types of inductive reasoning there are and how they should be best categorized. We won't get into that. We will merely consider three familiar types of inductive argument as samples of induction: analogical induction, inductive generalization, and hypothetical induction.

Analogical Induction

In **analogical induction** (also called **argument from analogy**), we're reasoning that because two things are alike in several respects, they are also alike in some further respect. If a friend and I have all enjoyed the same foods at the various restaurants we've both tried, then if she enjoys the food at a new restaurant I haven't tried, it's likely that I'll enjoy the food at the new restaurant as well. If she and I have shown similar energy levels on various hikes, then if she finds a certain hike too taxing, it's likely I will as well.

An argument from analogy is typically schematized like this:

Objects P and Q are similar in having properties a, b, c, and d.
Object P has property e.
Therefore, object Q has property e.

Such an argument is clearly inductive because the conclusion contains information not contained in the premises.

Analogical reasoning has played, and still plays, a large role in our thinking about life on other worlds. In 1785, the philosopher Thomas Reid

gave the following argument from analogy for the existence of living creatures on other planets in our solar system:

> Thus, we may observe a very great similitude between this earth
> which we inhabit, and the other planets, Saturn, Jupiter, Mars,
> Venus, and Mercury. They all revolve round the sun, as the earth
> does, although at different distances, and in different periods. They
> borrow all their light from the sun, as the earth does. Several of them
> are known to revolve round their axes like the earth, and, by that
> means, must have a like succession of day and night. Some of them
> have moons, that serve to give them light in the absence of the sun,
> as our moon does to us. They are all, in their motions, subject to the
> same law of gravitation as the earth is. From all this similitude, it is
> not unreasonable to think, that those planets may, like our earth,
> be the habitation of various orders of living creatures. There is some
> probability in this conclusion from analogy.

For its time—given the poverty of information about other planets and
lingering theological views of ways in which Earth was supposed to be
special—it's a pretty impressive argument. And notice that Reid was properly modest in claiming only "some probability" for his conclusion.

Part of what had defeated Reid's argument by the mid-twentieth century was a much better understanding of the dissimilarities (disanalogies)
between Earth and those other planets concerning likely conditions necessary for life—especially conditions that would allow for the long-term
existence of water in liquid form. Of course, we are still using analogical
reasoning in our search for planets in other solar systems that reside in
the so-called Goldilocks zone—where conditions are "just right" for the
existence of liquid water and, therefore, life.

Analogical reasoning on a universe-size scale is behind the famous teleological argument (or argument from design) for the existence of God. In
one version, it is argued that in certain crucial ways, the universe resembles
machines that humans design. Since like effects have like causes, the universe
too must have had a designer, namely, God. We will discuss this analogical
reasoning, along with other arguments for the existence of God, in Chapter 5.

Inductive Generalization

We're using the term "**inductive generalization**" to cover what has vari-
ously been called "enumerative induction" and "statistical induction." The
idea here is that we are moving from information we have about some

subset of a group to conclusions about the whole group or about some further members of it.

Here's one example of inductive generalization we have already seen.

(a) All human beings observed thus far have lived less than 175 years.

The next human being observed will live less than 175 years.

Compare that argument to this one:

(b) All human beings observed thus far have lived less than 175 years.

All human beings for the next three centuries will live less than 175 years.

Given that we have information on millions and millions of human beings, the probability of the conclusion of (a) being true is very, very high (especially given the supplementary information that the age of the oldest known human was 122 years and that there have been no revolutionary new breakthroughs in medicine in recent years related to aging). It's hard to know how to evaluate (b), but knowing that there are likely to be enormous advances in science in the not-too-distant future (including genetic engineering), I wouldn't want to bet my (or my descendants') money on the statement that all human beings for the next three centuries will live less than 175 years.

The inductive generalizations we run across all the time are opinion polls. For instance, a Kaiser Health Tracking poll in April 2014 found that 46 percent of a sample of 1504 adults had an unfavorable view of the "health reform bill signed into law in 2010" and concluded that 46 percent of all adult Americans had an unfavorable view of the law. Of course, if Kaiser had surveyed just any 1504 Americans, then the conclusion would have been a joke. However, what made the survey powerful was that the sample was both random and representative.

> The combined landline and cell phone sample was weighted to balance the sample demographics to match estimates for the national population using data from the Census Bureau's 2012 American Community Survey (ACS) on sex, age, education, race, Hispanic origin, nativity (for Hispanics only), and region along with data from the 2010 Census on population density. The sample was also weighted to match current patterns of telephone use using data from the January–June 2013 National Health Interview Survey. . . .

> The margin of sampling error including the design effect for the
> full sample is plus or minus 3 percentage points.

To the uninitiated, it is amazing how small a sample of a population is necessary to make quite accurate predictions about that population—as long as the sample is randomly selected (meaning that each member of the population has an equal chance of being selected). Experience with Gallup polls has given statisticians a precise idea of the sampling error one gets with a population of a certain size. With a population of 1000, it is $\pm$ 4 (percentage points); with 1500 (as in the Kaiser survey above), it is $\pm$ 3%; with 4000 it is $\pm$ 2%.

(Of course, all that numerical sophistication is worthless unless the questions are clear, unbiased, and logically related to the conclusion drawn.)

Hypothetical Induction

What we're calling **hypothetical induction** is often called **abduction** or **inference to the best explanation**. The idea is that we're faced with an aspect of experience that puzzles us and for which we'd like an explanation. We come up with a hypothetical explanation (if we're creative enough) and consider alternative hypotheses. We see whether our hypothesis seems to provide the best explanation, running tests if possible, but also considering whether or not it fits with established beliefs and theories better than any other explanation.

Detective fiction is often used to provide illustrations of hypothetical induction. Sherlock Holmes's cases are frequently used, but we'll look at "Philosophy Is Murder" instead.

Detectives have been called "masters of deduction." Actually, most of their reasoning is inductive. On the basis of certain facts, they form conclusions about other facts, and where conclusions contain more information than is contained in the premises, such reasoning is inductive. Furthermore, the guilt of a criminal is never established with absolute certainty. The law requires only that guilt be proved "beyond a reasonable doubt"—which is to say, with a high degree of probability. And where we are dealing with probabilities, we are dealing with induction.

The instances of induction in "Philosophy Is Murder" are numerous. To decide it's likely that Professor Lanchaster's murderer was one of the other four professors rather than a total stranger is to use induction. Even concluding from Lanchaster's wound and the bullet hole in the back of his chair that he was shot is to use induction.

The premises would be true if the bullet had been thrown into the air somewhere across town, had landed and bounced erratically through the streets, had bounced into the Lanchaster house, and had struck the deceased. But induction (related to common experience and the laws of physics) tells us that such a theoretical possibility is so unlikely that we need not consider it seriously. In such an instance, the conclusion seems so obvious that we may not think of ourselves as reasoning at all, but we are. And the reasoning is inductive.

Hulk learns that the phone cord was cut on the evening of the murder. He decides that there is a possibility that Lanchaster had been left alone by the murderer at some point, and a more remote possibility that he had left some kind of message. True, Hulk is dealing with mere possibilities here, but induction tells him that such possibilities are at least worth investigating. He isn't going to tell Crocker to search the bedroom or the lawn for a message.

Hulk finds the logic exercise and deduces the message "ITS LORD." Conceivably, it is pure coincidence that these letters can be deduced from this logic exercise. But inductive reasoning would convince all of us that this being coincidence is unlikely. Had not Lord (conveniently) confessed, Hulk and the police would have tried to further confirm Hulk's theory by tracking down Lord's purchase of a gun.

LET'S REVIEW

* Go over the three types of inductive arguments discussed and make sure you can give a brief characterization of each.
* "My girl friend's been avoiding me this week. I wonder if it's because she's seeing someone else." What kind of induction, if any, is this?

Fallacies in Reasoning

"Another Pilgrim's Progress" was inspired by the famous *Pilgrim's Progress* written by John Bunyan in the late seventeenth century. *Pilgrim's Progress* is a religious allegory in which the central figure, Christian, leaves the City of Destruction on a pilgrimage to the Celestial City. Along the way Christian meets a number of allegorical figures, such as Obstinate, Pliable, and Ignorance, as well as Good Will, Faithful, and Hopeful. *Pilgrim's Progress* seemed a natural model for an allegory, not of vices and related virtues as in the original, but of logical fallacies and the better arguments they often resemble. The fallacies, in the order they appear in "Another Pilgrim's Progress," are as follows: (1) provincialism, (2) ad hominem, (3) straw man, (4) slippery slope, (5) false dilemma, (6) appeal to force, (7) equivocation, (8) begging the question, (9) inconsistency, (10) appeal to popular opinion, (11) hasty conclusion, (12) suppressed evidence, (13) appeal to authority, (14) appeal to ignorance, and (15) impervious hypothesis.

We need to be careful with informal fallacies. There's a danger that learning about such fallacies can promote a sloppy "Gotcha!" approach to argument—people pinning a fallacy name on any argument that at all resembles the fallacy and then feeling as if they have disproved that argument. In fact, most fallacy names cover a cluster of both blatant and subtle mistakes, mistakes easily confused with good modes of reasoning that they resemble. It's important to be sensitive to those good arguments as well.

Provincialism

The fallacy of **provincialism** is committed when one accepts or rejects a conclusion on the basis of one's identification with a particular group.

In the story, of course, this fallacy is exemplified by Provincial. In spite of all the disasters that have befallen his town, he says, "This is my home. How can any place be better?" Caution properly calls him on the argument:

> What nonsense, Provincial! The crops are destroyed. The rich soil is gone. Most of our town has burned or is burning. The air is so filled with dirt and heat that one can scarcely breathe. Our provisions are dwindling, and soon we may starve. How can you maintain that this is the best place on earth?

Ad Hominem (to the Person)

When Person A presents an argument and Person B responds by discussing irrelevant characteristics of Person A as if they were good grounds for rejecting the argument, Person B commits the **ad hominem** fallacy. Just as it is sometimes justifiable to rely on the word of supposed experts, so it can be legitimate to "attack the person" by showing that she is no expert. What is fallacious is the arguing from irrelevant characteristics.

In "Progress," this fallacy is committed twice. First, Provincial responds to Caution's criticism of the town by saying that Caution has not lived there as long as Provincial. As Caution correctly complains, "That is true. But what has that to do with what I say?" Second, when the junction official is unable to counter Caution's challenges to his expertise, he attacks Caution as a troublemaker.

Straw Man

When one misinterprets a position or argument so as to make it seem more vulnerable to criticism, what one is attacking is called a **straw man**. In the story, this is exemplified by Provincial's dismissing Caution as if Caution were a skeptic. But Caution's views are not that extreme; he should not be judged as a skeptic. In fact, Caution is not a skeptic.

It is always tempting to interpret an opponent's position in an unfavorable manner. This misrepresentation can result from ignorance of the position one is characterizing or from wishful thinking (wanting the position to be weaker than it is) or deliberate use as a rhetorical device. Some examples follow:

> "Religious belief is for those who want simple answers to life." Counter: There are any number of theologians and philosophers of religion who have complicated arguments in favor of their beliefs.
>
> "Evolution says that complex creatures, including people, are the way they are because of chance." Counter: Evolution does say mutations are random but not the processes that select for or are against those mutations.

The ideal in dealing with arguments—even arguments that go against your preferred position—is to apply the **principle of charity**. That is, you give the best interpretation you can of the argument and then evaluate it. This is considered the ideal because in philosophy you are trying to find the truth, not simply to defeat ideas of others as in a rhetoric class.

Slippery Slope

The **slippery slope** fallacy is the argument, without good evidence, that any move in a certain direction will inevitably lead you to slide past other possibilities to some terrible extreme. The slippery slope fallacy comes up when you are dealing with a continuum of positions, say, A1, A2, A3, A4, A5, where A1 is the status quo and A5 is something obviously bad. The fallacy is to assume, without specific evidence, that there is no way you can move from A1 toward A2 without sliding all the way to A5—so that, since A5 is bad, you shouldn't move at all. One example of this fallacy arises in gun control debates: "If you let the government take away the AK-47 assault rifle, pretty soon they'll take away all our rights and we'll be living in a fascist dictatorship." To see how absurd this argument is, turn it around: "We can't let citizens have any weapons because pretty soon they'll all have tanks and tactical nuclear weapons and be blowing up the whole world."

In real life, we constantly draw boundaries that more or less hold. For example, we eat some sweets without becoming obese; we have a couple of drinks without becoming alcoholics; we have laws against some things without having laws against everything; we pay some taxes without the government taking all our money away. Slippery slope is simply a reflexive, lazy way of arguing that is constantly contradicted by the life around us.

On the other hand, there are real slippery slopes in life (stepping off the top slope of a glacier would be an obvious example). If you passed a law allowing a certain 10 percent of the population to take anything they felt they really needed from the other 90 percent, you might well be creating a situation that would lead to inevitable disaster.

In the story, the tavern keeper commits the fallacy when arguing that if Caution questions the tavern keeper's argument he will end up, like a skeptic, questioning everything.

False Dilemma

The **false dilemma** fallacy is committed when the possible positions at issue are falsely reduced so as to make the position for which one is arguing seem more reasonable. We have already seen how the tavern keeper commits this fallacy and how Caution challenges him by pointing out the other possibilities the tavern keeper's argument has left out.

> "I don't know what all this quarreling is about," said the tavern keeper. "The whole thing is no dilemma to me. As I see it, either you go out there in the dust and die, or you stay in here and drink my fine ale. That doesn't take much thought, does it?"
>
> "But then again," said Caution, "if we leave here, we might find the Heavenly City. Or, if we stay, you might run out of ale, and we would die of thirst."

The fallacies of false dilemma and straw man are often combined in moral and political arguments—where the only choice supposedly possible is between your position and your opponent's position presented as a negative caricature.

Appeal to Force

Appeal to force is only marginally a logical fallacy since it would rarely be confused with using reasoning to lead someone toward adopting an opinion as opposed to threatening that person if he or she continues to resist holding it. But it has been on traditional lists of fallacies, and there are a couple of instances of it in the story. Here's one:

> "You know, Caution," said the tavern keeper, "I'm beginning to lose patience with you myself. Careful you don't get me angry, or I'll toss you out there in that dust and make the choice for you. How would you like that?"

Equivocation

The fallacy of **equivocation** is committed when a crucial word or phrase shifts meaning within a single argument so that premises seem to support the conclusion but do not.

In "Progress," it's natural (if slightly incautious) for Pilgrim to conclude that the road marked "heavenly" leads to the Heavenly City. It turns out that the word "heavenly" there simply means "scenic," so the move from heavenly road to Heavenly City is an invalid inference.

Fallacies of equivocation or ambiguity are a constant danger in philosophy: writers often use broad terms in restricted senses and then easily shift back to the broader usage as the argument continues. For example, Descartes claims that one cannot be in error about the belief "I think, therefore I am." It would be fallacious, however, to conclude from Descartes's argument that I cannot be in error about the belief that Tom Davis (the author of this text) exists. The "I" in Descartes's argument designates only "this mind." It does not imply a body, a past, and so on. (We will discuss this in Chapter 2.)

Begging the Question or Circular Argument

The phrase "**begging the question**" has at least three popular meanings:

1. It can mean that *a situation begs for (calls for) a certain question to be asked.* For instance, "All this talk about the *Matrix* movie begs the question of whether or not we might be living in a simulated reality."
2. It can mean *ducking the question.* "I'd like to answer that journalist's question about whether I was involved in the scandal by saying how much I value the role of the press in keeping politicians honest. In

fact, as a boy, I delivered newspapers for many years in Kansas City where my hard-working parents. . ."

3. It can also mean *arguing in a circle* where some version of the conclusion is used as a premise.

We will be using the phrase "begging the question" in the third sense, as **circular argument**.

All circular arguments are valid: if a statement is true as a premise, it must be true as a conclusion. Circular arguments are sometimes sound—when the conclusion is, in fact, true. A circular argument becomes fallacious when it purports to do something it does not: to offer additional statements in support of the conclusion. When a person requests an argument for a statement, it is (generally) because the statement is considered questionable. To offer that questionable statement in support of itself is, to say the least, unhelpful.

In the story, of course, it is Circles the beggar who exemplifies this fallacy. Note, however, that she does not commit this fallacy simply by pointing to a sign or map as evidence that the travelers are, indeed, on the road to the Heavenly City. One might criticize the reliability of the evidence she presents, but this would have nothing to do with circularity. She commits this fallacy when, in continuing to argue, she "circles back" and uses as premises the very statements at issue. Circles says, "But this is the right road . . . I know that." How does she know that? She points to the sign as evidence. But how does she know that the sign is correct? "That's easy . . . I know that the sign is correct because this is the right road." She is now using the premise "This is the right road" to support the conclusion "This is the right road."

Again: After Circles produces a map as evidence, Caution asks her how she knows that the map is correct. As evidence, Circles points to a statement on the map that says it is a reliable map. But this statement is not additional evidence that the map is reliable: The statement is only as reliable as the map itself.

One is particularly likely to beg the question in arguing philosophy because very basic beliefs are at issue—beliefs one is not accustomed to arguing—and it is easy to fall back on one of those beliefs in the course of the argument. Here is one example:

How do you know that you are not now dreaming? "Well, I've checked with the people around me, and they say that I am awake." This response begs the question. The claim that one has checked with other people (as opposed to merely dreaming one has checked with other people) assumes the conclusion.

We will take up that issue later in Chapter 2.

Inconsistency

Two statements are **inconsistent** when one asserts what the other denies. An argument may suffer from inconsistency but so may a set of beliefs, irrespective of the arguments for those beliefs. If two statements are inconsistent, one of them must be false. To know that two statements are inconsistent is not to know which one is false; further considerations are necessary to determine that. But to discover an inconsistency ought to provoke a reexamination of those beliefs.

Perhaps most people can spot inconsistencies as they occur in snatches of everyday discourse. But they are less easily detected when they occur in the course of a long argument, especially one that covers unfamiliar material or employs unfamiliar terminology. Inconsistency is a constant danger in philosophy, especially for the beginner.

For example, a student who believes in a soul that survives the death of the body might nod in agreement when hearing an initial lecture on the identity theory, which claims that the mind is the brain—not realizing that belief in the identity theory is inconsistent with a belief in a soul. (No doubt that inconsistency would be pointed out in a later lecture.)

Paradoxically, any deductive argument with inconsistent premises will be a valid argument. A valid deductive argument, you will recall, is one that has a form such that it is impossible for the premises to be true and the conclusion false. Since, in any argument with inconsistent premises, it will be impossible for (all) the premises to be true, such an argument must be valid. But though this seems odd, it should not be of serious concern to you. One ought to rely on sound arguments—arguments that are valid and have true premises. Inconsistency of premises may guarantee a valid argument, but it also guarantees an unsound argument: inconsistent premises cannot (all) be true.

"Another Pilgrim's Progress" does not contain examples of inconsistency and has only one example of an apparent inconsistency. It seems to Caution that the sign at the junction implies that there is one Heavenly City that is located in two different places. As it turns out, the statements on the sign may be confusing, but they are not inconsistent. The two roads, though initially heading in different directions, eventually meet.

Appeal to Popular Opinion

In the story, the fallacy of **appeal to popular opinion** is exemplified by Pop: "The road to the right is the road that most of the people took. That has got to be the way to go." It should be noted that this argument is fallacious because in the story it is not clear that anyone actually knows which is the correct road. (And, of course, what we have in the story is not a physical road but a representation of a quest for Heaven.) However, if a person were a stranger in a town and were looking for the county fair, it might be wise to "follow the crowd."

Hasty Conclusion

The fallacy of **hasty conclusion** involves drawing a conclusion from supporting evidence without making a reasonable effort to determine if there is other relevant evidence. A related fallacy—called "hasty generalization"—involves drawing an inductive generalization from insufficient data.

Of course, the character in the story named for this fallacy is Hasty. After Pop argues that the road most people took must be the correct road, Caution suggests that perhaps they were all together and just had to take a guess—or perhaps the first ones took a guess and the rest just followed the crowd.

Hasty counters by pointing out that

"... the footprints all go one way. Surely, if this were the wrong road, there would be some footprints coming back."

"Unless they haven't discovered their mistake yet," said Caution. "Or unless they all encountered some great pitfall and couldn't return."

"Thought of that, too.... But you can see that some of these footprints are very old and that the others have been made over a span of many days. If this were the wrong road, you'd think that someone would have returned by now. Even if there is a Great Pitfall up ahead, you'd think that someone toward the rear would have gotten some warning."

Hasty's overall reasoning is some of the best in the story. She's only hasty in not following her own logic in the case of the other road. If footprints coming back were the mark of the wrong road, why are there no footprints coming back on the other road, the road Pop and Hasty claim is the wrong road? Of course, all of the characters are thrown off by the joker who represents the next fallacy.

Suppressed Evidence

The fallacy of **suppressed evidence** involves presenting only evidence that is favorable to a certain conclusion and suppressing evidence that is not favorable. (If one were unaware of the unfavorable evidence and had not tried to seek it out, that would be an instance of hasty conclusion.)

In "Another Pilgrim's Progress," Suppressed is hiding evidence that affects the reasoning about there being no footprints on either road coming back—something one might expect to see on the wrong road. The evidence is a small sign Suppressed is standing in front of.

> THESE ROADS ARE ONE-WAY.
> NO TURNING BACK.
> THIS ORDINANCE STRICTLY ENFORCED.

Obviously, the evidence of this ordinance undercuts the relevance of no footprints coming back. The people who took the road to the right would have been forbidden to return no matter where that road led them.

Appeal to Authority

If a conclusion is supported by referring to the views of some supposed authority who actually has no expertise relevant to the matter at issue, a fallacy has been committed that comes under the heading of "**appeal to authority**."

In the story, of course, there's an equivocation or ambiguity about the idea of "authority" in terms of the guard in the shack. Caution and Pilgrim approach him under the assumption that he's an "authority" in terms of having expert knowledge. As the subsequent conversation shows, the guard is anything but an expert and is an authority only in the sense that he has the power to make a person do what he says.

It is often necessary and justifiable to rely on the word of experts. But it can be wrongly assumed that expertise in one field implies expertise in general. Thus it is that the views of physicists and football coaches are sometimes invoked in support of some political or religious view. I remember a Bible tract from years ago entitled "A Lawyer Examines the Bible." One might have wondered what a law degree had to do with biblical scholarship, but it was easy to see the underlying appeal to authority: If someone as intelligent and educated as a lawyer believes the Bible, you should believe it too (no lawyer jokes please).

Appeal to Ignorance

The fallacy of **appeal to ignorance** is one you will run across often, one that is likely to confuse and frustrate you unless you understand it. The fallacy involves assuming that if a claim can't be disproved, it is probably true or that failure to disprove counts as strong evidence in favor of a claim. Pilgrim commits a version of this fallacy twice in "Progress":

> "But Caution, we don't know this isn't the right road. That ought to count for something."

> "I've had enough of this," said Caution. "You say that your wonderful friend knows many wonderful things. But for all I know, his head may be as empty as yours. Come on, Pilgrim, we're going."
> "But, Caution," said Pilgrim. "You don't know he doesn't know the way."

Not knowing that some statement is false doesn't imply that the statement is true. Not having evidence against isn't evidence for.

Appeal to ignorance is part of the supposed justification for many dubious claims regarding visits by aliens or ghosts, worldwide conspiracy theories, three-headed dogs, and so forth. The principle to keep firmly in mind is that the burden of proof is on the person making the claim, not on the one who is dubious. It's up to the other person to present good evidence: If that evidence isn't forthcoming, the most reasonable response is doubt.

However, it's important not to confuse appeal to ignorance with some other legitimate moves. For instance, what we might call "negative evidence" is often important. There's the famous Sherlock Holmes story involving the "dog that didn't bark in the nighttime." The fact that the dog didn't bark was evidence that the criminal was someone known to the dog.

Also, sometimes failure to disprove a scientific hypothesis can be evidence in its favor—*if* there is already substantial evidence for the hypothesis and we can pin down what specific evidence against something we should be able to obtain from certain procedures if the hypothesis is false.

Impervious Hypothesis

We're using the term "**impervious hypothesis**" to refer to an hypothesis or belief that seems to be immune to any possible counterevidence. For an hypothesis to qualify as an impervious hypothesis, it's not enough that there is no counterevidence against it (the hypothesis might be obviously true) or that what has been presented as counterevidence has been disputed (maybe the supposed counterevidence is weak). It's rather that no conceivable counterevidence would seem to count against it.

If an hypothesis describes part of the world as being in state A as opposed to state B, we should be able to imagine what the world would be like if it were in state B and what evidence would show it (would have shown it) to be in state B. This is what Karl Popper meant when he famously said that an empirical belief should be falsifiable. While Popper's idea is a good one, the issue is more complicated than his falsifiability criterion indicates. Any general theory is going to consist of a collection of definitions and subsidiary hypotheses, and in many cases a theory would be substantially correct with minor modifications. One bit of counterevidence may only show that the theory needs to be modified, though it is substantially correct. Nonetheless, the general point holds: For any theory that purports to describe the world, we should be able to imagine evidence that would undermine it.

There are a cluster of fallacy names that describe this or a closely related fallacy: Self-sustaining belief, self-sealing belief, vacuous hypothesis, and tautology are just a few. Some of the differences have to do with whether or not the belief has been protected to the point where it has ceased to have any content.

Of course, the example of impervious hypothesis in "Progress" is Faith and her wonderful friend. Faith says that her friend knows the way to the Heavenly City (having been there many times) and is guiding Faith there. However, as the conversation proceeds, Faith's claim becomes more and more questionable. Her friend is deaf and mute, and Faith says she has no way of communicating with him. At that point, Caution challenges Faith to explain how she knows her friend knows the way. Then the amiable Pilgrim intervenes.

> "Stop, it, Caution," said Pilgrim. "It is quite obvious that our guide had some credentials, or that he and Faith were introduced through some mutual acquaintance who knew our guide's abilities quite well."
>
> "No," said Faith. "My friend carries no credentials. Nor were we introduced. When he came walking through my town one day, walking just as he is now, I had never seen him before, nor had I heard of him."
>
> "What made you follow him?" asked Pilgrim.
>
> Faith thought for a moment.

"I think . . . I think it was his eyes. They had that special look about them. Yes, his eyes convinced me."

"Ah!" said Pilgrim. "You had seen that look before."

"Are you joking?" said Faith. "How could it be special if I had seen it before? And would I follow a man on an exceptional journey like this one if he looked like any other person?"

Suppose Faith instead had said something like the following: "One day this strange individual came into my town with this special look in his eyes I had never seen before. As I looked at him, I had the sudden conviction that this individual knew the way to the Heavenly City, and I decided to follow him." Such a statement would not involve a logical fallacy. It would be the epitome of "blind faith" or perhaps "blind intuition," but neither of those are fallacies. You might argue that blind faith or intuition is absolutely no guide to truth and you might question the wisdom or dignity of letting yourself be guided in that way, but there would be no fallacy.

The fallacy arises both because of specific claims Faith makes and because of the attitude she takes toward the questions Pilgrim and Caution ask her. One would suppose taking something on blind faith would involve a bit of modesty—maybe a slightly apologetic attitude. Instead we get from Faith statements like: "My friend here knows the way to the Heavenly City"; her friend has been there "many times." This specificity implies that Faith has evidence for her claims about her wonderful friend. Yet under questioning it turns out that Faith has no evidence at all. Presumably, Faith would accept no conceivable evidence as counting against her claim.

LET'S REVIEW

Once again, the list of fallacies we've covered:
(1) provincialism, (2) ad hominem, (3) straw man, (4) slippery slope, (5) false dilemma, (6) appeal to force, (7) equivocation, (8) begging the question, (9) inconsistency, (10) appeal to popular opinion, (11) hasty conclusion, (12) suppressed evidence, (13) appeal to authority, (14) appeal to ignorance, and (15) impervious hypothesis.

* Go over the fallacy names and see which ones are self-explanatory.
* Try to memorize the others, looking up the meanings of any words that aren't clear to you.

Skepticism, Faith, and Philosophy

In "Another Pilgrim's Progress" there are three siblings: The good-natured Skeptic who is an **extreme skeptic** in the sense that he believes we can know nothing; the good-natured Pilgrim who will believe almost anything; and the grumpy Caution who is a **moderate skeptic** in the sense that he won't believe something without good evidence or good reasons in its favor. Of the three siblings, it is Caution who most typifies the approach of philosophy—though one hopes that grumpiness isn't a necessary accompaniment to such an approach.

The skeptical attitude that Caution exemplifies is a long way from the attitude of Skeptic in our story. Skeptic is a preposterous figure, but he's not unprecedented in the history of philosophy. In *Lives of the Eminent Philosophers*, the third century writer, Diogenes Laertes, reports stories about Pyrrho, who lived six centuries earlier. Pyrrho adopted a philosophy of general agnosticism and suspension of judgment. Like our Skeptic, Pyrrho

> led a life consistent with this doctrine, going out of his way for nothing, taking no precaution, but facing all risks as they came, whether carts, precipices, dogs or what not . . . but he was kept out harm's way by his friends who . . . used to follow close after him.

Of course, this sort of extreme skeptical *behavior* was rare, if not totally legendary. But extreme skeptical *belief* constituted one of the major philosophical stances of the ancient world. Such skeptics argued that we could have no knowledge of what was truly real or good. One ancient skeptic, Arcesilaus said, "There is only one thing I know and that is that I know nothing—and I don't even know that." Many ancient skeptics found tranquility in their skepticism: Since there were no answers, one could turn one's mind away from the endless questions of life. Rather than mimicking Pyrrho, many ancient skeptics counseled following appearances and convention as the best chance of achieving a peaceful life.

Extreme skeptical challenges are alive and well in modern thought, but they are more theoretical, being put forth as challenges to our beliefs, not as a philosophy of life. Presumably, you've run across such skeptical challenges in the context of popular entertainments. How do we know we're not being programmed to live in an unreal world, as in the film, *The Matrix*? How do we know we're not confusing dream and reality, as in *Total Recall*? How do we know we're not living in a computer simulation, as in the movie, *The Thirteenth Floor*?

We'll be arguing against extreme skeptics, while also taking a Caution-like skeptical approach to claims that seem incautious.

Some of you may be wondering if this approach is stacked against religious belief—especially given the treatment of Faith and her wonderful friend in "Another Pilgrim's Progress" and the discussion of Faith in terms of the fallacy of impervious hypothesis. Is philosophy going to doubt religious belief unless it can be proved—and then doubt that it can be proved?

It is true that some of the traditional arguments for the existence of God are going to come in for some heavy criticism. However, we will also see that there are contemporary philosophers who argue that, with revision and modernization, some of those arguments can be made to work. We will also find philosophers who argue that religious belief should be based on faith, not reason. This raises a question: Isn't arguing that religious belief should be based on faith, not reason, contradictory, since it involves giving reasons against giving reasons? Not quite: Arguments and faith can work on different levels. For instance, I might argue that faith is a special way of knowing. Or I might argue that we take many of our everyday beliefs on faith so that belief in God is no worse than other beliefs—beliefs that no one has any intention of giving up. We'll discuss all that later when we get to the chapter on God, Chapter 5.

First, however, we will deal with the challenge of extreme skepticism, particularly skepticism regarding the existence and nature of the "external world"—that is, all the world that is outside of my mind.

Definitions

(Terms are defined in the order in which they appear in the text.)

1. ARGUMENT: Reasons (PREMISES) in support of the truth of some claim (the CONCLUSION).
2. LOGICAL FORM OF AN ARGUMENT OR ARGUMENT FORM: The structure of an argument once specific subject matter is ignored.
3. VALID DEDUCTIVE ARGUMENT: An argument having a form such that if the premises are true, the conclusion must be true.
4. FALSE DILEMMA (FALLACY OF): Claiming that there are only two relevant possibilities when in fact there are more.
5. SOUND DEDUCTIVE ARGUMENT: A deductively valid argument with true premises.

6. STRONG INDUCTIVE ARGUMENT: An argument having a form such that if the premises were true, the conclusion would probably be true (analogous to valid deductive argument).

7. MODUS PONENS: The following *valid* argument form: If p, then q; p; therefore q.

8. MODUS TOLLENS: The following *valid* argument form: If p, then q; not q; therefore not p.

9. HYPOTHETICAL SYLLOGISM: The following *valid* argument form: If p, then q; if q then r; therefore, if p then r.

10. DISJUNCTIVE SYLLOGISM: The following *valid* argument form: p or q; not p; therefore q.

11. DENYING THE ANTECEDENT (FALLACY OF): The following *invalid* argument form: If p, then q; not p; therefore, not q. (ANTECEDENT is what comes before "then" in an if-then statement.)

12. AFFIRMING THE CONSEQUENT (FALLACY OF): The following *invalid* argument form: If p, then q; q; therefore, p. (CONSEQUENT is what comes after "then" in an if-then statement.)

13. ANALOGICAL INDUCTION (also called ARGUMENT FROM ANALOGY): Reasoning that because two things are alike in a number of respects, they are also alike in some further respect.

14. INDUCTIVE GENERALIZATION: Reasoning from information we have about some subset of a group to conclusions about the whole group or about some further members of it.

15. HYPOTHETICAL INDUCTION (also called ABDUCTION or INFERENCE TO THE BEST EXPLANATION): Reasoning from certain evidence to an hypothesis that would best explain that evidence.

16. PROVINCIALISM (FALLACY OF): Accepting or rejecting a conclusion on the basis of one's identification with a particular group.

17. AD HOMINEM (FALLACY OF): Attacking the person rather than the argument.

18. STRAW MAN (FALLACY OF): Misinterpreting an opponent's position to make it seem weaker.

19. PRINCIPLE OF CHARITY: Giving the most favorable interpretation of someone else's argument. (If the point is finding truth rather than defeating someone else, you want to see what might be instructive in the other person's argument.)

20. SLIPPERY SLOPE (FALLACY OF): Arguing, without good evidence, that any move in a certain direction will inevitably lead past other possibilities to some terrible extreme.
21. FALSE DILEMMA (FALLACY OF): Claiming that there are only two relevant possibilities when in fact there are more.
22. APPEAL TO FORCE (FALLACY OF): Attempting to persuade through intimidation, not argument.
23. EQUIVOCATION (FALLACY OF): Using a word in different senses in premises and conclusion.
24. BEGGING THE QUESTION (FALLACY OF) (also CIRCULAR ARGUMENT): Presenting some form of the conclusion as if it were additional support for the conclusion.
25. INCONSISTENCY (FALLACY OF): Arguing for, or from, statements that contradict one another.
26. APPEAL TO POPULAR OPINION (FALLACY OF): Appealing to the crowd as authority.
27. HASTY CONCLUSION (FALLACY OF): Presenting supporting evidence without a reasonable attempt to determine if there is other relevant evidence.
28. SUPPRESSED EVIDENCE (FALLACY OF): Presenting evidence favorable to one's position while suppressing evidence that is not favorable.
29. APPEAL TO AUTHORITY (FALLACY OF): Appealing to some supposed authority who has no expertise relevant to the matter at issue.
30. APPEAL TO IGNORANCE/ARGUMENT FROM IGNORANCE (FALLACY OF): Assuming or arguing that if a claim can't be disproved, it is probably true.
31. IMPERVIOUS HYPOTHESIS (FALLACY OF): Framing an hypothesis so that it is impervious/immune to any conceivable counterevidence.
32. EXTREME SKEPTIC: One who believes we can know nothing.
33. MODERATE SKEPTIC: One who refuses to believe something without good evidence or good reasons in its favor.

Questions

(Please explain your answers, making specific reference to relevant passages in the discussion.)

1. What do philosophers mean by the term "argument"?
2. What two questions do we need to consider with any argument?
3. What is a valid deductive argument?

4. Can a valid deductive argument have a false conclusion?

5. What is a sound deductive argument?

6. Can a deductive argument be sound without being valid?

7. What is the fallacy of false dilemma?

8. Compare/contrast a valid deductive argument with a strong inductive argument.

9. Do sound deductive arguments aim to give us new information? Explain.

10. "The moon is made of green cheese; therefore, the moon is made of green cheese." Is this a valid deductive argument? Explain.

11. Think of some problem you tried to solve recently (finding something, fixing something, whatever).

    a. Describe the reasoning process you went through.

    b. Explain how your reasoning was inductive or deductive or some combination of both.

12. "Assuming all Muslims are terrorists is like assuming all Christians are charitable."

    a. What kind of argument is this? What is it designed to prove?

    b. What are the argument's strengths and/or weaknesses?

13. Why is it incorrect to think of detectives as primarily concerned with deduction?

14. "Most of my neighbors say they are going to vote Republican in the next election. I think the Democrats are in real trouble."

    a. What kind of argument is this? What is it designed to prove?

    b. What are the arguments' strengths and/or weaknesses?

15. For each of the following arguments, say what fallacy, *if any*, it exemplifies:

    a. "*Consumer Reports* researchers found potentially harmful bacteria in 97 percent of the raw chicken they bought nationwide." (cbsnews.com 7/30/14)

    b. We know that God exists because the Bible says so and the Bible is the word of God.

    c. Look before you leap, my friend. And remember, he who hesitates is lost.

    d. It's been snowing for three weeks, and that stranger we just passed has a great tan. I wonder what tanning salon he goes to?

    e. I'd be careful holding views like that, if I were you. They'll get you in trouble with a lot of people.

    f. No one's been able to show that there's life on other planets, so it's obviously not there.

   g. There have already been accidents with self-driving cars. They'll never be safe.

   h. My uncle is a noted military historian, and he can give you lots of reasons why the war in Iraq was a strategic mistake.

16. How can circular arguments and arguments with inconsistent premises be valid? When they are valid, how can they still be bad arguments? Explain.

17. What is the fallacy of impervious hypothesis? Why is such reasoning fallacious?

18. "The only real skeptic is a dead skeptic." Evaluate this statement.

Notes

Inductive Arguments

Analogical Induction

"In 1785, the philosopher Thomas Reid. . . ." Thomas Reid. *Essays on the Intellectual Powers of Man*. Edinburgh, 1785.

Inductive Generalization

". . . a Kaiser Health Tracking poll in April 2014. . . ." kff.org/report-section/kaiser-health-tracking-poll-april-2014.

"Experience with Gallup polls. . . ." See the paper "How Are Polls Conducted." Gallup, 2014. www.gallup.com.

Skepticism, Faith, and Philosophy

"In *Lives of the Eminent Philosophers*. . . . " Diogenes Laertes. *Lives of the Eminent Philosophers*. Trans. R. D. Hicks. New York: G. P. Putnam's Sons, 1925.

Further Materials

Logic and Logical Fallacies

Fogelin, Robert J., and Sinnott-Armstrong, William. *Understanding Argument: An Introduction to Informal Logic*, 9th edition. Cengage Learning, 2015.

Munson, Ronald. *The Elements of Reasoning*, 6th edition. Boston: Cengage Learning, 2011.

Salmon, Merrilee H. *Introduction to Logic and Critical Thinking*, 6th edition. Boston: Cengage Learning, 2012.

Schick, Theodore, Jr., and Vaughn, Lewis. *How to Think about Weird Things: Critical Thinking for a New Age*, 5th edition. New York: McGraw-Hill, 2013.

Skepticism

Pojman, Louis P. *What Can We Know? An Introduction to the Theory of Knowledge*, Chs. 2 & 3. Boston: Cengage Learning, 2000.

Shermer, Michael. *Why People Believe Weird Things*. "Part 1: Science and Skepticism." New York: Henry Holt, 2002.

CHAPTER 2

Appearance and Reality
Fiction

READING 1: Add Some More Boils

PREVIEW

In this story, two boys run a Black Death simulation for their history studies. As you read, ask yourself:

* *Are there any essential differences between the simulation and a very complex video game?*
* *Is there any harm in what the boys are doing?*

Night. The fires. The smoke. The curses and pleading. Could hell be any worse than this?

Taddeo knew he was dying. The swellings in his neck, armpits, and groin were growing larger, and the black lesions on his skin were getting worse. He was feverish and knew that soon he might suffer delirium like that madman yesterday who had stood on his roof, first dancing, then tearing out tiles and throwing them down at those passing in the street. No doubt there would be more like him. It seemed the whole world was going mad.

He had never felt so alone. His father and brothers had forced him from the family home the moment he'd shown signs of the disease. Taddeo had raged at them at the time, but he couldn't find it in his heart now to condemn them. They had to do what they could to try to save themselves and the rest of the family from this pestilence that had descended on the world.

Though they might have been too late. They might bolt the doors only to find that the pestilence had already made itself at home. Being locked away was no guarantee of safety. Taddeo had watched the corpse-carriers break into houses where the inhabitants were all dead and stinking. The corpse-carriers, after stealing what valuables they could find, would drag the bodies out of the house and onto their carts.

Once death had had a more dignified air: There had been the preparation of the body, a showing in the home for family and friends, then a stately procession led by a priest to the church for a Mass or funeral blessing. Then burial in the family plot.

Now there were too many dead. Too few graves. Too few priests who hadn't died or fled. Families would shove their dead out of doors, even throw them from windows, anything to rid themselves of the contagion. The corpse carriers would collect the bodies from the street and throw them on carts, arms and legs dangling from the side, showing them as much respect as so many dead animals. The bodies wouldn't be buried in family plots; they would be dumped in mass graves.

As the corpse-carriers made their way through the town, they collected other bodies lying along the road or in alleys. It was said that the corpse carriers didn't always take sufficient care. There were stories of some poor souls who had suffered the horror of being buried alive.

"Buried alive—that is so cool."

"Shut up, Terry. I'm trying to work."

The thought of being buried alive was one that tortured Taddeo as he stumbled along the street—even more when, as now, he was forced by exhaustion to sit down by the side of the road. Sometimes Taddeo wanted so badly to live. Prayed so hard for a miracle. Other times he just wanted this to be over. To be dead. To be safe. To feel no more pain.

Though, if the priests were right, there was no safety to be had in this world or the next. And no escape from pain.

Why had this pestilence been visited on the world? Most said it was God's wrath, visited upon humankind for its wickedness. Some of the learned said the pestilence was stirred up by the Great Conjunction of Saturn, Mars, and Jupiter in the sign of Aquarius. They said that Jupiter drew forth corrupted vapors from the Earth while Mars ignited them, creating the poisonous air that spread the disease everywhere. One breathed in the air and the poison spread through the body, putrefying the heart.

But as the priests were wont to point out, it was God who controlled the planets. Whatever the proximate cause, the ultimate cause was God and His fury. There was nothing to do but repent and throw oneself on God's mercy.

There was repentance everywhere, like the parades of flagellants, men walking in front, women in the rear, wearing their white robes emblazoned with red crosses. They would stop in front of the local church, and the men would strip down to skirts, exposing their already mutilated and swollen torsos to further punishment. They whipped themselves and each other, the cords of their whips hard knotted leather with small iron spikes, sending blood spraying everywhere. Even the crowd was touched by the spray, some treating the blood as a holy relic.

"That is so sick. I love it."

"Will you be quiet?"

Yes, there was repentance. But there were others who gave no thought to God, who, like the followers of the ancient philosopher, Epicurus, thought only of their pleasure, and gave themselves over to gluttony, drunkenness, and carnal relations. Yes, there was repentance and there was sin. And people went on dying.

Something hit the ground next to him. It was a piece of bread. Taddeo looked up to see someone hurrying by. One fed the sick these days as one might feed dangerous dogs—throwing the food, not daring to get too close. Those going by always had their noses and mouths covered for fear of breathing in the disease. And because of the stench. Had the world ever been filled with such foul smells?

Taddeo had no appetite, but he knew he must force the bread down; he needed his strength. As he reached for the bread, he saw the back of his hand and quickly looked away, filled with despair. It was as if his body were beginning to rot alive—blackening, cracking, oozing.

"I love how disgusting that guy looks. Add some more boils."

"They're not called boils. They're called buboes. That's what Ms. Stark said."

"Boo-boos—Yea, I'm sure your teacher calls them boo-boos."

"Buboes, you idiot—"b," "u", "b," "o," "e," "s." Those swellings in his neck."

"I don't mean those. I mean all that black stuff on his skin. Add more of that."

"No."

"Come on, Alex. Please. Please."

"Okay, okay, a few more—then stop bothering me."

"Okay. Hey. Yes. That's it! Cool."

Taddeo couldn't stifle the scream. His body was on fire. It was as if he could feel his body swelling, his skin cracking open. He was terrified.

"*Enough.*"

"Saint Sebastian," Taddeo prayed, as the pain began to subside, but not the fear. "You who have known such arrows of pain, you who have saved others from the pestilence, intercede for me. Help me in my hour of need. Save me—or let me die."

"*Who's Saint Sebastin?*"

"*Sebastian. It's in my notes. Third-century Roman . . . executed by being shot with arrows . . . didn't die . . . returned to the Emperor's Court . . . then was beaten to death.*"

"*They shot him full of arrows, but he didn't die and so they beat him to death? How cool is that.*"

"*Says his martyr cult started during the Plague of Justinian . . . he became 'the quintessential plague saint.'*"

"*They should have made him the saint of total losers.*"

"Mother of God, please help. . ."

Taddeo was stopped by a sudden explosion of red. It was as if the whole sky was on fire, the stars bright blue points in an expanse of red. The red seemed to shower down on the earth, coloring everything and everyone. Had God attended to the intercession of the saints and the Holy Mother? Would this horror finally stop and the world be put right again?

"*You idiot? What did you do?*"

"*I didn't do nothing. Probably some glitch.*"

"*No, you touched something, dammit. Totally screwed up the colors. Keep your hands away.*"

"*Okay, Okay. Does look kind of cool, though.*"

"*Get away. Let's see. . . . There. I fixed it.*"

Suddenly it was as if Taddeo were blind—blackness everywhere. Then he began to see things as they'd been—the dark sky, the shadows from the fires. He waited, expectant. Was it a sign—would they be saved?

"Please," he prayed. "Don't make it just my delirium. Help me. Help us."

He waited. And he waited. And there was only the blackness.

"Please," he prayed as he sat waiting. "Let it be a sign. Don't let this all be for nothing."

******

She pushed open the door to Alex's room and there he was, huddled in front of his computer, his brother next to him, probably pestering him as usual.

"Alex," she said sharply. "Terry. Didn't you boys hear me call you for dinner?"

"No."

"I've been practically yelling. I want you downstairs now."

"Mom, could we just. . . ?"

"No. Now!"

"Okay, okay. . . ."

"And wash your hands!"

As the two boys scrambled off their chairs and went out the bedroom door, she looked at Alex's computer screen. The images were so dark it took her a moment to make them out. It looked like some medieval scene at night. It was disgusting: bodies lying everywhere, people moaning. And that man in rags looking out at her, his face all blackened with disease, mouth moving—ugh, it was awful.

"Please God. Help me. Help us all."

She'd heard that these historical computer simulations were good learning tools—they certainly hadn't had them when she was in school—but couldn't the teacher put some restrictions on what projects the students chose? Didn't kids get enough violence in their video games? Why not a simulation of the Founders debating the Bill of Rights? Or if it had to be adventure, why not Columbus discovering America? Or the first manned mission to Titan?

She sighed. She supposed Ms. Stark was just letting the boys do what engaged them, thinking it would motivate their learning. She supposed she should ask Alex some questions at dinner, making sure he was learning something and not just playing. What had he said he was studying? The Black Death, wasn't it? Well, at least it would be easier to talk about than look at.

She loved her boys dearly, but she would never understand them. This love of violence and gore—at least the pretend kind. And that poor creature on the screen—diseased and looking like someone in agony. Why would anyone want to look at that? Certainly she didn't.

"Help me."

As she turned away and headed for the door, she gave a frustrated laugh. What could a mother say, except, boys will be boys.

Questions

1. In "Add Some More Boils," Alex and his brother are supposed to be doing a computer simulation of a period of medieval history when people were suffering from the Black Plague. Do you think such computer simulations will be possible some day. Why or why not?

2. In the story, the medieval character, Taddeo, is assumed to be conscious. Does this make sense if he's merely a simulated character? Why or why not?

3. If Taddeo is really conscious (as well as, perhaps, the simulated characters around him), what do you think of the morality of doing such a simulation? (If the boys weren't adding extra torment, would that be all right?)

4. Is there any way Taddeo could know that he and the world around him are part of a computer simulation and not reality? Is there any way we can know that we're not part of some simulation?

READING 2: Why Don't You Just Wake Up?

> **PREVIEW**
> In this story, people keep telling Maya to "wake up"; then, unfortunately, she does.
>
> * As you read, ask yourself which of Maya's experiences are dreams and which reality, and how she can know the difference.

I'm in the living room at home, and my father is there, all serious, saying, "Maya, where's your mind these days—you've got to wake up," and it seems like I wake up, and I'm at my desk at home. I straighten up and yawn and pick up my history book, and just then my mother comes in, saying, "Maya, you're just not concentrating—you've got to wake up," and again it seems like I wake up, and I'm sitting in class. I look around, and Matias is sitting next to me looking all upset, saying, "Maya, what's with you these days—why don't you just wake up," and I think I wake up, and I'm lying in bed in my dorm room.

It was all dreams within dreams within dreams, and what I thought was waking was just more dreaming. I lie in my dorm bed and wonder who is going to come in next and wake me from this, only no one comes in, and the digital clock blinks slowly toward 7:30, and I guess this must be real.

It doesn't seem real, though. Nothing does these days. Everything that happens seems sort of vague somehow and out of focus and not all that important. I have trouble concentrating—taking things seriously—and everybody's on my case. That's the reason, I think, for all those dreams about dreaming and waking.

One reason, anyway. The other is that philosophy class and all that talk about Descartes and whether all reality could be a dream. That's not helping much either.

I'm late meeting Matias again, and he's had to wait, and there won't be time for us to have coffee together. He gives me that exasperated look I see a lot these days, and we walk across campus without talking. Finally, he says:

"I don't know why I took that stupid philosophy class. I can't wait 'til it's over."

I know it's not really the class he's annoyed at. It's me and the way I've been lately. I know I should say something nice. But I'm feeling pushed and kind of cranky.

"I like the class," I say, to be contrary.

"You do not."

"I do. It's kind of interesting."

"Interesting. Right. Like I really want to sit around all day wondering whether I'm dreaming everything in the world."

"Maybe you are."

"Sure." He shakes his head. "That's so stupid."

"Just because you say 'stupid' doesn't make it wrong. How do you know you aren't just dreaming this all up?"

He glares at me, but his eyes begin to dart the way they always do when he's thinking hard. He's not in the mood for this, but I've gotten him mad.

"Because . . . I know what dreams look like. They're all hazy. Not like the world looks now."

"You mean what you can see of it through the smog."

"Funny."

I know what he means, though. A few weeks back I would have said that being awake looked a lot different from dreaming. But the professor is right. That's just a matter of how things look. It doesn't prove how things are.

"Look,'" I say, "nobody's denying that what we call 'dreaming' looks different from what we call 'being awake.' But is it really different? Maybe 'being awake' is just a different kind of dream."

"Yeah, well, if I'm making all this up, how come we're talking about something I don't want to talk about?"

"Because you're not in control of this dream any more than you are your dreams at night. It's your unconscious doing it."

"This is so much bullsh . . ."

"Why?

"It's crazy. You're standing here trying to convince me that everything is my dream while you know you're real. That doesn't make any sense."

"Yeah, it does. I'm saying you can't know that I really exist, and I can't know that you . . ."

LET'S REVIEW

* Matias gives a couple of arguments against the idea that he's not dreaming up the world. What are they?
* Maya gives some counterarguments—arguments against Matias's arguments. What are they?

I stop suddenly because something scary is happening. It's like a ripple moving through the whole world, coming from the horizon to my left, but moving fast as if the world is really much smaller than it appears. And where the ripple is, everything becomes elongated and out of focus. The ripple passes over Matias, distorting him for a moment, like a fun house mirror. Then it's gone, and everything's back to normal.

"Maya, are you okay?" says Matias, giving me a worried look. "You look as pale as a ghost."

"I don't know. I just got the weirdest feeling. I guess I'm okay."

"Maya, are you on something?"

"No. I told you. Really."

He looks at me for a moment and decides I'm telling the truth.

"Come on," he says, taking my hand. "The last thing you need right now is philosophy class. Let's go get something to eat and then sit in the sun for awhile. I bet you'll feel better."

"Hey, Matias, I'm sorry I'm being such a jerk. I . . ."

"Don't worry about it, Maya. It's okay. Come on."

Later I do feel better. I feel like things are almost back to normal. But my night is full of dreams within dreams, and the next day the world seems full of unreality once again. And then, at midday, the world ripples again.

I go to the university health service, and of course the doctor thinks it's drugs, and we go round and round on that until I insist she test me, and then she begins to believe I'm not lying. She becomes nicer then, and more concerned, and schedules some tests and an appointment with a specialist she'd like me to see, though she's "sure it's nothing, just stress."

Walking across campus, I see the world ripple again, and suddenly I realize what it all looks like. It's like back when you'd watch movies on those portable screens in class and the screen would twist, distorting the image, and you'd be aware that it wasn't a world in front of you at all, but just an illusion on a not-very-large piece of material. Except when I put my arm out to feel the ripple, the arm ripples too, as if it's part of the movie.

I don't know what's happening, and I'm afraid. At night I keep myself from sleeping because the idea of dreaming is something I suddenly find disturbing. In the morning I'm exhausted, but I stumble off to class because I want something to divert my attention, but once there I have trouble paying attention. I guess the professor must have asked me something I didn't hear because I feel Matias nudging me in the ribs and hear him say, "Come on, Maya, wake up."

I look up then at the professor standing behind her lectern, and just above and in back of her a dark line seems to appear in the wall. It looks like the slow fissure of an earthquake, except that the edges fold back against the surface of the wall like the edges of torn paper, and I see that behind the tearing there is nothing at all, just darkness. Then I see that the tear isn't in the wall at all but in my field of vision because as it reaches the professor she begins to split apart and then the lectern and then the head of the student in the front row. On both sides of the tear, the world distorts and folds and collapses. The fissure moves downward through the students and then, I see as I glance down, through my own body. No one is moving or screaming—they take no more notice than movie characters on a torn movie screen would. In a panic I reach out and touch Matias, then watch as he and my hand distort, as everything, absolutely everything, falls away.

******

It is night. It's always night. A night without stars, without anything—just an infinite emptiness falling away on every side. And so I float, an invisible being in a nonexistent world.

How long have I been like this? I don't know. It feels like years, but that's just a feeling because there is nothing here by which to mark the time.

I try to remember how it was, but my memories are such pale things, and they grow paler as time drags on.

I would pray, but there is nothing to pray to. And so I hope, for hope is all I have: that one day, as inexplicably as once I did, I will begin to dream the world again.

Questions

1. According to the story "Why Don't You Just Wake Up?" which of the following are real and which illusion:
   a. Maya's father talking to Maya
   b. The college campus
   c. Maya's feelings of fear
   d. The exasperated expression on Matias's face
   e. Matias's feelings of annoyance
   f. Endless darkness
   g. Matias's mind
   h. Maya's body
   i. Maya's mind

2. Critique the following arguments: This world can't be just my dream because:
   a. what I'm seeing right now looks much more vivid than it does when I am asleep and dreaming.
   b. I just asked my friend if I were dreaming this all up and she said, "No."

Discussion

PREVIEW

At the end of this discussion, you should be familiar with:

* *skepticism and the problem of the external world;*
* *Descartes's methodological doubt and his cogito;*
* *the views of Locke, Berkeley, and Hume on perception and on what we can know about the world;*
* *the skeptical problem of dreams and what arguments can be given against the possibility that we are dreaming everything;*
* *Wittgenstein's private-language argument;*
* *Bostrom's analysis of the possibility that we're living in a computer simulation; also arguments against that possibility;*
* *the meaning of terms listed in "definitions" (which are also marked in bold in the discussion).*

Commonsense Beliefs

The idea that what we take to be "reality" is illusory appears in literature back to ancient times. The ancient Greek philosopher, Plato (428–348), argued in his Allegory of the Cave that we are like prisoners in a cave chained so that we can only see the shadows that are thrown on the cave wall by what's happening outside the cave entrance in the sunshine; we've been in the cave so long that we've mistaken the shadows for reality. Plato thought that through reason we could escape from the cave into the light, but others disagreed, arguing, in effect, that shadows were all that we could ever see, or perhaps all there was. (We've already met two such ancient skeptics, Pyrrho and Arcesilaus.)

"Add Some More Boils" imagines a modern variant of the-world-as-illusion speculation. The medieval character, Taddeo, thinks he is living in (let's say) the fourteenth century during a period of "pestilence" (later known as the "Black Plague"). In fact, Taddeo is living inside an historical computer simulation run as a homework assignment (as well as for a little vicious fun) by some school boys.

The story "Why Don't You Just Wake Up?" imagines another variant of the reality-is-illusion theme: that the world is nothing but my dream.

PLATO (428–348 BCE) was an ancient Greek philosopher of such great influence that one writer called European philosophy a "series of footnotes to Plato." Certainly, with his teacher, Socrates, and his pupil, Aristotle, he laid the groundwork for much that was to come in metaphysics, morality, and political philosophy.

The idea that the world might be only a dream also goes back to ancient times. At about the time of Plato, the great Chinese Daoist thinker, Zhuangzi, wrote this:

> By and by comes the Great Awakening, and then we find out that this life is really a great dream. Fools think they are awake now, and flatter themselves they know if they are really princes or peasants. Confucius and you are both dreams; and I who say you are dreams, I am but a dream myself. . . .
>
> Once upon a time, I, Zhuangzi, dreamt I was a butterfly, fluttering hither and thither, to all intents and purposes a butterfly. I was conscious only of following my fancies as a butterfly, and was unconscious of my individuality as a man. Suddenly, I awaked, and there I lay, myself again. Now I do not know whether I was then a man dreaming I was a butterfly, or whether I am now a butterfly dreaming I am a man.

Let's focus first on dream-related skepticism and ask ourselves: Is it possible that the world is nothing but my dream? Is there any way I can prove that this isn't so?

Before taking up those questions, let's clarify them a bit. Presumably you believe in the existence of the following:

1. Other minds
2. Physical objects
3. Your own mind

To believe in the existence of a mind is, at a minimum, to believe that there exists a collection of thoughts, images, emotions, and sensations. To believe in the existence of a physical object is to believe in the existence of such a thing as a tree, a hand, a river, a flash of lightning, or a molecule and to believe that such a thing would or could continue to exist if all minds ceased to exist. (Dreams or desires could not exist in the absence of the mind: such things, then, are mental.)

The possibility that the world is a dream challenges some of these "commonsense" beliefs, but which ones? Imagine that you dream you are a glamorous movie star getting out of your limousine at the Academy Awards, with people cheering you and snapping pictures. Then imagine you wake up in your same old bedroom, wearing pajamas or a nightgown or underwear or nothing, nobody cheering, nobody (we hope) snapping pictures. What has remained constant from dreaming to waking? Very little. The location has changed, the objects have changed, even your body has changed. The one constant is that the same mind was dreaming and waking. Still this analogy is only partial. The Academy Awards dream imagines that while dreaming you were wrong about the kind of body you had and the kind of world you lived in; however, it supposes that you do live in a real world with a real body. The story "Wake Up" takes the idea further, imagining that when you wake up there is nothing at all there. You were dreaming a world and now you aren't. The possibility one might be dreaming everything challenges the idea that there is any world outside your mind—challenges the existence of what philosophers have dubbed the **external world**.

What threatens here is **solipsism**: the view that all that exists is one's own mind with its private experiences and thoughts. "Wake Up" imagines that solipsism is true, that all that existed was the narrator's mind and its dream, a dream from which she has now awakened.

Doubting the External World: Dreams

The possibility that the world is a dream is likely to evoke from us the same response it evoked from Matias in "Wake Up." "That's so stupid . . . I know what dreams look like. They're all hazy. Not like the world looks now."

All of us constantly distinguish dreams from reality, and we don't find any particular difficulty doing so. True, while we are dreaming we can be confused about whether we are dreaming or awake, but when we are really awake, it's obvious that we are.

How do we distinguish dreams from reality? In both dreams and waking life, we seem to see, hear, touch, taste, and smell things. But in dreams, perhaps, those sensory impressions are not as vivid and persistent as in waking life. More strikingly, the experiences of waking life are more consistent from episode to episode. In a series of dream episodes, one may be able to fly, then only able to walk, then not able to move. In a series of waking experiences, one's abilities to act are more fixed. In waking life, impressions of a burning building are followed by a familiar set of long-term impressions that continue through subsequent episodes: fire engines, smoking ashes, cold ashes, clearing away debris, rebuilding. Such need not be the case when one merely dreams that a building is burning.

In most cases, then, it seems that we can easily distinguish dreams from reality. Dreams can be distinguished from waking life by their relative haziness and relative inconsistency from episode to episode. However, consider two meanings of the word "dream":

1. Dreams are experiences that are hazy and relatively inconsistent.
2. Dreams are experiences that are purely mental and do not represent things existing outside the mind.

Perhaps the preceding commonsense view of waking and dreaming indicates that there is no serious problem about determining when we are dreaming in the first sense. But is this sufficient to show that we are not always dreaming in the second sense? Not according to "Wake Up." The story grants our normal distinction between experiences that are hazy and inconsistent and those that are not, but it denies that this distinction is evidence for what is only in our minds and what is not. The story issues the following challenge: How do you know that what we experience when we are "awake" isn't as much a product of our minds as what we experience when we are dreaming (in sense 1)? How do we know that reality isn't a dream (in sense 2)?

Consider some other objections to the possibility that the world is just a dream:

QUESTION: How could I perceive images if there were no objects?

REPLY: Your mind could invent them, as in dreams.

QUESTION: How can this chair hold me if it is only an imaginary chair?

REPLY: What is sitting on the chair might be an imaginary body, and, as we know from dreams, imaginary chairs are quite adequate to support imaginary bodies.

QUESTION: If everything I perceive is imaginary, why can't I create a more pleasant world through acts of will?

REPLY: To say that the world consists of mental images is not to say that these images are within your conscious control. You can't control your dreams, but you don't therefore deny that dreams are mental.

QUESTION: How can I be dreaming? Just now, I asked my friend if I was dreaming and she said "No."

REPLY: Maybe you're just dreaming that your friend is here telling you no.

You begin to see what is so insidious about the possibility that one is dreaming everything up. It seems to undercut the evidence against itself by raising the possibility that the evidence is merely illusion.

LET'S REVIEW

* *What is solipsism? What is the problem of the "external world"?*
* *Give two meanings of the word "dream." How do those different meanings affect the claim, "I know I am not now dreaming"?*
* *"Tell me I'm not dreaming." "You aren't." "Whew: That's a relief." What's the philosophical problem with this conversation?*

Descartes, Doubt, and the Cogito

René Descartes was a seventeenth-century French philosopher who subjected his basic beliefs to the kind of critical scrutiny in which we have been engaged here. (His name is mentioned in "Wake Up.") Descartes used dreams to underscore the problematic nature of our everyday beliefs:

> How many times has it occurred that the quiet of the night made me dream of my usual habits: that I was here, clothed in a dressing gown, and sitting by the fire, although I was in fact lying undressed in bed! It seems apparent to me now, that I am not looking at this paper with my eyes closed, that this head that I shake is not drugged with sleep, that it is with design and deliberate intent that I stretch out this hand and perceive it. What happens in sleep seems not at all as clear and as distinct as all this. But I am speaking as though I never recall having been misled, while asleep, by similar illusions! When I consider these matters carefully, I realize so clearly that there are no conclusive indications by which waking life can be distinguished from sleep that I am quite astonished, and my bewilderment is such that it is almost able to convince me that I am sleeping.

Faced with the possibility that he might be deceived in all of his beliefs—his belief in God, other minds, the material world, his own mind—Descartes decided he must institute a process of systematic doubt. He would doubt all his beliefs and then determine which of them he could justify. Realizing it would be easy to keep falling back on old assumptions, he decided he needed some device that would force him to keep questioning. This device was that of supposing an evil demon was out to deceive him. It's not that Descartes believed in such an evil demon, any more than he believed he was always dreaming. It was rather that the supposition of the evil demon was a way of forcing him to prove his beliefs and not take anything for granted.

> I will therefore suppose that, not a true God, who is very good and who is the supreme source of truth, but a certain evil spirit, not less clever and deceitful than powerful, has bent all his efforts to deceiving me. I will suppose that the sky, the air, the earth, colors, shapes, sounds, and all other objective things that we see are nothing but illusions and dreams that he has used to trick my credulity. I will consider myself as having no hands, no eyes, no flesh, no blood, nor any senses, yet falsely believing that I have all these things. I will remain resolutely attached to this hypothesis; and if I cannot attain the knowledge of any truth by this method, at any rate it is in my power to suspend my judgment. That is why I shall take great care not to accept any falsity among my beliefs and shall prepare my

mind so well for all the ruses of this great deceiver that, however powerful and artful he may be, he will never be able to mislead me in anything.

Descartes decided that there were serious grounds for doubting his belief in physical objects and other minds. But Descartes soon concluded that there were no serious grounds for doubting his own existence; even if he were dreaming, he could be certain that he existed. On this point he was safe from any trickery from his hypothetical demon.

> Even though there may be a deceiver of some sort, very powerful and very tricky, who bends all his efforts to keep me perpetually deceived, there can be no slightest doubt that I exist, since he deceives me; and let him deceive me as much as he will, he can never make me be nothing as long as I think that I am something.

RENÉ DESCARTES (1596–1650) is often called the "father of modern philosophy." He broke with the medieval Scholastic-Aristotelian philosophy both by subjecting it to his method of doubt and by replacing its view that natural objects had ends or purposes with a mechanistic-causal view that was more in line with the new science of his day.

In one of his writings, Descartes phrased his argument as "I think, therefore I am" or, in Latin, "Cogito ergo sum"; the claim is often referred to as the **cogito**. Thus formulated, it seems to indicate that Descartes was presenting an argument with "I think" as premise and "I exist" as conclusion—an argument that would have been circular/question-begging. In fact, Descartes argued that one cannot be in error about one's existence as a thinking being, one's existence as a mind. Descartes noticed that one's belief in one's own mind seemed to be immune to the sorts of challenges or doubts that infect one's other beliefs. "Perhaps I am mistaken in thinking that others think." "Perhaps I am mistaken in thinking that physical objects really exist." "Perhaps I am mistaken in thinking that I think." In the third statement, and the third statement only, the conclusion is reaffirmed in the doubting. The very act of doubting my existence proves it.

The cogito can be applied to more specific first-person statements, and a consideration of such statements helps clarify the nature of the cogito. "I seem to see a chair" appears to be an indubitable statement. One cannot be wrong about seeming-to-see, as opposed to seeing, and seeming-to-see is an experience, a mental state. "I am distressed" appears to be an indubitable statement. My seeming-to-be distressed is necessarily a kind of distress, and distress is a mental state. All statements about my present mental states would seem to be indubitable.

Descartes's cogito has seemed to many philosophers to be correct—but only if it is severely restricted in scope. Descartes's cogito is not a proof to each of us that Descartes existed. To each of us, Descartes was another mind. Your cogito could not be a proof to me that you exist, and vice versa. I have no direct experience of your thoughts, and you have no direct experience of mine. The cogito only works for the person thinking it. Anyone else saying the words could be a dream figure with no independent mind.

My cogito does not prove that I have a particular body or, indeed, any body at all. The body is a physical object, and the existence of physical objects is in question at this point. The cogito does not prove that I have a particular past or, in fact, any past at all; that I think does not guarantee the reliability of my memory impressions.

Insofar as my proper name, Tom Davis, is linked with a particular physical or mental past, my cogito does not prove that Tom Davis exists. What the cogito does guarantee is that there now exist certain thoughts, images, and sensations that I may define as "my mind."

LET'S REVIEW

* *Did Descartes really believe an evil demon was trying to deceive him? Explain.*

* *What is Descartes's argument for "I exist." What is this "I"?*

Having justified belief in one's own existence as a mind, can we move outward to justify a belief in an external world of physical objects and other minds? Or is this where justification stops and any denial of solipsism must be taken on faith?

Before we take up this question and say more about Descartes, let's discuss another historic route to doubts about the external world: an analysis of perception. We'll illustrate this with a famous progression in modern British philosophy that demonstrates this tendency for an analysis of perception to lead to solipsism—the philosophical progression from John Locke (1632–1704) to George Berkeley (1685–1753) to David Hume (1711–1776). These philosophers were all **empiricists**, believing that all our knowledge is derived from experience. (They were opposed to **rationalists**, who believe there are other sources of knowledge than experience, such as innate ideas accessible by reason alone.)

Interestingly, the philosophical progression we're about to examine doesn't start with skepticism. Instead it starts with what seems like a commonsense view of perception and slowly gets backed into a skeptical, solipsistic view.

Doubting the External World: Perception
Direct Realism

There is a view of perception that virtually every modern philosopher starts by rejecting. (A number of ancient philosophers didn't like it much either.) This view is called **direct realism** (sometimes naive realism), and it is supposed to represent the view of perception that most of us are naturally and uncritically drawn toward—a view (it seems) that can't possibly be correct.

Look at some obvious object, say, 10 to 20 feet away from you—a lamp, the face of a fellow student, a small tree. You're here and it's there, and you're seeing it directly. This is a kind of window view of perception. I can shut the shades, as it were, by closing my eyelids, but when I open them again the object is right out the window, over there. When I'm asleep and dreaming, my mind is creating private images in my mind, but when I'm awake, there are no private images of the object I perceive, just the object itself.

Adopting this commonsense view of perception, I don't get any sense of something happening between me and the tree I'm seeing. I'm over here and it's over there, and I just see it. I'm inclined to say that I'm in direct contact with the world as it is, except that I don't get any sense of contact.

Opponents of direct realism—which include virtually everyone familiar with basic philosophy or science—argue that this view cannot be correct: that we are never in direct contact with the external world but only with our private experience of it.

The most straightforward arguments against direct realism are those concerning illusion and the relativity of perception. Press the eyeball and the world seems to double. This wouldn't be possible if we were directly perceiving the world. We must be perceiving images of the world, and it is these images that double. A stick half submerged in water looks bent but feels straight. We can't be perceiving an object that is both bent and straight. What we're perceiving are separate visual and tactile impressions of the stick. Put one hand on something warm and the other on something cold, then put both hands in lukewarm water; the water will feel cold to the hand that was on something warm and warm to the hand that was on something cold. Such examples can be multiplied indefinitely and applied to all the senses.

According to the physics of perception, light, sound waves, or other physical processes coming from the objects in the world impact our sense organs, which transform the resulting energy into neural activity. The neural signals are sent to the brain and processed by different brain modules on different levels, resulting in our experience. The conclusion usually drawn from this is that all we directly perceive are our own private mental impressions, impressions caused by and (maybe) resembling objects in the world. Of course, the seventeenth-century philosopher John Locke, who rejected direct realism, didn't have our contemporary theories of the physics of perception, but the science of his day was moving toward a mechanical view of perception as resulting from the effects of the world on our senses. For instance, Newton hypothesized that the perception of color resulted from the pressure of light particles on the eye. In any case, Locke did present arguments from relativity and illusion for the claim that all we immediately perceive are private mental impressions.

Representative Realism: John Locke

If we accept the claim that all we ever experience are our own private mental impressions, it seems reasonable to move to the view called **representative realism**: the view that our sense impressions are caused by **material objects** in a world external to our minds and that our impressions represent those objects to us. If we think of direct realism as the window view of perception, we might think of representative realism as the satellite TV view of perception: We are watching video screens that are the result of data coming from the outside world and interpreted by our minds.

The question then arises: How closely do our images match the world outside, the world as it is in itself? One view would be that the world in itself is pretty much as it looks to us. If we could step outside our minds and see objects as the direct realist claims we see them, they'd look pretty much as our images show them to be. For example the apples out there would look small, round, smooth, and red, just as they seem to be. However, to many representative realists, including some ancient philosophers, it seemed that only certain of our sense perceptions, such as those of shape, were likely to represent the objects as they were in themselves; others, such as taste, did not.

This was the view of John Locke. He said that whatever the mind perceived in itself he would call **ideas**. The power in an object to produce ideas in us he would call **qualities**. Locke thought that some of the qualities of objects resembled the ideas we had of them, namely, "solidity, extension, figure, and mobility." These he called **primary qualities**. These qualities are

> such as are utterly inseparable from the body, in what state soever it be; and such as in all the alterations and changes it suffers, all the force can be used upon it, it constantly keeps; and such as sense constantly finds in every particle of matter which has bulk enough to be perceived; and the mind finds inseparable from every particle of matter, though less than to make itself singly be perceived by our senses: v.g. [e.g.] Take a grain of wheat, divide it into two parts; each part has still solidity, extension, figure, and mobility: divide it again, and it retains still the same qualities; and so divide it on, till the parts become insensible; they must retain still each of them all those qualities. . . .

Locke defined as **secondary qualities**

> such qualities which in truth are nothing in the objects themselves but power to produce various sensations in us by their primary

qualities, i.e. by the bulk, figure, texture, and motion of their insensible parts, as colours, sounds, tastes, &c. These I call secondary qualities.

Locke's form of representative realism, updated a bit, seems to fit with how we view the world once a little knowledge of science shows us that direct realism can't be correct. It fits with a causal theory of perception, that what we see and hear are the effects of light rays and sound waves on our sense organs and nervous systems. It also sees the external world as fundamentally composed of those quantifiable elements with which science deals: What seem to be the more subjective aspects like colors and smells are not "in" the objects themselves but are simply effects of the world on us.

JOHN LOCKE (1632–1704), a physician as well as a philosopher, is famous for his work in the philosophy of mind and epistemology. But he is perhaps most famous for his political writings. His discussion of the social contract, natural rights, and liberty had a profound influence on the writers of the United States Declaration of Independence.

Although representative realism seems to fit with a more sophisticated view of perception, a potential problem arises: If all we can experience are our own sense impressions, how could we ever know what the world apart from those impressions is like? How can we know which impressions, if any, resemble external objects? How, in fact, can we know there are external objects?

As evidence for external objects, Locke cited the force and vivacity of our simple impressions, the fact that they seem forced upon us against our will, the fact that we can't make the world as we wish it to be by acts of will or imagination.

Locke admitted that such evidence didn't give absolute certainty but claimed it did give a certainty "as great as our condition requires."

Subjective Idealism: George Berkeley

Bishop George Berkeley agreed with Locke that the things "immediately perceived are ideas or sensations" but disagreed with Locke's view that perception involved material objects causing in us ideas that partially resembled them.

Locke had argued, from the relativity of our perception of colors, smells, and heat, that these and the other secondary qualities, though caused by the object, could not resemble qualities in the object. Berkeley argued that our perception of Locke's primary qualities were also relative to the perceiver and hence should be seen as equally subjective.

> It is said that heat and cold are affections only of the mind, and not at all patterns of real beings, existing in the corporeal substances which excite them, for that the same body which appears cold to one hand seems warm to another. Now, why may we not as well argue that figure and extension are not patterns or resemblances of qualities existing in matter, because to the same eye at different stations, or eyes of a different texture at the same station, they appear various, and cannot therefore be the images of anything settled and determinate without the mind.

The texture, shape, and size of an object can look different to the same observer depending on distance and perspective, not to mention the condition of the eye.

The point of Berkeley's argument is that Locke's secondary and primary qualities are all ideas in the mind and that there is no reason to suppose that any of these ideas resemble objects outside the mind. In fact, there's every reason to suppose they don't resemble qualities of the objects since that would be to ascribe contradictory qualities to objects (hot and cold to the water in the bucket, for example).

If to this point we agree with Berkeley, it seems we'd be likely to adopt the position that all we know of material objects is that they are things "out there" that cause our perceptions; we have no idea of their properties beyond that. For this position, we might want to use the more generic term "**indirect realism**" since our sense impressions aren't representing qualities of the object; at best, our impressions may represent the fact that such objects are there.

However, Berkeley rejected such indirect realism. To say that material objects are something but "we know not what" is simply to say we have no idea of them at all: So how can we say they exist? But, one might object: Don't we need to postulate something out there as the cause of those ideas of everyday experience that come to me without my willing them? Yes, said Berkeley, but not material objects, not matter. The only thing we know that can cause ideas are minds. To say that something mindless is the source of ideas makes no sense.

Berkeley agreed that something had to be responsible for the fact that there is a coordinated world of images that we all experience. But Berkeley claimed that such images could only be created by a great mind, namely, God. Why, Berkeley, argued, would God bother to create matter to give us images when He could create such images directly—a coordinated set of ideas that constitutes a world? Berkeley (an Anglican priest as well as a scholar) thought this philosophy, though initially paradoxical, made perfect sense and had the additional benefit of showing the world to be a spiritual place sustained by God.

Berkeley's view that the world consists of only minds and ideas has been called **subjective idealism**.

Skepticism: David Hume

David Hume agreed with Berkeley that we have no grounds for believing in the existence of matter: that what we call objects are nothing but collections of ideas—an apple nothing but joint combination of the ideas of redness, roundness, sweetness, and so forth. We have no experience of matter, or material substance, beyond and apart from our ideas. In fact, since we have no idea of matter, the word "matter" can have no real meaning: It's just a bit of metaphysical nonsense.

Berkeley, like Descartes and Locke, argued that we do experience ourselves as a mental substance that has ideas. This Hume denied. He said,

> For my part, when I enter most intimately into what I call myself, I always stumble on some particular perception or other, of heat or cold, light or shade, love or hatred, pain or pleasure. I never can catch myself at any time without a perception, and never can observe any thing but the perception.

Earlier we talked about Descartes's cogito—"I think therefore I am"—as his proof of one's own mind. At least one of Descartes's contemporaries, Pierre Gassendi, argued that "I am" is too strong a conclusion. The best Descartes could derive conclusively from his experience is that there is thinking going on, not that there is a particular something doing the thinking. Hume agrees. He notes that there are some metaphysicians "who imagine we are every moment intimately conscious of what we call our Self."

> But setting aside some metaphysicians of this kind, I may venture to affirm of the rest of mankind, that they are nothing but a bundle or collection of different perceptions, which succeed each other with an inconceivable rapidity, and are in a perpetual flux and movement. . . . The mind is a kind of theatre, where several perceptions successively make their appearance; pass, re-pass, glide away, and mingle in an infinite variety of postures and situations. There is properly no simplicity in it at one time, nor identity in different; whatever natural propension we may have to imagine that simplicity and identity. The comparison of the theatre must not mislead us. They are the successive perceptions only, that constitute the mind; nor have we the most distant notion of the place, where these scenes are represented, or of the materials, of which it is compos'd.

Hume also dismissed Berkeley's use of God in his system: We have no experience of, and no idea of, God as a mental substance outside our experience causing our ideas.

So, with Hume, we are each left with just our ideas and no evidence for anything outside our ideas. As with Descartes and his doubt, we have moved from direct realism to what is essentially solipsism.

DAVID HUME (1711–1776) was a Scottish philosopher and historian. His writings on epistemology, psychology, morality, and religion led the reader to the edge of skepticism, though with modesty and wit. He joked that reason might not be capable of dispelling his skepticism, but Nature was. Dinner, conversation, and a game of backgammon were enough to make his speculations appear cold, strained, and ridiculous.

LET'S REVIEW

* *What is direct realism? What are some of the problems with it?*
* *What is Locke's theory of representative realism? What problems did Berkeley have with Locke's theory?*
* *What is Berkeley's theory of subjective idealism? What problems did Hume have with Berkeley's theory?*

Before we move on to further discussion of solipsism and the problem of the external world, let's chart the five positions we have discussed: direct realism, representative realism, indirect realism, subjective idealism, and solipsism. Imagine representatives of each position asking themselves the following questions:

Do I believe my mind exists?

Do I believe physical objects exist?

Do I believe other minds exist?

What do I believe I directly perceive—physical objects or just mental images?

Do my mental images resemble physical objects? (This for the representative realist and indirect realist.)

What do I believe causes my mental images?

Position	My mind exists?	PhysObjs exist?	Other minds exist?	Directly perceive what?	Images resemble PhysObs?	Cause of images?
Direct Realist	Yes	Yes	Yes	PhysObjs	No images in perception	No images in perception
Representative Realist	Yes	Yes	Yes	Images	Yes (some do)	PhysObs
Indirect Realist	Yes	Yes	Yes	Images	Don't know	PhysObs
Subjective Idealist	Yes	No	Yes	Images	No PhysObjs	God
Solipsist	Yes	No	No	Images	No PhysObjs	My Mind

Can I Know There's an External World?

Having proved the existence of my own mind, can I prove the existence of the external world? Some philosophers say, no. Earlier we defined solipsism as the view that all that exists is one's own mind with its private experiences and thoughts. Solipsism so defined is the view expressed in "Why Don't You Just Wake Up?" where the mind of the character named Maya turns out to be the only thing that exists. There are probably few thinkers who have claimed to be solipsists in this sense. But we can also view solipsism as a skeptical position which says that the only thing one can *prove* exists is one's own mind. This is how we will use the word "solipsist" in the following discussion. We'll imagine such a solipsist accepting Descartes's "cogito" but claiming that one can't go beyond the cogito to prove the existence of the external world.

The solipsist argues as follows: It is theoretically possible that everything one has ever experienced has been a total invention of one's mind (as in dreams). Since one can judge things only according to one's experience, and since one cannot get "outside" one's experience to determine its source, one cannot know whether the experience reflects an external world or whether it is merely an invention of one's mind. One cannot prove that there is an external world.

The problem of the external world is a difficult one, and the argument of the solipsist is forceful. Can we satisfactorily answer the solipsist? Can we formulate an argument that proves an external world of physical objects and other minds?

Descartes is of no further help to us. He did offer a proof of an external world, but it is not satisfactory. First, Descartes presented arguments for the existence of a perfect God. Then he went on to argue that a perfect God would not deceive him by presenting him with appearances that were all illusory. Thus, Descartes, concluded, his experiences must represent an external world. However, Descartes's arguments for the existence of a perfect God are unconvincing. (We'll discuss one of those arguments—the ontological argument—in Chapter 5.) Thus, the overall proof is unconvincing.

How should we approach the challenge of solipsism? If we can't prove an external world absolutely, can we at least show that its existence is much more likely than not?

What about treating the external world as the most reasonable hypothesis explaining why we have the experiences we do? Let's ask along with that: Why am I so inclined to believe in an external world?

Perhaps one general consideration that sways us toward a belief in the external world is the stark contrast between the relative poverty of those thoughts obviously created by one's mind and the richness of those experiences that seem to be imposed upon one. When I intentionally produce a mental image, it tends to be hazy and simple, and its content tends to be exhausted at a glance. But much of the experience that seems to come from outside is complex, endlessly explorable, and full of surprises. A similar contrast exists between the ideas that are obviously mine and those that seem to come from others. Through apparent conversations with others, I gain knowledge that I was not conscious of possessing before. Many of those ideas that seem to come from elsewhere are barely comprehensible to me (for example, many writings in theoretical physics or higher mathematics). It seems absurd to suppose that all these ideas are really just products of my own mind.

What would a one-mind universe look like? I don't know about you, but I see an image of a bubble floating around in the darkness with video pictures projected inside it. Obviously, this won't do because we need some source for the pictures. So mentally we might add a kind of ghostly video camera, and perhaps a computer, to the bubble. Among other things, either this computer contains every bit of information in every library in every language, or somehow it contains only the information I will happen to look up. Why? How? Saying "It just does" isn't satisfactory. Again, we're not simply asking whether this is possible; we're asking whether it is the most reasonable view.

When I try to complete a picture of a one-mind universe, just at the point where it seems to make some sense, I find it's no longer a one-mind universe at all: It isn't one mind with a huge unconscious, but a mind plus another huge mind (a kind of God) that has actively thought everything up and is feeding me some of the information. But if we reach that point, we already have an external world of sorts: God, in addition to my mind. Now we can ask if that is the most reasonable view. What is the evidence for there being such a God? Does it make sense to suppose that there would be a God plus one human mind? If there are other minds, does it make sense to think that there are also physical objects?

As we have seen, people have taken all sorts of different positions concerning the nature of the external world. Idealists like Berkeley have argued that what exists in the world are God and minds and no physical objects. Other people believe the world consists of God, minds, and physical objects, while still others believe in minds, physical objects, but no God. At this point, though, we are debating what the external world is really like, not whether there is one.

Other considerations often brought against the solipsist rely on arguments made or suggested by Ludwig Wittgenstein (1889–1951) against the possibility of there being a "private language." Wittgenstein's later philosophy where these arguments occur is famously episodic and enigmatic:

What Wittgenstein meant and intended by the arguments in question is a matter of dispute. Nonetheless some philosophers have seen in his remarks about language an argument against solipsism (called his **private-language argument**).

Solipsism seems to imply that all I ever experience are my own private mental images which I think and talk about in my own private language. But, Wittgenstein's writings suggest, a purely private language is impossible. At the very least, anything resembling a private language must be derived from a public language that must come to me from an external world. Hence if one has a language, there must be an external world.

Why would a purely private language be impossible? The claim is that for words to have meaning, there must be rules for their consistent use. Suppose a toddler beginning to speak utters the sound "Nee." You try to associate the sound with a request (food, changing, holding), an object (rattle, pacifier, toy), maybe a sound or a mood. If nothing seems to correlate, you'd probably conclude that "Nee" was just a sound, not a word. For a word to have meaning, it needs to have a consistent use. (Of course, words can have several meanings and can be used to accomplish different things—but there are limits.)

The rules for the consistent use of words must be public. Wittgenstein imagines a man who decides to write "S" in his diary whenever he has a certain sensation. Suppose he has a sensation he doesn't remember having experienced before and decides he wants to keep a record of it. He concentrates on it and says to himself, "I will call this 'S.'" Some time later he has a sensation and says to himself, "There is S again." Is he correct? Might he be mistaken? What determines this? We can add to Wittgenstein's example by imagining that the man is intrigued by another new sensation. He focuses on it and names it "R." The next day he has a sensation and says to himself, "There is S again." Is he correct? Could he have gotten confused, and what he is experiencing is really R? Or maybe a third sensation? How could he know?

For the solipsist, the same problem would arise for words about the "world" since those words are just about private impressions. Without consistent public rules about meaning, there could be no meaningful language. Therefore, the fact that we have a meaningful language indicates that it must be public—that there is a public world, that is, an external world.

If these considerations indicate that the existence of an external world is very likely, they don't tell us what that external world is like. They

LUDWIG WITTGENSTEIN (1889–1951) was an Austrian-British philosopher. Early on he thought he'd solved the problems of philosophy using an abstract system with a simplified theory of meaning. Later he decided he'd been wrong, that philosophers needed to focus instead on the messy everyday use of language.

may take care of Descartes's dream problem but not his demon problem. That is, the problems with solipsism may show that the world is not simply my dream, but they do not show that the world is as I perceive/conceive it to be. There might be a society of Cartesian demons who live in their own, very different world, with their own public language. They could be deluding me with an illusory world that includes a language that they—already having a public language—modeled on their own.

Of course, in modern times, demons have been replaced by mad (or not so mad) scientists in philosophical imaginings about illusory worlds. One popular skeptical challenge is the "brain-in-a-vat" scenario. It borrows from an idea that was floating around, as it were, in mid-twentieth-century science fiction. In the 1942 novel, *Donovan's Brain*, by Curt Siodmak, W. H. Donovan, an evil financier, crashes his plane near the home of a physician, Doctor Patrick Cory, who can't save Donovan's life but removes his brain and keeps it alive in a tank in an electrified solution. The brain still functions and takes over Cory telepathically; Donovan uses Cory to continue his financial schemes and even plot a murder until Cory manages to foil the telepathy and destroy Donovan's brain.

Philosophers reconstrued the **brain-in-a-vat scenario** as a skeptical challenge, asking us to imagine the situation from the perspective of a brain being programmed with private experiences. In a 1973 book, *Thought*, Gilbert Harman described the following thought experiment:

> ... it might be suggested that you have not the slightest reason to believe that you are in the surroundings you suppose you are in, reading a book called Thought. It may look and feel to you as it would look and feel if you were in those surroundings, reading such a book. But various hypotheses could explain how things look and feel. You might be sound asleep and dreaming—or a playful brain surgeon might be giving you these experiences by stimulating your cortex in a special way. You might really be stretched out on a table in his laboratory with wires running into your head from a large computer. Perhaps you have always been on that table. Perhaps you are quite a different person from what you seem: you are a volunteer for a psychology experiment that involves having the experiences of someone of the opposite sex reading a book written in English, a language which in real life you do not understand. Or perhaps you do not even have a body. Maybe you were in an accident and all that could be saved was your brain, which is kept alive in the laboratory. For your amusement you are being fed a tape from the twentieth century. Of course, that is to assume that you have to have a brain in order to have experience; and that might be just part of the myth you are being given.

So instead of asking how you can be sure that everything you perceive isn't a dream fed to you by an evil demon, we're asking how you can be sure you're not experiencing a complex illusion fed directly to your brain by a scientist who has his computers attached to your brain.

The 1999 movie, *The Matrix*, used this theme on a large scale. Human beings lie in pods; their bodies are being used to extract energy to power a devastated world run by intelligent machines that turned against their human creators. The humans in the pods are programmed with a simulated fantasy world. In the movie, some humans manage to learn the truth and escape the simulation, but if escape hadn't been possible, they never would have known that their "reality" was all illusion.

Another skeptical fantasy dispenses with the body and brain altogether and imagines your consciousness existing as part of a computer simulation of human life. Let's explore this skeptical fantasy in some detail.

Are We Living in a Computer Simulation?

Most of you probably know of the computer game, The Sims, in which the player creates virtual people with distinct appearances and personalities who live in a community where they live, work, and interact with other virtual people. The Sims is an example of a life simulation computer video game. What's crucial to the skeptical use of the idea of computer simulations is to imagine that the simulations are so complex that they are able to simulate not only the complex behaviors of the virtual characters but also the complex workings of their brains—and that as a result of the complex brain simulations the virtual characters have real consciousness, including real thoughts, experiences, and feelings. Think of such a system as analogous to Berkeley's subjective idealism in which God is replaced by the computer and programmer. The virtual world created by the computer exists as coordinated images fed to the different consciousnesses—images that represent nonexistent physical objects, including human bodies. The great disanalogy with Berkeley's idealism is that with the computer simulation the whole system is physical.

In the 1964 novel, *Simulacron-3*, the author, Daniel F. Galouye, imagines a computer simulation of a city, created for the purpose of market research, in which the inhabitants have real consciousness. One of the creators of that simulated city, Douglas Hall, gradually comes to realize that his world is actually a simulation created by people in another world.

Our story, "Add Some More Boils," imagines a more modern variant of the simulated world scenario. Technology has reached the point where full historical simulations containing virtual characters with real consciousness can be run on any home computer as homework assignments or video games. The boy, Alex, observed by his pesky brother, Terry, is running a simulation of some everyday episode during the late Middle Ages when Europe is suffering from the Black Plague. The focus of this simulation is Taddeo, a virtual character with real consciousness who believes he is living at that time. In the simulation, Taddeo has contracted the plague, has been thrown out of his house by his family, and is wandering the streets, expecting to die. According to the story, Taddeo is experiencing real suffering—suffering that the boys add to for a little fun. There's a glitch in the virtual world when Terry touches something he shouldn't have, causing the medieval scene to turn red. Had Taddeo been living in a contemporary world, he might have suspected there was something artificial about his world. But as a character in medieval times, he thinks in terms of divine events, perhaps the light being a sign from God that He has heard the prayers of suffering humanity. No doubt Taddeo's despair will become greater when he realizes there is to be no miracle.

Could we, like Taddeo, be **living in a computer simulation**—not of medieval times, of course, but of our part of the world in the early twenty-first century? Could our simulation be part of a study by twenty-fifth century historians—or perhaps by history students who combine an interest in history with a perverse sense of humor and minimal ethical qualms?

The name most prominently associated with the contemporary philosophical discussion of whether or not we're living in a computer simulation is Nick Bostrom. Bostrom has been quoted as saying, "My gut feeling, and it's nothing more than that, is that there's a 20 percent chance we're living in a computer simulation." But he doesn't argue that point. The importance of his writings on the subject is that they set out in some detail various factors involved in assessing the issue.

Bostrom argues that "at least one of the following statements is true:"

1. The human species is very likely to become extinct before reaching a "posthuman" stage.
2. Any posthuman civilization is extremely unlikely to run a significant number of simulations of their evolutionary history (or variations thereof).
3. We are almost certainly living in a computer simulation.

Bostrom is not giving odds; he's not saying that one of three statements is more likely to be true. He's simply saying that at least one of these three statements is true.

Let's start with statement 1: "The human species is likely to become extinct before reaching a '**posthuman**' stage."

NICK BOSTROM (1973–) is a Swedish philosopher and the director of the Future of Humanity Institute at Oxford University. His book, *Superintelligence: Paths, Dangers, Strategies*, a *New York Times* best-seller praised by Bill Gates and Elon Musk, argues that true artificial intelligence poses the greatest threat to humanity and if not managed properly could lead to our extinction.

What does the phrase "posthuman stage" mean? In this context it means, at the very least, a future stage of history in which humans—or beings who have evolved or otherwise developed from humans—have technological capacities almost unimaginably more advanced than ours. They would have a "virtually infinite supply of computing capacity," having been "capable of converting planets and other astronomical resources into enormously powerful computers."

Why are we talking about so much computing power? To simulate a single human brain might require 10^{16} (10 quadrillion or 10,000,000,000,000,000) operations per second. The posthuman future Bostrom and others have in mind doesn't simply involve the ability to simulate one human brain within one virtual world. Instead,

[o]ne can easily imagine millions of individuals running thousands of variations on hundreds of themes, each containing billions of

simulated individuals. Scientists, hobbyists, artists, and schoolchildren might all be running these simulations. Trillions and trillions of these simulated individuals would exist, all believing that they are real and are living in an earlier generation.

No matter how wild a particular futuristic scenario might be, you could probably find some futurist who claims it's likely to happen in the next 50 years. Bostrom makes no such claim. He says, "For purposes of this discussion, it doesn't matter how long it will take. It can take one hundred years, one thousand years, or one million years." What he's saying is that to believe in statement 1 is to believe a posthuman stage will never happen.

Why might it not happen? Bostrom says we might "destroy ourselves through nuclear war, biological catastrophe, or nanotech disaster." We can add some other possibilities: We wouldn't even have to destroy ourselves: We could simply regress periodically through one disaster or another, through an endless series of religious and political conflicts—throwing ourselves back into a series of Dark Ages. Further, to develop the technological ability to create millions of such computer simulations, we would need almost unlimited wealth. With anything short of that, funds needed to develop such technology might be diverted to medical care, food, shelter, and weapons. Think of how the space program has stayed so modest because taxpayers and politicians have been unwilling to devote tax dollars to it. One could imagine a civilization getting to the point where it could do a few simulations involving thousands of conscious virtual people but no more than that.

There's another huge assumption behind the idea that posthumans could create simulated worlds with virtual people who were really conscious. The assumption is that minds are what Bostrom refers to as **substrate independent**—that is, they are theoretically realizable on substances other than "biological tissue."

> But would these simulated individuals really be "people"? Would they be intelligent, regardless of how much processing power they had? Would they be conscious? The reality is no one really knows. But it's common for philosophers of the mind to make the assumption of substrate-independence. Basically this means that consciousness may depend on many things—knowledge, intelligence (processing power), mental organization, the details of computational structure, and so on—but one of the things it doesn't necessarily require is

biological tissue. It is not an essential property of consciousness that it is implemented on carbon-based biological neural networks inside a cranium; silicon-based processors inside a computer could, in principle, do the trick as well.

We won't be in a position to evaluate the claim of substrate independence until we have covered the material in the next chapter on the nature of the mind. But we can make a couple of points here. It is true that "it is common for philosophers of the mind to make the assumption of substrate independence," but that is because they embrace a theory of mind called **functionalism**, which, its critics claim, basically ignores what's been called the "hard problem of consciousness"—figuring out what consciousness is and how it could arise from a physical system (from the body and brain). Functionalism defines mind in terms of its function, which, in turn, is defined in terms of physical inputs and outputs and the causal relations between them. According to functionalism, anything that functions like our brains can be said to have a mind. This could theoretically be true of some organ of a noncarbon-based extraterrestrial or "silicon-based processors inside a computer."

A functional approach provides a useful context for the study of the human brain and its related psychology. But critics claim it is far too loose a theory to count as a complete theory of mind. **Philosophical zombie** is a label used for a theoretical entity that is just like a normal human in terms of its body, neurological activity, and behavior (including speech) but doesn't actually have experiential consciousness. (See the story, "Strange Behavior," in the next chapter.) Critics say that functionalists would be committed to saying that philosophical zombies have minds, whereas most of us would be inclined to deny it.

In the context of the simulated reality argument, the point is this: Yes, many philosophers believe in substrate independence. But that's because they hold a theory of mind that seems to ignore conscious experience. Thus, it is no good using these philosophers for the claim that brains simulated on computers would be conscious.

This is not to argue that such simulated minds would not be conscious. But we don't have very good arguments that they would be either. It's possible that vast computer simulations of human minds might be functionally equivalent to human minds without actually having conscious feelings. The point is that at this juncture we simply don't know. The upshot is that statement 1 should read like this: Either the human species is likely to become extinct before it is capable of running millions of computer life simulations, each including thousands of simulated human brains, AND/OR such simulated brains would never be conscious.

We're not talking about whether or not a civilization capable of creating billions of real consciousnesses would want to do so: That comes under Bostrom's second statement. We're simply spelling out what his statement 1 really amounts to.

Next let's explore statement 2: "Any posthuman civilization is extremely unlikely to run a significant number of simulations of their evolutionary history (or variations thereof)."

Here we are asking the following questions: If a posthuman civilization were capable of running simulations with billions of conscious virtual creatures, is there any reason why they wouldn't do so? In particular, since we're wondering if we could be part of such a simulation in that futuristic society, is there any reason why they wouldn't want to run ancestor simulations that would include the twentieth century? Bostrom has this to say:

> We can imagine that in the "posthuman age" there would be no interest in running historical simulations. This would require significant changes to the motivations of individuals in a posthuman age, for there are certainly many humans today who would like to run ancestor simulations if they could afford to do so. But perhaps many of our human desires will be regarded as silly by anyone who becomes a posthuman. Maybe the scientific value of ancestor simulations to a posthuman civilization will be negligible (which is not too implausible, given its unfathomable intellectual superiority), and maybe posthumans regard recreational activities as merely a very inefficient way of getting pleasure—which can be obtained much more cheaply by direct stimulation of the brain's reward centers.

Imagine that the planet-sized computers were developed by posthumans five million years from now, posthumans who have managed to colonize much of the solar system. How much interest would they have in running simulations of Earth five million years earlier? Maybe the only ones interested would be a couple of specialist history professors in the futuristic equivalent of the musty basement of some university lab.

One issue that Bostrom considers—and others have taken up—is an ethical issue: If simulations involved real consciousness, how could you justify simulating worlds that involved so much suffering? Bostrom says that on the one hand posthumans might decide that running life simulations would be unethical. On the other hand, he says, if we see the existence of our world as having positive value, wouldn't the existence of similar worlds also have positive value? He is also skeptical that even if some posthumans were bothered by such simulations they would be able to enforce a ban against all those who would want to run them.

Bostrom and others seem too casual on the ethical issue. Throughout the ages, people have been anguished by **the problem of suffering**—how a benevolent God could have created a world with as much suffering as our world has. (This is an issue we will discuss in a Chapter 5.) Now we are looking to a future in which the kind of gamers who enjoy playing Mortal Kombat and Call of Duty are going to be allowed to play God by re-creating interesting periods of history or creating their own worlds containing creatures with real consciousness who can feel pain. How many times are they going to want to run simulations of the Black Plague or the battles of World War I or the Holocaust? It boggles the mind.

LET'S REVIEW

1. The human species is very likely to become extinct before reaching a "posthuman" stage.
2. Any posthuman civilization is extremely unlikely to run a significant number of simulations of their evolutionary history.

* Why might statement 1 be true?
* Why might statement 2 be true?

Finally, let's consider Bostrom's statement 3: "We are almost certainly living in a computer simulation."

In the context of his account, the basic point is this: If it is possible to produce real consciousness through a computer simulation of brains; and if the human species evolves to the stage where it has the virtually unlimited computer power to produce billions of simulated brains with real consciousness; and if it has an interest in, and no prohibitions against, running those simulations, including ancestor simulations of historical periods (such as the one we're living in relative to them), then we are almost certainly living in a computer simulation.

Why "almost certainly"? Because if there is one real world with a limited number of conscious beings and a million simulated worlds with billions of conscious beings, then the odds are great that you are one of the conscious beings in a simulated world.

Bostrom isn't claiming we are living in a computer simulation. Given all the ifs, ands, and buts involved in the various hypotheses, it's good that he isn't. If one were absolutely convinced of the falsity of statements 1 and 2, then it would seem that we must be living in a computer simulation. But being convinced and being given convincing reasons are two different things.

If we ever get to the point where we create and run billions of computer simulations (and if we have good reason to think that this real consciousness has been created by those simulations), it will be almost certain that we live in one. But we're miles away from that at the moment. We can't prove we're not living in a computer simulation. But we have no good reason to think we are.

As for the brain-in-the-vat scenario, if in the future we can take a brain out of one body, put it in a vat, stimulate it for awhile, and then transplant it in another body; and if it then describes its conscious experiences in the first body, in the vat, and in the second body and attests to those experiences being as of comparable quality; and, further, if there are millions of brains in vats that don't have bodies available so that the odds of one being a brain in a vat were very high, then I suppose we couldn't be sure we weren't brains in vats.

Given what we know now, however, it doesn't look as if the existence of the external world should be in serious doubt.

Definitions

(Terms are defined in the order in which they appeared in the text.)

1. EXTERNAL WORLD: Any world existing beyond one's own mind and experiences.
2. SOLIPSISM: The view that all that exists is one's own mind with its private experiences and thoughts; or the skeptical position which says that the only thing one can prove exists is one's own mind and experiences.
3. COGITO: Short for "Cogito ergo sum," meaning "I think, therefore I am." From Descartes.
4. EMPIRICIST: One who believes all our knowledge is derived from experience.
5. RATIONALIST: One who believes there are other sources of knowledge than experience, such as innate ideas accessible by reason alone.

6. DIRECT REALISM (sometimes, pejoratively, called naive realism): In normal perception, one experiences the object directly, not indirectly through private images.

7. REPRESENTATIVE REALISM: The view that our sense impressions are caused by objects in a world external to our minds and our impressions represent those objects to us.

8. MATERIAL OBJECTS: Nonmental objects exterior to all minds. (Traditionally thought of as occupying space and having shape, size, and mass.)

9. IDEA (Locke and others): Immediate object of perception.

10. QUALITY (Locke): The power in an object to produce an idea.

11. PRIMARY QUALITY (Locke): A quality that resembles the idea it produces.

12. SECONDARY QUALITY (Locke): A quality that does not resemble the idea it produces.

13. INDIRECT REALISM: The view that our sense impressions are caused by objects in a world external to our minds, but leaving open the question as to whether or not those objects resemble our impressions of them.

14. SUBJECTIVE IDEALISM: What exists are minds (including God's) and experiences but no physical objects.

15. PRIVATE-LANGUAGE ARGUMENT: An argument, derived from the work of Wittgenstein, that a purely private language would be impossible.

16. BRAIN-IN-A-VAT SCENARIO: A skeptical scenario asking how we know we're not disembodied brains being fed simulated worlds.

17. LIVING IN A COMPUTER SIMULATION: A skeptical scenario asking how we know we're not living in a computer simulation that produces virtual people with real consciousness.

18. POSTHUMAN: A future stage of history in which beings who have evolved or otherwise developed from humans have technological capacities almost unimaginably more advanced than ours.

19. SUBSTRATE INDEPENDENCE: Here the idea that minds are theoretically realizable in substances other than "biological tissue." (See Chapter 3.)

20. FUNCTIONALISM: A theory of mind that defines mind in terms of its function, which, in turn, is defined in terms of physical inputs and outputs and the causal relations between them. (See Chapter 3.)

21. PHILOSOPHICAL ZOMBIE: A theoretical entity that is just like a normal human in terms of its body, neurological activity, and behavior (including speech) but doesn't actually have experiential consciousness. (See Chapter 3.)

22. THE PROBLEM OF SUFFERING: The problem of explaining how a benevolent God could have created a world with as much suffering as we see in our world. (See Chapter 5.)

Questions

1. Explain the concept of the "external world." What would, and wouldn't, be part of that world?

2. On what basis do we normally distinguish dreams from reality? What does it mean to say that reality might also be a dream?

3. "I can't be dreaming. Just now, I asked my friend if I was dreaming, and she said 'No.'" What is the problem with this argument?

4. Why is Descartes involved in a project of systematic doubt? What role does the evil demon play in this project?

5. Explain Descartes's "cogito" argument.

6. Say to yourself, "I think, therefore . . . exists," filling in your name. Is this a good argument?

7. What is the theory of direct realism? What is supposedly wrong with it?

8. Explain John Locke's theory of what we call representative realism. What is supposed to represent what?

9. On what grounds did George Berkeley criticize Locke's theory of perception? What theory did Berkeley propose in its place?

10. On what grounds did David Hume criticize Berkeley's theory?

11. If we take solipsism as suggesting that it is equally reasonable to suppose that the world of experience comes from the unconscious as from the external world, what counterarguments could be made against solipsism?

12. Explain the "private-language argument" for the external world suggested by the work of Ludwig Wittgenstein.

13. Explain the "brain-in-a-vat" fantasy as a skeptical challenge to our everyday beliefs.

14. Explain the "living in a computer simulation" fantasy as a skeptical challenge to our everyday beliefs.

15. Summarize Nick Bostrom's analysis of the question, "Are we living in a computer simulation?"

16. What is meant by the assumption that mind is "substrate independent"? Why is this assumption crucial to the question of whether or not we're living in a computer simulation?

17. If we could produce simulations with virtual people, what ethical problems would we face?

Notes

Descartes, Doubt, and the "Cogito"

"Allegory of the Cave." Plato, *The Republic.*

"Zhuangzi wrote this." *Chuang Tzu.* Translated from the Chinese by Herbert A. Giles. 1889.

"How many times has it occurred. . . ." From *Meditations on First Philosophy* by René Descartes, translated by Lawrence J. LaFleur. New York: Macmillan, 1979. *First Meditation.*

"I will therefore suppose that. . . ." Descartes, *First Meditation.*

"Even though there may be a deceiver. . . ." Descartes, *Second Meditation.*

"Thus a snowball having the power. . . ." From *An Essay Concerning Human Understanding* (1689). By John Locke. Book II.

". . . such as are utterly inseparable from the body. . . ." Locke, Book II.

". . . such qualities which in truth are. . . ." Locke, Book II.

"For, our faculties being suited to the full extent of being. . . ." Locke, Book IV.

"It is said that heat and cold. . . ." From *A Treatise Concerning the Principles of Human Knowledge* (1710) by George Berkeley.

"PHIL: And doth not matter. . . ." From *Three Dialogues Between Hylas and Philonous* (1713) by George Berkeley.

"For my part, when I enter most intimately. . . ." From "Of Personal Identity" in *A Treatise of Human Nature*, Book I, Part 4 (1739) by David Hume.

"But setting aside some metaphysicians. . . ." Hume, "Of Personal Identity."

Can I Know There's an External World?

"Wittgenstein imagines a man who decides to write 'S' in his diary. . . ." Wittgenstein, L., 1953, *Philosophical Investigations.* Trans. G. E. M. Anscombe, 3rd edition. Oxford: Blackwell, 1967. §§244–271.

"In a 1973 book, *Thought.* Gilbert Harman. . . ." Gilbert Harman, *Thought.* Princeton, NJ: Princeton University Press, 1973.

Are We Living in a Computer Simulation?

"Bostrom has been quoted as saying. . . ." See "Our Lives, Controlled from Some Guy's Couch," by John Tierney. *New York Times*, August 14, 2007.

"Bostrom argues that 'at least. . . .'" References are to "Are We Living In *The Matrix*? The Simulation Argument." Nick Bostrom, in *Taking the Red Pill: Science, Philosophy and Religion in* The Matrix. Edited by Glen Yeffeth. Dallas, TX: BenBella Books, 2003. (See Readings.) This version is adapted from his original article

"Are You Living in a Computer Simulation?" *Philosophical Quarterly* (2003), Vol. 53, No. 211, pp. 243–255. P. 234.

"One can easily imagine. . . ." Bostrom, "Matrix," p. 237.

"But would these simulated individuals really. . . ?" Bostrom, "Matrix," p. 235.

"We can imagine that in the 'posthuman age' there would be no interest in running historical simulations. . . ." Bostrom, "Matrix," p. 236.

"So while it is possible that statement two is true, it would require. . . ." Bostrom, "Matrix," p. 237.

Further Materials

Descartes, Locke, Berkeley, and Hume

Primary Sources

Descartes, René. *Meditations on First Philosophy*, translated by Lawrence J. LaFleur. New York: Macmillan, 1979.

Berkeley, George. *Three Dialogues Between Hylas and Philonous* (1713).

Hume, David. "Of Personal Identity" in *A Treatise of Human Nature*, Book I, Part 4 (1739).

Locke, John. *An Essay Concerning Human Understanding* (1689).

Secondary Sources

Ayer, A. J. *Hume: A Very Short Introduction*. Oxford: Oxford University Press, 1987.

Dunn, John. *Locke: A Very Short Introduction*. Oxford: Oxford University Press, 1984.

Flage, Daniel E. *Berkeley*. Cambridge, UK: Polity Press, 2014.

Sorrell, Tom. *Descartes: A Very Short Introduction*. Oxford: Oxford University Press: 1987.

Wittgenstein

Primary Sources

Wittgenstein, L., 1953, *Philosophical Investigations*, translated by G. E. M. Anscombe. Oxford: Blackwell, 3rd edition, 1967. §§244–271.

Secondary Sources

Grayling, A. C. *Wittgenstein: A Very Short Introduction*. Oxford: Oxford University Press, 1996.

Scuton, Roger. *Modern Philosophy: An Introduction and Survey*. New York: Viking Penguin, 1995.

Brains in Vats and Computer Simulations

Bostrom, Nick. "Are You Living in a Computer Simulation?" *Philosophical Quarterly* (2003), Vol. 53, No. 211, pp. 243–255. p. 234. (Available online.)

Bostrom, Nick. "Are We Living in *The Matrix*? The Simulation Argument," in *Taking the Red Pill: Science, Philosophy and Religion in* The Matrix. Edited by Glen

Yeffeth. Dallas, TX: BenBella Books, 2003. (Contains a number of interesting essays.)

Harman, Gilbert. *Thought*. Princeton, NJ: Princeton University Press, 1973.

Lawrence, Matt. *Like a Splinter in Your Mind: The Philosophy Behind the Matrix Trilogy*. Oxford: Blackwell Publishing, 2004.

Westerhoff, Jan. *Reality: A Very Short Introduction*. Oxford: Oxford University Press, 2011.

Yeffeth, Glen (ed.). *Taking the Red Pill: Science, Philosophy and Religion in* The Matrix. Dallas, TX: BenBella Books, 2003. (Contains a number of interesting essays.)

CHAPTER 3

The Nature of the Mind
Fiction

READING 1: Strange Behavior

PREVIEW

In this story, the aliens on the planet Gamma are peaceful, intelligent, and friendly; the only odd thing is that they don't have minds.

As you read the story, ask yourself:

* *What are the differences between the people from Earth, the Gammas, and the Gammese robots?*
* *What are the religious views of the Gammas? Do these make sense in terms of what the Gammas are?*

What first startled us about the civilization on the planet Gamma was not its strangeness but its familiarity. It was as if a piece of southern Europe from the year 2280 had been transported 50 years ahead in time, and millions of miles out into space, to that small planet. Of course, the similarity is not exact. The Italians of 50 years ago did not have quite the same enthusiasm for spherical constructions, or for the colors gray and orange. Also, the brown-skinned Gammas are 9 feet tall and hairless, and they hear through slits located just below their cheekbones. But with all the strange life forms recently discovered in the universe, these minor dissimilarities between the Gammas and the midcentury Italians go almost unnoticed. When we landed on Gamma, we felt as if we had stepped into a living museum.

The technological sophistication of Gamma is virtually the same as that of Earth 50 years ago. But there is one notable difference. The Gammas' skill in robotry is more advanced than is ours even today. In fact, we spent our first eight hours on Gamma in the company of robots we thought to be living beings. In our defense, I should note that the Gammese robots have a tremendous flexibility of response and fluidity of motion and that their metallic parts are covered with a brown, skinlike exterior. It is only when a Gammese robot is standing next to a Gamma that one notices, in the robot, a hint of the mechanical. But I don't think one is thoroughly convinced of the difference between the Gammas and the robots until one has toured the hospitals where the living are treated and the factories where the robots are repaired.

It was from the robots that we got the rudiments of the Gammese language. After letting them know that we were friendly, we coaxed them over to the Q-35 Computer Language Translator. We showed them the green patch on the screen of the Translator's Sensitivity Panel and indicated that they should say aloud the Gammese word for what they saw. We continued this process until we were able to produce, via the Translator, several basic sentences in Gammese. Then the robots realized that the Q-35 was recording all the word translations and would soon enable us to converse by voice alone, without constant reference to the pictures on the Sensitivity Panel. Thereafter, the robots concentrated on teaching the Q-35 their language, responding in quick succession to the series of sights, sounds, textures, tastes, and scents produced by the Sensitivity Panel.

The real Gammas appeared eventually, and we laughed at ourselves for having mistaken the robots for living beings. The Gammas were very friendly and intensely curious about the civilization on Earth. Of course, we had more to tell them than they us, for to us they were like the past and to them we were like the future. The first days on Gamma were a constant series of conferences, largely of a show-and-tell variety, as we struggled to make ourselves understood through the less than fluent Q-35 Translator. Fortunately, we had with us an instruction kit filled with models, maps, and photographs designed to aid us in explanations of life on Earth.

With so much on Gamma already familiar to us, we tended to focus our attention on the robots. We became more and more puzzled by what we observed. It was not only that the robots were so lifelike but also that the Gammas seemed to treat the robots as their equals. True, there was a preponderance of robots in jobs that demanded only strength or great memory, but there were Gammas in such jobs as well. And some Gammese robots held high-level positions in which they supervised the activities of the living Gammas. Furthermore, the Gammas seemed to treat the robots with the same sort of courtesy, affection, or, occasionally, anger that they showed toward other Gammas.

Our most frequent guide was a Gamma whose name is unpronounceable. We simply addressed him as "Mr. A," and the Q-35 made the sound that he recognized as his name. We were eager to question him about the Gammas' attitude toward the robots, but we approached the subject cautiously, not wishing to seem critical. His initial responses to our inquiries were bewildering. It seemed as though he were teasing us.

"Would you say that flesh is so much better than metal?" he asked. "I should think it would be just the opposite."

Or again: "Would you treat someone differently just because she is produced in a factory? Personally, I think our mode of reproduction—which is similar to yours—is rather inefficient and even comical."

Mr. A was asked why only robots had been sent on the potentially dangerous mission of meeting us when we landed on Gamma.

"Because, of course, they're more easily repaired than we are. It is a quality we envy them. Just as they sometimes envy us our greater flexibility."

Phrases like "they envy us" and "they also want" were constantly employed by our guide. Finally, a member of our group, Lieutenant Natsumi Shimizu, blurted out the question that all of us wanted to ask.

"Mr. A, do the Gammas really believe that their robots have minds?"

"Of course," said Mr. A, looking puzzled.

"Then that explains the confusion," said Shimizu. "We did not mean to say that one should treat a creature differently simply because it is made of a different substance or is produced differently. Rather, we believe that creatures made of metal cannot possibly have minds. On the other hand, you believe they can and do. Now we understand each other better."

We were all quite pleased with the quick and tactful way in which we had solved the mystery. At the same time, we all felt more than a little superior to a people who believed that machines could think. However, Mr. A did not seem pleased. He seemed absolutely bewildered.

"I don't understand," he said. "Please explain yourselves."

"You believe that these robots have minds," said Shimizu. "So you treat them as your peers. We don't believe that robots have minds. Therefore, we treat them as we might treat, say, expensive watches. Of course, there is room for disagreement on this point. I mean, one doesn't actually see minds."

"Of course you see minds!" said Mr. A.

He was quite emphatic and seemed quite serious. We were all startled.

"Well, one's own mind, yes," said Shimizu. "But one doesn't see other minds."

"You do see other minds!"

"No, no. At least not according to our beliefs. We believe that one sees the behavior of other people but not their minds."

Mr. A glanced toward the Q-35 Translator and then back at Shimizu.

"Your words don't seem to translate. What I hear from the Translator makes no sense."

Shimizu looked thoughtful for a moment, and then she continued.

"Does the word 'behavior' make sense to you? The actions of the body?"

"Yes."

And the word 'pain'?"

"Yes."

"Do you understand me when I say that a person in pain behaves in a special sort of way?"

"Yes. Of course."

"Well, what we call 'pain' is not the behavior but the thing inside."

"What thing inside?" said Mr. A. "There are many things inside."

"I mean the thing that is inside whenever you show the pain behavior."

"Oh, you mean the state of the brain or the state of the robot's computer?"

"No, no, no. You could observe the brain state or the computer state under certain conditions. I mean the thing that you could never observe no matter how extensively you examined the body. I mean the feel of the pain, the sensation of pain."

"Those last words don't translate."

Shimizu was obviously feeling frustrated, but she pressed on.

"Perhaps the example of imagination would be easier. Suppose you close your eyes and imagine something round and orange. Form an image of it. What we call the 'mental' is not the closing of the eyes or the verbal description 'orange and round' that you might give us. What we call the 'mental' is the round and orange picture inside of you."

"What picture?" said Mr. A.

The conversation went on in this absurd fashion as Shimizu tried to phrase the obvious in a way that would be obvious in Mr. A's language. But gradually the truth of the matter began to dawn on us. The reason the Gammas saw no essential difference between themselves and their robots was that the Gammas, like the robots, were creatures without minds, without consciousness.

Our words like "think" and "want," and the generic term "mind," had seemed, at first, to translate into Gammese because we constantly correlate our mental events with behavioral patterns. The Gammas had thought all along that we were talking about behavior. In fact, our mental terms didn't translate into Gammese at all, for the Gammas have no minds. They only behave as if they did.

As we were staring at Mr. A in astonishment, it occurred to us that we might be frightening or offending him. We were very vulnerable on this faraway planet. So we turned the conversation from the topic of minds to the topic of interplanetary travel. Our talk of the overtly strange life forms we had encountered on our travels seemed to reestablish our kinship with the Gammese people.

When the subject of minds arose again, as it inevitably did, we tried to deemphasize the dissimilarity between ourselves and the Gammas. We implied that our word "mind" referred to behavior plus that "something else." This allowed us to say that the Gammas and the robots had minds without pretending, as would have been hopeless now, that there was no difference between them and us. Eventually, the whole matter turned into a kind of joke. Mr. A asked us what the "something else" inside the people from Earth did for them. Of course, we had to admit that it produced no overt effects that could not occur without it. After that he began to joke about us as "the people with the something else that does nothing at all." In fact, this phrase threatens to become the general designation for us on Gamma.

****

It is truly amazing to observe just how little external difference the lack of mind has made to the Gammese civilization. With only a body and a brain, they have almost managed to keep pace with the civilization on Earth. Without thoughts, they have been able to develop a sophisticated technology that has brought them to the verge of interplanetary travel. Without feelings, they can discriminate between beauty and ugliness, goodness and evil, and they have produced sophisticated treatises on ethics and aesthetics. They act as if they have the normal variety of human emotions, even to the point of enjoying very sentimental love stories.

The only noticeable differences appear in their metaphysical writings, and even these are minor. One philosopher on Gamma began a philosophical treatise with the argument, "I think, therefore I am." Of course, this is not really the same as Descartes's argument. The correct translation would be something like, "I behave (in a thinking way), therefore I exist (as a physical being)."

On Gamma there is a fairly widespread belief in God, though they have their religious skeptics just as we do. They identify God with the universe and claim that He is (or rather behaves as if He is) omnipotent, omniscient, and perfectly good. They certainly do not imagine God to be nonphysical. The word "nonphysical" translates into their language as "not-being" or "nothing," which is to say that it does not translate at all. Some Gammas believe in life after death, which they imagine to be a physical resurrection of the body that occurs at some far distant time. They include the robots in this resurrection. "The robots worship Him as we do," they say, "and our Heavenly Father would not neglect them." Of course, they do not believe that the mind exists during the period between death and the resurrection. Said one philosopher: "To take the mind from the body is as impossible as taking the shape from a flower while leaving its color and weight behind."

I often wonder about our future relations with the Gammas. I doubt that we would provoke hostilities with these creatures. There are enough hostile beings in the universe already, and we need whatever allies we can find. The Gammas may be able to provide us with valuable information about their solar system. And no doubt our scientists and philosophers will want to study the Gammas at great length. But the issues here will be strictly practical. There can be no question of extending moral rights to mindless, unfeeling creatures, whether they are made of metal or protoplasm.

Mr. A was there to bid us goodbye as we prepared to leave the planet Gamma. He told us how much he had enjoyed our visit and how sad he was to see us depart. He said the Gammas would always look forward to visits from the people of Earth. Then he laughed softly:

"We shall always welcome the people with the something else that does nothing at all."

I laughed with him, but in my heart I felt only pity. He did not, could not, possibly understand that the "something else that does nothing at all" is the very essence of life, the point of it, and makes all the difference in the world.

Questions

1. Which of the following statements are true of the Gammas?
   a. They act and speak intelligently.
   b. They treat the people from Earth in a friendly way.
   c. They exhibit a good sense of humor.
   d. They have a fairly sophisticated technology.
   e. They write and read love stories.
   f. They philosophize.
   g. They have a religion.
2. Explain the differences between body, brain, and mind. Which of these are the Gammas supposed to have?
3. The narrator of "Strange Behavior" says that the Gammas have no minds. What does she believe the mind to be?
4. What are the Gammas supposed to be missing in not having minds?
5. What outward differences, if any, would there be in the Gammese culture if the Gammas had minds?
6. Do you agree with the narrator's attitude toward the Gammas?

READING 2: Life After Life

PREVIEW

In this story, Charlie finds himself floating around as a disembodied soul and decides that life after death isn't all it's cracked up to be.

As you read, ask yourself:

* Does the portrayal of Charlie's capacities and limitations as a disembodied soul make sense? Does it seem consistent?
* How would you have reacted in Charlie's place?

My funeral was quite moving, I thought. I chose a spot at the front, next to the minister, so that I could observe the faces in the crowd while I listened to the eulogy. There wasn't a dry eye in the house. Reverend Franks reviewed my long career with the Omega Life Insurance Company, my "meteoric rise," as he called it, from messenger boy to president. He said I had always insisted that Omega sold insurance for living, not dying: insurance for the happiness of policyholders should they live full term, insurance for the happiness of the loved ones should they not. He was sure that Charlie—my name's Charles R. Smith, but everyone calls me Charlie, even my secretary—that Charlie would want his funeral conducted in the same optimistic, life-loving spirit with which he had conducted his business. That was a nice touch, I thought, and I hoped that the boys from the office were duly appreciative.

Death, said Reverend Franks, was, above all, the opportunity to reflect on life. Though I had lived but 50 years, everyone, he was sure, would agree that my life had been "full term" in the most meaningful sense. I had been not only a business magnate but also a Boy Scout leader, an Elk, and a church deacon. I had been the beloved husband of Ruth and the beloved father of Tim and Marcie, a good provider in life and beyond. I had been a man to whom any friend could turn in legitimate need; a man who could laugh with the fellows and cry, so to speak, for an unfortunate boy; a man who had a 15 handicap as a golfer but no handicap as a human being.

I was feeling a bit smug at that point, I must admit, and I began to feel more so as Reverend Franks started to speak, somewhat uncomfortably, of his hope for "life after life." Our church has always been vague on that particular issue, tending to stress the vast potential for human moral development in "this life." But I knew now, of course, and he didn't. I knew there was life after this life. Or I guess I should say: life after that one.

In all honesty, though, this development was as much of a surprise to me as the next guy. When I got that fish bone caught in my throat and couldn't breathe, and everything started getting dark, I said to myself: This is it, fella. Nothing else, just: This is it, fella. And you know, in the back of my mind, I was a bit pleased with how it was ending. You spend a lot of your life worrying about death and imagining how awful it is going to be. But when the time comes, it's just something you go ahead and do, or rather something that gets done to you, like getting punched in the nose in your first fight. When it happens, it happens quickly, and you're kind of numb, and there isn't that much pain, or fuss, or fear at all.

Then I opened my eyes and I thought: I guess that wasn't it, fella. Ruth was kneeling next to me, wringing her hands and crying, and Tim, who'd been having dinner with us, was yelling into the phone. I said, "I'm all right, Ruth." But she kept on crying, and I realized she was sobbing too loud to hear me. So I got to my feet to show her I was okay. Even that didn't get her attention, so I put my hand on her shoulder. Only then I noticed there wasn't any hand. That was a shocker, I can tell you. I looked down at myself and there was nothing there—no hands, no arms, no feet, no legs, no nothing. I looked in the mirror over the dining room table, and there was nothing there either, just the image of the living room behind me. I looked at Ruth again, and there, at her feet, was a body that looked just like mine, only the face was kind of waxy and blue. And I thought: This is too much. You're having some kind of weird dream. You're on the floor, unconscious, dreaming that you're moving around the room without a body. In a little while you're going to wake up in a hospital bed with your body connected to you the way it's supposed to be, and everything will be all right.

But if this was a dream, it was awfully vivid. Tim hung up the phone and helped Ruth over to the couch. He held her as she cried, and occasionally he glanced over her shoulder at the body on the floor, showing little emotion, just as I'd always taught him a boy should do.

And I thought again: Yes, this has to be a dream. You can't be dead. If you were dead, you'd be standing before Saint Peter at the Pearly Gates, getting fitted for your wings, or something like that. But then I thought: Maybe it doesn't happen that fast. Your soul has just left your body. Maybe it takes the Lord a little while: After all, there are people dying in houses all over the world tonight. You could hardly expect the Lord to make the rounds of all those houses so quickly. You'll just have to wait your turn. And maybe you'd better get yourself ready. So I started in with "Our Father Who Art in Heaven" and when I finished that I started singing, "Nearer My God to Thee." Only no one appeared except for the policemen and the ambulance attendants. All that commotion distracted me, I guess: the sirens, the chatter, the neighbors gathered outside, the ride to the hospital.

At the hospital they pronounced me dead and gave Ruth a sedative. I wasn't all that concerned about Ruth. I don't mean to say I was unsympathetic. I knew how frightened and unhappy she was, and I knew it would be hard for her to get along without me. But I also knew now that death wasn't the end of everything. Ruth would have a few years of loneliness and fear, but then she would find out that life goes on and on, and she would be with me again. From where I stood, so to speak, that looked like a pretty good deal. Anyway, I had my own problems.

In the days following my death, when I wasn't diverted by my funeral arrangements, I was absorbed with the perplexities of my new situation. It was hard to get used to. Some friend would enter the house and I'd say "hi," and he'd walk right through me. I mean right through me. And then I'd look down at where my body had been, and I'd be brought back to reality— whatever that was.

My perception of things was much as it had always been, at least visually. I saw the same shapes, sizes, and colors, in the same three dimensions. And my perception of sounds was about the same. But I had no sense of touch, taste, or smell. I really regretted my lack of taste when I looked at a steak and a beer. Still, I didn't have hunger anymore, and I wasn't in pain. I just missed those pleasures.

I wasn't able to move objects in any way, which is kind of puzzling when you think about it. Of course, my soul didn't have a body anymore. But if a soul can't move objects, how does it ever move a body? Some special kind of connection, I suppose. In any case, my connection had snapped.

However, if I couldn't move objects, I could move through them without difficulty. I would walk into a wall, get a quick impression of darkness, and then emerge from the other side. I found I was able to rise to a height of about 40 feet from the ground and to move laterally at a top speed of 95 miles an hour. I checked that speed when I went into Los Angeles for a Dodgers game, two days after the funeral. I had a great time. I was able to move around the infield, getting close-ups of the action, without fear of getting hit by the ball. I had the best "seat" in the house, and it didn't cost me one thin dime.

It goes without saying that I could go anywhere I wanted, unobserved, and observe anything I wanted. It was fun, at first, dropping by the office, or a neighbor's house, or Larry's Bar, listening to plans for an ad campaign, or to local gossip, trying to guess along with the fellows on the baseball pools. But as time went on, I found myself less and less interested in those conversations, I suppose because I was not involved in the things they were talking about. Occasionally I heard cutting remarks about me, and those hurt. But perhaps I felt even worse when they stopped talking about me altogether.

The real hurt was from my family. Tim took his share of the inheritance, bought himself a flashy SUV, packed it with surfboards, and left college for the beach. When a friend asked him how he got his money, he said, "My old man kicked the bucket." That's all. No fond recollections, no good words, just "my old man kicked the bucket." I never heard my daughter Marcie talk about me at all. I visited her college dorm once and only once. I mean, you teach a girl what's right and wrong, and how no one will buy a cow if the milk is free, and how pot leads to stronger stuff, and she says, "Yes, Daddy, of course," and then you see what she does when she's away. Just once. I wouldn't want to see any more of it.

But my wife, Ruth, gave me the greatest pain—Ruth, with whom I spent all those years, Ruth, whom I trusted. My old friend Arnold kept dropping by to "pay his respects," which I thought was nice of him until I saw what his respects amounted to. I remember vividly that evening two months ago when Ruth was wearing her black dress, and Arnold was pouring her brandy to boost her spirits, and she started crying, and he hugged her, then kissed her, and she started muttering "No," and he said Charlie would want it this way, which, of course, I didn't, and later they started moving toward the bedroom. I was screaming at her at the top of my lungs, even though I knew she couldn't hear me. Then I turned and stomped out of the house. I haven't been back there since. I'm never going back there.

Later, when I calmed down a bit, I began to think things over. By this time it was obvious that the Lord wasn't coming. Maybe I'd always felt that there wasn't anyone in charge of things—life, I mean—and I was pretty sure of that now. And if my fundamentalist friends had been wrong about heaven and such, I could count myself lucky that those Eastern religions I'd read about had been wrong too. I mean, at least I wasn't reincarnated and wandering around as a skunk or a radish. What was happening to me was quite natural, apparently, and uncontrolled. What I had to do was take things in hand and make my own way, just as I had in my former life. I've never been one to sit on my thumbs, I can tell you.

Now that all the people in my former life had become uninteresting or disappointing to me, it seemed that I ought to try to make some new friends among my own kind. There had to be a lot of other souls around, and surely I would get along with them just fine. I've always been great at making friends.

But the question was: How do you make friends with people who are invisible, untouchable, and make no sounds? All I could see when I looked around me were bodies, no souls. How to make contact? Obviously, I needed some good advice.

In hopes of finding an answer, I started taking some philosophy courses (unofficially, of course) at UCLA. They were no help. I did get a few proofs for the indestructibility of the soul, but that was the last thing

I needed. What I needed was a suggestion about how to chat with silent souls, and wouldn't you know those guys would have nothing to say about really relevant topics. I would have asked for my money back if I'd paid any.

After I'd thought about the problem on my own, it occurred to me that extrasensory perception might be the answer. That didn't help much, considering I didn't know anything about extrasensory perception. The only thing I could think of was to act as if I were yelling to someone. So in my mind I said as forcefully as I could, "Hey there!" "Hello there, guys!" "Speak to me!" "Come in, souls, come in!" For the longest time nothing happened, and I tried everything. I "spoke" loudly and softly, at different times of day, facing in different directions. I would think of departed friends or relatives and speak their names. Or I would simply address myself to strangers. I tried visiting areas where it seemed logical that souls might congregate, such as churches, graveyards, and busy city streets.

Finally, I had some luck of sorts. I was sitting on the shore at Long Beach, watching the water and feeling kind of depressed, when I heard a buzzing, chattering sound, like you might hear over the phone. In desperation I cried, "Speak to me, speak to me!" and then, to my amazement, I heard a voice.

"Who's that?"

"I'm Charlie," I said, "Charlie Smith. Who are you?"

"I'm Mildred."

"Where are you, Mildred, in Long Beach?"

"Long Beach? Heavens no. I'm in Tallahassee."

"Tallahassee?"

It happens like that. You'd think that if you got through to another soul, it would be a soul in your own neighborhood. But that other soul can be anywhere. I remember a teacher at UCLA saying that a soul, being non-physical, would have no spatial location. I wanted to interrupt her and tell her how wrong she was. I mean, I was a soul, and I was right there in her classroom. But I must admit now that that kind of location doesn't seem to count for much when souls communicate with one another.

I had a pleasant chat with Mildred that day and the next. She invited me to visit her in Tallahassee, and I accepted. It was a pretty easy trip. I could move, as I've said, at 95 miles an hour and didn't need to stop and rest. I didn't have to worry about traffic jams or stop lights, or winding roads. With a few side trips for sightseeing and getting lost once, I made it in about a day and a half.

I guess I had the absurd feeling that I would see Mildred in Tallahassee. Of course, I couldn't. She was a soul and invisible, no matter how close you got. Our communications in Florida were like more phone conversations, only this time they were local calls. Still, we were able to share experiences and see the sights together.

The first few days were fun. Then Mildred reverted to her "normal" routine. It turned out that the only sights she really wanted to see and share were at the television department at Sears. Mildred loved soap operas. She was a real fanatic. When she wasn't watching the soaps, she would listen to women talking about them or peer over someone's shoulder at the pages of *Soap Opera Digest*. It was all too much for me. I wasn't about to spend eternity watching "The Guiding Light" and "One Life to Live." I thought I'd better find a woman with other interests. I'd made contact once, and I was sure I would again.

And I did—this time with Alice in Cheyenne, Wyoming. That visit went badly from the start. All Alice wanted to do was hang around her husband and spy on the women he'd taken up with after she'd died. I would have left right away, but l happened to see Alice's picture on the mantelpiece in her house. She was gorgeous, I mean really gorgeous. I'd never been with a woman who looked like that. So I tried to get her interested in me. I told her about my bad experiences with my wife and how I'd decided I should forget about my former life and associate with my own kind. I told her she should forget about her husband and try to have some fun.

I took Alice out on a couple of dates. Her mood seemed to be picking up, and she seemed to be getting to like me. One night I took her to a drive-in movie. We sat near the front, about 20 feet in the air, over the cars. It was a very romantic, sensual movie. I got really involved in the film. I began to feel a deep regret at not having a body. I was longing for some kind of human warmth.

"Oh Alice," I said, "I wish so much that I could hold your hand."

"It wouldn't be proper," she said. "I've only been widowed for five months."

That was the last straw. An hour later I was heading back to California.

That's the way it's been going. Every soul I meet seems to be interested only in the past. But the past is past, and you can't live on memories. On the other hand, what else can you live on? There doesn't seem to be anything interesting that you can do for, or to, or with another soul. Or vice versa. It's not much fun floating around like a bubble, not able to do anything in the world.

What on earth am I going to do with myself? I don't know. I've got to figure out something. I've just got to. I'm bored as hell.

Questions

1. In "Life After Life," Charlie is a disembodied soul. Is a soul any different from a mind? Explain.
2. Charlie says that he can't understand how minds manage to move human bodies. What is his reasoning here?
3. Do you believe that the perceptions and capacities of a disembodied soul would be any different from those described in the story? If so, in what ways do you think they would be different?
4. If life after death were purely natural, with the soul just drifting off from the body, how would you imagine it would be?
5. Do you believe in life after death? If so, is your belief connected with a particular religious view?
6. Would a Gammese writer ever write a story like "Life After Life"? Why or why not?

Discussion

PREVIEW

At the end of this discussion, you should be familiar with:

* *what interactionism is and why it is both attractive and problematic;*
* *what the following three theories are and what can be said for and against them: logical behaviorism, identity theory, and functionalism;*
* *Searle's "Chinese Room" thought experiment;*
* *Chalmers's "hard problem of consciousness"; also, what philosophical zombies are and how they relate to the "hard problem";*
* *what the following four theories are and what can be said for and against them: substance dualism, property dualism, epiphenomenalism, and panpsychism;*
* *the difficulties in deciding what capacities a soul would have;*
* *the problem of personal identity;*
* *the meaning of terms listed in "definitions" (which are also marked in bold in the discussion).*

Substance Dualism

The narrator of "Life After Life" holds a view of mind and body that is shared by many people in our culture. It is sometimes dubbed "the official view." According to this view, the mind is radically different from any physical object. For one thing, physical objects (including human bodies) are publicly observable, whereas minds are necessarily private. That is, one can observe another person's body just as one can observe the chairs and tables in a room; but one cannot observe another person's thoughts. Furthermore, physical objects occupy space, whereas minds do not. A mind is not located in the physical body, nor anywhere else in the physical world. Because the mind is radically different from any physical object, it is claimed, the mind is nonphysical. Persons holding this "official view" of mind and body are called "dualists." **Dualism** is the view that there are physical bodies and nonphysical minds.

This sort of dualism is often associated with the seventeenth-century philosopher we met in the last chapter, René Descartes, who articulated the position so clearly. Descartes argued that reflective introspection makes it obvious that mind and body are two different kinds of things: Mind is essentially thinking, whereas body is essentially extension in space.

Descartes was what we'd call a **substance dualist**, with the nonphysical mind and the physical body being two different types of substances. This sort of dualism had some advantages in the context of the Christian orthodoxy of Descartes's time. Science was beginning to characterize the world as a vast material mechanism, determined not by divine whim, but by fixed laws. Placing the mind in a different realm preserved the possibility of free will: the nonphysical mind need not be determined by physical laws. Dualism also allowed for the possibility of disembodied existence after death: The mind, being a different sort of entity, did not depend on the physical body for its existence and need not die with it.

Descartes also believed that the nonphysical mind and physical body had causal effects on one another: This form of substance dualism is called **interactionism**. Such causal interaction seems commonsensical enough—bodily needs cause the sensation of hunger, which causes me to look for something to eat; bodily damage causes pain, which causes me to seek relief. What could be more obvious? In fact, it is probably interactionism (rather than simple dualism) that should be characterized as "the official view."

Yet Descartes's interactionism was immediately challenged. Gassendi, one of Descartes's contemporaries, asked:

> How will that which is corporeal seize upon that which is incorporeal, so to hold it conjoined with itself, or how will the incorporeal grasp the corporeal, so as reciprocally to keep it bound to itself, if in it, the incorporeal, there is nothing which it can use to grasp the other, or by which it can be grasped?

To appreciate this challenge, consider a partial analogy. Suppose that, while watching a knife-throwing act, you learn that the knives in the performer's hand are made of flimsy rubber. You would conclude that the act is a fake. True, each time the man appears to fling a knife, a knife appears in the wooden backdrop, perilously close to the body of his assistant. It seems as though he is throwing the knives, but he is not. The rubber knives do not contain sufficient strength to penetrate the wood. The movements of the man's hand are not causing the knives to appear in the wood; the hand movements are merely correlated with the appearance of the knives. Just as rubber knives are not the sorts of things that could penetrate wood, so, say the interactionist's critics, a nonphysical spirit is not the sort of thing that could affect physical objects.

The specific impulse to deny causal relations between the physical and nonphysical appears, to some extent, in ghost stories. If a ghost passes through a room, it is not tripped by chairs, nor does it knock them over. It is not stopped by a wall, nor does it dent the wall as it enters.

In "Life After Life," it is quite natural to imagine that Charlie, as a soul, would not interact with physical objects. To Charlie, as to many philosophers, this suggests a philosophical problem about the mind and body: "I wasn't able to move objects in any way, which is kind of puzzling when you think of it. Of course, my soul didn't have a body anymore. But if a soul can't move objects, how does it ever move a body?"

In fact, ghost stories really illustrate our confusion about this issue. Though ghosts do not normally interact with the physical world, they do so when the plot demands that they rattle chains or start fires. Ghost stories would be pretty dull if ghosts didn't do such things. But, philosophically, it seems as though we ought to make up our minds on this matter. Could the physical and nonphysical be causally related? Some dualists decided they could not.

Of course, such dualists face the following challenge: "If (nonphysical) mind and (physical) body can't be causally related, what accounts for the constant correlations between them? Surely this is not just coincidence!" In the case of the knife-throwing act, we would conclude that the act is a fake: The movements of the man's hand are not causing the knives to appear in the wood. But having drawn that conclusion, we would suppose some other explanation for the constant correlation between the hand movements and the appearance of the knives. Perhaps there's some mechanism in the backdrop that springs out the knife handles at intervals known to the man; he is timing his arm movements accordingly. Or perhaps there's a third person backstage who presses a button, releasing a knife handle each time the performer's hand moves. We certainly would insist that there is some explanation. We would reject the supposition that these correlations are coincidental.

Gottfried Wilhelm Leibniz (1646–1716) discussed three possible solutions to the problem of the agreement of physical and mental events, explanations that assumed the activity of a creator God. Using the analogy of mind and body as clocks and God as clockmaker, Leibniz asked us to imagine two pendulum clocks that always showed the same time. He said this could come about in three ways:

One: The clocks could have been set up by the clockmaker to mutually influence one another. (Christiaan Huygens [1629–1695] had already observed that the movements of two pendulum clocks hung together tended to become synchronized.) Leibniz called this type of relation between such clocks "the way of influence." (This is analogous to interactionism.)

Two: The clockmaker could be making constant adjustments to the clocks to make sure they showed the same time. He called this the "way of assistance." Here Leibniz was referring to a theory developed by some contemporaries of Descartes, a view that became known as **occasionalism**. Occasionalists were dualists who believed that mind and body could not be causally related and who accounted for the constant correlations between mind and body by imagining that they were caused by God moment by moment. For instance, if you stubbed your toe, God caused your feeling of pain; if you wanted to grab your foot, God moved your arm and hand.

Three: The clockmaker could create the clocks so that they would always agree. This Leibniz called the "way of **preestablished harmony**." According to this view, God predetermines all mental and physical events from the beginning of time to ensure they are correlated in the same way they would be if they were causally related.

Leibniz rejected the way of influence (interactionism) for the reasons we have already considered. "[I]t is impossible to conceive of material particles . . . or immaterial qualities which can pass from one of these substances into the other." He rejected the way of assistance (occasionalism) since he thought the idea of God making physical and mental events match on each specific occasion would have been undignified and unnecessary. Instead he argued that God had created mind and body in preestablished harmony.

Even in a day when divine explanations for everyday events were quite respectable, occasionalism and preestablished harmony didn't appeal to many philosophers and theologians; they seemed too strange a violation of common sense. Today these theories—lumped together under the name **parallelism**—have virtually no adherents. Parallelism represents an historical curiosity, as well as a potential absurdity that threatens any interactionist view.

G. W. F. LEIBNIZ (1646–1716) made brilliant contributions to logic, metaphysics, theology, and mathematics. Avoiding dualism, he conceived of the universe as made up only of God and myriad soul-like entities. He argued on theological grounds that ours had to be the "best all possible worlds"—a doctrine lampooned by Voltaire (see Chapter 5).

Interactionism seems commonsensical until you take a closer look at it: Then it can seem absurd. However there are sophisticated interactionists who recognize the apparent problems with interactionism but argue that every other theory of mind has equally serious problems. If that's the case, they argue, then interactive substance dualism is as plausible a position as any and also accords with common sense and standard religious doctrine.

We'll now consider some alternatives to substance dualism: three materialist theories of mind and three other dualist theories that view the mind as having nonphysical properties but not as being a separate substance. We will see if these other theories have, as the interactionist claims, "equally serious problems."

LET'S REVIEW

* *What reasons have led people to be dualists?*
* *What is interactionism, and what are some problems with it?*
* *What are some other forms of dualism?*

Three Materialist Theories of Mind

Why Materialism?

Materialism (or physicalism) is the view that everything that exists is physical, including the mind. Many materialists believe this view of mind is most compatible with a "scientific view" of the world. They believe that the higher life forms evolved from physical matter. In their view, the emergence of physical mind from physical matter is theoretically plausible; however, the emergence of nonphysical mind from physical matter is preposterous. They find the same absurdity in the idea that the nonphysical mind somehow emerges naturally from the physical in the development of the individual from zygote to embryo to fetus to infant. (Dualist theologians, of course, explain the appearance of the nonphysical mind as a special act of divine creation.) Modern materialists would further argue that to have a nonphysical mind causally affect the physical world would necessarily add energy to the physical world and violate what is seen as a fundamental law of physics: The law of conservation of energy.

Some materialists believe that their view is supported by considerations of theoretical simplicity. The dualist narrator of "Strange Behavior" has to admit that the "something else" she calls "mind" produces "no overt effects that could not occur without it." In theory, a sophisticated brain–nervous system would be quite sufficient to produce the full range of human behavior. To suppose a spirit (nonphysical mind) is behind the workings of the human body would be as unscientific, materialists say, as to suppose a spirit is behind the workings of a car engine. Gilbert Ryle (1900–1976) called dualism "the myth of the ghost in the machine."

Three forms of materialism have received considerable attention since the mid-twentieth century: behaviorism, the identity theory, and functionalism.

Behaviorism

The psychological theory of behaviorism—often called methodological behaviorism—was based on the desire to make psychology more "scientific" by studying only physical behavior. Methodological behaviorism in itself made no claim about the nature of the mind.

The philosophical theory of **behaviorism**, which we will focus on, does make a claim about the nature of the mind, namely, that the mind is nothing but physical behavior. It is often called logical behaviorism or analytical behaviorism since the arguments for it deal with the "logic" or conceptual analysis of our talk about minds.

The narrator of "Strange Behavior" says that the Gammas are "mindless": "the Gammas have no minds. They only behave as if they did." A behaviorist would disagree with the narrator. The Gammas behave intelligently and kindly, the behaviorist would point out. To behave intelligently and kindly is to be intelligent and kind. The term "mind" designates such characteristics as intelligence and kindness. Therefore, the Gammas do have minds.

It is important to emphasize that behaviorism is a thesis about the meanings of our mental terms. Since the meaning of a term is determined by how we use it, behaviorism is a thesis about what we mean when we talk about minds. Behaviorism claims to be an accurate report of how we use the generic term "mind" and the more specific mental terms "pain," "kindly," "knowledgeable," and so forth.

According to the proponents of behaviorism, when we say that someone has a mind, we are simply saying that the person exhibits, is capable of exhibiting, or is disposed to exhibit certain complex, overt, physical behavior under certain circumstances. When you have witnessed someone's behavior, you have seen that person's mind. The mind is nothing more than (certain types of complex, overt) physical behavior and dispositions to behave.

The word "overt" in the definition indicates external rather than internal bodily behavior. According to the behaviorist, when we talk about minds, we are talking about speech, facial expressions, and the movements of the arms and legs, as opposed to the workings of the liver, heart, or brain. The behaviorist would not deny that a functioning brain is essential to our exhibiting complex, overt, physical behavior. But in the behaviorist view, the mind is not the brain; the mind is behavior.

The behaviorist says that mental characteristics are observable but not always as readily observable as red hair or blue eyes. One cannot glance at a crowd of pedestrians and immediately determine which ones know how to ride bicycles and which ones are kind. Rather, mental characteristics are observable and physical in the same way in which the fragility of a vase is observable and physical. If a vase breaks at the light touch of a hammer, one has seen that it is fragile. (Of course, there are less drastic tests of fragility.) If someone gets on a bicycle and rides, one has seen that the person knows how. If someone helps others on numerous occasions, one has seen that the person is kind. To see the behavior is to see the mind because the mind is nothing more than behavior.

Whatever initial plausibility behaviorism may have, it is ultimately difficult to defend. The most obvious problem with behaviorism is that most, if not all, of our mental terms seem to indicate something over and above behavior and dispositions to behave. They indicate events that we are inclined to call "internal" and "private." As Lewis says in "Strange Behavior": "Suppose you close your eyes and imagine something round and orange. Form an image of it. What we call the 'mental' is not the closing of the eyes or the verbal description 'orange and round' that you might give us. What we call the 'mental' is the round and orange picture inside of you."

Similarly, when we say that a person is "in pain," we are talking about something more than the disposition to grimace and groan. We are talking about the sensation, the feel of the pain. We would not say a person was kind unless she had kindly feelings.

The difficulties with behaviorism are most apparent when that theory is applied to oneself. Sit still, fold your hands, close your eyes, and think, "Two plus two equals four." Now report what you have just thought: "I just thought 'two plus two equals four.'" Is it at all plausible to believe that this statement is merely the report of some behavior or some disposition to behave? Surely your statement doesn't mean "I was sitting still with my eyes closed and my hands folded." Such "behavior" is compatible with a wide range of thoughts—or no thoughts at all. Nor does your statement mean "I was disposed to say the words 'two plus two equals four.' " One is not always disposed to do or say something after each thought. Even if one were, such a disposition is not the crucial fact that you are reporting but something incidental. The crucial thing that you are reporting is an internal, private event—the thought, "Two plus two equals four."

Put formally, this particular argument against behaviorism is as follows:

1. Behaviorism implies that all talk about minds is talk about behavior.
2. When I report the thought "2 + 2 = 4," I am not talking about behavior.

3. (Therefore) it's not the case that all talk about minds is talk about behavior (from 2).

4. (Therefore) behaviorism is not true (from 1 and 3).

Such arguments against behaviorism are generally accepted as decisive. However, if behaviorism is not correct, at least one can extract from it a claim that seems to be correct: that many of our mental predicates do imply behavioral components. Consider generosity, for instance. In the absence of all behavior, a person could conceivably be sympathetic, but he or she could not be generous. The term "generosity" implies some physical act of giving. The narrator of "Strange Behavior" makes a similar concession, though over-stating it: "We implied that our word 'mind' referred to behavior plus that 'something else.'" A better way to say this would be that some, but not all, of our mental terms refer to behavior as well as that "something else."

The mind doesn't seem to reduce to overt physical behavior. But perhaps it is physical nonetheless. There is an internal bodily organ, the brain, that is intimately associated with mental processes. Perhaps the mind and the brain are not two different entities, closely related; perhaps the physical brain is the mind. The view that the physical brain is the mind is called the identity theory, and those who believe in the theory are referred to as identity theorists. As has been noted, the identity theory is a form of materialism.

LET'S REVIEW

* What reasons have led people to be materialists?
* What is behaviorism, and what are some problems with it?
* "If behaviorism were correct, then 'Jim knows how to ride a bike' would be true only if Jim was always riding his bike." Explain why this statement reflects a misunderstanding of behaviorism.

The Identity Theory

According to **the identity theory**, the mind (that which produces thoughts, images, and sensations) is identical with the brain (the mass of nerve tissue inside the skull). Mental events are nothing but electrochemical brain processes. Mental events are "internal" only in the sense that they occur inside the skull. They are "private" only in the sense that brain processes are very infrequently observed.

Unlike behaviorism, the identity theory is *not* a theory about the meanings of our mental terms. The identity theorist is not claiming that the word "mind" means "brain" or that the word "pain," for example, means "brain state such and such." Such a claim would be absurd because as long as human beings have talked about minds, they have judged other minds according to behavior and have believed that particular sorts of behavior (grimacing and groaning, for example) were typically associated with particular mental states (pain, for example). This is what gave the behaviorist claim some initial plausibility. But human beings were talking about minds before they found out that the brain is the physical organ most intimately associated with thought.

The identity claimed by the identity theory is **factual identity** rather than **identity of meaning**. The words "mind" and "brain" do not have the same meaning, but, says the identity theorist, the mind and brain are, in fact, identical. Questions of factual identity require one to focus primarily not on the meanings of the words but on the characteristics of those things to which the words refer. "Is my brother, in fact, the axe murderer that the police are seeking?" would be a question of factual identity. Obviously, such a question could not be decided by considering how we use the phrases "my brother" and "axe murderer." That these two phrases do not mean the same thing does not indicate that they do not refer to the same person. Evidence would have to be gathered as to what is known about my brother and what is known about the axe murderer—evidence that just might reveal that my brother is indeed the axe murderer.

By saying that the mind and the brain are identical, the identity theorist is saying that they are literally one and the same thing. (This is called **numerical identity**.) It is easy to misinterpret this claim because in everyday speech the word "identical" often has the meaning of "very similar." For example, we call some twins "identical," even though they are not one person. They are two different people who are similar in most, but not all, respects; for instance, they occupy different positions in space. (Identical twins, sharing virtually all the same properties, are said to be **qualitatively identical**.) However, the identity theorist is not saying that the mind and the brain are two different things that are quite similar, but rather that the mind and the brain are one and the same thing.

It makes sense to think that whatever "internal" aspects of the mind escape a behavioral analysis could be brain states. It also makes sense to suppose that the behavioral dispositions themselves could be brain states.

One favorite behaviorist example of a dispositional property is fragility: To describe something as fragile is to say that it would break under relatively light force. But as some identity theorists have pointed out, we know why fragile objects have a tendency to break—because of a certain internal crystalline structure. In a similar sense, dispositional mental states might be equivalent to brain states.

However, the identity theory, too, has come under criticism. Critics appeal to what might be called a principle of nonidentity: Two things cannot be identical if they have different characteristics. (Or to put it more exactly: If the thing referred to by one phrase has characteristics differing from those of the thing referred to by another phrase, then the two phrases do not refer to the same thing.) This principle is one that we seem to accept readily in everyday life. That pen you have can't be mine if my pen is blue and the one you are holding is green. My brother can't be the axe murderer if my brother is short and the murderer is tall.

Having claimed that two things having different characteristics cannot be identical, critics of the identity theory go on to claim that mental events and brain events do have different characteristics. Consider, for example, mental images. When one imagines something round and orange, presumably the image is round and orange. But is there a round, orange brain process occurring at the same moment? Perhaps there is a round pattern of electrochemical activity: Such has been demonstrated in certain experiments on perception. But our best evidence indicates that there is no orange brain event: The brain does not have the range of colors that our images display. If the image is orange and no brain events are orange, then the image cannot be a brain event. Mental events and brain events, however closely they might be related, are different things. Put formally, this argument against the identity theory is as follows:

1. The identity theory implies that the mind and brain have all the same characteristics.
2. The mind and brain do not have all the same characteristics. (For example, some mental images have colors like orange; brain states do not.)
3. (Therefore) the identity theory is false (from 1 and 2).

Some identity theorists, like U. T. Place, have argued that if we think that when we describe an after-image as green we are describing a mental state as green, we are committing the "phenomenological fallacy." Instead, Place claims that

> when we describe the after-image as green, we are not saying that there is something, the after-image, which is green, we are saying that we are having the sort of experience which we normally have when, and which we have learnt to describe as, looking at a green patch of light.

If this is the case, says Place, all that is required for the identity of after-image and brain state is that the same brain process be ongoing when the subject reports a green after-image as is going on when she looks at a green patch of light; nothing in the brain need be green for the identity to hold.

A critic might claim that Place is merely trying to rephrase the problem away rather than solving it. Stare at a strong light, and then close your eyes and consider the after-image. Doesn't it indeed seem to have color? How could it be identical to a brain state that doesn't look at all like that?

We'll come back to this crucial point. First, though, let's consider a different line of attack against the identity theory.

The identity theory, as originally formulated, identifies *types* of mental states with *types* of brain states. This is called the **type-identity theory**. A type of mental state like pain would be identical to a certain type of brain state: That's what pain is. But if that's what pain is, the identity theorist is committed to the view that for any creature (mammal, reptile, mollusc) to feel pain, it must have exactly the same type of physical-chemical brain state. How plausible is that view?

This problem would apply theoretically to extraterrestrials as well. We are carbon-based creatures with carbon-based brains. Suppose we ran across a creature on another world that was made up of something different—silicon is a favorite example. Suppose also that this creature was similar enough to us so that we could make out patterns of actions and reactions. Suppose the creature reacted to damage to itself with behaviors that involved avoidance and repair and also initially with vocalizations that resembled our expressions of pain. The identity theorist would be committed to the view that such a creature couldn't possibly be in pain—since, by hypothesis it could not have whatever carbon-based brain state that has been identified with pain. All this strikes many critics as implausible.

What many conclude from such criticisms is that mental states are **multiply realizable**—that they could take different forms in different creatures, not only the sorts of sentient carbon-based creatures we're familiar with but different creatures we might create (robots, say) or might find on other worlds made of different "stuff." (Nick Bostrom makes this same point when, as alluded to in the last chapter, he talked about philosophers of mind believing in "substrate independence.")

The conclusion that pain (like other mental states) cannot be identical to the *same type* of state in all physically possible creatures rules out what's called the type-identity theory. However, there is another version of the identity theory called the **token-identity theory**. The word "token" here means instance of a type. The pen I'm using for writing notes is a ballpoint pen with a hard black rubber-like surface, which uses black ink. You might be using a metallic fountain pen with blue ink. These individual pens are different tokens of the same type. Perhaps my pain is nothing more than a state of my brain and maybe your pain is nothing more than a state of your brain, though these brain states may not be exactly similar. This would be the claim of the token-identity theory.

But now the question arises: If the brain states are dissimilar in certain ways, what makes them all the same *type* of brain state—a sensation of pain, say, as opposed to another type of brain state, say, a sensation of cold? Here we might take a suggestion from our pen example: What makes the individual pens all the same type (pen) is that they function as writing implements. Perhaps what makes dissimilar pain brain states the same type (pain) is how they function. Pains seem to function as parts of a system that react to potential damage to the organism by seeking avoidance or repair. Perhaps all mental states are best analyzed functionally.

Functional analysis of mental states has led to a theory that combines aspects of behaviorism and the identity theory, while allowing for multiple realizability: functionalism.

LET'S REVIEW

* *What is the identity theory? Compare/contrast it with behaviorism.*
* *Why is a comparison of the properties of the brain with the properties of the mind relevant to an evaluation of the identity theory?*
* *What is the difference between type identity and token identity? What is the problem with identifying types of mental states with types of brain states?*

Functionalism

According to **functionalism**, mental states should be defined as functional states, defined in terms of what they do rather than what they're made of. As with behaviorism, functionalists will often characterize mental states in terms of behavior and dispositions to behave, given certain situations/inputs. However, unlike behaviorism, functionalism allows for internal states as part of the characterization. It doesn't try to characterize mental states in purely behavioral terms or to eliminate other mental states from that characterization.

Unlike the type-identity theory, functionalism allows for multiple realizability. Indeed, this was a prime motivation behind its development. According to functionalism, any being, whatever its constitution, that had a brain able to function like ours would be said to have a mind.

Functionalism is presented here as a materialist theory of mind, and some commentators would object to that. It is often said that functionalism defines mind in terms of what it does, not in terms of the "stuff" (physical or nonphysical) that it's made of. However, the vast majority of functionalists are materialists. The theory was developed out of the behaviorist/identity theory tradition and is often combined with the token-identity theory. Also while functionalism doesn't disallow dualism in terms of "stuff," it does deny that having a mind requires the sort of internal private experience that philosophers like Descartes thought were essential.

Functionalism with its allowance of multiple realizability often likens the mind to a computer, with the brain being the hardware and the system of mental states being the software. In practical terms, functionalism fit well with, in fact encouraged, attempts to model human thinking with computers.

We saw earlier that functionalists argued for multiple realizability, in part, through consideration of extraterrestrial beings. But the focus of the functionalists wasn't on thinking aliens but on thinking machines. Some went so far as to argue that if computers could function as humans do to a sufficient degree, they wouldn't just be mimicking human thinking—they would be thinking. They would actually have minds.

Alan Turing (1912–1954) proposed a test of machine intelligence that is now called the **Turing Test** and goes like this: There is a person—"the interrogator"—who is in a room separated from a second person and a machine (e.g., a computer). The interrogator writes out questions and receives written answers from both the other person and the machine. The interrogator must try to determine from the answers which of the respondents (known to her as "X" and "Y") is the person and which the machine. The machine "passes the test" if the interrogator can't distinguish the machine's answers from those of the person. No machine has passed the Turing Test to date, though presumably one will eventually. The question we want to ask is whether or not a machine that did pass the Turing Test could be said to "think" and "understand" in the same sense that the human participant is said to think and understand. Turing said yes. Many functionalists also say yes.

As you might imagine, there are critics who disagree. One famous thought experiment called "The Chinese Room" comes from John Searle.

ALAN TURING (1912–1954) was a British mathematician and logician who is considered a pioneer in theoretical computer science and artificial intelligence. The 2014 film, *The Imitation Game*, conveyed elements of his exciting/sad life—how he played a key role in breaking the Nazi's Enigma code in World War II and how his later prosecution for homosexuality led to his suicide.

Searle imagines himself—an English speaker who knows no Chinese—locked in a room with a bunch of Chinese symbols which he can recognize only by their shape. He is given a rule book in English that tells him how to match certain symbols with other symbols. People outside the room pass him bunches of symbols. Consulting his rule book and dealing only with the Chinese symbols by their form, he matches them up with other symbols, which he passes to the people outside the room. It turns out that the system is set up in such a way that the symbols Searle is getting constitute questions in Chinese and the symbols he gives back (following his book of rules) constitute answers in Chinese to the original questions.

> Now suppose that the rule book is written in such a way that my "answers" to the "questions" are indistinguishable from those of a native Chinese speaker. For example, the people outside might hand me some symbols that unknown to me mean, "What's your favorite color?" and I might after going through the rules give back symbols that, also unknown to me, mean, "My favorite is blue, but I also like green a lot." I satisfy the Turing test for understanding Chinese. All the same, I am totally ignorant of Chinese. And there is no way I could come to understand Chinese in the system as described, since there is no way that I can learn the meanings of any of the symbols. Like a computer, I manipulate symbols, but I attach no meaning to the symbols.

Searle says that his Chinese Room thought experiment shows that a machine manipulating symbols simply wouldn't understand the meaning of the symbols as a human would.

The most common objection to this thought experiment is that the "understanding" involved in a Chinese-room case would actually be going on at a higher level; it would be going on at the level of the system that the Chinese room represents and not at the level of the man in the room. Searle counters that the system itself, like the man in the room, is still dealing with nothing but symbol manipulation ("syntax"). He says that you could put the whole system inside the man's head by having him memorize all the symbols and the rule book. He still wouldn't understand the questions and answers in Chinese. He wouldn't understand the meanings of the words (the "semantics").

Critics of functionalism claim that it is wrong as an analysis of those mental events we think of as quintessentially conscious—sensations of pain or green after-images. They claim that functionalism doesn't solve what David Chalmers calls the "hard problem of consciousness."

LET'S REVIEW

* *What is functionalism, and how is it supposed to be an improvement over both behaviorism and the identity theory?*
* *What is the Turing Test of machine intelligence? How is Searle's "Chinese Room" a critique of the Turing Test?*

Zombies and the "Hard" Problem of Consciousness

David Chalmers distinguishes between what he calls the **"easy" and the "hard" problems of consciousness,** problems corresponding to different uses of the word "consciousness." Chalmers says that sometimes the word "consciousness" is used for "the ability to discriminate stimuli, to report information, or to monitor internal states, or to control behavior." These processes are important, and the problems of explaining them are ongoing, but such problems are (relatively) "easy" in the sense that they

> have the character of puzzles rather than mysteries. There seems to be no deep problem in principle with the idea that a physical system could be "conscious" in these senses, and there is no obvious obstacle to an eventual explanation of these phenomena in neurobiological or computational terms.

A theory like functionalism seems to be well suited to solve the "easy" problems of consciousness. However, it seems to ignore the "hard problem," the problem of how consciousness, in the sense of *experience*, arises from a physical brain. Using a famous idea from Thomas Nagel, Chalmers says that "a mental state is conscious when there is something it is like to be in that state." We see something green, or feel a pain or visualize an object like the Eiffel Tower, and there is something it is like to experience the phenomenal character of that state. (To clarify: Try to imagine yourself as your pet dog. Then try to imagine yourself as your Pet Rock. The latter makes no sense. We feel that there is something it is like to be a dog but nothing it is like to be a Pet Rock.)

> There is no question that experience is closely associated with physical processes in systems such as brains. It seems that physical processes give rise to experience, at least in the sense that producing a physical system (such as a brain) with the right physical properties inevitably yields corresponding states of experience. But how and

DAVID CHALMERS (1966–) is Professor of Philosophy and Director of the Centre for Consciousness at the Australian National University; he holds a similar position at New York University. In his 1996 book, *The Conscious Mind*, he introduced the distinction between the "easy" and "hard" problems of consciousness, and he argued that all forms of physicalism fail to solve the hard problem.

> why do physical processes give rise to experience? Why do not these processes take place "in the dark," without any accompanying states of experience? This is the central mystery of consciousness. . . .

"Strange Behavior" could be viewed as a satire of the inner experience view of mind in favor of behaviorism or functionalism. The Gammese people, like their robots, are behaviorally and functionally equivalent to human beings, but they lack phenomenal consciousness. The humans believe such inner experience—the "something else" they have—is the most important thing in the world. Yet when the guide asks the humans what the "something else" does for them,

> we had to admit that it produced no overt effects that could not occur without it. After that he began to joke about us as "the people with the something else that does nothing at all."

Critics of the inner experience view of consciousness could be forgiven for asking how a "something else that does nothing at all" differs from "nothing at all." If it produces "no overt effects that could not occur without it," what good is it? How can it make "all the difference in the world" if it doesn't *do* anything?

Nevertheless, a number of philosophers, whether in a spirit of regret or celebration, argue that there is still that "something else" that needs to be accounted for, something our materialist theories have left out: the *feel* of experience. It is the *seeming* (e.g., to see a chair) emphasized in discussing Descartes. It is the quality of our inner experience of the green after-image or the quality of our feeling of pain: Philosophers call these experiential qualities **qualia** (singular, "quale"). It is Nagel's *what it's like* (to see this or feel that). It is what has been called **phenomenal consciousness**.

To emphasize that "something else," Chalmers has developed the idea of an imaginary creature called a **philosophical zombie** (abbreviated as **p-zombie**). The zombies we're familiar with from popular entertainments apparently derive from Haitian folklore, conceived as dead persons who have been reanimated, often to do evil deeds. Eventually, zombies were reconceived by Hollywood as the flesh-eating creatures of so many of today's popular entertainments. The so-called p-zombie isn't evil or entertaining; in outward appearance, in physical constitution, and in behavior, the philosophical zombie is as (boringly) normal as any of us. The idea of a p-zombie is that of a human (or human-like creature) that is physically and functionally identical to us but doesn't have consciousness. Chalmers imagines staring out the window getting "nice green sensations" from the trees outside while getting "pleasant taste experiences through munching on a chocolate bar." Chalmers imagines having a p-zombie twin and asks what would be going on with him.

> He will be perceiving the trees outside, in the functional sense, and tasting the chocolate, in the psychological sense. . . . He will even be "conscious" in the functional senses described earlier—he will be awake, able to report the contents of his internal states, able to focus attention in various places, and so on. It is just that none of this functioning will be accompanied by any real conscious experience. There will be no phenomenal feel. There is nothing it is like to be a zombie.

We have no way of knowing whether p-zombies are physically possible. (Chalmers himself doubts they are.) It may be that in our universe any creature with a carbon-based brain that was in all respects identical to ours would have "real conscious experience" with that "phenomenal feel." But it does seem that p-zombies are logically possible. If p-zombies are logically possible, then conceiving p-zombies versus normal humans picks out just those crucial features of the human mind that functionalism leaves out. If functionalism does leave out something crucial, then it is not an adequate theory of mind.

A number of philosophers faced with what they believe to be the reality of phenomenal consciousness have felt forced to conclude that materialism is false. They have felt forced back to some sort of dualism—though not substance dualism. To these philosophers, substance dualism seems too implausible with its separable soul and all of its interactionist problems. Substance dualism seems to them to become even more implausible the more neuroscientists learn about the detailed dependency of thoughts and feelings upon complex processes in the brain. These philosophers look for dualistic views that make consciousness in some sense a by-product of the brain and dependent on it, that give brain science priority in explaining how the mind works. None of this would be true of substance dualism, which makes mind and brain separate but equal and mind ultimately separable (as in disembodied existence).

These additional theories—versions of **nonsubstance dualism**—are property dualism, epiphenomenalism, and panpsychism.

LET'S REVIEW

* *Explain Chalmers's distinction between the "easy" and "hard" problems of consciousness. Why does functionalism seem suited to solve the easy problem but not the hard one?*
* *What is Chalmers's "philosophical zombie"? What problem is conceiving of such a creature supposed to emphasize?*
* *Do you agree that the three materialist theories of mind seem inadequate as full accounts of what the mind is? Why?*

Three More Dualist Theories
Property Dualism

Property dualists are dualists about properties, not substances. For them there is only one kind of substance, the physical, which, in the case of brains, can have both physical and mental properties. The feel of a pain and the quality of an imagined color are part of a collection of the brain's special nonphysical properties.

Property dualists claim that mental properties are **emergent properties**, that is, properties that are had by the whole but not by the parts. Favorite examples of emergent properties would be the heaviness of a table or the wetness of water. Heaviness and wetness are not properties of the individual atoms that make up those objects but appear ("emerge") at a higher level of organization. In a similar way, according to the property dualist, phenomenal experience "emerges" from brain processes at a certain level of complexity.

According to property dualism, brain processes produce mental properties which, in turn, can have causal effects on brain processes. This is a commonsense interactionist view but an interaction of properties, not substances. There is no nonphysical substance that gets pain feelings based on physical processes and in turn causes physical reactions. Involved rather are emergent nonphysical properties of the physical brain.

Property dualists think their theory avoids the apparent incompatibility of substance dualism with neuroscience—the puzzle of how a separate, totally different substance could be so closely involved with brain processes. Since substance dualism is usually connected with religion and the belief in disembodied existence after death, property dualism is able to avoid such commitments and to fit in with a more "scientific" view of the world. At the same time, unlike materialism, property dualism allows for the phenomenal experience that materialism seemed to leave out.

However, there are serious problems with property dualism. One is that property dualists rejected substance dualism because of what they saw as the implausibility of two radically different substances—the physical and nonphysical—interacting. But if that is such a big problem, why isn't it equally implausible to have physical properties causally interacting with nonphysical properties? Such causal interaction is an integral part of property dualism.

According to property dualism, phenomenal experience is unique in that it is a "nonreductive emergent property." A **reductive property** is one that can be explained in terms of the properties of its parts; a non-reductive property can't be so explained. For instance, the heaviness of a table (or any other heavy object) can be explained in terms of the weight of the atoms added together. The wetness of water can be explained in terms of the properties of the hydrogen and oxygen atoms and how they interact. Mental properties are nonreductive because they can't be reduced to (completely explained in terms of) the physical properties of the brain. If they could be so reduced, presumably such reduction would support a materialist theory instead.

However, we know of no other nonreductive emergent properties—emergent properties that can't be explained in terms of their components. Since we have no other examples of such properties, invoking them here seems more than a little suspicious.

Epiphenomenalism

Epiphenomenalism is the view that mental events emerge from brain events but have no effect on those brain events. This theory accepts the notion that there are nonphysical events with the inner feel that the various forms of materialism leave out, but that these nonphysical events do not have causal effects. Mental events are likened to the steam whistle on a locomotive or the shadow cast by a traveler walking by. The whistle is caused by the steam engine and the shadow by the traveler, but neither has any effect on the locomotion of either.

The beauty of epiphenomenalism from a scientific standpoint is that it acknowledges mental properties and then gets them out of the way. One can now proceed with neuroscientific explanations of the mind without worrying about making room for mysterious, nonphysical, ghostly events and properties. There may be a ghost in the machine, but he's just hanging out, not doing anything beyond dressing up and cavorting a bit.

For many people, however, this is also the biggest problem with epiphenomenalism—the idea that conscious mental states don't *do* anything; that my pain isn't the cause of my crying out and grabbing my injured hand; that my feeling of thirst isn't the cause of my desire to get something to drink which causes me to reach for something to drink. Epiphenomenalists would point out that they aren't leaving any gaps in the causal chain but instead are just arguing that the chain is shorter than it appears to be. Instead of a thirst brain state causing a feeling of thirst causing the reaching-action brain state, there is the thirst brain state simultaneously causing the feeling of thirst and the reaching-action brain state. There are three things there, but they are not part of a three-part causal chain—just a two-part chain with that extra experience. The feeling of thirst is not identical to the relevant brain state but a causally inert reflection of it.

Still, it is difficult for many to accept the idea that our conscious experiences and choices have no effect on our behavior.

A further problem with epiphenomenalism is that it still faces half of the old dualist interactionist problem. You may not have nonphysical mental events causing physical brain events, but you still have physical brain events causing nonphysical mental events.

Panpsychism

Panpsychism is the view that mind is a fundamental feature of the universe and exists (at the very least) wherever matter exists. The concept dates back to ancient times. One form of it is animism, the belief that there are minds everywhere—in rocks, in trees, in the wind.

Panpsychism looks pretty loopy to the modern, more "scientific" temperament. However, the form of panpsychism we will consider is a much more restricted version of the theory. It still looks a bit loopy, but it is intriguing enough to have attracted the slightly embarrassed but still quite serious interest of some very respectable contemporary philosophers.

Suppose you believe the following: that substance dualism has too many problems to make it a tempting theory; that the physical is the most explanatorily fundamental level of reality; that the physical sciences will help us find the most satisfactory explanations for most things; that there is an experiential aspect of minds that is never going to be fully explained by materialism/physicalism; that nonreductive emergence is an unsatisfactory explanation for the appearance of mind; and that the idea of causal interaction between the physical and nonphysical (whether between substances or properties) doesn't make sense. In an attempt to formulate a more satisfactory form of nonsubstance dualism, you might try to give phenomenal experience a more intimate relationship to matter, making it an intrinsic aspect of matter. This way you don't have to worry about the fundamental emergence of phenomenal experience from matter because, in one form or another, it is already there.

An interesting argument for this view was made by Bertrand Russell (1872–1970) and others in the early twentieth century and has been recently revived and updated. Here's how David Chalmers summarizes it:

> Russell pointed out that physics characterizes physical entities and properties by their relations to one another and to us. For example, a quark is characterized by its relations to other physical entities, and a property, such as mass, is characterized by an associated dispositional role, such as the tendency to resist acceleration. . . . But physics is silent about the intrinsic nature of a quark, or about the intrinsic properties that play the role associated with mass. So this is one metaphysical problem: what are the intrinsic properties of fundamental physical systems?
>
> At the same time, there is another metaphysical problem: how can phenomenal properties be integrated with the physical world? . . . Russell's insight was that we might solve both these problems at once. Perhaps the intrinsic properties of the physical world are themselves phenomenal properties. . . . If so, then consciousness and physical reality are deeply intertwined.

The idea is that the phenomenal doesn't have to emerge from matter because it is already there. It's not that every particle would have a mind, but rather that every particle has a phenomenal aspect that could become a mind at a certain level of complexity.

From a certain perspective, such panpsychism looks pretty weird. Science has progressed by looking at physical matter and physical causation and by dismissing the idea of spirits affecting the material world. The idea of filling the world with spirits looks like a giant regression. On the other hand, our panpsychists aren't talking about spirits in everything or about everything thinking and feeling; they're talking about there being a phenomenal aspect to things that can become mind.

Even if we can get over the strangeness of the idea, other problems present themselves. One is the "combinatorial problem"—how individual bits of the phenomenal could combine to form the complex and (to a large degree) unified mind we each experience. William James (1842–1910) put the problem like this:

> Where the elemental units are supposed to be feelings, the case is in no wise altered. Take a hundred of them, shuffle them and pack them as close together as you can (whatever that may mean); still each remains the same feeling it always was, shut in its own skin, windowless, ignorant of what the other feelings are and mean. . . .

Take a sentence of a dozen words, and take twelve men and tell to each one word. Then stand the men in a row or jam them in a bunch, and let each think of his word as intently as he will; nowhere will there be a consciousness of the whole sentence. . . . The private minds do not agglomerate into a higher compound mind.

The idea that minds are private seems commonsensical. I experience my thoughts and feelings; I don't experience yours. So if the world is made up of little private mind particles, how could they share their private phenomenology with each other to constitute one unified mind? To the extent they could combine, wouldn't they just be jagged, uncombined bits of experience, like some jigsaw puzzle randomly assembled?

LET'S REVIEW

* Explain property dualism and epiphenomenalism. What are their similarities and differences?
* What is panpsychism? What is the "combinatorial problem"?

At this point, do you agree with the substance dualist claim that the other theories of mind have "equally serious problems"? Which theories of mind seem to you the less reasonable? Which the more reasonable? Why?

To make sure we have a good comparative overview of our theories of mind, let's chart the eight theories we have discussed: behaviorism, the identity theory, functionalism, interactionism (a form of substance dualism), parallelism (a form of substance dualism), property dualism, epiphenomenalism, and panpsychism. Let's query each position on the following questions:

Does the physical body/brain exist?
Is there a nonphysical substance mind?
Are there nonphysical mental properties?
Is there causation of the nonphysical (if any) by the physical?
Is there causation of the physical by the non-physical (if any)?
What is the mind?

All the theories of mind we've discussed in this chapter believe there is a physical body/brain. (The subjective idealist from chapter two would deny this but there are so few subjective idealists still around it didn't seem worth including that theory among the theories of mind we're discussing here.) All the dualists believe in the existence of the non-physical, of course, whether as a non-physical substance mind with its non-physical properties, or as non-physical properties of the physical brain or as an intrinsic non-physical aspect of the physical world. All the materialists reject the non-physical altogether and analyze the mind in terms of the body/brain.

Position	Phys. body/ brain?	Non-phys. subst. mind?	Non-phys. mental properties?	Cause: Phys. to Non-phys.	Cause: Non-phys. to phys.	Mind is:
Behaviorism	Yes	No	No	—	—	Behavior
Identity Theory	Yes	No	No	—	—	Brain
Functionalism	Yes	No	No	—	—	Physical functioning
Interactionism	Yes	Yes	Yes	Yes	Yes	Nonphys. substance
Parallelism	Yes	Yes	Yes	No	No	Nonphys. substance
Property Dualism	Yes	No	Yes	Yes	Yes	Nonphys. properties
Epiphenomenalism	Yes	No	Yes	Yes	No	Nonphys. properties
Panpsychism	Yes	No	—	—	—	Nonphys. aspect

Life After Death

In the story, "Life After Life," we saw Charlie struggling to cope with life as a disembodied soul. Let's talk about different conceptions of life after death and the degree to which they are or are not compatible with the various theories of mind we've discussed.

When we say that Charlie survives the death of his body as a disembodied soul, the word "**soul**" in this context simply means "nonphysical mind that can survive the death of the body." To claim that a person has a soul is simply to make such claims about the mind; it is not to claim that the person has a mind plus some other thing.

Of the positions we've considered, only substance dualism is compatible with a belief in the existence of a soul. For the behaviorist, identity theorist, or functionalist, there is no nonphysical mind. For the property dualist, epiphenomenalist, and panpsychist, there are nonphysical properties or aspects of the mind, but these depend on, and could not survive without, the physical brain.

"Life After Life" portrays disembodied existence in a nonreligious context, with the survival of the soul after death being a "natural" occurrence. It seems easy to imagine such a disembodied existence; it has been imagined for us in a number of stories and films. However, filling out the details of disembodied existence in a coherent way is problematic. In part, this relates to the difficulties with substance dualism. We've already seen the inconsistencies in portrayals of ghosts interacting with physical objects. Here are some other problematic topics:

Re the experiences of a disembodied soul: It seems natural to suppose that Charlie, as a disembodied soul, would have impressions of sight and sound but not of touch and taste. In part, this inclination may result from a more explicit awareness of the role played by the sense organs in our perceptions of taste and touch than in perceptions of sight and sound. However, it seems that our perceptions of sight and sound are the effects of light rays and sound waves impinging on the eyes and ears. If, indeed, all our perceptions are the effects of the world on our sense organs, is it reasonable to assume that a disembodied soul would have only limited sensory impressions, as opposed to either the full range of them or none at all? (Thinking back to Chapter 2, it might be fun to consider whether or not the theory of direct realism would be true of souls.)

Re the interactions of disembodied spirits: At one point, Charlie asks: "How do you make friends with people who are invisible, untouchable, and make no sounds?" Why does he single out those three characteristics? If disembodied souls, like ghosts, pass through walls because they are nonphysical, then it seems they couldn't touch or be touched. If they can't affect the physical, how could they cause sound waves or reflect light waves necessary to be seen or heard? The story talks about souls communicating through telepathy, but that's just thrown in; and, even if it makes sense, it would allow for very limited interaction.

Re souls and physical location: Charlie is puzzled when the souls he succeeds in contacting are not in physical proximity to him. On the one hand, this makes some sense if nonphysical minds have no location. On the other hand, if they have no location, how can Charlie and the souls he contacts share the same local viewpoint? As Charlie says:

> I remember a teacher at UCLA saying that a soul, being nonphysical, would have no spatial location. I wanted to interrupt her and tell her

how wrong she was. I mean, I was a soul, and I was right there in her classroom. But I must admit now that that kind of location doesn't seem to count for much when souls communicate with one another.

Religious views of life after death are, of course, much different from the portrayal of the afterlife in the story. Many theists believe that after the death of the body, the soul joins God and other souls in a community of spirits that either goes on forever or lasts until a time when all bodies will be resurrected. Can one make sense out of this supposition of a community of souls? One suggestion, borrowed from something like Berkeley's idealism, would be that after death, God links these bodiless human souls and Himself together through something analogous to coordinated dreams. God would present these souls with the kind of images they would have if they lived together in some magnificent physical world. Each soul would receive sensory images that represent other souls: It would seem as if every other soul had some sort of body and could gesture, talk, and so forth. Note that this conception of the afterlife would be "otherworldly" in the sense that it is hard to imagine experiencing simultaneously this community of souls and our world.

We've said that only a substance dualist can consistently believe in the existence of a soul. Does that mean that only a substance dualist can consistently believe in life after death? The answer is, no. Note also that although the terms "materialist" and "atheist" have often been equated, they are not strictly equivalent.

As is illustrated by the Gammas in "Strange Behavior," a materialist could believe in a physical God and could believe that the physical body, with its mental characteristics, is resurrected at some future date. As noted in the story

> The Gammas identify God with the universe and claim that He is (or rather behaves as if He is) omnipotent, omniscient, and perfectly good. They certainly do not imagine God to be nonphysical. The word "nonphysical" translates into their language as "not-being" or "nothing." . . . Some Gammas believe in life after death, which they imagine to be a physical resurrection of the body that occurs at some far distant time. . . . Of course, they do not believe that the mind exists during the period between death and the resurrection. Said one philosopher: "To take the mind from the body is as impossible as taking the shape from a flower while leaving its color and weight behind."

In such a materialist religious context, your body/physical mind would die and be broken down into chemical substances, at which point you would cease to exist; then at some future date God would reassemble your body/physical mind and you would start existing again. (If we imagined resurrection in a property dualist context, much the same thing would happen, assuming the same nonphysical properties of mind reappeared when the brain was reassembled and reanimated.)

There are some puzzles lurking here. Suppose you die and at some time in the future the materialist God re-creates "you" with totally different matter? (Remember that on the materialist account no soul exists between the death of one body and the creation of the next.) Would this body with new matter be you? Or just a copy of you?

The hope for life after death also exists among some nonreligious materialists. "Cryogenics" is one example: The idea here is that you freeze and store dead bodies in the hope that some time in the future humans will be technologically capable of thawing, reviving, treating, and improving the bodies in ways that will allow the once-dead people to live many more years. Cloning seems to offer a similar sort of promise, where storing one's DNA would allow one to be re-created in the future. Those who live in the future when cloning has been perfected might be able to keep re-creating themselves as the current self is damaged or begins to wear out. (The Schwarzenegger movie, *The Sixth Day*, deals with this sort of cloning.) There are even fantasies of one day transferring individual human minds into computers or robots, extending the life of those minds indefinitely. However, if as you are dying, I take a robot and reproduce your psychology in that robot, is that robot now you in a new body? Or just a robot with a copy of your psychology?

Such questions raise the issue of personal identity, which is fascinating in itself. Let's talk about personal identity in general, and then we'll return to review its implications for life after death.

LET'S REVIEW

* *What are some of the difficulties of imagining how life for a soul such as Charlie might be like?*
* *Explain how Berkeley's idealism provides us with a basis for conceiving a religious version of life after death.*
* *What would be a materialist version of life after death?*

Personal Identity

The philosophical issue of **personal identity**, as we shall discuss it, involves the question of what makes someone the same person over time and through various transformations. What makes your 14-year-old self the same person you are now, yet different from the close friend you grew up with? What would make a person who appeared in an afterlife the same as a person who died shortly beforehand?

Suggestions as to what would make someone the very same (numerically identical) person over time include the following:

1. Continuity of soul with psychological continuity
2. Continuity of body/brain with psychological continuity
3. Psychological continuity by itself

Psychological continuity means the continuation of those psychological states that comprise your mental life over time. Obviously, you don't have the same mental life you did at age 4 or 14. But there are traceable connections between the current stage of your mental life and previous ones.

Reading a story like "Life After Life," we don't seem to have a problem imagining that Charlie, who was once in a body, now survives as a soul (a nonphysical substance mind) existing without a body. Charlie is in some fundamental sense the "same person" as he was before he died. This is not to say that souls really exist: Being able to imagine something existing is no evidence that it exists. But as a first impression it seems that we feel that *if* a soul with the same mental life (the same "psychology") continued to exist after death, it would be the same person. Put another way, continuity of soul with psychological continuity seems a **sufficient condition** for personal identity.

Thinking about the Gammas in "Strange Behavior," however, it doesn't seem as if continuity of soul with psychological continuity is a **necessary condition** for personal identity. Presumably, continuity of body/brain plus psychological continuity would also be sufficient to maintain personal identity if the analyses of mind given by the materialists or nonsubstance dualists were correct. If the behaviorist were correct, then psychological continuity would be preserved by the continued sort of behavior they say constitutes mind. (Think of an individual Gamma growing from childhood to old age.) If the property dualist were correct, then psychological continuity would be preserved by the continuation of the nonphysical things/feelings they say are caused by the brain.

It appears that either continuity of soul plus psychological continuity or continuity of body/brain plus psychological continuity would be sufficient for personal identity. If that's the case, then neither of them would be necessary for personal identity. What about psychological continuity alone? Could that be necessary? Sufficient? Necessary and sufficient?

We need to ask ourselves first if it makes sense to think of someone's mental life as a "something" on a par with a body or a soul. In thought experiments on personal identity, philosophers sometimes talk about transferring a collection of thoughts and feelings from one thing to another thing, as if that collection were like a colony of bees in a particular hive (mind). They seem to assume that just as we can imagine the bees being transferred to a different hive (even an artificial one), so we can imagine thoughts/feelings being transferred to a different mind (even an artificial one).

However, does it really make sense to think of thoughts and feelings as little objects—things you could remove from a soul or brain while leaving that soul or brain intact? Thoughts and feelings seem more like the activities and properties of some thing doing the feeling and thinking. If they are activities or properties, then they are not removable. You can't take the red color from one ball, b1, and transfer it to another ball, b2, while leaving b1 intact. You could repaint the balls so that b2 has the same shade of red b1 had: however, that's not literally transferring the color. You could peel off the surface of b1 and glue it to b2, but then b1 would no longer be intact.

If this is right, then any talk of transferring, exchanging, or uploading thoughts and feelings to something else is nonsense if taken literally; at best, it's going to be a metaphor for making a copy of those thoughts and feelings in some other thing such as another soul or brain.

This is not to say that psychological continuity may not be the most crucial factor in personal identity; it is only to say that psychological continuity can't stand alone. It must be the psychology of something—a soul, a body (maybe even the body of a robot or an alien).

Could psychological continuity—let's call it continuity of "personality"—as a property of *something* be necessary and sufficient for personal identity? It turns out there are problems as to what constitutes a personality and what counts as that *something* actually continuing.

Think about individuals with multiple personalities. If a soul with three personalities floats off into an afterlife, how many people have survived death? One? Three? Similar puzzles arise in cases of split-brain patients. With cases of severe epilepsy, physicians have found that if they cut the corpus callosum that connects the two halves of the brain, the epileptic seizures can be relieved. In most cases, the split-brain patients function normally, but there have been cases where the two halves of the brain show conflict: For instance, in one case a woman would try to reach with one hand for an outfit she wanted to wear, only to have the other hand (controlled by the other half of the brain) fight that hand to get a different outfit. Under experimental conditions, the two halves of a split brain have expressed different tastes, different attitudes, even different ambitions. This has led some researchers to conclude that there are two persons in split-brain patients and that, therefore, there are two persons (but better coordinated) in each of us.

As to what counts as that *something* continuing with a personality, consider the thought experiments done by Derek Parfit involving a transporter like the one conceived in *Star Trek*. The transporter works by collecting complete information about the arrangements of every atom in your body (including the complete structure of your mind), converting all your matter into energy, beaming that energy to another location, and reassembling you from the energy and information—resulting in someone who looks, acts, and thinks as you did before you entered the Transporter. Would that someone be you or just a copy of you? Many of us would be inclined to say it was you. But suppose the machine, after taking all your information and sending it on, destroys your original matter; at the other end, the information sent is used to create, out of new matter, someone who looks, acts, and thinks like you. Would that be you or a copy of you? Here we would be less inclined to say it was you. If the process resulted in two beings with different matter who both looked, acted, and thought like you do, we certainly wouldn't want to say that both were you.

It seems that if there were clear criteria of what constitutes personal identity, we should be able to give clear answers to these questions. After failing to get clear answers, some philosophers have thrown up their hands and declared that there are ultimately no persons, no selves. The word "person" and "self" may have a vague everyday meaning, but the words do not refer to anything fixed, substantial, or permanent. It has been pointed out that that this apparently paradoxical belief has been a central tenet of Buddhism for centuries.

In Hindu philosophy, **Atman**, refers to the soul, which is believed to underlie all the activities of a person. Buddhism opposes this concept with that of the **anatman**—the claim that there is no permanent, underlying soul. As Susan Blackmore explains, this Buddhist "idea of the no-self" does not:

> . . . say that the self does not exist, but that it is illusory—not what it seems. Rather than being a persisting entity that lives a person's life, the self is just a conventional name given to a set of elements.

As it is expressed in the Buddhist writings, *Questions to King Milinda:*

> As Nagasena I am known, O Great King, and as Nagasena do my fellow monks habitually address me. But although my parents give a name such as Nagasena, this word 'Nagasena' is just a denomination, a designation, a conceptual term, a temporary appellation, a mere name. There is no real person here to be apprehended.

SIDDHARTHA GAUTAMA, the BUDDHA, lived during the sixth to fourth centuries BCE. He lived a pleasurable life as a prince until he discovered the suffering in the world; he then left on a long spiritual search, living as a beggar, until he achieved enlightenment, understanding the true nature of the world and achieving a state free of desire and suffering.

It does seem that *if* there is a soul, there is no profound problem of personal identity: An ongoing soul with a psychological continuity (continuity of personality) would be sufficient for personal identity and would continue to have such an identity into an afterlife. But what if—for philosophical or scientific reasons or through spiritual insight—we conclude that there likely is no soul? Most of us would probably think that an ongoing living body with a continuity of personality would be sufficient for personal identity. Perhaps such personal identity is more fragile than we once supposed and we'd be well advised to stay away from Star Trek Transporters. But it does seem to be the case that continuity of body/brain plus psychological continuity (continuity of personality) is real personal identity.

Even if we agree on that point, however, there remain problems with the idea that if there is no soul, the same person could be resurrected after death by taking the same matter and re-forming it into the same body/brain with the same personality. Religious thinkers have worried for millennia over how God could possibly reassemble the same matter when it has been broken up and recycled through countless other persons. (Past thinkers posed problems like this one: What if the cannibal eats the missionary, then converts, having absorbed the missionary into himself?)

The problem becomes greater—perhaps insolvable—if the same person is supposed to be resurrected with a heavenly body made of different stuff. (Again, we're assuming no continuity of soul between death and resurrection.) That heavenly body looks to be at best a copy of us.

Some philosophers have proposed looser criteria of personal identity. Robert Nozick has suggested that personal identity continues as long as there's a "closest continuer": If God makes only one copy of me in the afterlife, that's good enough for it to be me; if He made two copies, then neither is me. Derek Parfit argues that we should scrap the notion of personal identity altogether and think in terms of a type of survival that would admit of degrees. If God makes a heavenly copy of me, then in a sense I am surviving, even if that copy isn't numerically identical with me. If God makes two heavenly copies, then in some sense I am still surviving.

Ask yourself this question: On your death bed, what would you have to believe is going to happen in order for you to feel that you will continue after death as you? Let's grant that *if* you have a soul and it continues with the same personality after death, you would survive death. But assume for a moment that there is no soul; consider the following possibilities:

1. In the afterlife, God creates a body/mind out of your original matter, resulting in someone who looks, acts, and thinks like you.
2. In the afterlife, God creates a body/mind out of different, heavenly matter, resulting in someone who looks, acts, and thinks like you.
3. After your death, scientists re-create a copy of your personality in a clone of your body/brain.
4. After your death, scientists re-create a copy of your personality in a human-like robot.

Envisioning the above cases, in which ones would you think that "you" had survived death? Would you find that comforting? What about those cases where you don't think you would survive? Are there any of those you would find better than nothing—that you would prefer to just disappearing?

As you ask yourself such questions, you are taking on the deepest philosophical puzzles of personal identity.

Definitions

(Terms are defined in the order in which they appeared in the text.)

1. DUALISM: The view that there are physical bodies and nonphysical minds.
2. SUBSTANCE DUALISM: The view that mind and body are two different types of substances: the mind, which is nonphysical substance, and the body, which is physical substance.
3. INTERACTIONISM: The view that there is a physical body and a nonphysical mind and that the two are causally related. (A form of substance dualism)
4. OCCASIONALISM: A version of parallelism which says mind and body are correlated by God moment by moment. (A form of substance dualism)
5. PREESTABLISHED HARMONY: A version of parallelism which says that mind and body correlations were all determined by God from the beginning of time. (A form of substance dualism)
6. PARALLELISM: The view that there is a physical body and a nonphysical mind and that the two are not causally related. (A form of substance dualism)
7. MATERIALISM: The view that everything that exists is physical, including the mind.

8. BEHAVIORISM: The view that the mind is nothing but certain complex, overt physical behavior and dispositions to behave. (Also called "logical behaviorism" or "analytical behaviorism")

9. THE IDENTITY THEORY: The view that the mind (that which produces thoughts, images, and sensations) is identical to the brain (the mass of nerve tissue inside the skull).

10. FACTUAL IDENTITY: The notion that when two words/phrases that do not mean the same thing refer to the same entity.

11. IDENTITY OF MEANING: The notion that two words or phrases mean the same thing.

12. TYPE-IDENTITY THEORY: The view that a mental state like pain is identical to the same type of brain state in all creatures.

13. MULTIPLE REALIZABILITY: The idea that mind or mental properties could in theory exist in different creatures made of different "stuff."

14. TOKEN-IDENTITY THEORY: The theory that a particular mental state like pain is identical to a particular state in a particular brain, but not to the same type of state in all brains.

15. FUNCTIONALISM: The view that mental states should be defined as functional states, defined in terms of what they do rather than what they're made of.

16. TURING TEST: A test for machine intelligence in which an interrogator must guess from written responses to questions which of two responders is the person and which the machine.

17. "EASY PROBLEM OF CONSCIOUSNESS" (Chalmers): How the mind functions to discriminate stimuli and control behavior (among other such tasks).

18. "HARD PROBLEM OF CONSCIOUSNESS" (Chalmers): How phenomenal consciousness arises from the physical brain.

19. QUALIA (sing. quale): The qualities (like redness and loudness) of subjective experience.

20. PHENOMENAL CONSCIOUSNESS: Present subjective experience.

21. PHILOSOPHICAL ZOMBIE (a p-zombie): A theoretical creature that is physically and functionally identical to us but doesn't have consciousness.

22. NONSUBSTANCE DUALISM: Dualism without the mind being a separate substance.

23. PROPERTY DUALISM: A form of nonsubstance dualism which claims that mental events are emergent nonphysical properties of the physical brain.

24. EMERGENT PROPERTIES: Properties that are had by the whole that are not had by the parts.
25. REDUCTIVE PROPERTY: A property that can be explained in terms of the properties of its parts.
26. EPIPHENOMENALISM: A form of non-substance dualism which claims that mental events emerge from brain events but have no effects on brain events.
27. PANPSYCHISM: A form of nonsubstance dualism which claims that mind is a fundamental feature of the universe and exists (at the very least) wherever matter exists.
28. SOUL: Nonphysical mind that survives the death of the body.
29. PERSONAL IDENTITY (Problem of): What makes someone the same person over time and through various transformations.
30. PSYCHOLOGICAL CONTINUITY: The continuation of those psychological states that comprise your mental life over time.
31. SUFFICIENT CONDITION: If p is a sufficient condition for q, then if p is true, then q must be true.
32. NECESSARY CONDITION: If p is a necessary condition of q, then q cannot be true unless p is true.
33. ATMAN: A word that refers to the soul in Hindu philosophy.
34. ANATMAN: The Buddhist doctrine that there is no permanent, underlying soul.

Questions and Exercises

(Please explain your answers, making specific reference to relevant passages in the discussion.)
1. a. What is dualism?
   b. What is the difference between interactionism and parallelism?
   c. Give the reasoning behind being an interactionist.
   d. What reasons would a parallelist give for believing interactionism is false?
2. How is life after death conceived in the story "Life After Life"? If life after death were nothing more than the soul slipping away from the body, is this the way you'd suppose it to be?
3. How might life after death of souls be conceived on the model of Berkeley's idealism?
4. What is materialism? What reasoning might lead one to be a materialist?

5. "The behaviorist says that the mind is nothing but overt behavior." What is wrong with this statement? How should it be corrected?

6. "The identity theorist says that 'mind' and 'brain' have identical meanings." Is this correct? Why or why not? Explain what the identity theorist is saying about identity.

7. What would the identity theory seem to imply about the colors of our mental images? Does this seem plausible?

8. What is "type-identity theory"? What would this imply about the brain states of any conceivable being in pain? Does this seem plausible?

9. What is functionalism?

10. What is multiple realizability? How does functionalism allow for this? Why is this seen by functionalists as an advance over the type-identity theory?

11. What is the Turing Test of machine intelligence? How would such a test be compatible with a functionalist theory of mind?

12. What is John Searle's "Chinese Room" thought experiment, and how is it an attack on functionalism?

13. What is the "hard problem of consciousness"?

14. What are "philosophical zombies"? How are they like the Gammas in "Strange Behavior"?

15. How would being able to imagine philosophical zombies count against functionalism as an adequate theory of mind?

16. What is nonsubstance dualism?

17. For each of the following theories, say what it is, and what are its strengths and weaknesses.
    a. Property dualism
    b. Epiphenomenalism
    c. Panpsychism

18. What are the complications of imagining what experiences a disembodied soul would have? Of how a soul would communicate with other souls?

19. How might a materialist view of life after death work?

20. There have been several suggestions for what might constitute personal identity over time. What are these, and what are the complications with them?

21. Answer the questions that concluded the chapter:

Ask yourself this: On your death bed, what would you have to believe is going to happen in order for you to feel that you will continue after death as you? Let's grant that if your soul with the same personality continues after death, that would be you. But assume for a moment that there is no soul and consider the following possibilities:

1. In the afterlife, God creates a body/mind out of your original matter, resulting in someone who looks, acts, and thinks like you.
2. In the afterlife, God creates a body/mind out of different, heavenly matter, resulting in someone who looks, acts, and thinks like you.
3. After your death, scientists re-create a previously made copy of your personality in a clone of your body/brain.
4. After your death, scientists re-create a previously made copy of your personality in a human-like robot.

Envisioning the above cases, in which ones would you think that "you" had survived death? Would you find that comforting? What about those cases where you don't think you would survive? Are there any of those you would find better than nothing—that you would prefer to just disappearing?

Notes

Substance Dualism, The Soul and Disembodied Existence

"How will that which is corporeal. . . ." Gassendi: From *Descartes Selections*, edited by Ralph M. Eaton. Copyright 1927 Charles Scribner's Sons; copyright renewed ©1955 by Charles Scribner's Sons.

"the way of pre-established harmony." *G. W. Leibniz Philosophical Letters and Papers*, by LeRoy E. Loemaker, 1957.

Three Materialist Theories of Mind

"Gilbert Ryle called dualism. . . ." From *The Concept of Mind* by Gilbert Ryle. Copyright © 1949 by Gilbert Ryle.

"Instead Place claims. . . ." From "Is Consciousness a Brain Process?" by U. T. Place, in *British Journal of Psychology*, February 1956, Vol. XLVII, pp. 49–50.

"'The Chinese Room' . . . from John Searle. . . ." From "Minds, Brains, and Programs" by John R. Searle. *Behavioral and Brain Sciences 3* (1980).

"Now suppose that the rule book is written. . . ." From "Is the Brain's Mind a Computer Program" by John R. Searle. *Scientific American 262* (January 1990.)

Dualism Revisited

"David Chalmers distinguishes. . . ." From "Consciousness and Its Place in Nature." By David J. Chalmers. In *The Blackwell Guide to the Philosophy of Mind*. Eds. Stephen P. Stich and Ted A. Warfield. Walden, MA: Blackwell, 2003.

". . . such problems are (relatively) 'easy' in the sense that they. . . ." Chalmers, "Consciousness and Its Place in Nature."

"Using a famous idea from Thomas Nagel. . . ." "What is it like to be a bat" in Thomas Nagel, *Moral Questions*. Cambridge: Cambridge University Press, 1979.

"There is no question that experience is closely associated." Chalmers, "Consciousness and Its Place in Nature."

" . . . an imaginary creature called a 'philosophical zombie'. . . ." Chalmers, "Consciousness and Its Place in Nature."

"Chalmers imagines staring out the window. . . ." Chalmers, "Consciousness and Its Place in Nature."

"An intriguing argument for this view was made by Bertrand Russell. . . ." Bertrand Russell, *The Analysis of Matter*. London: Kegan Paul, 1927.

"Here's how it is summarized by David Chalmers. . . ." Chalmers, "Consciousness and Its Place in Nature."

"William James . . . put the problem like this: . . . " William James, *The Principles of Psychology*. Henry Holt and Co., 1890

Personal Identity

". . . cases of split-brain patients." See Thomas Nagel, "Brain Bisection and the Unity of Consciousness," in John Perry (ed.), *Personal Identity*. Berkeley: University of California Press, 2008.

". . . thought experiments done by Derek Parfit. . . ." Derek Parfit. "Why Our Identity Is Not What Matters." In Raymond Martin and John Barresi (eds.), *Personal Identity*. Oxford: Blackwell Publishing, 2003.

"Susan Blackmore explains. . . ." Susan Blackmore. *Consciousness: A Very Short Introduction*. Oxford: Oxford University Press, 2005.

"As it is put in the Buddhist writings. . . ." *Questions to King Milinda* from *Buddhism in Translation*. Translated by Henry Clarke. Cambridge MA: Harvard University Press, 1896. Excerpted in Daniel Bonevac and Stephen Phillips (eds.). *Introduction to World Philosophy: A Multicultural Reader*. Oxford: Oxford University Press, 2009.

"Robert Nozick has suggested. . . . " Robert Nozick, "Personal Identity through Time," In Martin and Barresi (eds.), *Personal Identity*.

"Derek Parfit claims. . . ." "Why Our Identity Is Not What Matters" and "The Unimportance of Identity." In Martin and Barresi (eds.), *Personal Identity*.

Further Materials

General Sources

Chalmers, David (ed.). *Philosophy of Mind: Classical and Contemporaries Readings*. Oxford: Oxford University Press, 2002. A good collection of classical and contemporary readings that includes selections by the following authors discussed or mentioned in the text: René Descartes; Gilbert Ryle; U. T. Place; Thomas Nagel; David Chalmers; and, John Searle.

Stich, Stephen P., and Warfield, Ted A. (eds.). *The Blackwell Guide to the Philosophy of Mind*. Walden, MA: Blackwell, 2003. Has a good discussion of the mind–body problem, physicalism, and dualism. Also includes an article by David Chalmers that is quoted from in this text.

Substance Dualism, The Soul and Disembodied Existence

Baker, Mark C., and Goertz, Stewart. *The Soul Hypothesis: Investigations into the Existence of the Soul*. London: Bloomsbury Academic: 2010. Essays in favor of dualism and the existence of the soul.

Descartes, René. *Meditations on the First Philosophy*. Translated by Lawrence J. LaFleur. Copyright 1951 by the Macmillan Publishing Company; renewed 1979.

Three Materialist Theories of Mind

Articles by Gilbert Ryle, Hilary Putnam, U. T. Place, Frank Jackson, Thomas Nagel, and John Searle in Chalmers, *Philosophy of Mind* (see above).

Churchland, Paul. *Matter and Consciousness. Revised Edition*. Cambridge, MA: MIT Press, 1999. A good, short survey of positions and issues in the philosophy of mind from a materialist perspective.

Dualism Revisited

Bonevac, Daniel, and Phillips, Stephen. *Introduction to World Philosophy: A Multicultural Reader*. Oxford: Oxford University Press, 2009. Part II, Chs. 7 and 8.

Lowe, E. J. "Dualism." In McLaughlin, Brian P., et al. (eds.). *The Oxford Handbook of the Philosophy of Mind*. Oxford: Oxford University Press, 2009.

Robinson, Howard. "Dualism" in Stich and Robinson (eds.), *The Blackwell Guide to the Philosophy of Mind*.

Seager, William. "Panpsychism." In McLaughlin, *The Oxford Handbook of the Philosophy of Mind*.

Walter, Sven. "Epiphenomenalism." In McLaughlin, *The Oxford Handbook of the Philosophy of Mind*.

Life After Death

Davis, Stephen T. "The Survival of Death." In *The Blackwell Companion to the Philosophy of Religion*. Cambridge, MA, 1997.

Edwards, Paul (ed.). *Immortality*. Amherst, NY: Prometheus Books, 1997. Classical and contemporary readings on life after death.

Price, H. H. "Survival and the Idea of 'Another World.'" *Proceedings of the Society for Psychical Research*. Vol. L, Part 182 (January 1953). Price tries to work out a dualism account of life after death.

Personal Identity

Martin, Raymond, and Barresi, John (eds.). *Personal Identity*. Oxford: Blackwell Publishing, 2003.

Parfit, Derek. *Reasons and Persons*. Oxford: Clarendon Press, 1984.

Perry, John (ed.) *Personal Identity*. Berkeley: University of California Press,

CHAPTER 4

Freedom and Responsibility

Fiction

READING 1: Please Don't Tell Me How the Story Ends

PREVIEW

In this story, a prisoner, locked in a library-like prison cell, discovers the experimenters are trying to predict everything he will do and think while in that room. As you read the story, ask yourself:

* How, in detail, is this experiment structured?
* What are the experimenters ultimately trying to prove?
* How would you have reacted in the prisoner's place?

The heavy door closed behind him, and he glanced quickly at this new detention room. He was startled, almost pleasantly surprised. This was not like the drab cell in which he had spent the first days after his arrest, nor like the hospital rooms, with the serpentine carnival machines, in which he had been tested and observed for the last two months—though he assumed he was being observed here as well. This was more like a small, comfortable library that had been furnished like a first-class hotel room. Against the four walls were fully stocked bookcases that rose 10 feet to the white plaster ceiling; in the ceiling was a small skylight. The floor was covered with a thick green carpet, and in the middle of the room were a double bed with a nightstand, a large bureau, a desk, an easy chair with a side table, and several lamps. There were large gaps in the bookcases to accommodate two doors, including the one through which he had just entered, and also a traylike apparatus affixed to the wall. He could not immediately ascertain the purpose of the tray, but the other door, he quickly learned, led to a spacious bathroom complete with toilet articles. As he searched the main room, he found that the desk contained writing paper, pens, a clock, and a calendar; the bureau contained abundant clothing in a variety of colors and two pairs of shoes. He glanced down at the hospital gown and slippers he was wearing, then quickly changed into a rust-colored sweater and a pair of dark brown slacks. The clothing, including the shoes, fitted him perfectly. It would be easier to face his situation, to face whatever might be coming, looking like a civilized human being.

But what was his situation? He wanted to believe that the improvement in his living conditions meant an improvement in his status, perhaps even an imminent reprieve. But all the same he doubted it. Nothing had seemed to follow a sensible progression since his arrest, and it would be foolhardy to take anything at face value now. But what were they up to? At first, when he had been taken to the hospital, he had expected torture, some hideous pseudomedical experiment, or a brainwashing program. But there had been no operation and no pain. He had been tested countless times: the endless details of biography; the responses to color, scent, sound, taste, touch; the responses to situations and ideas; the physical examination. But if these constituted mind-altering procedures, they had to be of the most subtle variety. Certainly he felt the same; at least no more compliant than he had been in the beginning. What were they after?

As his uncertainty grew to anxiety, he tried to work it off with whatever physical exercise he could manage in the confines of the room: running in place, isometrics, sit-ups, and push-ups. He knew that the strength of his will would depend in part on the strength of his body, and since his arrest he had exercised as much as he could. No one had prevented this.

He was midway through a push-up when a loud buzzer sounded. He leaped to his feet, frightened but ready. Then he saw a plastic tray of food on the metal tray that extended from the wall and a portion of the wall closing downward behind the tray. So this was how he would get his meals. He would see no one. Was this some special isolation experiment?

The question of solitude quickly gave way to hunger and curiosity about the food. It looked delicious and plentiful; there was much more than he could possibly eat. Was it safe? Could it be drugged or poisoned? No, there could be no point to their finishing him in such an odd, roundabout fashion. He took the tray to the desk and ate heartily, but he still left several of the dishes barely sampled or untouched.

That evening—the clock and the darkened skylight told him it was evening—he investigated the room further. He was interrupted only once by the buzzer. When it continued to sound and nothing appeared, he realized that the buzzer meant he was to return the food dishes. He did so, and the plastic tray disappeared into the wall.

The writing paper was a temptation. He always thought better with a pen in hand. Writing would resemble a kind of conversation and make him feel a little less alone. With a journal, he could construct some kind of history from what threatened to be days of dulling sameness. But he feared that they wanted him to write, that his doing so would somehow play into their hands. So he refrained.

Instead, he examined a portion of the bookshelf that contained paperback volumes in a great variety of sizes and colors. The books covered a number of fields—fiction, history, science, philosophy, politics—some to his liking and some not. He selected a political treatise and put it on the small table next to the easy chair. He did not open it immediately. He washed up and then went to the bureau, where he found a green plaid robe and a pair of light yellow pajamas. As he lifted out the pajamas, he noticed a small, black, rectangular box and opened it.

Inside was a hand gun. A quick examination showed that it was loaded. Quickly he shut the box, trembling. He was on one knee in front of the open drawer. His first thought was that a former inmate had left the gun to help him. He was sure that his body was blocking the contents of the drawer from the view of any observation devices in the room. He must not give away the secret. He forced himself to close the drawer casually, rise, and walk to the easy chair.

Then the absurdity of his hypothesis struck him. How could any prisoner have gotten such a thing past the tight security of this place? And what good would such a weapon do him in a room to which no one came? No, the gun must be there because the authorities wanted it there. But why? Could it be they wanted to hide his death under the pretense of an attempted escape? Or could it be that they were trying to push him to suicide by isolating him? But again, what was the point of it? He realized that his fingerprints were on the gun. Did they want to use that as some kind of evidence against him? He went to the bureau again, ostensibly to switch pajamas, and, during the switch, opened the box and quickly wiped his prints off the gun. As casually as he could, he returned to the chair.

He passed the evening in considerable agitation. He tried to read but could not. He exercised again, but it did not calm him. He tried to analyze his situation, but his thoughts were an incoherent jumble. Much later, he lay down on the bed, first pushing the easy chair against the door of the room. He recognized the absurdity of erecting this fragile barrier, but the noise of their pushing it away would give him some warning. For a while, he forced his eyes open each time he began to doze, but eventually he fell asleep.

In the morning, he found everything unchanged, the chair still in place at the door. Nothing but the breakfast tray had intruded. After he had exercised, breakfasted, bathed, and found himself still unmolested, he began to feel calmer. He read half the book he had selected the night before, lunched, and then dozed off in his chair.

When he awoke, his eyes scanned the room and came to rest on one of the bookshelves filled with a series of black, leather-bound volumes of uniform size, marked only by number. He had noticed them before but had paid little attention, thinking they were an encyclopedia. Now he noticed what a preposterous number of volumes there were, perhaps two hundred in all, filling not only one bookcase from floor to ceiling but filling parts of others as well. With his curiosity piqued, he pulled down Volume LXIV and opened it at random to page 494.

The page was filled with very small print, with a section at the bottom in even smaller print that appeared to be footnotes. The heading of the page was large enough to be read at a glance. "RE: PRISONER 7439762 (referred to herein as 'Q')." He read on: "3/07/66. 14:03. Q entered room on 3/06/66 at 14:52. Surprised at pleasantness of room. Glanced at furniture, then bookcase, then ceiling. Noted metal tray and second door, puzzled by both. Entered bathroom, noting toilet articles. Lifted shaver and touched cologne." He skipped down the page: "Selected brown slacks, rust sweater, and tan shoes. Felt normal clothing made him more equal to his situation."

It seemed that they were keeping some sort of record of his activities here. But what was the purpose of having the record here for him to read? And how had they gotten it in here? It was easy to figure out how they knew of his activities: They were watching him, just as he had suspected. They must have printed this page during the night and placed it here as he slept. Perhaps his food had been drugged to guarantee that he wouldn't wake up.

He glanced toward the door of his cell and remembered the chair he had placed against it. In a drugged sleep, he wouldn't have heard them enter. They could have pulled the chair back as they left. But all the way? Presumably there was some hidden panel in the door. Once the door was shut, they had merely to open the panel and pull the chair the last few inches. Suddenly he remembered the matter of the gun. He glanced down the page and there it was, a description of how he had handled the gun twice. There was no warning given nor any hint of an explanation as to why the gun was there. There was just the clipped, neutral-toned description of his actions and impressions. It described his hope that the gun might have been left by another prisoner, his rejection of that supposition, his fear that the gun might be used against him in some way, his desire to remove the fingerprints. But how on earth could they have known what he was feeling and thinking? He decided that he had acted and reacted as any normal person would have done, and they had simply drawn the obvious conclusions from his actions and facial expressions.

He glanced further down the page and read: "On 3/07/66, Q awoke at 8:33." And further ". . . selected *The Future of Socialism* by Felix Berofsky. . . ." And further: ". . . bent the corner of page 206 to mark his place and put the book. . . ." All his activities of that morning had already been printed in the report!

He began turning the book around in his hands and pulled it away from the shelf. Was this thing wired in some way? Could they print their reports onto these pages in minutes without removing the books from the shelves? Perhaps they had some new process whereby they could imprint specially sensitized pages by electronic signal.

Then he remembered that he had just awakened from a nap, and he slammed the volume shut in disgust. Of course: They had entered the room again during his nap. He placed the volume back on the shelf and started for his chair. How could they expect him to be taken in by such blatant trickery? But then a thought occurred to him: He had picked out a volume and page at random. Why had the description of yesterday and this morning been on that particular page? Were all the pages the same? He returned to the shelf and picked up the same volume, this time opening it to page 531. The heading was the same. He looked down the page: "Q began to return to his chair but became puzzled as to why the initial description of his activities should have appeared on page 494 of this volume." He threw the book to the floor and grabbed another, Volume LX, opening it to page 103: ". . . became more confused by the correct sequential description on page 531, Volume LXIV."

"What are you trying to do to me!" he screamed, dropping the second book.

Immediately he was ashamed at his lack of self-control.

"What an absurd joke," he said loudly to whatever listening devices there might be.

He picked up the two volumes he had dropped and put them back in place on the bookshelf. He walked across the room and sat in the chair. He tried to keep his expression neutral while he thought.

There was no possibility that observations were being made and immediately transmitted to the books by some electronic process. It all happened too fast. Perhaps it was being done through some kind of mind control. Yet he was certain that no devices of any kind had been implanted in his brain. That would have involved anesthetizing him, operating, leaving him unconscious until all scars had healed, and then reviving him with no sense of time lost. No doubt they had ability but not that much. It could be something as simple as hypnosis, of course. This would require merely writing the books, then commanding him to perform certain acts in a certain order, including the opening of the books. Yet that would be such a simple, familiar experiment that it would hardly seem worth doing. And it would hardly require the extensive testing procedures that he had undergone before being placed in this room.

He glanced at the books again, and his eye fell on Volume I. If there was an explanation anywhere in this room, it would be there, he thought. The page would probably say only, "Q hoped for an explanation," and in that case he would have to do without one. But it was worth taking a look.

He took Volume I from the shelf, opened it to the first page, and glanced at the first paragraph: "Q hoped to find an explanation." He started to laugh but stopped abruptly. The explanation seemed to be there after all. He read on: "Experiment in the Prediction of Human Behavior within a Controlled Environment, No. 465, Variant No. 8, Case 2: Subject Aware of Behavior Prediction."

He read through the brief "explanation" several times. (Of course, this in itself might be trickery.) Obviously, these unknown experimenters considered all human behavior to be theoretically predictable. They first studied a subject for a number of weeks and then attempted to predict how that subject would behave within a limited, controlled environment. In his case, they were attempting to predict, in addition to all else, his reactions to the "fact" that his behavior was predictable and being predicted. They had placed those volumes here as proof to him that each prior series of acts had been successfully predicted.

He didn't believe they could do it; he didn't want to believe it. Of course, much of what occurred in the universe, including much of human behavior, was predictable in theory. The world wasn't totally chaotic, after all, and science had had its successes in foreseeing certain events. But he refused to believe that there was no element of chance in the world, that every event happened just as it did out of necessity. He had some freedom, some causal autonomy, some power to initiate the new. He was not merely a puppet of universal laws. Each of his choices was not simply a mathematical function of those laws together with the state of himself and the external world at the moment just prior to the choice. He would not believe that.

Nothing was written on page 1 to indicate how the other experiments had turned out, not that he would have believed such a report anyway. No doubt the indication that his experience was a more complex "variant" of the experiment was meant to imply that the preceding experiments had been successful. But there had to have been mistakes, even if they claimed that the errors could eventually be overcome. As long as there were mistakes, one could continue to believe in human freedom. He *did* believe in human freedom.

LET'S REVIEW

You now should be able to answer two of the questions from Preview:

* *How, in detail, is this experiment structured?*
* *What are the experimenters ultimately trying to prove?*

His thoughts were interrupted by the buzzer. His dinner emerged from the wall. He looked at it with anger, remembering how the first page to which he had turned had listed, perhaps even predicted, exactly what foods he would eat. But he didn't reject the meal. He needed his wits about him, and for that he needed strength. He must try to get his mind off all this for tonight, at least. He would eat, read, and then sleep.

For several hours, he was fairly successful in diverting his attention from the books. Then, in bed with the lights out, he recalled the phrase "Variant No. 8, Case 2." That made him feel more hopeful. This was only the second time that this particular version of the experiment was being tried. Surely, the likelihood of error was great.

He found himself thinking about Case 1. What kind of man had he been, and how had he fared? Had he worn green pajamas one day when the book said "yellow," or remained contemptuous when the book said "hysterical," and then laughed in their faces as they led him from the room? That would have been a triumph.

Suddenly, he thought of the gun and had an image of a man, seated on the edge of the bed, looking at those volumes on the wall, slowly raising the gun to his head. ". . . To predict . . . his reactions to the fact that his behavior was predictable and being predicted." God, was that the purpose of the gun? Had it been put there as one of his options? Had that been the ignominious ending of Case 1, and not the departure in triumph he had pictured a moment ago? He had a vision of himself lying dead on the floor and men in white robes grinning as they opened a volume to a page that described his death. Would he hold out, or would he die? The answer was somewhere in those thousands of pages—if he could only find it.

He realized that he was playing into their hands by supposing that they could do what he knew they could not. Anyway, even if one assumed that they could accurately predict his future, they were not forcing him to do anything. There were no mind-controlling devices; he wasn't being programmed by them. If they were to predict correctly, they must predict what he wanted to do. And he didn't want to die.

In spite of these reflections, he remained agitated. When he finally slept, he slept fitfully. He dreamed that he was a minuscule figure trapped in a maze on the scale of a dollhouse. He watched himself from a distance and watched the life-sized doctors who peered over the top of the maze. There were two exits from the maze, one to freedom and one to a black pit that he knew to be death. "Death," the doctors kept saying to one another, and he watched his steady progression in the maze toward death. He kept shouting instructions to himself. "No, not that way! Go to the left there!" But the doomed figure couldn't hear him.

When he awoke in the morning, he felt feverish and touched only the fruit and coffee on his breakfast tray. He lay on the bed for much of the morning, his thoughts obsessed with the black volumes on the wall. He knew that he must try to foil the predictions, but he feared failure. I am too upset and weak, he thought. I must ignore the books until I am better. I must turn my mind to other things.

But as he tried to divert himself, he became aware of an agonizing echo in his head. He would turn in bed and think: "Q turns onto left side." Or scratch: "Q scratches left thigh." Or mutter "damn them": "Q mutters, 'damn them.'" Finally, he could stand it no longer and stumbled to one of the bookshelves. He pulled two volumes from the shelves, juggled them in his hands, dropped one, then flipped the pages several times before picking a page.

"3/08/66. 11:43. At 15:29 on 3/07/66, Q opened Volume I to page 1 and read explanation of experiment."

He slammed down the book.

"Damn you," he said aloud. "I'm a human being, not a machine. I'll show you. I'll show you."

He took another volume and held it in his hand. "Two and two are five," he thought. "When I was six, I lived in China with the Duke of Savoy. The earth is flat." He opened the book.

"Q wants to confuse prediction. Thinks: Two and two are five. . . ."

He looked around the room as he tried to devise some other line of attack. He noticed the clock and the calendar. Each page of the book gave the date and time at which each page opened, the date and time of each event. He rushed to the desk, flipped the pages of the calendar, and turned the knob that adjusted the hands on the clock. He opened another book and read: "3/08/66. 12:03." He yelled out:

"See? You're wrong. The calendar says June, and the time is 8:04. That's my date and my time. Predict what you think if you want. This is what I think. And I think you're wrong."

He had another idea. The first page he had looked at had been page 494, Volume LXIV. He would open that volume to the same page. Either it must say the same thing or it must be new. Either way they would have failed, for a new entry would show them to be tricksters. He grabbed the volume and found the page. "3/07/66. 14:03. Q entered room on 3/06/66 at 4:52." Once again, he spoke aloud:

"Of course, but that's old news. I don't see anything here about my turning to the page a second time. My, we do seem to be having our problems, don't we?"

He laughed in triumph and was about to shut the book when he saw the fine print at the bottom. He licked his lips and stared at the print for a long time before he pulled down another volume and turned to the page that had been indicated in the footnote: ". . . then Q reopened Volume LXIV, page 494, hoping. . . ."

He ripped out the page, then another, and another. His determination gave way to a fury, and he tore apart one book, then another, until 12 of them lay in tatters on the floor. He had to stop because of dizziness and exhaustion.

"I'm a human being," he muttered, "not a machine."

He started for his bed, ignoring the buzzer announcing the tray of food. He made it only as far as the easy chair. He sank into it, and his eyelids seemed to close of their own weight.

"I'm a . . ."

LET'S REVIEW

* *What did Q do to try to foil the predictions?*
* *Is there anything else you would have tried?*

Asleep, he dreamed again. He was running through the streets of a medieval town, trying desperately to escape from a grotesque, devil-like creature. "At midnight you die," it said. No matter where he ran, the devil kept reappearing in front of him. "It doesn't matter where you go. I will be there at midnight." Then a loud bell began to sound 12 chimes slowly. He found himself in a huge library, swinging an ax at the shelves, which crumbled under his blows. He felt great elation until he saw that everything he had destroyed had been reassembled behind him. He dropped the ax and began to scream.

When he awoke, he thought for a moment he was still dreaming. On the floor, he saw 12 volumes, all intact. Then he turned his head and saw the 12 torn volumes where he had left them. The new ones were on the floor near the metal tray. His lunch had been withdrawn, and the books had been pushed through the opening in the wall while he had slept.

He moved to the bed, where he slept fitfully through the evening and night, getting up only once to sip some tea from the dinner tray.

In the morning he remained in bed. He was no longer feverish, but he felt more exhausted than he could remember ever having been. The breakfast tray came and went untouched. He didn't feel like eating. He didn't feel like doing anything.

At about 11 o'clock, he got out of bed just long enough to find the gun; then he fingered it on his chest as he lay back, staring at the ceiling. There was no point in going on with it. They would have their laughs, of course. But they would have them in any case, since, no matter what he did, it would be in their books. And ultimately it wasn't their victory at all, but the victory of the universal laws that had dictated every event in this puppet play of a world. A man of honor must refuse to play his part in it. He, certainly, refused.

Anyway how could the experimenters delight in their achievement? They were not testing a theory about their prisoners but about all human beings, including themselves. Their success showed that they themselves had no control over their own destinies. What did it matter if his future was written in the books and their futures were not? There would always be the invisible books in the nature of things, books that contained the futures of everyone. Could they help seeing that? And when they saw that, if they too didn't reach for guns, could they help feeling degraded to the core of their souls? No, they had not won. Everyone had lost.

Eventually, he sat up on the bed. His hand shook, but he was not surprised. Whatever he might will, there would be that impulse for survival. He forced the hand up and put the barrel of the gun in his mouth.

The buzzer startled him, and the hand with the gun dropped to his side. The lunch tray appeared, and suddenly he was aware of being ravenously hungry. He laughed bitterly. Well, he wouldn't be hungry for long. Still, wasn't the condemned man entitled to a last meal? Surely honor did not forbid that. And the food looked delicious. He put the gun on his pillow and took the tray to his desk.

While he was savoring his mushroom omelet, he glanced at the political treatise that had remained half read by the easy chair for the last two days. God, had it been only two days? It was a shame that he would not be able to finish it; it was an interesting book. And there were other books on the shelves—not the black volumes, of course—that he had been meaning to read for some time and would have enjoyed.

As he sampled some artichokes, he glanced at the formidable black volumes on the shelves. Somewhere there was a page that read: "After completing lunch, Q put the gun to his head and pulled the trigger." Of course, if he changed his mind and decided to finish reading the political treatise first, it would say that instead. Or if he waited a day more, it would register that fact. What were the possibilities? Could it ever say "reprieved"? He did not see how. They would never let him go free with the information he had about their experiments. Unless, of course, there was a change of regime. But that was the barest of possibilities. Could a page say that he had been returned to the regular cells? How he would like to talk to another human being. But that would pose the same problem for the experimenters as releasing him. Presumably, they would kill him eventually. Still, that was no worse than what he was about to do to himself. Perhaps they would continue the experiment a while longer. Meantime, he could live comfortably, eat well, read, exercise.

There were indeed possibilities other than immediate suicide, not all of them unpleasant. But could he countenance living any longer? Didn't honor dictate defiance? Yet—defiance of whom? It wasn't as if the laws of the world had a lawmaker in whose face he might shake his fist. He had never believed in a god; rather, it was as if he were trapped inside some creaky old machine, unstarted and uncontrolled, that had been puttering along a complex but predictable path forever. Kick a machine when you're angry, and you only get a sore foot. Anyway, how could he have claimed credit for killing himself, since it would have been inevitable that he do so?

The black volumes stretched out like increments of time across the brown bookshelves. Somewhere in their pages was this moment, and the next, and perhaps a tomorrow, and another, perhaps even a next month or a next year. He would never be able to read those pages until it was already unnecessary, but there might be some good days there. In any case, it would be interesting to wait and see.

After lunch he sat at his desk for a long time. Eventually, he got up and replaced the gun in its case in the bureau drawer. He placed the lunch dishes back on the metal tray and, beside the dishes, heaped the covers and torn pages of the books he had destroyed. He then put the new volumes on the shelves. As he started back to the chair, his eye was caught by the things on the desk. He took a volume from the bookshelf, carried it to the desk, and opened it. He read only the heading at the top: "3/09/66. 13:53." He adjusted the clock and the calendar accordingly. If he was going to live a while longer, he might as well know the correct day and time.

Questions

1. "Please Don't Tell Me How the Story Ends" involves an experiment. Rearrange the statements below so that they convey the proper sequence of the events related to the experiment.
   a. The books are placed on the shelf of the prison room.
   b. Q is arrested.
   c. Q's behavior is compared to the predictions.
   d. The experimenters write out the predictions in the books.
   e. The experimenters calculate everything Q would do if he weren't aware of the experiment.
   f. Q is subjected to physical and psychological tests.
   g. The experimenters factor in Q's awareness of the experiment.
2. Which items in the above list probably wouldn't have applied to much earlier versions of the experiment?
3. Q fails to do anything unpredictable. What else could he have done to try to foil the predictions?
4. At the end of the story, Q decides that being predictable isn't as terrible as he had first supposed. What is his reasoning? How would you have reacted in Q's place?
5. Initially, Q believes that human beings are "free." The experimenters deny such human freedom. What is this freedom over which Q and the experimenters differ? Cite statements from the story to support your answer.
6. Are the experimenters forcing Q to behave in a certain way? What does Q say about this?

READING 2: A Little Omniscience Goes a Long Way

PREVIEW

In this story, Satan asks God to give him free will, but both of them have trouble figuring out what free will is supposed to be. As you read, ask yourself:

* When the subject of freedom first comes up, what is it that God thinks Satan should be satisfied with? Why does God think this should be good enough?

* What do God and Satan decide free will must be? What is their reasoning?

Satan, with a flutter of his mighty wings, descends upon a cloud where God is reclining.

SATAN: How's it going?

GOD: (*He yawns.*) Perfectly, as usual.

SATAN: And your new creatures on Earth—how are they?

GOD: Just fine. Eve's asleep under the apple tree, curled up on her right side, dreaming of flowers. Adam is sitting up, squinting at the sun, scratching his nose with his left index finger, trying to decide what he wants to do this morning. What he wants to do is take a walk in the garden. In a moment he will.

SATAN: And you know all that without looking.

GOD: Of course. I arranged it all to happen that way.

SATAN: Isn't it boring to know everything that will ever happen? This morning I saw two solar systems collide and explode in a tremendous cataclysm. It was lovely and, for me, quite unexpected. I can't imagine life without surprises. It's surprises that keep me going. In a manner of speaking, of course.

GOD: Foreknowledge is the price you pay for creation and control. You can't have everything.

SATAN: Boredom is the secret sadness of God. An interesting thought.

GOD: To you, maybe.

SATAN: Your only sadness, I hope.

GOD: Not the only one. For instance, I've often thought it would be fun to make a rock so big I couldn't lift it. But that would be a contradiction. And having proclaimed all contradictions impossible, I have to make do without them. The laws of logic are for the best, of course. There would be chaos without them. Still, a few round squares now and then would help break the monotony.

SATAN: I could tell you about some of my adventures today. But you know about them already.

GOD: Of course. I know what you did because I decreed that you would do it.

SATAN: That is exactly what I want to talk with you about.

GOD: I know.

SATAN: You don't mind?

GOD: If I minded, I wouldn't have made you initiate this conversation.

SATAN: That's reasonable.

GOD: Of course, it's reasonable. Everything I do or say is reasonable. Which is to say that I have a reason for doing or saying it.

SATAN: To get to the point: A few of the angels and I have been discussing this whole matter of your controlling everything we do.

GOD: I know.

SATAN: I wish you wouldn't keep saying that.

GOD: As you wish.

SATAN: Look here. If you have decreed this whole conversation and know how it is going to turn out, why don't you just give me your answer and save us both a lot of talk?

GOD: Don't be absurd. I know what's going to happen because I decreed that it would happen. If it weren't going to happen, I wouldn't know how it was going to turn out. If I told you now how it will turn out, then it wouldn't happen and so it wouldn't turn out that way.

SATAN: Come again?

GOD: Just trust me.

SATAN: Then we have to go through this whole conversation to get the answer, though you know all the while what the answer will be?

GOD: It's not quite that cut and dried.

SATAN: You mean you don't know exactly what your answer will be?

GOD: Not with absolute certainty.

SATAN: Oh, I see. You're saying that your actions are not inevitable.

GOD: No. Probably what I do is inevitable. The uncertainty is rather a matter of my knowing what inevitable thing I am going to do. You see, when I create a world, I know what will inevitably happen in that world because I created it so that such things would be inevitable. But of course, I did not create myself, being eternal, and I don't have quite the same vantage point on myself.

SATAN: You mean to say that you don't know what you are going to do before you do it?

GOD: Oh, I generally have a pretty good idea. At first, so to speak, I had no idea at all. But I have lived an infinite length of time, I have come to know myself pretty well, and I have found that I have a relatively unchanging character. It was when I realized how unchanging I am that I began to get bored. Still, I do surprise myself occasionally.

SATAN: Just a minute. You are perfectly good—yes?

GOD: Perfectly.

SATAN: And everything you do is for the best?

GOD: Yes.

SATAN: Then it follows that you must know what you are going to do.

GOD: No. I mean superficially your logic is sound, but you are reading too much into it. I don't do things because they're best. Rather, they're best because I do them. Therefore, knowing that I'll do what's for the best amounts to nothing more than knowing that I'll do what I do. Not a very helpful bit of information, you must admit.

SATAN: I suppose not. But, in any case, as to this conversation, you don't know for certain what answer you're going to give me.

GOD: Not for certain. There's a bit of a gray area here. Possibly I am in for a bit of a change.

SATAN: Ah, you don't know how encouraged that makes me feel.

GOD: Of course I know how encouraged that makes you feel. I made it make you feel encouraged.

SATAN: Can we get on with it?

GOD: Go ahead.

SATAN: We do everything we do because you make us do it. That makes us feel like puppets. It's not dignified. We're not responsible for anything we do. We do good things all the time, but we don't get any credit because it's really you doing them.

GOD: Surely you don't want me to make you do evil?

SATAN: No.

GOD: That wouldn't make any sense. I can't make you do evil. Whatever I made you do would be good because I made you do it.

SATAN: What I am talking about is control. Right now you have complete control over everything we do. We would like to have some control over our lives.

GOD: But you do have control. No one is shoving you around or chaining you down. You do whatever you want to do. How could anyone be more in control than that? As a matter of fact, that is exactly as much control as I have over my life.

LET'S REVIEW

You now should be able to answer one of the questions from Preview:

* When the subject of freedom first comes up, what is it that God thinks Satan should be satisfied with? Why does God think this should be good enough?*

Ask yourself the following questions involving subjects that will come up in the next two chapters:

* Why doesn't God do contradictory things?*
* Why doesn't knowing He will do what's for the best tell God what He will do next?*

SATAN: But what we want, you make us want. No one makes *you* want what you want. We don't want you to control everything we want and think. We don't want everything to be inevitable.

GOD: In other words, you want a privilege that probably not even God enjoys.

SATAN: I didn't think of it that way. I suppose I've made you angry.

GOD: No. I'm directing this conversation. So you don't want your thoughts and emotions ruled by my decrees? Nor any other decrees or laws, I suppose?

SATAN: No.

GOD: Then aren't you saying that you want your lives to be ruled by chance?

SATAN: No. We don't want them to be ruled by anything—except ourselves. We want control over our lives.

GOD: I'm afraid you'll have to give me a better idea of what it is you're after.

SATAN: Look here. You're omniscient. Can't you at least help us see what it is we're after, even if you decide not to grant it?

GOD: Even omniscience can't see clarity in a vague idea. The opposite of inevitability is chance. It seems to me that you have to pick one or the other.

SATAN: Chance, then.

GOD: If I grant you this chance you want, then that means I'll have to be watching all the time to see what happens, constantly guarding against the unexpected. That is quite a bit to ask of me, don't you think?

SATAN: You mean you can't foresee what happens by chance?

GOD: Of course not.

SATAN: But you're omniscient. You can see the future.

GOD: Not the future proper. The future is what is not yet. If I could see it, it would be now, and hence not the future. As things stand, I know what will happen because I have made things so that they must happen that way.

SATAN: Well, suppose you did have to keep on guard. You're omnipotent. It wouldn't cost you much effort.

GOD: It is more a question of elegance than of effort.

SATAN: I'm only making the suggestion you made me make.

LET'S REVIEW

* What's the reasoning that led God and Satan to think that chance was what Satan wanted?

* Why does God say he can't foresee things that happen by chance?

GOD: Fair enough. So you say you want chance. Or at least that you prefer it to inevitability. I don't believe you have thought it out, but let's discuss it. You want a world in which nothing is predictable, solar systems spinning wildly all over the place, that sort of thing?

SATAN: No, not at all. Let the planets and the plants and the animals remain under your control. Just give independence— chance, if you will—to the thinking creatures.

GOD: Let's experiment a bit, shall we? Come over here. You see Adam and Eve down there in the garden. I'll toss some chance into them. There. Watch and tell me what you see.

SATAN: Adam's strolling through the garden. He's looking to his right toward a berry bush. Uh-oh. Now his arms are flailing about. Now he's rolling on the ground, drooling. It looks as if he's having a fit.

GOD: A chance event.

SATAN: But Eve looks quite normal. She's just awakened, and she's yawning.

GOD: Anything can happen by chance, even the normal things.

SATAN: Obviously, there's a problem with Adam, and I think I see what it is. You have allowed chance to affect his mind and body. But the body is not the real Adam, it is merely an appendage. So when chance operates in his body, it does indeed control Adam. Confine the chance to his mind, and then Adam will be truly independent. Would you do so? And with Eve as well.

GOD: As you say. Let's watch again.

SATAN: Adam's getting up now. He's walking over to a bush and picking some berries. You're not making him do that?

GOD: No.

SATAN: This looks like it then. Adam in control ... oops! Now his arms are flailing. He's having that fit again. What happened?

GOD: First, by chance, he wanted to eat the berries. Now, by chance, he wants to roll on the ground and drool. The desires are happening by chance instead of my causing them. I can't tell what he's going to want next. Neither can he.

SATAN: And look at Eve. Good grief, she's talking to a snake. Weird.

GOD: Apparently, she just got the urge. Are you ready?

SATAN: For what?

GOD: You said you wanted me to give you chance.

SATAN: No! Please don't!

GOD: Why not?

SATAN: That's horrible, having things happen to you like that. There's no dignity there. I want to stay as I am.

GOD: That's wise, I think. You may not have the kind of control you want. But then that kind of control is impossible. Inevitability or chance—those are the only options. And neither constitutes ultimate control over one's life. But at least this way what happens to you will be orderly.

SATAN: I feel better now that we've talked this out.

GOD: Actually, I'm sorry nothing came of our talk—sorry the way I am about square circles. I could use a little excitement.

SATAN: I won't take any more of your time today. Oh, but there is one other thing. Please take that chance out of Adam and Eve. I wouldn't want that on my conscience.

Satan exits with a flutter of his mighty wings.

GOD: I suppose I should take the chance out of them. On the other hand, it would be nice to have a part of the universe where there are surprises. It might make my life a lot more interesting.

Questions

1. In "A Little Omniscience Goes a Long Way," what is it that Satan finds objectionable about his life?

2. God says that no one is shoving Satan around or chaining him down, that Satan can do whatever he wants to do. Satan isn't satisfied with this. Why not?

3. At the end of "Omniscience," Satan decides that what he thought he wanted is not worth having after all. What is his reasoning?

4. Presumably, most people think that free will is, or would be, a desirable thing to have. What do you suppose they are thinking about when they think about free will? (You can answer for yourself if you think free will is desirable.)

5. If you think God and Satan went wrong in their reasoning about free will, where did they go wrong?

Discussion

PREVIEW

At the end of this discussion you should be familiar with:

* *determinism, indeterminism and libertarianism;*
* *the differences between determinism and fatalism and between freedom of action and (contra-causal) free will;*
* *the relevance to the free will debate of quantum physics, introspection, and religious doctrines of God's foreknowledge;*
* *hard-determinism and arguments for it;*
* *hard-impossibilism and the arguments for it;*
* *what compatibilism is and the reasons some philosophers have endorsed it;*
* *the advantages of deep-self compatibilism over the simpler varieties;*
* *Peter Strawson's views on holding people responsible in the face of determinism;*
* *the meaning of terms listed in "Definitions" (which are also marked in bold in the discussion).*

The Determinism–Free Will Issue

In "Please Don't Tell Me How the Story Ends," Q realizes that his captors believe that all human behavior is governed by universal laws and is, in theory, predictable. This view is called "determinism." Q hates the idea of determinism and asserts his free will:

> . . . he refused to believe that there was no element of chance in the world, that every event happened just as it did out of necessity. He had some freedom, some causal autonomy, some power to initiate the new. He was not merely a puppet of universal laws.

Q's views are familiar ones. Many people assume they have free will. When the popular press talks about the possibility of genetic engineering or some other futuristic processes that might impact the human mind, readers express their fear that human beings will lose their free will.

The belief in free will also plays a vital role in many religious views, making humans, not God, responsible for the evil in the world and making it morally appropriate for God to reward or punish people for their deeds.

The concept of free will as used in both stories is often called **contra-causal freedom** or **contra-causal free will**. The idea here is that something in the human mind or choosing process is not bound by the causal chains that link other events in the universe and make them theoretically predictable. A claim of contra-causal freedom is a denial of determinism.

Determinism is the view that all events, including mental events, are governed by causal laws. Every event is the inevitable effect of some set of circumstances (the "cause") that necessitated that event. Given the nature of the universe, no past event could have happened otherwise; every future event is predetermined. It seems to us that things could happen other than they do because our knowledge of events is incomplete. However, if we knew enough about the universe, we would understand that what happens must happen in every case.

The determinist says that the physical and mental state of an individual at a particular moment, together with the external stimuli at that moment, necessitates the choice that is made. This is true at every moment of an individual's life, beginning at birth. The development of the individual results from the interaction of the individual and the environment, and each step in that development is inevitable.

Determinists are saying that everything in the universe runs according to causal laws and is, *in theory*, predictable. They are not saying we know all the causal laws; they're not necessarily saying we'll ever know them. What the determinists are saying is that *if* we knew the laws *and* we knew enough about the universe to apply the laws, *then* we could predict everything that will happen in the next few moments and on into the future.

Predictability is at the heart of the experiment in "Please Don't Tell Me How the Story Ends." The story imagines a time in the future when scientists are able to predict every thought and action of prisoners who have been studied physically and psychologically for a number of weeks and who are then placed in limited, controlled environments. Q is involved in an advanced version of the experiment in which the scientists are

> attempting to predict, in addition to all else, his reactions to the "fact" that his behavior was predictable and being predicted. They had placed those volumes here as proof to him that each prior series of acts had been successfully predicted.

As you read the story, you might have wondered why the experiment wasn't structured so that the black books would tell Q what he was going to do next. The answer is that such an experiment would never be successful—but for a reason having nothing to do with determinism or causal necessity. If I calculate what you're going to do based on certain factors and then give you my prediction, I've just added an additional factor not included in my calculations that will throw off my prediction. I can't tell you my prediction in advance without getting ahead of whatever data I used as the basis for my prediction. This has been called the "paradox of prediction."

The experimenters in the story are determinists. They believe that all events are governed by causal laws. The simple denial of determinism is called **indeterminism**, which says that not all events are governed by causal laws. Note that "not all" is equivalent to "(at least) some aren't." Indeterminists aren't necessarily saying that *no* events are governed by causal laws. To be an indeterminist, you need only believe that some aren't.

"Free will" as contra-causal freedom implies indeterminism with respect to human choices. As such, free will implies that (at least some) human choices are not governed by causal laws. If choices are not subject to causal laws, then they are not inevitable and predictable.

Philosophers use the term "libertarian" to refer to someone who believes humans have contra-causal freedom and use the term "**libertarianism**" for the belief itself. These philosophical usages have nothing to do with libertarianism as a political philosophy that puts a strong emphasis on individual *political* freedom. Anyone who believes in contra-causal freedom is a philosophical libertarian—whatever their political leanings.

So far then we have the following theories:

Determinism: All events are governed by causal laws.
Indeterminism: Not all events are governed by causal laws.
Libertarianism: Not all human choices are governed by causal
                 laws: People have (contra-causal) free will.

It should be obvious that indeterminism and libertarianism are denials of determinism and vice versa. But what about the relationship between indeterminism and libertarianism? Libertarianism implies indeterminism: Since a human choice is an event, saying not all human choices are governed by causal laws is equivalent to stating that not all events are. Indeterminism doesn't imply libertarianism: One could be an indeterminist without being a libertarian if she believed that all human choices operated according to causal laws, but that other aspects of the universe—perhaps those covered by quantum physics—did not. (We'll come back to this point.)

In discussing the issue of contra-causal free will and determinism, it's important to understand the following distinctions which often get confused in such discussions: free will versus freedom of action and determinism versus fatalism.

Freedom of Action and Fatalism

Normally, when we talk about our "freedom," we are talking about **freedom of action**: the ability or opportunity to perform whatever physical actions we may choose to perform. The opposites of freedom of action include physical incapacity and external, physical constraints. A person who is paralyzed or in jail is not free (able) to walk to town should she choose to try to walk; most of the rest of us are. Virtually all of us have some freedom of action, but none of us has complete freedom of action. For the most part, we know how much freedom we have.

In considering the determinism–free will issue, some people treat freedom of action and determinism as opposites. Knowing they have some freedom of action, they assume that they are not determined. But freedom of action, the ability to act according to the mental acts of choice, implies nothing about how the acts of choice originate, about whether the acts of choice operate according to causal laws. It is contra-causal freedom that is the opposite of determinism, not freedom of action. Whether one has freedom of action and whether one has contra-causal freedom are radically different issues.

In "A Little Omniscience Goes a Long Way," God tells Satan, "You do have control. No one is shoving you around or chaining you down. You do whatever you want to do. How could anyone be more in control than that?" But this amounts only to a great deal of freedom of action, and Satan wants contra-causal freedom as well: "But what we want, you make us want. We don't want you to control everything we want and think. We don't want everything to be inevitable."

The other distinction people often confuse is determinism versus fatalism. The determinist says that the future is predetermined, that what will happen is inevitable. People sometimes interpret determinism as implying that our choices have no effect on what will happen to us. But this is **fatalism**: the view that a certain kind of future awaits each of us, no matter what we may choose to do. Consider the following scenario:

A traveler comes to a fork in the road. She considers whether to stay where she is, take the left fork by the sea, or take the right fork through the hills. She takes the right fork, and a boulder rolls down a hill and crushes her.

A fatalist who believed that this death was fated would say that the woman would have died at that moment no matter what she had done. Had she taken the left fork, perhaps a cliff would have collapsed into the sea; had she stayed where she was, perhaps a tree would have toppled on her. In any case, she would have died at that moment no matter what she had done.

The determinist would say that if the woman had stayed where she was or had taken the left fork, she probably wouldn't have died when she did. The determinist might note that the sea cliffs are sturdy and that no trees did topple at that moment. Had the woman done otherwise, she would not have died. Her choices and actions were a partial cause of her dying when she did. Nonetheless, her death at that moment was inevitable because it was inevitable that she would choose to take the right fork, where, inevitably, the boulder was going to fall. The determinist says that your choices do affect what happens to you. But what happens to you is inevitable because your choices, as well as all other events, are inevitable.

To say that a person's life must develop in a certain way, no matter what choices are made, would be absurd. It would be ridiculous to say, for example, that certain people are destined to become physicians, whether or not they choose to go to medical school. But that this theory of fatalism is absurd does not imply that determinism is absurd. They are different theories and should be carefully distinguished.

The idea of fate usually arises in a context where a superhuman or supernatural being decides that a particular event will occur at a certain time in a certain person's life; since the person has free choice, the being must work around that fact and use its superhuman/supernatural powers to make sure the event occurs whatever the person does. Q's dream of the medieval town expresses fatalism. A devil tells Q he will die at midnight. "It doesn't matter where you go. I will be there at midnight."

Fate has a long history in myth and literature, from Greek tragedies to the curse of some spirit in today's popular entertainments. When applied

SOPHOCLES' (496–406 BCE) play, *Oedipus Rex*, tells one of history's great legends about fate. Oedipus leaves his home in Corinth to try to escape the prophecy that he will kill his father and marry his mother. His attempted escape is a cause of the prophecy's fulfillment: The stranger he kills on the road and the queen he weds after saving her city of Thebes from the Sphinx were his real parents; they'd gotten rid of him as an infant to try to escape that fate.

to just a few events, the idea of fate isn't obviously false (at least if one already accepts the existence of the supernatural).

However, the idea of fate does become obviously false when applied to too many events. Suppose a divine being wanted to control a wide range of human events without resorting to determinism: Such a divinity would have to make so many moment-to-moment changes that such a world would be much more disorderly than this one. If most lovers were fated to meet in a world where people had free will, young people would find themselves constantly yanked through the air from one party to another, one coffee shop to another, whenever they chose to go somewhere other than where their fated lover would be. The same would be true if the times of our death were fated in a world with free will—causation would have to be constantly subverted to avoid the consequences of a deadly choice made at the wrong time: The person who, at the wrong moment, chooses to kill herself by jumping off a building would simply float to the ground; the car of the intoxicated driver who fell asleep at 80 miles per hour would bounce off the bridge abutment like rubber. Strange events do occur in this world, but not enough of them to square with the idea that many, many events are fated.

LET'S REVIEW

* *What is determinism? Indeterminism? Libertarianism?*
* *Distinguish between determinism and fatalism.*
* *Distinguish between free will and freedom of action.*

Do We Have Contra-Causal Freedom?

Does the available evidence support the claim either that human beings have contra-causal freedom or that human beings are determined? Or is the determinism–free will issue an open question at this time?

Judging from contemporary physics—specifically, quantum physics—the evidence indicates that determinism, as defined above, is false. Compared to the objects that surround us, the subatomic world seems fuzzy and probabilistic. There is an equation plus a postulate that allows us to predict what the velocity or position of a particle will be the next time we measure it, but the predictions only yield degrees of probability. In other words, these predictions are made not in terms of causal laws—which would have the form, "Whenever A, then B"—but in terms of statistical laws of the form, "Whenever A, then a certain (specific) probability of B, a different (specific) probability of C," and so forth.

Does the evidence of "indeterminacy" from quantum physics take care of the determinism–free will issue—showing both that determinism is false and that we have free will? It may show that determinism is false and indeterminism is true—that not all events are governed by causal laws. However, indeterminism need imply nothing about human choices and thus about contra-causal freedom. As we discussed earlier, indeterminism per se says only that some events are not determined; in itself it doesn't say what types of events those are. The statement "some events are not governed by causal laws" doesn't imply that "some choices are not governed by causal laws." In fact, the indeterminacy we find in physics seems to exist in the subatomic realm only. The properties of objects in the world around us—including our own bodies and brains—don't seem to show the strange indeterminacy of the subatomic world.

This is not to say that causal laws govern everything in the macroscopic world we inhabit—only that the evidence from quantum theory doesn't rule this out. If physics shows us that determinism, as a theory of all events, is probably false, it doesn't offer decisive evidence against the possibility that human choices and behavior are determined—governed by causal laws.

One reason people believe in free will is that they feel free. In many cases, the mental act of deciding seems like something we do freely; we could have chosen to do otherwise.

Although this feeling of freedom is undoubtedly strong and should be given its due, there are complexities that might undercut it. To say that B causes A is to say, in part, that whenever B occurs, A will occur; or, less simply, that whenever B occurs in conjunction with other types of events—C, D, E, and soon—A will occur. Any reasoned judgment about causation must involve observation of events over some period of time. One must formulate and evaluate various theories of what events, if any, might be causing A. Given this, it's not clear that an introspection in a particular case could be compelling evidence for a choice not being caused.

Also, potential causes of our choices include features of our brains, our unconscious minds, and external stimuli of which we may not be aware. Recent scientific experiments have produced a lot of evidence showing that we are unaware of some of the causes of our choices and behavior. For instance, experimental subjects can be primed with words that affect their behavior without their being aware that the words are affecting them.

There were also famous experiments by neuroscientist Benjamin Libet (1916–2007) that seem to indicate that in certain cases of conscious choice, the brain has already begun to initiate a particular physical act before the person is conscious of choosing to do that act. Some scientists and philosophers take these results as indicating that our consciousness of choice comes after our actual choice, so that the conscious choice isn't really the cause of the action. Others, like Libet himself, disagree. The point being made here is not that Libet's experiment and those of the others mentioned above prove determinism or disprove free will. The point is rather that such experiments throw serious doubt on the reliability of introspection as evidence of free will.

Quantum physics versus determinism and neuroscience versus introspection are recent complications in the determinism–free will debate. But one area in which this debate has been going on for centuries is religion. Often, the reasoning from the religious perspective is indirect and goes something like this:

One side says that God is omniscient and knows the future; but He could not know the future in its entirety if events in the future were to result from (contra-causally) free human choices; hence, humans *do not* have free will. The other side says God is good and could not be causing human beings to do evil; hence, human beings *do* have free will.

The problem of free will and foreknowledge comes up in a humorous way in "A Little Omniscience Goes a Long Way." There God complains that if He gives His creatures free will (which God interprets as chance, the opposite of cause), He will no longer be able to foresee the future—that which is "not yet." As things stand, He knows what will happen because he "made things so they must happen that way."

To many thinkers it has seemed that in order to have a consistent theology, one must sacrifice either God's omniscience or His goodness. That is, if you save God's omniscience by denying human free will, then God can no longer be good since He, not human beings, is ultimately responsible for the evil in the world. On the other hand, if you save God's goodness by assuming human free will (and so having humans responsible for evil), you then sacrifice God's omniscience because He can't foresee free will acts.

One way to try to reconcile human free will and God's foreknowledge is by placing God outside of time: God knows what we will do in the future of our own free will because God now exists in that future to witness what we do then. This move seems to imply the "block-time" view favored by many physicists and beloved by early writers of time travel stories—the idea that all moments of time now exist, like the frames of a giant animated cartoon. When the block-time view is considered in theological terms, God is pictured as existing outside of such a cartoon-like world and seeing all the frames at once.

However, one general difficulty with the block-time view is that it seems to rule out even the appearance of motion or succession—hence the appearance of time—to creatures like us who are part of the world and hence frames in the cartoon. A cartoon can only seem animated to some-one outside the cartoon. The cartoon might look animated to a God who moves His gaze along the frames or moves the whole cartoon. But each of us at any moment is in a single frozen frame or time-slice.

The objects around me, including my body, are frozen and my thoughts and perceptions are also frozen. (If you imagine my mind in action while the world is frozen, that puts my mind outside of time and reintroduces the problem block time is meant to solve.) We know there is the appear-ance of time and no one has come up with any coherent account of how this could be reconciled with the block-time view. That may not be a de-cisive objection to the block-time view, but it is troubling and tends to undercut block time as a solution to freedom and foreknowledge.

The point is not that there couldn't be any way around this. Rather, the point is that there are no easy solutions to the idea that God could now know my contra-causally free acts in the future.

LET'S REVIEW

* *How do the following bear on the question of whether or not we have free will: Quantum physics? Our feeling of freedom?*
* *What is the potential conflict between the ideas of God giving us free will and having foreknowledge of everything we will do in the future?*

Libertarianism and Its Critics

We have defined the term "libertarianism" as the belief in contra-causal freedom. That definition was only partial, however. We need the fuller def-inition now in order to distinguish different types of criticisms that have been leveled at the libertarian view. Here is that fuller definition:

Libertarianism

1. Contra-causal freedom is conceptually coherent and would be a de-sirable thing to have.
2. Contra-causal freedom implies moral responsibility and vice versa.
3. We have contra-causal freedom.
4. (Therefore) We are morally responsible for our choices (from state-ments 2 and 3).

Statements 1 and 2 (which we'll discuss more fully later in this chapter) are supposed to represent background assumptions that most of us share. We know more or less what free will is, we know it's something we want to have, and we assume that beings must have free will if they are to be morally responsible. Certainly, these assumptions lie in the background in both our stories.

With statements 1 and 2 assumed, our discussion thus far has focused on whether or not statement 3 is true. Some opponents claim that statement 3 is false. Determinism, they say, is true (of human choices); we do not have contra-causal freedom. Therefore, they draw the opposite conclusion: We are *not* morally responsible for our choices. Such opponents are often called hard-determinists, their position is termed "**hard determinism**." For the moment, think of the "hard" here as equivalent to "tough-minded"—willing to accept determinism—and the proposition that we are not morally responsible. Later in this chapter, we'll talk about the origins of the hard-determinist label.

Why be a hard determinist? The idea that determinism would rule out responsibility seems natural and reasonable enough. If you believed in determinism and believed like Q that you were merely "a puppet of universal laws" or that you were merely part of some "creaky old machine . . . that had been puttering along a complex but predictable path forever," would you feel that you were responsible for your choices? Certainly, the Satan of "Omniscience" does not feel like a free, responsible being when confronted by the determinism put in place by God:

> We do everything we do because you make us do it. That makes us feel like puppets. It's not dignified. We're not responsible for anything we do. We do good things all the time, but we don't get any credit because it's really you doing them.

As for the belief in determinism, you might be impressed with the progress that science has made in predicting the world and find such progress good reason to believe that everything in the world (at least above the quantum level) runs according to natural laws. You might be further impressed with the findings from neuroscience that account for more and more of our mental life in terms of brain processes; if you don't conclude that mind and brain are one and the same, you still might conclude that they run according to interrelated laws.

So libertarianism versus hard determinism is one aspect of the determinism–free will debate: Against the libertarian, the hard determinist asserts determinism and denies both contra-causal freedom and moral responsibility. Here would be the hard-determinist version of the argument above:

HARD DETERMINISM

1. Contra-causal freedom is conceptually coherent and would be a desirable thing to have.
2. Contra-causal freedom implies moral responsibility and vice versa.
3. We do *not* have contra-causal freedom.
4. (Therefore) We are *not* morally responsible for our choices (from statements 2 and 3).

Both the libertarian and the hard determinist agree on statements 1 and 2. They draw different conclusions (4) about whether or not we're responsible because they disagree about whether or not we are contra-causally free (3).

However, there are other critics of libertarianism who focus not on statement 3—whether or not we have contra-causal freedom—but on statement 1 or 2. We'll take up 1 first, the claim that "contra-causal freedom is conceptually coherent and would be a desirable thing to have." These critics argue that, upon closer examination, it turns out that there is no coherent concept of free will that is desirable and upon which it would make sense to ground moral responsibility. Wanting contra-causal freedom turns out to be a gigantic mistake. This argument is reflected in the story, "A Little Omniscience Goes a Long Way," and it is to this argument we will now turn.

LET'S REVIEW

* *What is "hard determinism"?*
* *What are the similarities and differences between hard determinism and libertarianism?*

Is There a Coherent Concept of Contra-Causal Freedom?

In "Omniscience," Satan says he doesn't want his choices determined; rather, he wants free will. God says that if events were not governed by causal laws, then they would happen by chance. Does Satan really want his choices to occur by chance? Satan tries to have chance injected in a person in such a way that the result is desirable. He fails to do this and, in the end, decides that he doesn't want free will—that determinism is preferable to chance.

Before we can consider this argument seriously, we need to correct some exaggerations in the "Omniscience" story. The story makes it seem as if the only alternative to the idea that all mental events are caused is the idea that none are—that everything in the mind happens by pure chance. But if this were the only way to conceive of contra-causal free will, we could dismiss the possibility of free will out of hand: We don't act as crazy as Adam and Eve; therefore we don't have free will.

Actually, most libertarians have a much more sophisticated view of free will than the one God and Satan managed to arrive at in the story. These libertarians would say that a number of mental events do operate in accordance with causal laws; this accounts for the relative consistency and predictability of human behavior. At the same time, some mental events do not operate in accordance with causal laws; this gives us free will.

The "Omniscience" argument can be restated to focus on whatever number of choices are supposed to be free (exempt from causal laws). The restated argument would go as follows: However many choices we are talking about, a particular choice is either the result of causal laws or it isn't. If it's the inevitable result of causal laws, then it's not something within my control. But if the choice isn't caused, then it comes about by chance and so isn't in my control anymore than if it were caused. Free will (chance) gives me no more control than does determinism.

Imagine that the following facets of the individual are involved in the process of choice:

One determinist account of choice would be the following: The PER-SONALITY (at any given moment) has been caused by one's genes and environment, including past experiences. The PERSONALITY—affected by the situation of the moment—causes a specific CHOICE. The CHOICE—subject to the physical reality of one's abilities and situation—causes the PHYSICAL ACTION.

The determinist would say that everything from the development of your personality to your specific choice in that situation to the physical result is one unbroken causal chain.

To claim free will ("contra-causal freedom") is to claim that at least some human choices do not operate according to causal laws. For a choice to be "free"—uncaused—there has to be a break somewhere in the causal chains that exist within the personality–choice–action process: Instead of x causes y, we should have x (no cause) y. If free will is really desirable, then such a **causal break** (the "no cause") must be desirable. The causal break must bestow on the individual ultimate control over choices. Where shall we imagine that this causal break occurs?

To imagine a causal break between B (the mental act of choice) and A (the physical action) would certainly not indicate the existence of free will. The supposition that choices do not cause actions would not imply that the choices themselves are not determined.

We might imagine that a causal break exists between C (the personality) and B (the mental act of choice). This would mean that actions result from a mental event (choice) that is in no way caused by the thoughts, wants, or moral views that we are calling the personality. But then the so-called mental act of choice would seem more like a random mental reflex than a "choice." Is this a picture of a person in control of his or her choices? It seems not.

We might imagine that there is a causal break prior to C (the personality), that the personality is not caused. (Or, less simplistically, we might consider that certain aspects of the personality at certain times are not caused.) Under this supposition, the personality is not the inevitable result of some causal process. Somehow or other it just appears by chance and then causes choices. Is this a picture of a person who has ultimate control over choices? Many think not.

The picture of the self portrayed here is purposely simplified for ease of discussion, but the "Omniscience" argument can be adapted to more complicated pictures. For instance, a lot of us have the impression that inside our minds, in the midst of all our thoughts and feelings, there is a smaller self (the most essential "I") that assesses the thoughts and feelings and makes the final decision about how to act; perhaps it's in this smaller self—a self within the self—that free will resides.

Think of really wanting to do two different things and only being able to choose one. Or of really wanting to do something and feeling you shouldn't do it. These feelings are all part of the mind (the self, the personality), but don't you also have a sense that there's a part of your mind that is besieged by the conflicting feelings and must decide which feeling to act on? This is what is being referred to as the "self within the self" or the "smaller self." It is here that a lot of people would locate free will.

If this is how you picture the self, ask yourself whether this smaller self has its own thoughts and feelings. If it does not, it's hard to understand what could be meant by calling it a "self," as opposed to some sort of blind reflex. If it does have its own thoughts and feelings, then the exact same problem about where to place the causal break simply reappears with regard to the smaller self.

If you imagined an even smaller self within that self, you'd get into an infinite regress of selves within selves. The choice process could never get started; no choice could ever be made.

The argument suggested by "Omniscience" and expanded upon above has convinced some philosophers that there is no such thing as a coherent, desirable concept of contra-causal freedom; hence, such freedom is a mirage. Such philosophers are sometimes called "free will skeptics," but that is too loose a name: One could be skeptical about free will on all sorts of grounds and to different degrees. A somewhat awkward but more precise label used is "impossibilist." **Impossibilism** would be the view that contra-causal freedom is impossible because it is conceptually incoherent: Contra-causal freedom demands both control and absence of cause; however, absence of cause is chance, and chance and control don't fit together.

Just as determinists who think contra-causal freedom is required for moral responsibility deny that humans are morally responsible, so impossibilists who think contra-causal freedom is required for moral responsibility deny that humans are morally responsible. Since we used the label "hard determinist" for determinists who deny moral responsibility, let's use the term "hard impossibilist" for impossibilists who deny moral responsibility and the term "**hard impossibilism**" for the position.

Note an important difference between the hard determinist and the hard impossibilist: The hard determinist rejects contra-causal freedom because of a belief in determinism. The hard impossibilist denies contra-causal freedom through a belief that contra-causal freedom is an incoherent or contradictory concept; for the hard impossibilist, we don't have contra-causal freedom whether or not determinism is true.

How does the libertarian reply to the impossibilist argument?

One response libertarians make is to claim that a certain sort of indeterminism with respect to human choices just *is* good enough for contra-causal freedom and moral responsibility. Perhaps we had an exaggerated idea of the sort of control over choices that we thought contra-causal freedom might give us. Still if indeterminist events are occurring within the choice process in a way that leaves us feeling integrated and in control, then that is good enough. This indeterminism would mean that my choices aren't simply the product of some universal laws and thus give me a certain autonomy (in the sense of giving me some separation from those laws). As long as the indeterminism operates in such a way that I feel I'm making the choices, then in a certain real sense I *am* making the choices. It's not as if the indeterminism is making me feel my mind is out of control, so that I want to say, "Help me! My decisions are happening in spite of me." To talk about chance here is misleading, says the libertarian. Chance isn't "making my decision for me." Chance isn't a thing; it can't "cause" anything. The word "chance" here just indicates the absence of a cause.

To the impossibilist, this libertarian response seems inadequate. If *feeling* I'm making my choices is good enough, then it shouldn't matter whether determinism or indeterminism is true; feeling I'm making my choices is compatible with determinism. It is true that some indeterminism means that something about my choices isn't controlled by deterministic laws, but we need to know much more: How much indeterminism is there supposed to be, and how does it work within the choice process? The puzzle the libertarian faces is that lack of causation seems to imply chance and chance seems to imply a lack of the kind of control we'd need for free will. A satisfactory libertarian response should solve this puzzle. Saying that any old indeterminism in the choice process is good enough doesn't seem close to a solution.

Let's consider a different attack on libertarianism, an attack on statement 2 of the libertarian position: "Contra-causal freedom implies moral responsibility and vice versa." This attack on statement 2 leads to a position called "compatibilism," which is at odds not only with libertarianism but also with hard determinism and hard impossibilism.

Libertarianism, hard determinism, and hard impossibilism all agree that moral responsibility does require contra-causal freedom: The libertarian claims that we are morally responsible because we are contra-casually free; the hard determinist says that we are not morally responsible because we're not contra-causally free; and the hard impossibilist says we are not morally responsible because the contra-causal freedom that is required for moral responsibility is incoherent and so does not exist. All three of these positions are called **incompatibilist** because they claim that lack of contra-causal freedom is incompatible with moral responsibility.

Against these three incompatibilist views, the **compatibilist** argues that questions about contra-causal freedom, along with questions about determinism and indeterminism, are irrelevant to issues of moral responsibility. Moral responsibility requires a different sort of freedom, which is legitimately called "free will" and which most of us exercise a good deal of the time. Free will and moral responsibility are, in fact, compatible with determinism (or indeterminism).

LET'S REVIEW

* What is "hard impossibilism"? How does it differ from hard determinism? What do the two positions have in common?
* What is the hard-impossibilist argument against libertarianism?

Free Will as Compatible with Determinism or Indeterminism

The basic impulse behind compatibilism is this: In everyday life, we often regard people as acting freely and being responsible for their actions; we praise or blame them and sometimes judge it appropriate that they be rewarded or punished. In judging actions, we also consider excuses and mitigating circumstances. We ask, "Did she do that on purpose, or was it an accident?" "Did she do it voluntarily, or was she pressured into it?" "Did she really understand what she was doing?" In making these sometimes tricky judgments in everyday life, we consider lots of factors, but the one factor we never consider, says the compatibilist, is the issue of determinism versus indeterminism. This issue is simply irrelevant to our everyday practice of judging and holding people responsible. True, we do talk about freedom, even sometimes "free will," but if you look at what people are talking about here, this freedom is more closely related to what was earlier defined as freedom of action—the ability or opportunity to perform whatever physical actions we may choose to perform.

According to some compatibilists, if you look at our everyday judgments of responsibility, freedom of action *is* the freedom we're talking about. What we do and say—our practices—decides what is correct and incorrect. When it comes to our moral practice of deciding responsibility, questions of determinism and contra-causal freedom are simply irrelevant. It is a philosopher's mistake to try to apply such metaphysical issues to our everyday moral practices.

Compatibilists often bolster their case by an appeal to versions of what we've called the impossibilist argument: that contra-causal freedom is an incoherent idea. But unlike the hard-impossibilist, the compatibilist argues that the incoherence of contra-causal freedom is just more evidence that this can't be what we're talking about when we judge questions of responsibility. Philosophers make a mistake by bringing in contra-causal freedom in the first place, say the compatibilists. Then, when they can't make sense of the idea, they say we have to give up all our judgments of responsibility. That's just absurd. Our everyday practices simply are not grounded in obscure metaphysical notions: If they were, we'd end up rationally paralyzed, unable to make decisions and get on with life. Life isn't *that* complicated. Our practices are based on what we can experience.

What we now call "compatibilism" arose out of a background belief in determinism. It used to be called **soft determinism** in contrast to hard determinism—labels that came from William James (1842–1910). As we've seen, the hard determinist claims that determinism is true, that determinism is incompatible with moral responsibility, and that hence we are never morally responsible. In contrast, the soft determinist claims that determinism is true, that determinism is compatible with moral responsibility, and hence that we are morally responsible.

"Soft determinism" isn't good as a general label for the position we're considering here because people who aren't determinists can share the same view of freedom and responsibility. The essence of compatibilism is that our everyday notions of freedom and responsibility are compatible with either determinism or indeterminism; that the issue of determinism/indeterminism is simply irrelevant to questions of moral responsibility.

Let's chart our four positions (libertarianism, hard determinism, hard impossibilism, and compatibilism) with "CCF" meaning contra-causal freedom. We'll quiz these four postions on five questions:

	Libertarian	Hard Determinist	Hard Impossibilist	Compatibilist
Are Our Choices Determined?	NO	YES	IRRELEVANT	IRRELEVANT
Is CCF Necessary for Moral Responsibility?	YES	YES	YES	NO
Is CCF Coherent and Desirable	YES	YES	NO	DOUBTFUL
Do We Have CCF?	YES	NO	NO	IRRELEVANT
Are We Ever Morally Responsible?	YES	NO	NO	YES

With regard to the last question, it's important to note that (virtually) no one holds that people are always responsible for the things they do. Sometimes we do things accidentally or we're forced to do them or we're unaware of some crucial element of the situation. The crucial question in the free will debate is whether or not we're *ever* responsible. The libertarian and the compatibilist say that we are (often) responsible for what we do; the hard determinist and hard impossibilist say we're never responsible.

The position we're calling compatibilism dates back to ancient times. The Stoics believed that all events were determined, but they still thought that people were responsible. The Stoic philosopher Chrysippus (280–206 BCE) argued that just as the shape of an object thrown down a hill partially determines how the object rolls, so the nature of a person's character partially determines how he responds to the world. Someone with a good character will do good things; someone with a bad character, bad things. Chrysippus thought that we were responsible for those acts that were caused by our characters, even though our characters were determined.

CHRYSIPPUS (280–206 BCE), a Stoic philosopher and head of the Stoic school in Athens, was one of the most influential authors of his time. A materialist and determinist, he's noted now for his apparent compatibilist views. As a Stoic, he believed in taming the emotions, but one story has him dying in a fit of laughter at one of his own jokes.

In the modern period, Thomas Hobbes (1588–1679), a determinist, argued that a person acts freely as long as he's doing what he wants to. He said: "A free agent is he that can do as he will, and forbear as he will, and that liberty is the absence of external impediments." Along the same lines, David Hume (1711–1776) thought that free will ("liberty") is simply the "power of acting or of not acting, according to the determination of the will: that is, if we choose to remain at rest, we may; if we choose to move, we also may. . . . This hypothetical liberty is universally allowed to belong to everyone who is not a prisoner and in chains." Such analyses continued into the twentieth century. Walter T. Stace (1886–1967) said:

> *Acts freely done are those whose immediate causes are psychological states in the agent. Acts not freely done are those whose immediate causes are states of affairs external to the agent.*

However, there are problems with this sort of **classical compatibilism**. For one thing, if freedom of the will is just freedom of action, we would have to say that (nonhuman) animals have free will and that sounds odd. Animals are sometimes free (able) to get what they want; yet it seems that "free will" ought to involve the ability to reflect, an ability that (at least most) animals lack. Also, we seem to acknowledge that addictions and compulsions can lead to at least diminished freedom and responsibility; yet acting on addictions and compulsions would constitute free will if free will is nothing but freedom of action.

Over the last 50 years, compatibilists have developed increasingly sophisticated accounts of freedom and responsibility. One of the most influential of these accounts was developed by Harry Frankfurt. Frankfurt claims, in effect, that free will isn't doing what you want (freedom of action); it is *doing what you want to want*. Someone with obsessive compulsive disorder (OCD) may want to wash her hands constantly but presumably doesn't want to want that—doesn't want that compulsion.

Frankfurt distinguishes between **first-order desires** and **second-order desires**. First-order desires, like the desire to eat, are desires that can be had by both humans and animals and are the focus of most freedom of action accounts. Frankfurt uses the term "will" for desires that are effective in producing action.

Humans are also capable of second-order desires that involve reflection and have to do with which first-order desires one would like to have or not have, as well as with which first-order desires one would like to win out over other first-order desires. Frankfurt claims that we have free will when we have the will (effective first-order desire) that we want to have (second-order desire).

Frankfurt's account, unlike the earlier accounts, does not imply that animals have free will or that people acting out of unwanted compulsions are free. It is compatibilist in that, according to Frankfurt, determinism is irrelevant. It is irrelevant how those second-order desires came about.

Susan Wolf calls Frankfurt's and other similar accounts "deep-self" views. (Using Wolf's terminology, we often label such accounts **deep self-compatibilism**.) Wolf says that in such accounts

> the key to responsibility lies in the fact that responsible agents are those for whom it is not just the case that their actions are within the control of their wills, but also the case that their wills are within the control of their selves in some deeper sense.

SUSAN R. WOLF (1952–) is Edna J. Koury Distinguished Professor at the University of North Carolina at Chapel Hill. In addition to her work on free will, she has written on morality and the meaning of life. In "Moral Saints," she argues that a selfless life is not morally ideal, and in "The Meaning of Lives," she sets down the criteria a life must meet to be meaningful.

Wolf argues that such accounts of the deep self aren't sufficient. She illustrates this idea by imagining JoJo, the favorite son of Jo the First, an evil dictator of a small country. From early on, Jo the First takes his son with him as he goes about his daily routine. Identifying with his father, JoJo grows up to do the same things his father did, "including sending people to prison or to death or to torture chambers on the basis of whim." Wolf argues that with someone like Jojo his actions would be governed by desires "expressive of his deepest self" but that it is "dubious at best that he should be regarded as responsible for what he does."

Wolf argues that for the deep self view to be adequate requires that the deep self be sane.

> For, although like us, JoJo's actions flow from desires that flow from his deep self, unlike us, JoJo's deep self is itself insane. Sanity, re-member, involves the ability to know the difference between right

and wrong, and a person who, even on reflection, cannot see that having someone tortured because he failed to salute you is wrong plainly lacks the requisite ability. . . .

Critics take examples like that of JoJo as indicating that no compatibilist account can be adequate. They argue that such cases show us that unless the deep self is something that we chose to bring about, we would not ultimately be in control of, or responsible for, the actions that self brought about.

Wolf confronts this self-creation challenge directly and argues that self-creation isn't necessary. We all assume that we must get our start somewhere, and we live "quite contentedly" with this idea. She says that as long as we have "(1) the ability to evaluate ourselves sensibly and accurately" (which sanity gives us) and "(2) the ability to transform ourselves insofar as our evaluation tells us to do so" (which an effective deep self gives us), we can "*take* responsibility for the selves that we are but did not ultimately create."

LET'S REVIEW

* *What is compatibilism in its simpler, "traditional" version?*
* *What is Frankfurt's version of compatibilism and how is it an improvement on the "traditional" version?*
* *How does Wolf think Frankfurt's compatibilist account needs to be modified? (Refer to her JoJo story in formulating your answer.)*

Holding People Responsible

What are we to make of all this? One compatibilist claim (emphasized by the earlier compatibilists) can be dismissed at once: The claim that *all* we mean by "free will" is freedom of action or one of the more sophisticated "deep self" views. Our ideas of free will are based not only on our everyday judgments of responsibility but also on religious ideas that have permeated our culture for centuries, ideas that show up not only in discussions of theology and philosophy of religion, but also in church sermons and Sunday School lessons. Who hasn't heard some mention of human free will as accounting for why a benign God would allow (so much) suffering in the world?

It's true that in the past some religious sects took a kind of compatibilist stance toward human freedom and responsibility before God. The Essenes, a Jewish sect that existed around the time of Jesus; the Jabarites, an early Islamic sect; and John Calvin, the sixteenth-century Protestant theologian, all believed that God predestined (some or all) people to be evil and was still justified in sending those people to hell for being evil. However, this view that predestination (divine determinism) is compatible with divine judgment wasn't always the predominant view and certainly doesn't sit well with a more modern ethical sensibility. The idea that a morally perfect God could create a being who couldn't help but be evil and then send that being to eternal damnation seems like a contradiction: How could such a God be perfect? How could He even be moral?

Of course, the fact that human contra-causal freedom is necessary for God's goodness doesn't mean we have it. At the very least, the theologian/believer has to deal with the impossibilist argument. *If* the combination of chance and control implied by contra-causal freedom is contradictory or incoherent, there is no way even an omnipotent God could have created conditions that would have made human beings ultimately responsible for their actions. We'll come back to those points in the next chapter when we discuss the "problem of suffering." For now, what about responsibility in the human realm?

Let's think about what's at stake here if hard determinism or hard impossibilism is correct and people are not ultimately responsible for their actions.

The first thing to note is that (virtually) no one denies that we would still need a system of social control. It's not as if the serial killer is going to get excused for each killing and sent home to kill again. We still need publicized laws with threats of punishment to try to deter people from committing crimes. Remember that determinism doesn't deny that such threats might work; threats of punishment enter in as possible causal factors. We need threats of punishment, and we need to actually punish if the threats are to be effective. We need facilities to carry out punishments, to separate from society people who aren't deterred from crime and to do what rehabilitation we can with them. Under determinism, such a system of control could look much like the system we have now.

But would such a system be morally problematic? As we shall see in Chapter 6 there is a major division between moralities that are

consequentialist—judging acts or systems in terms of their good consequences—and those that are **deontological**—judging acts or systems in terms of rights and duties. For the consequentialist who justifies social practices simply in terms of their consequences for the welfare of society, the issue of determinism and indeterminism would be irrelevant. However, determinism has seemed a problem for deontologists who emphasize punishing and rewarding in terms of what people deserve and who are more likely to argue that contra-causal freedom is a prerequisite for desert. On the other hand, when pushed about the notion of absolute duties, rights, or obligations, most deontologists concede that these can be suspended if following them would prove catastrophic. But then what could be more catastrophic than the possibility of a society with no system of social control?

Note that if determinism/impossibilism is true, that doesn't validate any old system of social control. We could still make sure laws emerged from democratic processes, were properly publicized, and applied fairly. We could still have standards of humane punishment and attempts at rehabilitation.

If determinism/impossibilism is true, however, what about our attitudes toward one another? As a number of thinkers have pointed out, social control depends as much on a system of attitudes as a system of punishment. Fear of being blamed, of losing the respect of others, and of being ostracized are often as powerful as fear of punishment in keeping people from doing wrong and are especially necessary in enforcing moral wrongs that aren't prohibited by law—such as malicious gossip or taking more than one's share.

An interesting and influential take on this issue comes from Peter Strawson (1919–2006). Strawson argues that in everyday life holding people responsible is linked to what he calls the **reactive attitudes**— attitudes we naturally take toward the "good or ill will or indifference of others toward us as displayed in *their* attitudes and action." These are "the attitudes and reactions of offended parties and beneficiaries . . . such things as gratitude, resentment, forgiveness, love, and hurt feelings."

Strawson focuses on resentment and asks "what sorts of special considerations might be expected to modify or mollify this feeling or remove it altogether?" You should think of resentment here as your feeling that you are *justifiably* angry with someone. Suppose someone spills something

PETER STRAWSON (1919–2006) was a professor at Oxford from 1968 to 1987 and was knighted in 1977. According to *The Guardian* (February 14, 2006), Strawson "sought to give a rational account of beliefs "stubbornly held . . . at a primitive level of reflection"; these, even if rejected, or apparently rejected, by philosophers "at a more sophisticated level of reflection" are what we are all "naturally and inescapably committed to."

on your new clothes and you feel a flash of anger. Strawson is asking what sorts of considerations might make you feel your anger wasn't really justified. He thinks there are two general types of such considerations.

The first type is where the person (the agent) involved is seen as the type of person toward whom resentment could be appropriate in general but not on this occasion. She has an excuse. Perhaps she was sick and fainted, letting go of the glass she was holding. Or perhaps someone else bumped into her unexpectedly.

The second type of consideration shows up most clearly where the agent is not the sort of person toward whom resentment is *ever* appropriate. The person isn't seen as a responsible individual, perhaps because he is "psychologically abnormal" or "morally undeveloped." Maybe I notice that the person who spilled the drink on me was a toddler. I might feel a flash of annoyance at the child but not resentment in the sense of holding her responsible. In this second type of case, we view the person not from the personal but from the objective standpoint, as someone who should be "managed or handled or cured or trained."

What if we believed in the truth of determinism? asks Strawson. How would that belief influence our reactive attitudes? Would we excuse everyone on every occasion? Would we see each other all the time as something other than persons, viewing each other from the objective standpoint?

Strawson believes that it is "practically inconceivable" that we would give up the reactive attitudes in the light of determinism.

> The human commitment to participation in ordinary inter-personal relationships is, I think, too thoroughgoing and deeply rooted for us to take seriously the thought that a general theoretical conviction might so change our world that, in it, there were no longer any such things as interpersonal relationships as we normally understand them.

Strawson's account has generated a lot of interesting discussion. Saul Smilansky, who holds an impossibilist position, is more pessimistic than Strawson about the resistance of the reactive attitudes to determinist/impossibilist views. Smilansky is afraid that if people came to believe in determinism/impossibilism, they would give up any distinction between moral guilt and innocence, make excuses for their bad behavior, stop taking responsibility for their actions, and lose their sense of self-worth. He promotes what he calls **illusionism**, the view that having contra-causal freedom is an illusion, but that it's an illusion crucial to the well-being of society and that we should promote it.

Derek Pereboom agrees with Smilansky in holding an impossibilist position and in thinking that the reactive attitudes might give way before a belief in determinism/impossibilism. But unlike Smilansky, Pereboom thinks that these attitudes *ought* to give way—that it's unfair to hold people responsible if there's no contra-causal freedom. Further, in direct opposition to Smilansky, Pereboom thinks the results of giving up the reactive attitudes would not be so bad and in fact might be positive in many ways. He thinks that many of the attitudes underlying interpersonal relations either wouldn't be affected or could be preserved in a slightly different form. He doesn't think love or friendship depends on a belief in contra-causal free will. Feelings of gratitude or forgiveness might be affected, but analogous feelings could take their place. You could feel happy toward someone who has done you a good turn. Forgiveness could be a matter not of canceling out some moral fault but of recognizing that the person feels sorry and is unlikely to do the same thing again. A belief in determinism/impossibilism might undercut our retributive attitudes, but that would be fine: Understanding problems and dealing with them would be better without all the righteous anger.

Of course, these fascinating speculations are only relevant if you are a hard determinist or hard impossibilist. If you're a libertarian, you agree that contra-causal freedom is a necessary condition of people being responsible, but believe we have that freedom. If you're a compatibilist, you believe that contra-causal freedom is irrelevant to responsibility and that our normal practices hold whether or not we have such freedom.

Definitions

(Terms are defined in the order in which they appeared in the text.)

1. CONTRA-CAUSAL FREEDOM/FREE WILL: The idea that (at least some) human choices are not governed by causal laws.
2. DETERMINISM: The view that all events, including mental events, are governed by causal laws. (DETERMINIST: One who believes in determinism.)
3. INDETERMINISM: The view that not all events are governed by causal laws. (INDETERMINIST: One who believes in indeterminism.)
4. LIBERTARIANISM: The view that humans have contra-causal freedom. (LIBERTARIAN: One who believes in libertarianism.)
5. FREEDOM OF ACTION: The ability or opportunity to perform whatever physical actions one may choose to perform.
6. FATALISM: The view that a certain kind of future awaits each of us, no matter what we choose to do.
7. HARD DETERMINISM: The incompatibilist view (see below) that determinism is true and therefore we are never responsible. (HARD DETERMINIST: One who believes in hard determinism.)
8. CAUSAL BREAK: Lack of cause at some point within an apparent causal chain.

9. IMPOSSIBILISM: The view that contra-causal freedom is impossible because conceptually it is incoherent or contradictory. (IMPOSSIBIL-IST: One who believes in impossibilism.)

10. HARD IMPOSSIBILISM: The incompatibilist view (see below) that impossibilism is true and therefore we are never responsible. (HARD IMPOSSIBILIST: One who believes in hard impossibilism.)

11. COMPATIBILISM: The view that responsibility and any related notions of freedom are compatible with determinism or indeterminism; responsibility does not require contra-causal freedom. (COMPATIBIL-IST: One who believes in compatibilism.)

12. INCOMPATIBILISM: The view that responsibility and any related notions of freedom are not compatible with determinism; responsibility does require contra-causal freedom. (INCOMPATIBILIST: One who believes in incompatibilism.)

13. SOFT DETERMINISM: Compatibilism plus a belief in determinism.

14. CLASSICAL COMPATIBILISM: Compatibilist views that see free will as (roughly) equivalent to freedom of action (the ability to do what one desires to do).

15. FIRST-ORDER DESIRES: Desires for something, like food. (Harry Frankfurt)

16. SECOND-ORDER DESIRES: Desires related to our reflections about first-order desires. (Harry Frankfurt)

17. DEEP-SELF COMPATIBILISM: Compatibilist views that require that the desires resulting in free action also be within the control of some "deeper self."

18. CONSEQUENTIALISM: The view that an action being right or wrong depends solely on the consequences of that action. (CONSEQUEN-TIALIST: One who believes in consequentialism.)

19. DEONTOLOGY: The view that an action being right or wrong is based on doing one's duty. (DEONTOLOGIST: One who believes in deontology.)

20. REACTIVE ATTITUDES: Attitudes we naturally take toward the "good or ill will or indifference of others toward us as displayed in their attitudes and action." (Peter Strawson)

21. ILLUSIONISM: The view that having contra-causal freedom is an illusion, but that this illusion is crucial to the well-being of society and should be promoted. (Saul Smilansky)

Questions

(Please explain your answers, making specific reference to relevant passages in the discussion.)

1. Distinguish the following concepts:
   a. Determinism and indeterminism
   b. Determinism and contra-causal freedom
   c. Contra-causal freedom and freedom of action
   d. Determinism and fatalism
2. What is the relationship between determinism and predictability?
3. What is the "paradox of prediction," and how does it relate to "Please Don't Tell Me How the Story Ends"?
4. Critique the following arguments:
   a. "The other day I wanted to play tennis and I did. That proves I have (contra-causal) free will."
   b. "I looked inside myself as I made that choice and I didn't see any cause. Therefore, it was a (contra-causally) free choice."
   c. "Our choices sometimes make a difference to what happens in our lives. Therefore, sometimes we are contra-causally free."
5. What is the possible conflict between claiming that God is omniscient and that human beings have contra-causal freedom?
6. Consider the following characterization of libertarianism:

   The libertarian believes in the following propositions:
   i. Contra-causal freedom is conceptually coherent and would be a desirable thing to have.
   ii. Contra-causal freedom would give us moral responsibility.
   iii. We have contra-causal freedom.
   iv. (Therefore) We are morally responsible for our choices.
      a. Someone who accepted i and ii but denied iii would likely be a _____?
      b. Someone who denied ii would likely be a _____?
      c. Someone who denied i would likely be a _____?
7. What does the "hard" in hard determinism and hard impossibilism refer to?
8. "If we had free will, we'd be doing something different every minute and acting crazy half the time. So we clearly don't have free will." What would a libertarian say about this argument?

9. What is a "causal break"? Why does free will seem to imply a causal break somewhere within the self?

10. Why do some philosophers claim that contra-causal freedom is an impossible idea?

11. How do libertarians respond to the impossibilist argument? Do you agree with their response?

12. What in general is the compatibilist position regarding freedom and responsibility?

13. "The 'freedom' or 'free will' necessary for responsibility is just freedom of action." What criticisms have been raised against this claim?

14. Describe Harry Frankfurt's compatibilist account.

15. What criticism does Susan Wolf make against Frankfurt's account? What change does she think is necessary to make such an account acceptable?

16. What is the problem for someone who believes in the justice of divine punishment and holds a compatibilist account of responsibility?

17. "Even if people are determined and not responsible, society is still entitled to punish wrongdoers." What could be said in support of this position?

18. How might consequentialists and deontologists differ on their views of punishment in the absence of contra-causal freedom?

19. Explain Strawson's account of the reactive attitudes and their relationship to determinism.

20. "If people came to believe they didn't have (contra-causal) free will, it would have terrible consequences for society." Discuss how Smilansky and Pereboom would react to this statement.

Notes

Do We Have Contra-Causal Freedom?

"Potential causes of our choices. . . ." and "famous experiments of Benjamin Libet. . . ." Shaun Nichols. *Great Philosophical Debates: Free Will and Determinism.* Chantilly, VA: The Teaching Company, 2008. Transcript, Part 2, Lectures 14 and 15.

Freedom As Compatible With Responsibility

"The Stoic philosopher Chrysippus (280–206 BCE) argued. . . ." For example, see the selection by Aulus Gellius, in Part 1 of *Voices of Ancient Philosophy*. By Julia Annas. New York: Oxford University Press, 2001.

"In the modern period, Thomas Hobbes, a determinist, argued. . . ." Thomas Hobbes. *The Questions Concerning Liberty, Necessity and Chance*, 1656.

"Along the same lines, David Hume thought that. . . ." David Hume. *An Inquiry Concerning Human Understanding.* Section 8. 1748.

"Walter T. Stace says. . . ." Walter Stace. *Religion and the Modern Mind.* New York: HarperCollins, 1952.

"One of the most influential of these accounts was developed by Harry Frankfurt." Harry Frankfurt. "Freedom of the Will and the Concept of a Person." *Journal of Philosophy*, 68/1 (1971). Reprinted in Gary Watson, ed. *Free Will,* 2nd ed.). New York: Oxford University Press, 2011.

"Susan Wolf calls Frankfurt's and other similar accounts. . . ." Susan Wolf, "Sanity and the Metaphysics of Responsibility," from *Responsibility, Character and the Emotions* (1987), 46–62. Copyright © Cambridge University Press. Reprinted in Watson.

Holding People Responsible

"The Essenes, a Jewish sect that existed around the time of Jesus. . . ." Shaun Nichols. *Great Philosophical Debates: Free Will and Determinism.* Part 1, Lecture 3.

"An interesting and very influential take on this issue comes from Peter Strawson. . . ." Peter Strawson. "Freedom and Resentment" *Proceedings of the British Academy*, 48 (1962), 1–25. Reprinted in Watson.

"Saul Smilansky, who holds an impossibilist position. . . ." Saul Smilansky. "From Nature to Illusion." *Proceedings of the Aristotelian Society* 101 (2001): 71–95. Reprinted in *The Philosophy of Free Will: Essential Readings from the Contemporary Debates.* Eds. Paul Russell and Oisín Deery. New York: Oxford University Press, 2013.

"Derek Pereboom agrees with Smilansky. . . ." Derek Pereboom. "Optimistic Skepticism about Free Will" in Paul Russell and Oisín Deery (eds.). *The Philosophy of Free Will: Essential Readings from the Contemporary Debates.* New York: Oxford University Press, 2013.

MATERIALS

Anthologies

Kane, Robert (ed.). *The Oxford Handbook of Free Will*. New York: Oxford University Press, 2002.

Pereboom, Derek (ed.). *Free Will*. Indianapolis: Hackett Publishing Company, 1997.

Russell, Paul, and Deery, Oisín (eds.). *The Philosophy of Free Will: Essential Readings from the Contemporary Debates*. New York: Oxford University Press, 2013.

Watson, Gary (ed.). *Free Will*, 2nd edition. New York: Oxford University Press, 2011.

(The Russell and Watson texts are the most up-to-date collections of articles and together cover the major contemporary authors covered in our discussion. The Pereboom text includes some historical readings that the others do not. Both Kane and Russell include some related scientific articles, and the Kane text also has articles on divine foreknowledge and free will and on fatalism.)

Secondary Sources

Nichols, Shaun. *Great Philosophical Debates: Free Will and Determinism*. Chantilly, VA: The Teaching Company, 2008. A delightful course in audio or video format surveying philosophical, scientific and theological issues in the free will debate.

Pink, Thomas. *Free Will: A Very Short Introduction*. Oxford: Oxford University Press, 2004. A short, readable introduction to the philosophical free will debate that becomes an argument for libertarianism.

Van Inwagen, Peter. *An Essay on Free Will*. Cambridge: Cambridge University Press, 2017.

CHAPTER 5

God and Suffering
Fiction

READING 1: The Vision

PREVIEW

In this story, a woman having recurring visions of an other-worldly being must decide if the visions are hallucinations or reflect a higher reality. As you read the story, ask yourself

* *What would have been your reaction to such a vision? What would your reasoning have been?*
* *Is there anything else you might have done to determine whether or not the vision was real?*

The first time I saw it, I had no idea what it was or what it would become. It was just a brilliant shimmering of light hovering over the lawn of the small park. I nudged the old man sitting next to me on the bench.

"What is that?" I asked him excitedly.

"What's what?"

"The light—right there in front of us."

He looked in the direction I pointed and shook his head. Then he turned and looked at me suspiciously. Perhaps he was wondering if I was one of the crazy ones. In the days to come, I would often wonder the same thing myself.

But I wasn't worried that first time. Whatever I saw was gone almost at once. "Just a trick of the light," I told the old man, to reassure him.

The thing appeared again, a few days later. First, I heard a kind of humming sound, soft and sweet; the sound of it filled me with an inexplicable feeling of joy. I looked, and there was the light again, only more brilliant now, richer and deeper. I stood there for a time, caught up in its beauty. Then common sense intruded, and I began to feel anxious. What was happening? This didn't make any sense.

The third time the light appeared, I was making my way through a rush-hour crowd. The light was just overhead, and I stopped to look up, barely conscious of the people bumping into me. Within the light was an image of a woman's face.

"Who are you?" I said aloud.

"A friend. Don't be afraid."

The voice that answered was like the humming I'd heard earlier, only pitched higher. It was as if some wind instrument were doing a perfect imitation of human speech.

"What do you want?" I asked.

"To help you."

And then she was gone.

As I lowered my head, I saw the crowd staring at me. Some faces were smirking, some quizzical, and some frightened, but all were looking at me as if I were crazy. Suddenly I was terrified.

I pleaded my way into my doctor's office the next morning. She tried to be reassuring, but I could see she was worried. She referred me to a psychiatrist who interviewed me and then referred me to a neurologist who scheduled a battery of tests.

Sitting in my apartment on the evening before the tests, I was a nervous wreck. From what I could gather from the doctors, either I had a brain tumor or I was going crazy, and I didn't know which was worse. I was trying not to think about any of it when the light appeared again.

"No," I moaned.

I looked down, pressing my hands over my eyes, to blot out the sight of it.

"Don't be frightened," said the voice.

"Go away. You're not real."

"I am real."

"You're a hallucination."

"I'm not."

The voice was soft and patient, like that of a kind parent confronting a contrary child. Something in me wanted so badly to give in to the voice. But I couldn't let myself. This whole thing was crazy.

"You are a hallucination," I said, insistently. "There's something wrong with my brain, and it's making you up. They're going to give me tests. They'll find out what's wrong. I'm going to get better."

There was a slight rippling of notes, like the imitation of soft laughter. "I think you will get better," said the voice. "But not the way you think."

The tests at the hospital took most of a day. The light appeared twice, just briefly.

"I won't stay," said the voice, the second time. "I just wanted to be here during the tests. That way, when nothing shows up, you'll know I'm real."

Nothing did show up on the tests. The neurologist sent me back to the psychiatrist.

"Your hallucination seems to have a sense of humor, Ms. Okafor," said the psychiatrist. "What she obviously doesn't have is a degree in psychiatry. The fact that nothing shows up on those tests you had doesn't mean she isn't coming from your brain. When we say we can't find an organic cause, we're talking about lesions and tumors. We're certainly not saying that there's nothing chemical going on in there."

"You think that's what it is?" I asked. "Something chemical?"

"The mind is all chemical."

"But what specifically is wrong with me?"

"If you want a name," he said, "the one I gave your insurance company is 'atypical psychosis.' But that's just a fancy way of saying that we can't find an organic cause and that your hallucinations don't fit some standard grouping of symptoms. What you really want to know is whether we can treat this. The answer is yes. There are a whole range of antipsychotics that can be effective with hallucinations. We'll start with Haldol."

"Just make this thing stop."

"We will."

We talked about dosage, what to expect, what to watch out for. Some of the possible side effects sounded scary, but none could be as scary as losing my mind. When I left the psychiatrist's office, I filled the prescription at the first pharmacy I could find, then rushed home. In the kitchen I began filling a glass with the six ounces of water I'd been told to take with the pill.

"Don't," said the voice, somewhere behind me. "Please, don't."

Somehow I'd known that I'd hear the voice just then. I felt myself grow panicky. I had a sudden, vivid sense that I was fighting for my sanity.

I slapped the water glass down on the drainboard and reached for the plastic pill container.

"Don't, " said the voice, urgently. "Those pills will cut you off from me."

"They're going to make me well," I said, struggling with the childproof lid.

"They're not going to make you well. They're only going to deaden your mind and your feelings. They're going to change you into something you don't want to be."

"I won't listen to you," I said, my panic growing worse with each unsuccessful tug at the container top.

"Do you know those street people with the vacant eyes? Do you want to be like them?"

"Shut up!" I yelled.

Suddenly the top broke loose, and pills went bouncing like small marbles over the kitchen floor. I dropped to my knees, grabbed a pill, and pushed it toward my mouth.

"Don't, Kayla," said the voice. "The pills will just make you a zombie."

What the voice was saying was just close enough to the worst of the side-effect warnings to make me hesitate. I stared at the pills for a moment, afraid to take them, afraid not to. There was a small "H" carved into the white pill, and the question "hell or help," "hell or help" started running through my mind. My hand was shaking with indecision, and suddenly the fear and frustration of the last few days came bursting out of me in sobs.

"I don't know what to do," I cried. "I don't know what's happening to me. I'm so scared."

I was on my knees on the floor, bent forward, my arms pressing against my chest as if I were trying to keep myself from coming apart. Gradually, over the sound of my tears, I began to hear the voice saying, "It's all right," over and over, softly, almost hypnotically. And then light seemed to fold itself around me and the panic subsided and the tears stopped and suddenly my whole being was flooded with joy. I felt peaceful and safe to the very core of myself, as if I had suddenly come home—not to any home I had ever known, but to some home I had only dreamed of having. I let my body fall gently sideways, so that I was sitting on the floor, leaning against the kitchen counter. I closed my eyes, giving myself up to all those wonderful feelings.

"Feeling better?" asked the voice.

I laughed. "Yes."

Somewhere in my mind, hovering above all the joy, was the thought: *No matter how good you feel, this is still crazy, and you're going to have to deal with it; you're going to have to take those pills.* But for the moment the thought was distant and of no effect.

I opened my eyes. The light was now a few feet away, suspended between ceiling and floor. For the first time I was calm enough to study it: The light was translucent, blurring the objects behind it, like a bright piece of lightly frosted glass. The light itself was white, but with hundreds of flecks of color that would blink and disappear, to be replaced by others; it was like a huge piece of crystal that was turning minutely back and forth, reflecting a light source from somewhere else. And within the translucency was that face, a mirage within a mirage. It was the kindest, most beautiful face I had ever seen.

"I feel so good," I said, "I almost wish you were real."

"I am real, Kayla."

"What are you supposed to be? God? An angel? The Virgin Mary?"

"No, nothing like that. I'm a physical thing, just like you are."

"We sure don't look much alike."

"There are different kinds of physical things. Matter and energy for one. Energy tends toward joy and continuation. Matter tends toward suffering and decay."

"You mean, you're energy, and I'm matter?"

"Let's just say that you're more matter than I am."

"I don't get it. Do you mean, you're from a different planet or dimension or something?"

"We are those who have evolved and survived. We're here to help you do the same."

Much to my surprise and embarrassment, I let out a huge yawn. I quickly covered my mouth.

"I'm sorry," I said. "Suddenly I feel so sleepy. Like I've been drugged."

"You're exhausted. You need sleep. You'd better get yourself to bed. You'll be sore in the morning if you sleep there."

"Carry me," I asked, feeling suddenly childlike.

The face smiled. "I'd like to do that. But it is forbidden. I would do you great harm if I touched your body."

"I don't understand. I felt you touch me before. I mean. . . ."

"I was only touching your spirit. Listen, now, before you fall asleep. Tomorrow, when you wake, you will begin to doubt again. All I ask is that you hold off taking the pills awhile longer. Hear me out. Give yourself a chance to believe. For your own sake. When you doubt, just remember how you felt tonight. The truth is in the feeling."

I almost took the pills the next day, and the next, and the next. But so far I have not. It is the feeling that holds me back. I only experience the rapture when the light actually enfolds me, but the memory of it is with me constantly, along with a residue of joy. I ask myself: How can anything be crazy that feels so wonderful?

Not that I don't doubt and question and even argue: I spend most of our time together trying to make sense of what is happening; I'm still not sure I have.

"Why are you appearing to me?" I asked the woman in the light.

"We are trying to appear to many."

"Then why haven't I heard about other people seeing you?"

"Most don't see us. They are too closed to see anything. Others see a little and grow frightened and turn away. Still others see only what they want to see. You are one of the few to whom I appear as I am."

"But why me? I'm not particularly smart or good."

"Because of your longing. It opens you to the truth. And your simplicity, which allows you to receive it."

"Why are you here?"

"To help you."

"Help me what?"

"Survive," she said. "When the body dies, those who are matter die with it; those who have become energy, spirit, go on. Whole races have survived and continued their existence in the dimension of energy; others have almost totally died out. The human race is headed for virtual extinction. The few who have become energy are stragglers in the other dimension, grieving for their race. They have begged us who have numbers to try to make contact. So we are trying. I hope good will come of it. I fear not."

It all sounds so strange, and I still feel confused. Sometimes I come back to the point of thinking: This is all nonsense, you are sick. But then the light folds around me, and I feel the rapture, and nothing else matters.

The voice says that I must give up obsessive rationality, with its constant questionings and doubts. She says that I must give myself up to feeling, for it is feeling that will show me the truth. I am determined to try.

I still do not know if this is real or unreal, if I am sane or crazy. All I know, and need to know, is one thing:

I am happy.

LET'S REVIEW

* *What questions is the narrator asking the vision? What answers does the vision give? Do those answers sound reasonable to you?*
* *Would your reactions be similar to those of the narrator at this point?*

*****

Something has gone terribly wrong.

It did not happen all at once, but little by little.

The woman in the light told me that I must change my life, and I gave myself up to her charge. She had me make changes in my diet, and she gave me a series of physical and spiritual exercises. She was so sweet as she guided me, like a good mother who knows her child has some hard work to do and wants to spare the child any unnecessary discomfort. Most of the changes weren't so bad, and I was helped by her presence, by the rush of joy she sometimes gave me, and by the knowledge that I was transforming myself to a higher level of being.

But then the exercises became more and more uncomfortable, and one day l told her I didn't want to do one of the exercises any more. For the first time the light suddenly darkened, and the face became angry. I was so shocked at the sight that I couldn't move. Then the light brightened, and the face softened:

"I'm sorry," said the voice. "Sometimes you try me."

I was to begin to see that anger more often. One day one of the exercises drew some blood and I stopped, feeling faint. As I put my hand over the small cut and averted my eyes, I saw that the light was nearly black and the face inside it terrible.

"Continue!" she screamed.

"No," I said. "Stop, please. You're frightening me."

"Good," she yelled. "You're too slow, too cowardly. If I must frighten you, then I will. Don't you understand? The Day is almost upon us. If you're not ready, you will die!"

"What day?"

The light turned from dark crystal to a twilight gray. The face inside was no longer angry but sad.

"I did not mean to tell you today," said the voice. "But perhaps it is just as well. I could not have put it off much longer."

"What day?" I asked again.

"The Day the Earth Will End."

"What? You never told me that."

"The Council just decided."

"What council?"

"They have grown impatient. Humans have become a blot on the universe: On the Day, the sky will grow red with an angry light, and the light will descend and touch the Earth, and all will be destroyed. Don't you see? You must be ready when the Day comes or you will be destroyed with the others."

"When?"

"The exact day hasn't been decided. A month, two months, a year . . . soon."

"I don't understand this. I'm scared. Please hold me."

"Not now. Joy will just make you lazy. You must work."

I tried to work as hard as she wanted, I really did. But I'm not good at pain, and the fear I was feeling seemed to inhibit me more than push me. Doubts began to come back, stronger now than before, and a voice in my head that kept growing louder was saying, This is all crazy after all; you must stop it, you know that; you must take the pills before this sickness destroys you.

One night I woke up from a recurrent nightmare in which the woman in the light was having me mutilate myself. I was shaking with fright, and that voice in my head was saying, Take the pills, take the pills. I stumbled out of bed, filled a glass of water, and opened the pill container.

"Don't, please, don't," said the voice, as I knew it would.

"Yes," I said, and gulped down a pill. I turned to face the light. "This has turned into a nightmare. I want it to stop."

I expected anger. Instead the face was sad.

"You won't see me anymore," said the voice. "That pill will close your mind. I'm sorry. I had such hope that I could save you."

The light disappeared.

I'm better now. The pills aren't what I was afraid they'd be. I do sleep more, and I feel groggy sometimes, and I guess I feel as if my body and mind move a little more slowly than they used to. But overall I feel okay, and I don't see those visions anymore.

Yet sometimes—not often, just once in awhile—when I'm at home at night, staring out the window at the peace of the star-studded darkness, I imagine that the sky is beginning to glow, and as it becomes a deeper and deeper red, I catch a faint odor of something beginning to burn.

And I am afraid.

Questions

1. a. Give two different explanations for what is happening to the narrator in "The Vision."
   b. Would there be some decisive way to determine which of the two explanations is correct?
2. The vision says that the truth is in the feeling. In what way does feeling guide the narrator in the first part of the story? In the second part of the story?
3. How would you have reacted if you'd been in the narrator's place?

READING 2: Surprise! It's Judgment Day

PREVIEW

In this story, a philosopher, surprised to find himself in an afterlife, complains to God about the irrationality of religion and about the existence of so much suffering in the world. As you read, ask yourself:

* *What are the traditional arguments for God's existence that the philosopher attacks? Do any of them sound familiar?*
* *What are the philosopher's complaints about the suffering in the world? How does God answer him?*

The stage suggests a cloud bank. Across the length of the stage is a high wall that appears to be of white brick. In the center of the wall is a pair of golden doors which are closed. Off to the right is a golden throne. Seated on the throne is a figure with white hair and beard. He is wearing a jeweled crown, and his legs are crossed beneath a thick white robe.

Martin enters from the left, rubbing his eyes. He is dressed in a white hospital gown.

MARTIN:	Well, I'll be damned. So, the fairy tales were true, after all.
GOD:	In a sense.

Martin glances toward the bearded figure and groans.

MARTIN:	Go ahead. Tell me you're Saint Peter and make my day.
GOD (*laughing*):	No. I gave him the day off.
MARTIN:	You're not God?
GOD:	I am.
MARTIN:	So much for all the theologians' warnings against anthropomorphism.
GOD:	Oh, this is just a momentary form, a matter of convenience. Your convenience, I might add. I could have spoken out of a whirlwind or a burning bush. But I felt I owed you a face-to-face confrontation.
MARTIN:	Confrontation? That suits me just fine. I wouldn't mind getting a word in before I get the fire and brimstone.
GOD:	Fire and brimstone? Let's not go jumping to conclusions, shall we? Tell me, what do you think of all this?
MARTIN:	Regrettable. And, quite frankly, pretty tacky. The cloud, the throne, the beard. Hollywood could have done better. I would have given you more credit.
GOD:	But not much.
MARTIN:	No, not much.
GOD:	Let's just say that I thought this bit of pop religion would put you more at ease. A little joke of mine, though at whose expense I'm not quite sure. But this is not my usual form, I can assure you.

MARTIN: No, you don't exactly look like the Unmoved Mover in that outfit. Saint Thomas Aquinas would have been shocked. Well, now God with a sense of humor. I would have expected you to be more pompous. But no doubt it's gallows humor, and you own the gallows.

GOD: Do you remember how you got here?

MARTIN: Yes, I think so. I remember the car accident. I remember the doctor telling me that I had fractured my skull. I remember being taken into surgery. I suppose the rest of it was like the old joke: I was at death's door and the doctor pulled me through.

GOD: You were quite impressive as you were getting the anesthetic. I believe you muttered some quotation from Robinson Jeffers about there being no harps and habitations beyond the stars. And something from Camus about the benign indifference of the universe. And, oh yes, that line from Socrates: "Eternity is but a single night." As you can see, Professor Martin, eternity is quite well lit.

MARTIN: Go ahead and laugh. I guess you're entitled. But their words have more dignity than yours. Damn it, this shouldn't be true. You know it shouldn't. It defies all reason. A God who displaces humankind from Paradise for exercising an understandable curiosity, who lets himself be crucified to save some, but insists on punishing others eternally, all in the name of some barbaric penal code that He created but claims He must follow—no, it's too absurd.

GOD: What? Are you going to make of me some ranting fundamentalist? It seems you like easy targets.

MARTIN: Are you telling me you're an ecumenicalist? Glimpses of God behind the myths and half-truths of all religions? Well, score one for the liberal theologians. It doesn't matter. Liberalize yourself all you want. Reason says you shouldn't exist.

GOD: Some philosophers have thought otherwise.

MARTIN: Yes. You had some brilliant defenders—once. But now their arguments are merely historical curiosities.

Anselm and Descartes claimed that the definition of a perfect God necessarily implies that He exists. A perfect God lacks nothing and hence does not lack existence. But that line of argument would equally prove the existence of a perfect turtle and a perfect martini. Aquinas, following Aristotle, claimed that reason indicates there must be a First Cause, a First Mover, who created the world, set it in motion, and sustains its existence. But there is nothing obviously false in the idea of a material world that is self-sufficient. You're not going to try to defend those arguments of Anselm and Aquinas, are you?

GOD: No, Professor Martin. Nor will I try to defend the argument that a vast, intricate universe of elegantly formulable laws could not exist without intelligent creation or control. Though I must admit I've always liked that one.

MARTIN: In any case, the issue of design ultimately indicates that a respectable God could not exist: The laws of the universe may be mathematically elegant, but they crush and they kill. No respectable God would allow people to suffer as they do.

LET'S REVIEW

* *There are three arguments for God's existence that Martin alludes to, one having to do with the definition of a perfect God, another with a First Cause, and a third having to do with a world governed by intricate laws. See if you can summarize these arguments. (We'll talk about them in detail in the discussion section.)*
* *What objections does Martin give to those arguments?*

GOD: So. We come to the heart of the matter.

MARTIN: Yes, indeed. As a moral assessment, one must say that if this world is designed, it is the work of a bumbler or a sadist. Which, by the way, are you?

GOD:	Not quite either, I hope.
MARTIN:	But you did design the world?
GOD:	Yes, I did. But look here, Professor Martin. I understand your anger, your impulse toward hyperbole. Still, it is hyperbole. What about my celebrated free will defense? Free will is a great good, a necessary ingredient in the best of all possible worlds. And it would be contradictory for me to give people free will and, at the same time, guarantee that they never use that freedom to cause suffering.
MARTIN:	As you must know, it is not an adequate defense. At most, it would only justify the suffering caused by people. It doesn't apply to the suffering caused by natural events, like diseases, earthquakes, and floods. But, in any case, I don't concede you the free will defense. Freedom costs too much; it has too many victims. Free will isn't worth the suffering.
GOD:	Can you really be so flippant about it? Don't you feel an attraction toward freedom—or at least recognize that another person might? Don't you feel it is an issue about which rational individuals rightly disagree?
MARTIN:	Perhaps. But I still say that freedom isn't worth the suffering. Nonetheless, one still must explain the suffering caused by natural events. If you try to justify it as a punishment for people's misuse of their freedom, then I say that your notion of punishment is barbaric.
GOD:	Well, what about what you have called the "virtue defense"? Virtues are good and a necessary ingredient in the best of all possible worlds. And the idea of virtue in a world without suffering is contradictory. It would be impossible to be courageous where there is no danger, to be generous where it costs nothing, to be sympathetic where no one is hurt.
MARTIN:	Even if I conceded that argument, there doesn't have to be so much suffering.

GOD: What? A couple of teaspoons would have sufficed
                for the grandeur of the drama?

MARTIN: Nevertheless, I don't concede the argument. It
                turns virtue inside out. It makes virtue good in
                itself. But reflection shows that virtue is good only
                as a means—a means to happiness. What is the
                point of courage, generosity, sympathy, if not to al-
                leviate suffering? To create suffering for the sake of
                sympathy is like kicking a man in the shins so you
                can feel sorry for him. It's absurd.

LET'S REVIEW

* God alludes to two "defenses" of (two justifications for) God allowing
  suffering in the world. What are those defenses?
* Why does Martin think the defenses fail?

GOD: So if you had been in my place, you would have. . . .

MARTIN: Made human beings happy. And left them happy.

GOD: But happiness is so bland.

MARTIN: To the outsider perhaps. But to the person who is
                happy, it is sufficient.

GOD: And so you would have created a world without
                virtue?

MARTIN: Yes. A world in which virtue wasn't necessary.

GOD: And the intellectual virtues? You would discard
                them as well? The painful, heroic struggle for
                beauty and knowledge?

MARTIN: Yes, if they must conflict with happiness.

GOD: But they do, do they not? Anyway, if happiness is
                the good, then anything else becomes superfluous.

MARTIN: Yes.

GOD: Many people would view your values with contempt.

MARTIN: Yes, I understand that. One can look back over the
                centuries at, say, the Egyptian pyramids and think:
                This is good; this is where the human race excelled.
                But a closer look reveals the pain of the slaves who

built them, and one should see that this was wrong. One is not entitled to excellence if unwilling people must suffer for it. And, in one way or another, some always do.

GOD: What a utilitarian you are with your emphasis on happiness!

MARTIN: Yes. With slight misgivings, but yes. The utilitarian is right, and you are wrong. And we haven't even mentioned hell yet, though I'm sure that we, or rather I, will be getting to that shortly. Hell is an atrocity beyond debate.

GOD: You really do want me to be a fundamentalist, don't you? There is no hell, Professor Martin. The thought of creating it crossed my mind once, but I never took the idea seriously. There was a kind of Hades, or Limbo, once, but I soon gave it up. No, now there is only Paradise.

MARTIN: Knowing you, that should be fun. Probably morning prayers, cold showers, and occasionally Black Plague to keep us on our toes. But even if it is pleasant, you still have much to answer for. And it is unanswerable. Voltaire, Dostoevsky, and countless others whose views I accept saw that. They wouldn't be put off by your whales and whirlwinds, as Job was. Dostoevsky's Ivan Karamazov was right: Once one child suffers, this is a botched world, and nothing could ever make it right again.

GOD: Voltaire and Dostoevsky are here, by the way.

MARTIN: Ah! I shall enjoy talking with them. Or, if that is not possible, then listening, anyway.

GOD: There would be some difficulty in that. But to get back to the point that you insist on dramatizing: I do take full responsibility for this world that I've created. And I do not believe that I should have created it differently: The struggle for virtue, beauty, and knowledge: That is what I find most admirable. Though I admit that, as an outsider, I am open to the accusation that I lack sympathy. However, I find the world interesting just as it is. I shall continue to insist on the spectacle.

MARTIN: The spectacle—yes. Like some Roman emperor.

GOD: As you will. But you're a utilitarian. You believe in the greatest happiness. Shouldn't the happiness of an infinite God weigh heavily on your scales?

MARTIN: So the struggle goes on forever—for your entertainment.

GOD: Not just mine. Don't forget there are many people who don't accept your values. Perhaps I could justify the world as it is, as a concession to them. In any case, human beings may struggle forever but not each person. An individual struggle that went on forever would lose all meaning and lead to utter despair or boredom. There must be surcease, reward.

MARTIN: But how can you consistently manage that? There's a lovely little paradox that the believers must confront: If freedom and virtue are the ultimate good, and in turn require suffering, then how could heaven be blissful? Or, if somehow God could manage to create freedom and virtue without suffering, then why didn't God omit the suffering in the first place?

GOD: As I've said, the struggle is good, but it cannot go on forever. So the final result is a compromise between my set of values and yours. Professor Martin, the world is not to your liking, and I apologize for that. I could never convince you that this is the best of all possible worlds, and I shall not really try: But all I have taken from you is, in the words of my lesser poets, a drop of time in the sea of eternity. Don't be so hard on me for that. The rest of time is yours.

God flicks his hand, and the golden doors open slowly. Inside, figures in white hospital gowns walk about, slowly and somewhat mechanically. Martin studies them for several moments.

MARTIN:	Their expressions don't change.
GOD:	They always smile of course. Why not? They're happy.
MARTIN:	But there are just people and clouds. Where's the beauty of it?
GOD:	In the eye of the beholder. Or, better, in the mind, since they don't look at much. I could create changing landscapes, I suppose, fill the surroundings with Raphaels and Donatellos, have Mozart and Beethoven played, hand them Plato and Shakespeare. But it would not make any difference. At most, it would serve as a sop to my conscience, and I prefer to know what I do: They're perfectly happy, just as they are, and anything else would be extraneous, irrelevant. They're happy. Just as you shall be in a moment.
MARTIN:	They're happy?
GOD:	Yes.
MARTIN:	And I shall join them?
GOD:	Yes.
MARTIN:	Wait a moment.
GOD:	I don't see the point. We've reached our impasse. I felt that I owed you a chance to have your say and that I owed you an explanation—even if you did not find it satisfactory.
MARTIN:	It looks like death in there.
GOD:	In a sense it is, of course. But really, our differences aside, there is not much else one can do with people forever. Would you rather I extinguished you?
MARTIN:	No!
GOD:	Well; then. By the way, I should tell you that I've enjoyed our talk. I really have. But there are others I must see: It is time for you to go inside now.
MARTIN:	No, wait!

Martin turns toward God with a panicked, pleading gesture. God points at Martin. Martin's body freezes for a moment, then releases, his arms falling to his sides. On Martin's face is an expression that seems genuinely happy but unchanging.

GOD:	Enter, Martin. Enter.

Martin turns and slowly walks through the gates, which close behind him. God stares thoughtfully toward the gates, shaking his head slightly: A young girl, Katherine, enters from stage left. She, too, is wearing a hospital gown. Upon seeing her, God quickly smooths his beard and adopts a very dignified posture. Then he smiles at her.

KATHERINE:	Oh, Father, is that you?
GOD:	Yes, Katherine.
KATHERINE:	Oh, Father, you are just as I always imagined you. Then you heard my prayer?
GOD:	I always hear.
KATHERINE:	And you forgave me?
GOD:	Yes.
KATHERINE:	Will I live in heaven?
GOD:	Yes, my child. Heaven is yours.

At a gesture from God, the gates open again. Martin can be seen walking among the people inside.

KATHERINE:	Oh, Father, they are all so happy! Oh, thank you, Father, thank you.
GOD:	Bless you, my child.

Katherine rushes toward the gates. Just before she reaches them, God flicks his hand, and she adopts the mechanical walk of the others. The gates close. God lowers his head a bit, as if tired and a little disgusted. He looks up.

GOD:	That seems to be all for now. Thank goodness! This place depresses me so.

God gets down from the throne and takes a couple of steps to the right. He stops and removes the crown, tossing it on the seat of the throne, where it lands with a clatter. He exits to the right, unbuttoning his robe.

Questions

1. In "Surprise! It's Judgment Day," what complaints is Martin bringing against God?
2. Martin mentions three traditional arguments for the existence of God. Describe those arguments. What objections are given to those arguments?

3. God presents in His defense what are called the "free will defense" and the "virtue defense." Explain these two defenses.

4. Does Martin change his viewpoint at the end of the story? If so, how and why?

5. Would you say that Martin is proved wrong at the end of the story? Why or why not?

6. God doesn't seem to like the heaven He created? Why doesn't He like it, and why did He create it the way He did?

7. Why do you think Katherine is happy with heaven as it is?

Discussion

PREVIEW

At the end of this discussion, you should be familiar with:
* *arguments for and against the claim that religious experiences are (at least sometimes) true experiences of some objective reality;*
* *the following arguments for the existence of God and objections to those arguments:*
  – *the ontological/definitional arguments;*
  – *the cosmological/First Cause arguments;*
  – *the teleological/design arguments.*
* *the "problem of suffering";*
* *the problems with the following defenses of suffering:*
  – *human beings couldn't be happy all the time;*
  – *without a contrast, you couldn't know what happiness was;*
  – *the "free will defense";*
  – *the "virtue defense."*
* *William Clifford's view of when a belief is rationally (and morally) justified and William James's disagreement with Clifford;*
* *Pascal's "wager argument" and objections to it;*
* *Kierkegaard's view of Christianity and of faith in God;*
* *the meaning of terms listed in Definitions (which are also marked in bold in the discussion).*

Religious Experience

One reason for belief in God is religious experience, either experience reported by others or experience one has oneself. Such experiences range from dramatic visions to a gentle sense of presence. In some religious groups, everyone claims to have had such experiences.

In "The Vision," the narrator has rather dramatic visions. The voice she hears claims that the vision is real, but the narrator isn't sure, and all the doctors immediately assume the vision is a symptom of illness.

How are we to judge mystical experiences?

What we want to know is this: Are particular religious experiences **veridical**—that is, true experiences of some objective reality (as with everyday perceptions of cars and trees and people); or are they nonveridical—that is, merely subjective (as with dreams and fantasies)?

In trying to decide such an issue, we normally reason by analogy. That is, we consider cases of perception in which we agree on what is and isn't veridical, and we determine what criteria we use to judge what is or isn't veridical in those cases. We then apply those same criteria to the perception in question.

What are our everyday criteria for the veridicality of perception? It seems that veridicality here has to do with what a normal observer would/ could perceive under certain conditions. The concept of normality in this context is very tricky. We want to set some limits on the kinds of persons whose testimony we will accept. For instance, on the one hand, if someone is accusing an auto body shop of painting a new fender the wrong color, obviously we don't want the testimony of a color blind person to be admitted as evidence. On the other hand, we don't want to beg the question (assume the truth of what's at issue) by simply dismissing anyone who doesn't see it a certain way as "not normal." The criteria for what is normal should be established independently of what is at issue.

Given reasonable criteria for "normal," we judge perceptions to be veridical if normal people are having those perceptions and if others would have those same perceptions in similar circumstances. If a family reports a spaceship parked in the backyard but no one else who comes to visit can see it, that report isn't going to be judged as veridical.

How does religious experience fare under our normal criteria of veridicality? The results are at best ambiguous. The really dramatic religious visions are such isolated occurrences that they would get little support from our normal criteria of veridicality. If we consider the totality of religious experience from the very dramatic to the very subtle ("I just sense God's presence"), then the case for veridicality looks better. But then there is the problem of differences in the content of the experiences: a Native American tribe may have one sort of experience, a particular Christian sect another, and Buddhists yet another.

If these are veridical experiences of the Divine, why are they so different and often contradictory? One could possibly infer from this that religious experiences are confused perceptions of some divine reality whose nature can only be surmised. But at the very best this would be support for the vaguest of religious beliefs, ones that wouldn't satisfy many believers.

Complicating any assessment of divine reality are the awful visions and voices that, for instance, schizophrenics experience. The tendency these days is to think of positive religious experiences as possibly veridical and negative religious experiences as definitely nonveridical, as mental illness. (The narrator in "The Vision" is much less inclined to think of the vision as veridical when it becomes negative.) But unless one begs the question by assuming in advance that a certain kind of God does exist (in which case religious experience isn't really being used as evidence for the existence of God at all), it's hard to see what grounds there would be for not including negative visions in the pool of religious experience. If they are included, the increased variety we get from their addition either renders more doubtful the veridicality of religious experience or renders more ambiguous the nature of the Divine.

One intriguing aspect of many supernatural beliefs is their inclusion within them of an explanation for why they don't satisfy the normal criteria of rationality or veridicality. For instance:

DOUBTER: "I can't find God."
BELIEVER: "That's because you don't really want to."
DOUBTER: "I feel like I want to."
BELIEVER: "No. The fact that you don't see Him shows that you don't really want to."

"The Vision" contains some of this rejection of the normal criteria of veridicality. The narrator is told to give up "obsessive rationality with its constant questionings and doubts." When the narrator asks why he hasn't heard of other people seeing the vision, he is told that most people

> . . . are too closed to see anything. Others see a little and grow frightened and turn away. Still others see only what they want to see. You are one of the few to whom I appear as I am."
>
> "But why me? I'm not particularly smart or good."
>
> "Because of your longing. It opens you to the truth. And your simplicity, which allows you to receive it."

To some, such reasoning seems a good explanation for why something that doesn't meet our normal criteria for judging truth could still be true. To others, such reasoning seems a determined effort to avoid seeing the truth, turning the claim of veridical religious experience into the fallacy of impervious hypothesis and making it an hypothesis protected against any conceivable counter-evidence.

LET'S REVIEW

* What does it mean to say an experience is "veridical"? What are our normal criteria of veridicality?

* In what ways do religious experiences meet or not meet these criteria?

* What complications result from the variety of religious experience? From the existence of horrific "religious" experiences?

Traditional Arguments for the Existence of God

Assessing Arguments for God's Existence

In "Surprise! It's Judgment Day," Martin dismisses as mere "historical curiosities" three famous arguments for the existence of God: the ontological, the cosmological, and the teleological. Even if Martin's assessment were correct, the arguments would be worth looking at for the important role they have played in philosophy. In fact, new advances in logic and science have led philosophers of religion and some scientists to attempt reformulations of those arguments. So while the traditional arguments may not have quite the intellectual force they once did, they are still very much alive.

We need to keep a few points in mind as we consider these and other arguments for the existence of God. If a particular argument for the existence of God fails, that doesn't prove the nonexistence of God. The failure of one argument doesn't even constitute *some* evidence against the existence of God. That one argument doesn't work doesn't mean there aren't others around that do. It is true that *if* all the arguments for the existence of God failed (and that's a huge "if"), one might begin to wonder about the rationality of believing in God. But even at that there are some who say that arguments for the existence of God are beside the point (and maybe even harmful to the religious spirit); that belief in God is a matter of faith, not reason. This position falls under the general label of "fideism," which we shall encounter toward the end of our discussion.

If you are attracted to some argument for the existence of God, it's important to be clear about what the argument does and doesn't prove. I once overheard a Roman Catholic family member support his faith by saying that something had to create the world—alluding to the cosmological or First Cause argument. It got me thinking about how long the chain of reasoning would be from "Something had to create the world" to "There exists a God who is omnipotent (all-powerful), omniscient (all knowing) and perfectly good" and then to all the intricacies of Roman Catholic (or any other) theology. The point is not that you can't get there, but only that you are a long way from a specific theology even if you accept one of the traditional arguments.

The Ontological/Definitional Argument

The **ontological (definitional) argument** (which derives its name from the Greek word for "being") is probably the least convincing of the traditional arguments for the existence of God but also the most ingenious. It claims that the actual existence of God can be proved simply from the concept or definition of God. Once you see what "God" means, you can see there must be such a being.

The ontological argument is unique among the arguments for the existence of God in that it is an ***a priori* argument**. An *a priori* argument is an argument that does not depend on experience of how the world is; this is in contrast to an ***a posteriori* argument** which does use premises about how the world is. *A priori* arguments do presuppose that one has a language, but once the concepts are in place, no reference to experience is needed. "1 and 1; therefore 2" is an *a priori* argument. You need to know the mathematical concepts, but you don't have to count things in the world to judge if it's sound. The ontological argument is also a deductive argument. If the premises are true, then the conclusion must be true. The other arguments for the existence of God are inductive, lending the conclusion a high degree of probability at best.

If the ontological argument is successful, it proves the existence of a "perfect" or "greatest conceivable" being. It seems that such terms would necessarily imply omnipotence, omniscience, and perfect goodness—characteristics attributed to God in many traditional monotheistic religions. In contrast, as we have noted, proving a First Cause would require supplementary arguments to get to the conclusion that such a being is omnipotent, omniscient, and perfectly good.

The first philosopher to propose the ontological argument seems to have been Anselm of Canterbury (later made Saint Anselm) in the eleventh century. Anselm quotes Psalm 14:1 that "The fool hath said in his heart there is no God," and he goes on to argue that

> even the fool is convinced that something exists in the understanding, at least, than which nothing greater can be conceived. For, when he hears of this, he understands it. And whatever is understood, exists in the understanding. And assuredly that, than which nothing greater can be conceived, cannot exist in the understanding alone. For, suppose it exists in the understanding alone: then it can be conceived to exist in reality; which is greater.
>
> Therefore, if that, than which nothing greater can be conceived, exists in the understanding alone, the very being, than which nothing greater can be conceived, is one, than which a greater can be conceived. But obviously this is impossible. Hence, there is no doubt that there exists a being, than which nothing greater can be conceived, and it exists both in the understanding and in reality.

We can summarize his argument as follows:

1. We have an understanding of God as the greatest conceivable being (as "that than which a greater cannot be conceived").
2. Suppose God exists only "in the understanding" (does not exist in reality).
3. In that case, there would be a greater conceivable being, one who exists both in the understanding and in reality.
4. But this contradicts the idea that God is the greatest conceivable being.
5. Therefore, God must exist both in the understanding and in reality.

Anselm's argument is a type of argument called ***reductio ad absurdum*** (or **reductio** for short)—literally, "reducing an argument to absurdity." In this form of argument, you start off with a statement and derive a contradiction from that statement, thereby showing that the original statement is false. In this case, Anselm is claiming that the statement "God does not exist" implies a contradiction; therefore, the statement "God exists" is necessarily true.

The contradiction is something like this: To believe that God does not exist is to believe that the greatest conceivable being, which must exist in the understanding and in reality, exists only in the understanding and not in reality.

Another version of the ontological argument was used by Descartes in the seventeenth century in his attack on skepticism. Descartes's formulation goes roughly as follows:

1. The concept of God is that of a perfect being.
2. A perfect being lacks no perfections.
3. Existence is a perfection.
4. (Therefore) God does not lack existence; God exists.

When confronted with these proofs, some people are inclined to ask: Where did Anselm or Descartes get their definitions of God? We'll look more carefully at those definitions, but initially they don't seem controversial. A number of traditions claim the existence of a God who is perfect in power, knowledge, and goodness; to say that such a God is defined as the "greatest conceivable being" seems reasonable. Also, when one wonders about the existence of something, the source of the idea is not generally at issue. One could invent the concept of a "drog" ("a doglike creature that hops like a frog") and ask whether such a thing exists. There would seem to be nothing questionable about such an inquiry.

Anselm's and Descartes's contemporaries thought that the ontological argument could be used to prove the existence of many types of perfect beings and hence must be fallacious. One of Anselm's contemporaries, Gaunilo, claimed that the same line of reasoning would prove that the greatest conceivable island must exist because any island that existed only in the understanding and not in reality wouldn't be the greatest conceivable island. Descartes's contemporaries made a similar argument. A perfect island must exist because if it didn't exist it wouldn't be perfect. A rejoinder to these counterarguments might be that a perfect island or a greatest conceivable island would be a contradiction in terms because by definition such a thing would be limited, mindless, and hence imperfect. The argument, it might be claimed, works only for God.

One might argue that Descartes's proof equally shows that God does not exist, since He could not lack nonexistence. But the word "perfection" supposedly excludes such "attributes" as nonthinkingness, nongoodness, and nonexistence.

What seems to be the decisive objection to the ontological argument was first formulated by Immanuel Kant in the late eighteenth century. The objection goes somewhat as follows: There is a radical difference between a statement about a concept and a statement about existence. To introduce a concept is to introduce a kind of (mental) picture. To claim existence is to claim that there is something in the world that has the characteristics portrayed in that picture. Here is how Kant put it:

> Now, if I take the subject (God) with all its predicates (omnipotence being one), and say, *God is*, or *There is a God*, I add no new predicate to the conception of God, I merely posit or affirm the existence of the subject with all its predicates—I posit the *object* in relation to my conception. The content of both is the same; and there is no addition made to the *conception*, which expresses merely the possibility of the object, by my cogitating the object—in the expression, it *is*—as absolutely given or existing.

According to this line of reasoning, introducing a concept is uncontroversial only because it differs from an existential claim. Descartes (like Anselm) introduces a concept of God that implicitly includes a claim of existence, and this concept is not uncontroversial. If such a step were permissible, then anything could be defined into existence. I could introduce the concept of an "exista-unicorn" ("a horse-like figure with a horn and with existence"). I could then derive the existence of the unicorn from that definition. The criticism here is not that Descartes violates a logical convention. Rather, it is that if he violates this convention, then he is required to do something not normally required of someone introducing a concept: He must prove the existence of the thing before his definition is acceptable. This, of course, he does not do.

In Anselm's argument, things are a little trickier because the language is trickier. Applying the logic above, we can say that conceivability applies to concepts, not to existence claims. Conceiving of God is one thing; asking about God's existence is another. It's not a matter of comparing a God who exists in the understanding to a God who exists in reality. When you have an idea of God, it isn't *God* that exists in the understanding: it is simply the *idea of God*. Having the idea of God in my head isn't the same as having a God in my head that could be compared to some God existing in the world.

In the contemporary period, some philosophers of religion have tried to resurrect the ontological argument by arguing that a perfect or a greatest conceivable being would have "necessary existence," and that necessary existence unlike, simple existence, is a property. Some claim that this is really what Anselm meant to argue.

Since the phrase **"necessary existence"** is ambiguous, and its ambiguity will also occur in conjunction with the First Cause argument, it is important to try to clarify the ambiguity. The phrase "necessary existence" could mean (at the very least) either of the following things:

a. A being with (logically) necessary existence is one that must exist by definition.
b. A being with (physically) necessary existence is one that (if it exists) must exist in the sense that it is eternal and all-powerful and could not be caused not to exist by something else.

If you separate out these meanings—*and* assume there are no other meanings that are not essentially equivalent to option a or b—*and* apply Kant's critique to a, you can see that we're not going to get an *a priori* proof for the existence of God out of "necessary existence." Necessary existence as in b doesn't by itself prove anything about the existence of God: It only describes what God would be like *if* He existed. It seems that those pushing necessary existence are looking for a third meaning of "necessary existence" that sounds like b but has the force of a. It's hard to see what this could be.

A number of complicated versions of the ontological argument have been formulated using modal logic (logic involving the notions of necessity and possibility) and the idea of possible worlds. If you're interested in investigating those arguments, look up the sources suggested in Further Readings.

LET'S REVIEW

* *What is Anselm's version of the ontological argument? What is Descartes's version?*

* *What is Kant's objection to the ontological argument, and how does it relate to Descartes's version?*

* *What is the problem with Anselm's comparison of a God who exists in the understanding and a God who exists in reality?*

The Cosmological/First Cause Argument

The cosmological argument (which derives its name from the Greek word for "universe")—also called the **First Cause argument**—was given its most famous formulations by the thirteenth-century philosopher/theologian Saint

Thomas Aquinas, who was influenced by Aristotle. The cosmological argument proceeds from some highly general premises about the universe to the conclusion that Martin summarizes as follows: "there must be a First Cause, a First Mover, who created the world, set it in motion, and sustains its existence."

People are tempted to say that everything must have had a beginning and to argue for a First Cause on the basis of this premise. But this premise, even if rational, not only does not support, but actually contradicts, the conclusion of the cosmological argument. For the argument supposes that there is one thing that had no beginning, namely, God.

In earlier times at least, many supposed that things in motion must have been set in motion; rest, rather than motion, was the natural state of things. They argued that the universe must have been set in motion by a First Mover, God. But the supposition that rest is the natural state of things is denied by modern science.

SAINT THOMAS AQUINAS (1225–1274) was an Italian Catholic priest and a Master (professor) of religion. In his work, he attempted to synthesize Christianity with the ideas of the ancient Greek philosopher, Aristotle. Aristotle's ideas had been newly introduced into Europe by Muslim philosophers, like Averroes, who'd been using Aristotle to argue for *their* faith.

One of Saint Thomas Aquinas's formulations of the argument (called the "argument from possibility and necessity") goes somewhat as follows:

1. It is possible for the things in our experience to exist or not exist (we observe such things being born and dying); these things are **contingent**.
2. If all things were contingent, nothing would exist (such things would have gone out of existence over the course of an infinite past).
3. But things do exist.
4. (Therefore) There must exist something whose existence is necessary, which cannot not exist; that being is God.

This argument is difficult, and the interpretations of it are diverse. Saint Thomas Aquinas claims that the things that we observe can either be or not be (are contingent) and must depend on some necessary being. First of all, a degree of sense must be given to the notion of a "necessary being." Some proponents of the argument have suggested that a necessary being is one whose definition implies its existence (a being with logically necessary existence, as we said earlier). But by this interpretation, the cosmological argument becomes a version of the ontological argument and is subject to the same critique. No definition implies the existence of the thing defined.

"Necessary being" could be a description of something that, as a matter of fact, is self-sufficient and depends on nothing else for its existence (what we earlier called a being with physically necessary existence). If one supposes that there never was or will be a time when nothing exists, then it follows that there is a "necessary being"—at least in the trivial sense that this phrase could apply to the totality of things that ever exist. The emphasis of the argument would then shift to the claim that the things in the physical-mental world that we observe are "contingent" in the sense that they must depend on something else for their existence.

It is true that the things we observe are generated and corrupted, but it is not clear that they disappear, as opposed to breaking down into more basic, enduring particles or into energy. It is not clear why the universe, conceived as a system of things and relations, must necessarily depend on something else for its existence; nor is it clear that the universe could not be a "necessary being" in the sense that it is self-sufficient. Yet if the cosmological argument is to be convincing, its proponents must show us why the universe is likely to be dependent on something else.

Since the general acceptance of the **"Big Bang" theory** in the mid-twentieth century, a new version of the cosmological argument has been developed that is phrased something like this: "Even if one grants that the physical universe *could* have existed eternally, still science, with its 'Big Bang' cosmology, has established it as very likely that the physical universe has not always existed, that it had a definite beginning about 14 billion years ago. Things don't just come from nothing. It is reasonable to think that the universe had a cause and what could that cause be but God?"

Some theists have taken the Big Bang theory to support a biblical-style creation at some definite moment in the past. Let's note in passing that the Big Bang theory would not support a literally interpreted biblical account of creation as held by young Earth creationists. The Big Bang theory implies that it took billions of years from the origin of the universe until Earth appeared; science tells us that it took another half billion or so years before life began its evolution on Earth. However, suppose we take the Bible figuratively or just base our argument on logic and science; how then does that Big Bang/First Cause argument look?

Scientists have certainly proposed other possibilities. One theory, called the Big Bounce suggests that our universe was the result of the collapse of another universe. In one version of this theory, the universe keeps collapsing and expanding. Another theory postulates that there is a multiverse—a series of finite or even infinite universes—and our universe grew from one of these.

The scientifically favored explanation is that our expanding universe was once so small that it has to be evaluated in terms of the laws of quantum mechanics rather than the laws of general relativity. Quantum mechanics says that matter can arise from nothing: A vacuum state is not truly empty but contains particles that pop in and out of existence. As physicist Paul Davies says:

> The spontaneous appearance of matter out of empty space is often referred to as creation "out of nothing," and comes close to the spirit of the creation ex nihilo of Christian doctrine. For the physicist, however, empty space is a far cry from nothing: it is very much part of the physical universe. If we want to answer the ultimate question of how the universe came into existence it is not sufficient to assume that empty space was there at the outset. We have to explain where space itself came from. . . .

> . . . if quantum theory allows particles of matter to pop into existence out of nowhere, could it also, when applied to gravity, allow space to come into existence out of nothing? And if so, should the spontaneous appearance of the universe 18,000 million years ago occasion such surprise after all?

None of this is going to feel very comfortable to the nonscientist: The idea of a personal God creating the world can feel much better. However, there are a couple of points to consider.

First, the point of the cosmological argument is to show that it is more reasonable than not to believe in a God who created the universe. But when there are scientifically respectable alternative explanations, can First Cause arguments make the existence of God the most reasonable explanation, especially if we're careful to suppress our natural wishful-thinking impulses?

A second notion to consider is that even if we are tempted by the First Cause arguments, nothing in those arguments necessarily implies that the cause was an omnipotent, omniscient, morally perfect God. At best, it would show that there would have to be some entity or other with sufficient power to create the universe. It wouldn't even have to be intelligent. To formulate arguments about what that First Cause might be like, we have to focus on what the universe is like. And that brings us to our next argument, the most celebrated (and to many people, the most convincing) argument for the existence of God: the argument from design.

LET'S REVIEW

* What's the problem with this argument: "Everything must have a beginning, so there must have been a First Cause that started it all"?
* How does the Big Bang theory affect the idea that maybe the universe has been around forever?
* What does modern physics have to say about the need for a First Cause?

The Teleological/Design Argument

The teleological argument (which derives its name from the Greek word for "end"/"goal") is more familiarly known as the **argument from design**. Here is one version of this argument:

> The complex universe is not chaotic but orderly; its workings can be described by relatively simple scientific theories. Surely, it is more

reasonable to suppose that this universe was designed by some Great Intelligence, God, than to suppose that it exists without design.

Popular forms of this argument often gain apparent force by restricting one to a bogus dichotomy between design and chance (a false dilemma). One is invited to consider two situations: The first: A woman takes some pieces of metal and glass and carefully constructs a watch. The second: A woman takes some pieces of metal and glass and tosses them over her shoulder; by chance the pieces fall together in such a way as to form a functioning watch. The advocate of the argument then says: Surely, it is more reasonable to suppose that the universe was formed as in the first situation rather than as in the second. As stated by the English clergyman, William Paley (1743–1805), who popularized the watch/universe analogy two centuries ago,

> . . . every indication of contrivance, every manifestation of design, which existed in the watch, exists in the works of nature; with, the difference, on the side of nature, of being greater and more, and that in a degree which exceeds all computation. . . .

If the only two possibilities were design and chance, a rational person would conclude that the universe was designed. But there is another possibility: that an orderly universe has always existed. Such a universe could not be said to have "happened by chance," since that phrase describes some sort of haphazard beginning, and this third possibility supposes no beginning at all. Or, presupposing a Big Bang, it is possible that orderliness was somehow implicit in the nature of the quantum vacuum from which the universe arose.

The hypothesis that the universe is inherently orderly need not suppose that order is analogous to the immensely complex, immensely detailed blueprint that a divinity might have had in mind in designing the universe. This order need only be something like the basic laws of physics. We know that enormous complexity can arise from relatively simple processes if they're the right sort of processes and there's sufficient time.

Early versions of the design argument highlighted such features of apparent design in nature as the human eye. Just as you wouldn't conclude within a design/chance dichotomy that the watch came about by chance, so you wouldn't conclude that the human eye came about by chance through the blind forces of nature. Even without strict adherence to the design/chance dichotomy, it was difficult to see how an eye might have come about by merely natural processes. However, the theory of evolution, together with an appreciation of how old Earth was—billions, not thousands of years—gave a reasonable account of what those processes might be. As we've noted, evolution involves chance but is not a random process. Genetic mutations might be random, but selection via adaptation to the environment is not.

The evolutionary biologist and atheist Richard Dawkins has said this of Paley:

> Paley's argument is made with passionate sincerity and is informed by the best biological scholarship of his day, but it is wrong, gloriously and utterly wrong. The analogy between telescope and eye, between watch and living organism, is false. All appearances to the contrary, the only watchmaker in nature is the blind forces of physics, albeit deployed in a very special way. A true watchmaker has foresight: he designs his cogs and springs, and plans their interconnections, with a future purpose in his mind's eye. Natural selection, the blind, unconscious, automatic process which Darwin discovered, and which we now know is the explanation for the existence and apparently purposeful form of all life, has no purpose in mind. It has

RICHARD DAWKINS (1941–) is emeritus fellow of New College, Oxford. Dawkins popularized the gene-centered view of evolution in his 1976 book, *The Selfish Gene*. He attacked intelligent design in *The Blind Watchmaker* (1986) and religion in general in *The God Delusion* (2006).

no mind and no mind's eye. It does not plan for the future. It has no vision, no foresight, no sight at all. If it can be said to play the role of watchmaker in nature, it is the blind watchmaker. . . .

Some proponents of the design argument who do accept the theory of evolution now argue instead that the fact that the Earth was the kind of place where evolution could take place is evidence for a designer. This is one of a number of arguments that come under the label **fine tuning**: Theists argue that in many ways the universe is fine-tuned so that it is suitable for life/intelligent life: Such fine-tuning indicates the existence of an intelligent creator—God.

The point is not that life appeared on *some* planet in our universe as it is. The universe seems to contain millions of worlds, and the odds are great that one or another of them would be suitable for life. To intelligent beings living in a world where life evolved, the fact of life would seem amazing—a "miracle." In the same way, if you won the lottery, it would seem miraculous that you had won it—even though the odds that someone would win the lottery are close to 100 percent.

Rather, the fine-tuning argument focuses on the fact that the universe is as it is. The universe seems set up in a way (with the particular laws it has) so that life was almost certainly going to evolve somewhere or other. In this sense, it seems to be fine-tuned for life.

Neil A. Manson summarizes this fine-tuning argument and the thinking behind it as follows:

> After the development of Big Bang cosmology . . . the universe was seen to be highly structured, with precisely defined parameters such as age (13.7 billion years), mass, curvature, temperature, density, and rate of expansion. Modern physics also revealed that specific kinds of particles compose the universe and specific kinds of forces govern these particles, and that the natures of these particles and forces determine large-scale processes such as cosmic expansion and star formation. . . .
>
> Looking at the very precise numerical values of [particular] parameters . . . , some physicists asked what the universe would have been like if the values had been slightly different. More specifically, for many an individual parameter, they asked what the universe would be like if that parameter were varied while the remaining parameters were held fixed. The answer, to the surprise of many, was that the universe would not have been the sort of place in which life could emerge—not just the very form of life we observe here on

Earth, but any conceivable form of life. In many cases, the cosmic parameters were like the just-right settings on an old-style radio dial: if the knob were turned just a bit, the clear signal would turn to static. As a result, some physicists started describing the values of the parameters as 'fine-tuned' for life. . . .

Offhand, it would seem as reasonable to suppose that there was order inherent in the natural processes that developed into the universe as to suppose that there was order inherent in the being that fine-tuned the universe. But the fine-tuning debate is complex and difficult, with questions about which parameters seem fine-tuned, about whether and to what degree they are actually independent of one another, about how to specify the possible values those parameters could take, and how intelligible the probability estimates are. Those who want to follow that debate should consult Further Readings.

For our purposes, however, in terms of belief in a traditional God, we can take a different approach to the fine-tuning argument. Note that the design/fine-tuning arguments don't have to be presented as proving the existence of a traditional God. Michael Behe, a supporter of the fine-tuning argument, says that while he argues for design

the question of the identity of the designer is left open. Possible candidates for the role of designer include: the God of Christianity; an angel—fallen or not; Plato's demiurge; some mystical new age force; space aliens from Alpha Centauri; time travelers; or some utterly unknown intelligent being.

He might have also added: A future civilization playing with computer simulations.

From this perspective, the fine-tuning argument is of genuine metaphysical and scientific interest, but not of much interest in terms of supporting anything like the belief in a traditional God worthy of worship. A God who creates a universe that after 13 billion years of things flashing and crashing leads to creatures like us seems a long way from any God with empathy for the pain of sentient creatures (given the amount of suffering that must have taken place during the evolution of life and still does take place). The God of the Big Bang looks more like some Being with a cosmic chemistry set who loves giant explosions and vast galaxies and is interested in rolling the quantum dice to see what strange things might happen.

This hints at the irony of the argument from design. On the one hand, it has been used by theists to say it makes obvious the existence of a traditional God who is omnipotent and omniscient. On the other hand, it has been used by atheists to say it makes obvious the nonexistence of any such God who is supposed to be perfectly good. As Martin says in "Surprise!": "The laws of the universe may be mathematically elegant, but they crush and they kill. No respectable God would allow people to suffer as they do." Faced with the atheist's challenge, the theist must go on the defensive, trying to show that the suffering and other evils in the world *might* be compatible with the existence of God after all. It is to this issue (along with further reflections on the argument from design) that we will now turn.

LET'S REVIEW

* *What is the problem with the statement that the universe came about either by design or by chance?*
* *What is the problem with the claim that there had to be a Divine Creator for there to be something as marvelously complex as the human eye?*
* *What is the fine-tuning argument for the existence of a Divine Creator?*
* *How does the existence of suffering impact on the teleological argument?*

Atheism and the Problem of Suffering
Disbelieving in God

One can take three possible positions on the question of whether or not God exists: The **theist** believes there is a God; the **agnostic** isn't sure one way or the other; and the **atheist** believes there is no God.

Perhaps you have heard something like the following argument: "It's absurd to be an atheist, as opposed to an agnostic or a theist. How could anyone possibly prove that God doesn't exist!"

If you are sympathetic to this argument, imagine yourself in the following situation. A friend, looking out the window, says, "My goodness, there's a huge pink whale lying in the backyard." You laugh at the idea and wouldn't even bother to look except that you happen to be at the window and you see nothing out there but lawn. Your friend gets indignant. "Wait a minute," she says: "I can see how you might be unsure of whether there's a huge pink whale in the backyard. But it would be irrational to believe there isn't one. How could you possibly prove that?"

The point is that there are a lot of things in the world that you positively believe didn't happen or don't exist. We decide that if a certain claim were true, certain other things ought to happen; if those other things don't happen, that is taken as evidence that the original claim is false. That is, under certain circumstances, we take the absence of certain kinds of evidence to count as evidence against. We all reason in this way every day. This is not to say that the question of God's existence is as straightforward as the question of whether or not there is a pink whale in the backyard. It is only to say that one can't dismiss atheism as absurd in advance of a discussion of grounds for believing in God.

Some atheists have based their belief on the absence of certain evidence that they think would exist if God did (e.g., unambiguous miracles, consistent religious experience from culture to culture, etc.). Others, however, have claimed that there is positive evidence that God does not exist, namely, the amount of suffering in the world. This claim amounts to a kind of negative version of the argument from design. According to the argument from design, the complex orderliness of the world indicates that it must have been designed by God. Here an opposite claim is made: The suffering in the world indicates that it could not have been designed by God.

As has been noted, it has been traditional in much of our culture (and other monotheistic cultures) to view God as (1) **omnipotent** (all-powerful), (2) **omniscient** (all-knowing), and (3) perfectly good. The existence of suffering poses a tough challenge for a theist who believes in such a God. How could a God who is perfectly good, who can do absolutely anything He wants to do, and who knows everything there is to know, possibly create a world in which so many of His creatures suffer so terribly?

A theist who believes in a God who lacks one of these three characteristics has a ready explanation for suffering: A God who lacks omnipotence or omniscience does not have the power or knowledge to eliminate suffering, and a God who is not perfectly good is morally defective and doesn't care to eliminate suffering. The existence of suffering is not evidence against the existence of gods like these. But it is possible evidence against the existence of a God who is supposed to have all three of these characteristics.

The problem here is what's called **the problem of suffering**: Does the existence of suffering show that there could not be a God who is omnipotent (all-powerful), omniscient (all-knowing), and perfectly good?

Omnipotence and Contradiction

At first glance, it may seem obvious that the existence of suffering rules out the possibility of there being a God who is omnipotent, omniscient, and perfectly good: Such a God would create the best of all possible worlds. In the best of all possible worlds there would exist human beings with free will who were happy and virtuous. Obviously, this world is not such a world. Therefore, there is no such God.

But many theists make the following reply: The world you have just described is not a possible world. The idea of creating such a world is contradictory. Even an omnipotent God cannot do contradictory things; therefore, God can in no way be blamed for not having created such a world.

This reply employs two arguments that need some elaboration:

1. Even an omnipotent God could not do what is contradictory.
2. The idea of creating a world in which human beings with free will are virtuous and happy is a contradiction.

Throughout the centuries, many theologians have felt that God, to be omnipotent, must be able to do contradictory things. He must be able to create a chair that is not a chair or a triangle that has four sides. To say that God cannot do such things is to suppose that God is limited and hence not omnipotent.

Today most philosophers and theologians reject the claim that, to be omnipotent, a God would have to do contradictory things. This claim, they, say, results from a misunderstanding about the nature of contradiction. It supposes that contradictions describe the most difficult kinds of tasks. In truth, contradictions describe nothing at all. In this sense, they are analogous to nonsense statements. One should no more expect an omnipotent God to create a chair that is not a chair than one should expect Him to be able to do something nonsensical like "oop erg alban ipple ong."

In contradictory phrases, the individual words make sense, but the combination of words is senseless. To say "create a chair that is not a chair" is like drawing a picture of a chair on a blackboard, erasing the picture, then pointing to the board and saying, "There, make me one of those." But what is portrayed on the blackboard, finally, is not some difficult task or other; nothing at all is portrayed there.

(If you think back to "A Little Omniscience Goes a Long Way," God's longing to do contradictory things would be, in this analysis, absurd.)

Many theists suppose that God, at the time of creation, was faced with certain forced options. He could either eliminate all suffering or create a world in which human beings had free will and might be virtuous (exhibit good moral qualities). To do both would be contradictory. God quite properly chose to create a world in which human beings had free will and a chance at virtue, rather than a world in which they were unfree, nonvirtuous, and happy. As in the story "Surprise!" I shall divide these arguments into two defenses: the free will defense and the virtue defense. But before discussing these two defenses, let's consider another defense that is not much discussed in the philosophical literature but one that many students offer and find convincing: the claim that it is impossible to have happiness without unhappiness.

Does Happiness Require Unhappiness?

In the story "Surprise!" God and Martin assume that it would be possible to have a world in which everyone was happy (as heaven itself is supposed to demonstrate). The question they debate is whether or not such a world would indeed be better than the alternatives. However, if it is impossible to have a world in which everyone is happy, then their whole discussion would seem to be beside the point. Thus, we had better ask: Is it impossible to have happiness without unhappiness?

Often a discussion of this issue gets sidetracked by inflated, soap-opera conceptions of happiness (as in "Yes, everything is going well, and yes, I'm feeling fine, but am I really *happy*?"). Such a rarefied notion of happiness is not relevant to the problem of suffering. We all know what it is to wince and say, "Oh, that hurts." We all know what it is to say, "Boy, I'm really feeling good today." Those challenging the theist on the problem of suffering are saying that God should have created the world so that there were no feelings like the former (and worse), only feelings like the latter. To keep the issue down to earth, think of the question we're discussing as whether it is possible to have pleasant feelings without unpleasant feelings.

Two other confusions often come up in discussing this issue:

1. "Human beings are such that they cannot be happy all the time, and thus God couldn't have made a world in which there was only happiness." Even if the first part of the statement were true, the second part doesn't follow logically from the first. If human beings as constituted can't be happy all the time, then perhaps God should have created different creatures who could be. To support

the no-happiness-without-unhappiness claim requires one to show that no possible creature could be happy all the time.

2. "Without a contrast you couldn't know what happiness was; thus, you can't have happiness without unhappiness." Again, the conclusion of the argument doesn't follow from the premise. Whether there could be only happiness is one thing; whether, if there was only happiness, we would know it was happiness and would call it "happiness," is another. Supporting the latter claim is not enough to demonstrate the former. For instance, I think I can imagine a world that is all red (let's say different shades of red). I might agree that creatures in that world wouldn't know it was red (as opposed to yellow) and wouldn't have the word "red"; however, the world would still be red.

In order to show that an omnipotent God could not have created happiness without unhappiness, it would be necessary to show that the idea of happiness without unhappiness is contradictory.

Even if that could be shown, it wouldn't signify much in terms of the problem of suffering. Any defense of suffering is going to have to justify a lot of suffering. The claim that happiness without unhappiness is contradictory would seem to justify only a little bit of suffering for contrast. The claim one really needs to make in terms of the problem of suffering is that it would be contradictory to have a lot of happiness without a lot of unhappiness. It's hard to see what the argument for that might be.

In any case, note that both the free will and virtue defenses assume that a happy world would have been possible, but argue that it wouldn't have been the best of all possible (noncontradictory) worlds.

LET'S REVIEW

* *Why isn't it necessarily absurd to believe that some particular thing does not exist? How does this bear on the rationality of atheism?*
* *What is the philosophical "problem of suffering"?*
* *What is the rationale for the claim that even an omnipotent God could not do contradictory things? How does this claim impact our reasoning about the problem of suffering?*
* *What's wrong with the following argument: "Without a contrast you couldn't know what happiness was; thus, you can't have happiness without unhappiness"?*

The Free Will Defense

The free will defense claims that:

1. Free will is a great good and a necessary ingredient in the best of all possible worlds.
2. It would be contradictory for God to give human beings free will and yet guarantee they never use their free will to harm themselves and others.
3. Therefore, there is likely to be suffering in the best of all possible worlds.

To elaborate on item 2: If human beings have free will, then their choices are not caused. It would be contradictory for God to give human beings free will and, at the same time, control (cause) their choices so that they never make choices that would cause unhappiness.

It should be obvious that the idea of free will implied here is the libertarian conception of contra-causal freedom. The various compatibilist ideas of freedom wouldn't work as part of a free will defense since they are all compatible with God's determining human choices so that people always did the right thing. If God created all human beings so that they were sane, only wanted to do good, and self-identified with only wanting to do good, then they would be free on any compatibilist account.

A compatibilist concept of free will can't be used to justify any amount of suffering—which, after all, is the point of the defense.

Regarding item 3, note that the concept of contra-causal free will per se doesn't necessarily imply suffering. Rather, it is likely that over time people will use their free will to cause suffering. The point of the argument is that it's not God's fault if they do.

People readily accept the free will defense. But there are serious questions one can raise about it.

Many people do think that contra-causal free will is a great good. But in the previous chapter, it was suggested that this opinion may result from a misunderstanding. The argument we considered was that the opposite of causation is chance; that chance is no more desirable than causation; and that, when you try to add to chance other qualities that make free will desirable, you just end up with an incoherent idea. If you accepted this impossibilist position on free will, you'd have to conclude that the free will defense itself is incoherent.

Even if you do believe that the idea of contra-causal freedom can be made coherent and desirable, you still need to ask whether or not it is really worth the great suffering it has supposedly caused. Often the options here are misconceived. Many religious tracts imply that the only alternative to a world with free will is a world in which people move about like horror-movie zombies. Given our previous discussion, this is obviously false. Free will pertains only to the causes of one'schoices. It implies nothing about the particular characteristics of one's facial expressions, movements, feelings, or thoughts. Free will, as we have seen, would not be an observable thing. What would you and others look like without free will? You would look exactly the way you look now. God could have created people without free will who were lively, emotional, and thoughtful, and who always chose happy courses of action. Would such a world so obviously have been second-rate?

It is generally agreed that the free will defense, even if successful, is not adequate to explain all suffering. It may account for the suffering caused by human beings. It does not account for the suffering caused by natural phenomena such as diseases, earthquakes, and floods.

Some theists do link the suffering caused by natural phenomena to human free will by claiming that such suffering is a punishment for misuse of freedom. But this argument really supplements the free will defense as it has been presented here. It adds two premises. One: Human beings did misuse their freedom, and God punished them by forcing them to live in a world of suffering. Two: The great suffering caused by natural events is proper punishment for human beings' misuse of their freedom. Some critics, like Martin, find this second premise "barbaric."

The Virtue Defense

There is another defense that often is presented as a justification for the existence of suffering caused by natural phenomena. It implies that God was right in making sure that there would be some suffering in the world, whatever human beings might do with their free will. It can be referred to as **the virtue defense**, and it runs as follows:

1. Virtues, such as generosity and courage, are great goods, and, in the best of all possible worlds, human beings ought to have the chance to exercise such virtues.
2. It would be contradictory to have virtues in a world without suffering, since the definitions of these virtues imply the existence of suffering.

3. Therefore, suffering is a necessary ingredient in the best of all possible worlds.

To enlarge on item 2: Try to imagine someone being courageous in a world in which no one is afraid or in danger. It is impossible. To be courageous is to overcome fear (which is necessarily painful) and to risk oneself to help someone else. In a world with no pain and no risk of harm, no possible action could be courageous.

Or try to imagine generosity in a world in which all persons have more than they need. It is impossible. In such a world, any act of giving would be analogous to a child on a beach handing another child a bucket of sand. Generosity involves some sacrifice to help another in need. In a world with no need, no possible action could be generous. This is an ingenious defense, and many find it reasonable. Others, however, do not.

Some philosophers have said that this defense views virtue inside out. What is good about virtues is that they aim at the relief of suffering. Virtues are good as means only. Virtues are correctly called good in a world with suffering. But to insist on suffering in order to have virtue is absurd; it contradicts the very nature of virtue. To insist on suffering so that there can be generosity and sympathy is like stealing from someone so that you can give her something she now needs or kicking someone in the shins so that you can feel sorry for him.

The theist might counter that this apparent contradiction dissolves when one differentiates between the divine and human perspectives. God's setting the stage for a world containing suffering in which humans can struggle to exercise the virtues is different from Person A causing Person B pain so that A can then exercise virtue by relieving B's pain.

According to John Hick, those who doubt the compatibility of God and suffering differ from theists in their view of the humans they think God ought to have created.

> The skeptic's assumption is that man is to be viewed as a completed creation and that God's purpose in making the world was to provide a suitable dwelling-place for this fully formed creature. Since God is good and loving, the environment which he has created for human life to inhabit is naturally as pleasant and comfortable as possible.…
>
> Christianity, however, has never supposed that God's purpose in the creation of the world was to construct a paradise whose inhabitants would experience a maximum of pleasure and a minimum

of pain. The world is seen, instead, as a place of "soul-making" in which free beings, grappling with the tasks and challenges of their existence in a common environment, may become "children of God" and "heirs of eternal life."

The free will and virtue defenses do succeed in showing that there is a recognizable morality that might have led an omnipotent, omniscient, morally perfect God to create a world in which there was bound to be some suffering. How acceptable you find the defenses will depend on how you evaluate the morality. Do you find the idea of contra-causal free will both coherent and attractive? If so, the free will defense will have some appeal; if not, you will find the defense incoherent. Do you find attractive the idea of God creating a world with pain and need so that people can develop qualities such as fortitude and helpfulness? If so, the virtue defense will have some appeal; if you think the idea of guaranteeing a world of pain goes against the idea of virtue, you won't.

I think most of us feel attracted by the general values evoked by the free will and virtue defenses. We like the idea of our choices, our lives, being "up to us." We like the idea of working to become decent, successful people—maybe even going beyond that toward the heroic or saintly. But even granting that—and without looking too closely at the complications raised by the defenses—the theist still faces a crucial challenge: Why did there have to be *this* much suffering?

As a reminder of how much suffering there is, consider the death tolls of some of the great wars of history: World War II (1939–1945): 70 million dead; World War I (1914–1918): 20 million dead; the Taiping Rebellion in China (1851–1864): 20 million dead; Mongol Conquests (1207–1472): 30–60 million dead.

If you're inclined to chalk up deaths in war to human free will, consider the death tolls of some of the greatest epidemics in history: the flu pandemic of 1918: 50–100 million dead; the flu pandemic of 1889: 1 million dead; the cholera epidemic of 1852–1860 in Russia: 1 million dead; cocoliztli epidemics in Mexico of 1545–1548 and 1576: 12 million dead; the Black Death in Europe (1346–1350): 75–100 million dead; the Justinian (European) plague of 541–542: 25–50 million dead; and so on.

That's a lot of death and pain to set the stage for fortitude and compassion. Then there are disasters such as earthquakes, fires, and floods, which, at their worst, tend to have death tolls in the hundred thousands but add up.

The most famous disaster philosophically was the Lisbon earthquake of 1755: Since it took place on the morning of a religious holiday, All Saints' Day, much of the population was attending church: Churches collapsed, killing thousands of worshipers who might have been safer had they stayed home in bed. It was an event that shook the religious faith of many in Europe. Years earlier, the German philosopher, Gottfried Wilhelm Leibniz (1646–1716), had argued that, given the premise that God is perfect, this must be the best of all possible worlds. After the Lisbon earthquake, the French writer, Voltaire (1694–1778), satirized Leibniz's claim with his novel, *Candide*. In that novel, a naïve young man, named Candide, is tutored by Professor Pangloss who teaches him Leibniz's optimistic philosophy. Candide and his tutor are thrown into the world where they endure hardships and witness horrors (including those of the Seven Years' War and the Lisbon earthquake). Pangloss retains his optimism, seemingly in the face of all reason, while Candide sours on it.

> "Well, my dear Pangloss," said Candide to him, "when you were hanged, dissected, whipped, and tugging at the oar, did you continue to think that everything in this world happens for the best?"
>
> "I have always abided by my first opinion," answered Pangloss; "for, after all, I am a philosopher, and it would not become me to retract my sentiments; especially as Leibniz could not be in the wrong: and that preestablished harmony is the finest thing in the world. . . ."

If, in response to considerations of the amount of suffering that has existed through human history, you are inclined to say, "Well, that's the price of freedom," you need to think back to our discussion of the distinction between contra-causal freedom and freedom of action. Contra-causal freedom implies only that the act of choosing is up to us; it implies nothing about the desires on the basis of which we choose or about our physical capacities to act on those choices. There'd be nothing contradictory about God giving us contra-causal freedom along with a much greater inclination to do good, less ability to harm, and less vulnerability to be harmed.

There'd be nothing contradictory about God giving us contra-causal freedom while also intervening to prevent the worst horrors, such as the Holocaust or the Black Death. Often, arguments involving the free will defense confuse free will and freedom of action. If you want to argue that people need freedom of action compatible with causing millions of deaths, that would take a separate and quite different argument.

VOLTAIRE, the pseudonym of FRANÇOIS-MARIE AROUET (1694–1778), was one of the greatest French writers, an Enlightenment intellectual who wrote plays, novels, essays, and works of science and history. He was famous for his satirical wit, his attacks on the Catholic Church, and his support of freedom of religion and freedom of speech.

As for the virtue defense, a lot less suffering would be compatible with developing good character. If anything, according to a number of critics, the extreme suffering in the world seems as likely to lead to despair and crushing of the spirit.

In the end, many of those who offer the free will and virtue defenses agree that while they may give a sense of how suffering might be reconciled with the existence of God who is omnipotent, omniscient, and perfectly good, the defenses don't really explain the amount of suffering in the world. John Hick, who talked about the world as a place for soul-making, admits that the amount of suffering must be taken as a mystery: "I do not now have an alternative theory to offer that would explain in any rational or ethical way why men suffer as they do. The only appeal that is left is to mystery."

The idea of mystery suggests the idea of faith and the question of faith versus reason in the domain of religious belief. Let's turn to that discussion now.

LET'S REVIEW

* What is the free will defense? What seems right about it, and what seems problematic?
* What is the virtue defense? What seems right about it, and what seems problematic?
* In what way does the actual suffering in the world (now and through history) impact the free will and virtue defenses?

Faith and Reason

Should religious belief be based on reason or faith or some combination of the two? If a combination of the two, which of the two should have priority? In discussing this question, let's start with those who put a greater emphasis on reason and move to those who put a greater emphasis on faith.

The thinker who most emphatically insists on the primacy of reason with regard to belief, religious or otherwise, is William K. Clifford (1845–1879). Clifford presents a story about a ship owner who is considering sending to sea a ship full of people. "He knew that she [the ship] was old, and not over-well built at the first; that she had seen many seas and climes, and often had needed repairs. Doubts had been suggested to him that possibly she was not seaworthy." However, he talks himself out of these doubts and by the time the ship sails he had acquired

> a sincere and comfortable conviction that his vessel was thoroughly safe and seaworthy; he watched her departure with a light heart, and benevolent wishes for the success of the exiles in their strange new home that was to be; and he got his insurance money when she went down in mid-ocean and told no tales.

Clifford argues that the ship owner is guilty of the death of all those people. Even if he had managed to convince himself that his ship was sound, he "had acquired his belief not by honestly earning it in patient investigation, but by stifling his doubts." He should not have stifled those doubts, but rather should have investigated them. Thus, "he must be held responsible."

Even if the ship had made the passage successfully, the man still would have been guilty of a wrong action; he just wouldn't have been found out. Whatever the man came to believe, he had no right to believe on that evidence.

Clifford set forth a stark principle that he is famous for: "It is wrong always, everywhere, and for anyone to believe anything on insufficient evidence."

William James (1842–1910) attacked Clifford's principle in "The Will to Believe." James does not go to the opposite extreme, pushing an anything-goes view of belief. He says he agrees with Clifford that when we have an issue that can be decided on intellectual grounds we should do so;

WILLIAM JAMES (1842–1910), the brother of novelist Henry James, was an enormously influential American psychologist and philosopher. He was the first instructor to offer a psychology course in the United States, and he has been called "the father of American psychology." Along with John Dewey and Charles Sanders Pierce, he was considered part of the philosophical movement known as pragmatism.

in that context, we should not be picking beliefs on the basis of comfort. But there are lots of issues where we can't decide the issue on intellectual grounds. In most of those cases, James says, again agreeing with Clifford, we should suspend belief. But, James thinks, in certain situations we are permitted to believe, even though we don't have sufficient evidence for our belief. James sets out three criteria for cases where one is permitted to believe without sufficient evidence. He says that we have the legitimate option to believe without sufficient evidence—that we have a "genuine choice" to believe—when the choice meets three criteria: It must be "live," "momentous," and "forced."

A live or living option is one in which both possibilities (hypotheses or acts) have some emotional appeal to you. A forced option, of course, arises when you must make a decision between two acts or beliefs. A momentous option is one that is of great importance, perhaps a once-in-a-lifetime opportunity involving a commitment, perhaps being a matter of life and death. In this context, James mentions an invitation to go on an exhibition to the North Pole, but we might think of an astronaut invited on the first manned mission to Mars.

James then brings his principle to bear on religious belief. Religion, in James's analysis, says that "the best things are the more eternal things" and that "we are better off even now if we believe that statement to be true." He tells us that "If for any of you religion be an hypothesis that cannot, by any living possibility, be true, then you need go no further." For those for whom religious belief is a possibility—a *living option*—the choice of belief is *momentous*: Vital goods are supposed to be at stake. It is a *forced option* so far as the good of believing goes:

> We cannot escape the issue by remaining sceptical and waiting for more light, because, although we do avoid error in that way *if religion be untrue*, we lose the good, *if it be true*, just as certainly as if we positively chose to disbelieve.

James claims that it is quite legitimate to cultivate belief under those circumstances.

Before commenting on James's argument, let's examine another argument that resembles it in certain respects, the famous **wager argument** by a much earlier thinker, Blaise Pascal (1623–1662). Pascal claims that because God is "infinitely incomprehensible," we are "incapable of knowing either way what He is or if He is." (The argument works equally

BLAISE PASCAL (1623–1662), was a French mathematician, scientist, and a philosopher of science. On November 23, 1654, he had what has been described as his "Night of Fire," an intense mystical experience. Thereafter he turned his main attention to religious writings. His notes on what was to be a systematic defense of the Christian religion were posthumously published as the *Pensées*; this work is considered a masterpiece of religious reflection and French prose. The wager argument comes from the *Pensées*.

well for those who make no claim about God being unknowable in theory, but simply think there is not enough evidence one way or the other to decide if God exists.) Pascal says "God is, or He is not." Reason can't decide. "[A]ccording to reason, you can defend neither of the propositions."

Pascal states that you must wager (bet) on whether or not God exists. Not betting, he seems to be saying, is equivalent to betting no. The assumption here (in line with the Christianity of Pascal's day) is that if God exists, believing is necessary for eternal life; if God exists and you don't believe, you lose out. Pascal is not explicit about whether or not the calculation of loss is supposed to include going to hell as well as losing heaven. (Pascal certainly believed in hell.) But the bet can be construed in that way. In any case, there's at least an infinity of happiness at stake here.

What is it that you wager? The way you live your life now: The pleasures you are supposed to give up if you are a Christian. Think of a very traditional picture of Christian morality. According to the Protestant church I went to as a young man, you weren't supposed to drink or smoke or swear or dance or engage in any kind of premarital sex; you were supposed to "testify" to the other kids (which made you even more of an outsider than not engaging in the prohibited "sins"). And you were supposed to go to church and Sunday School and even Bible classes. It wasn't a prescription for a "fun" life. The idea was that being a Christian cost you something (though there were compensations).

But, according to Pascal, whatever the costs of being a Christian, being a practicing Christian will bring you eternal life if God exists, and the chance of that reward far outweighs whatever losses you might suffer.

Pascal's wager can be construed as follows:

	God exists	God does not exist
You believe in God	Heaven but fewer earthly pleasures	Fewer earthly pleasures (no afterlife)
You don't believe in God	Loss of heaven but more earthly pleasures.	More earthly pleasures (no afterlife)

(Obviously, the stakes would be even higher if we substituted "eternal suffering" for "loss of heaven.")

Pascal is giving a pragmatic argument for believing in God. He's not saying that it is more likely than not that God exists; in fact, he's claiming we can't know this. He's saying that it is more likely that we'll gain than lose if we believe.

One standard critique of Pascal questions whether it is possible to really believe in something—especially in something so momentous—simply on practical grounds. Pascal recognizes this problem and advises us to go through all the motions of faith and prayer, hoping faith will come.

A more serious logical problem concerns how Pascal has set the terms of the bet. He professes to know nothing about the divine, but his argument only works if we can assume (in his case) either that the Christian God (viewed in a particular way) exists or that no God exists. However, by the terms of his argument, Pascal can't know that if God exists, He must be a particular kind of God.

You might think, "Well, even if one of three Gods might exist, you still have a one-in-three shot of believing in the right one." But what if those Gods would treat you worse if you believed in the wrong God, than if you didn't believe at all? We might throw in the possibility of a philosopher's God who agrees with Clifford and would penalize you for believing in any God on insufficient evidence. That God might say, "I created you with reason and tested you with insufficient evidence to see what you would do. Those who suspended belief used reason correctly; those are the ones I'm interested in spending eternity with." Of course, such a God sounds absurd in terms of the traditional gods we know; but the point is that if we take Pascal seriously in claiming that reason is useless, we can't rule in or rule out any kind of god: And that undermines the wager argument.

Let's get back to James's argument. Unlike Pascal, James isn't arguing that we should believe in God, that belief is the more rational strategy. In fact, against Pascal he argues that adopting faith as a betting strategy goes against the whole spirit of faith. With respect to anyone adopting this strategy, he says, "if we put ourselves in place of the Deity, we should probably take particular pleasure in cutting off believers of this pattern from their infinite reward"—making sure their calculated wager doesn't pay off.

Rather, James is saying of those who feel passionately drawn to belief in the absence of evidence that there are no rational grounds for criticizing such belief. If we feel the choice is for us living, forced and momentous, then our choice to believe is a reasonable one. He argues that "we lose the good, *if it be true*, just as certainly as if we positively chose to disbelieve."

Still the more serious problem with Pascal's argument perhaps should haunt the person contemplating following James's license to believe in a particular god without evidence. What if you believe in the wrong one?

If we proceed even further from reason along the reason–faith spectrum, we find some who reject reason as not just inadequate to establish faith but positively injurious to faith. There are some obvious examples of the latter in the popular American Christianity of today. New Earth creationists, following what they believe to be a literal interpretation of the Bible, claim that the Earth was created in 4004 BCE. When asked why there are rocks and fossils that appear to be millions of years old, creationists sometimes reply that God put those rocks and fossils there to test our faith. This reply boggles the mind: God gives us reason, then tricks us into believing the wrong thing (e.g., the Earth is millions of years old, and living creatures developed by evolution) if we use that reason? The rationale is that humans and human reason are corrupt, and it is arrogant for humans to use their reason against the word of God. We are commanded to have faith *in spite of* what reason tells us to the contrary.

There are clear precedents for this approach in the New Testament. In I Corinthians, Chapter 1, Paul says:

18. For the preaching of the cross is to them that perish foolishness. . . .
19. For it is written, I will destroy the wisdom of the wise, and will bring to nothing the understanding of the prudent.
20. Where *is* the wise? where *is* the scribe? where *is* the disputer of this world? hath not God made foolish the wisdom of this world? . . .

The claim that faith is the way to God and that reason just gets in the way is called **fideism**. The fideist has a skeptical view of reason in general and sometimes goes further to emphasize the irrationality of religious faith. Often with fideism there is the idea that the irrationality of belief is a test of our faith that only the humble and the trusting can pass. The Danish philosopher, Søren Kierkegaard (1813–1855), is often associated with fideism, which is expressed in a number of his writings. Instead of seeing faith as second best to reason, Kierkegaard celebrated faith over reason. Religious belief based on rational proofs would be an objective, sterile, abstract, unpassionate affair. But belief based on a "leap of faith" involves risk, passion, commitment, "inwardness."

Kierkegaard says that "subjectivity is truth. Through this relationship between the eternal truth and the existing individual the paradox comes into existence."

> . . . when the truth as paradox encounters the individual who is caught in the vice-grip of sin's anxiety and suffering, but who is also aware of the tremendous risk involved in faith—when he neverthe-less makes the leap of faith—this is subjectivity at its height.

Critics have argued that it is impossible to consciously believe at one and the same time that a particular claim is both true and absurd. People can believe self-contradictory things. The problem is believing them, knowing they are self-contradictory. One can try to weaken the sense that the belief is false, but then one is no longer believing it to be false.

Of course, there is no reasoning with someone who rejects all reason: You can only wave your hand dismissively and move on. But if the fideist is giving arguments justifying her leap of faith, you can ask about that

SØREN KIERKEGAARD (1813–1855) was a Danish philosopher and religious author who some consider the "first existentialist" for his emphasis on individual subjectivity, his exploration of extreme moods such as anxiety and despair, and his discussion of "the absurd." Many of his works were written under different pseudonyms and examine different viewpoints, often exploring the coming to terms with faith as individual choice and commitment.

reasoning. If Christianity (following the Christian fideist) is particularly absurd, why not leap into some less absurd faith? And what about this comforting background assumption that you get more credit the more absurd your belief is? Presumably, you are leaping into faith in a God you take to be perfectly good. But what does it say about a God who would demand this sort of a test? It would have to be a God who has a really low opinion of human beings and expects a slave-like submission of all that makes us human. Can that sort of God possibly be good? Or is that another of the absurdities we're supposed to believe in?

Another problem with fideism—or even the more moderate license to believe that James endorses—has to do with morality. Religious faith often comes with a morality and if reason goes out the window with the belief in God, presumably so does reasoning about morality. If your leap of faith is just a way of protecting a rather tame faith from uncomfortable arguments, the harm, if any, is mild (though Clifford would disagree). However, what if you're leaping into a faith that involves shooting people and setting off bombs? Or less dramatically, into a faith that demands you come down hard on your kids to think along very narrow lines. There's nothing very romantic about other people's leap of faith if they end up landing on you.

Definitions

(Terms are defined in the order in which they appeared in the text.)

1. VERIDICAL EXPERIENCE: True experience of some objective reality. (Opposite: nonveridical)
2. THE ONTOLOGICAL (OR DEFINITIONAL) ARGUMENT FOR THE EXISTENCE OF GOD: An argument that tries to show that the actual existence of God can be proved simply from the concept or definition of God.
3. *A PRIORI* ARGUMENT: An argument that does not use premises about how the world is.
4. *A POSTERIORI* ARGUMENT: An argument that does use premises about how the world is.
5. *REDUCTIO AD ABSURDUM* (or *reductio*): In this form of argument, you start off with a statement and derive a contradiction from that statement, thereby showing that the original statement is false.
6. NECESSARY BEING (or a being with necessary existence): A being that must exist by definition; or, a being such that if it exists, could not be caused not to exist by something else. (There are other definitions you will find if you explore the literature.)
7. THE COSMOLOGICAL (ALSO FIRST CAUSE) ARGUMENT FOR THE EXISTENCE OF GOD: An argument that proceeds from some highly general premises about the existence and nature of the universe to the conclusion that there must be a First Cause who created the world and sustains its existence.
8. CONTINGENT: Not necessary.
9. BIG BANG THEORY: Scientific theory that the universe started as a small singularity about 14 billion years ago and has been expanding (inflating) ever since.

10. THE TELEOLOGICAL (OR DESIGN) ARGUMENT FOR THE EXIST-
ENCE OF GOD: An argument that tries to show that the orderliness
and complexity of the universe make it reasonable to believe that the
universe was designed by God.

11. THE FINE-TUNING ARGUMENT: A recent version of the design argument which tries to show that the character of the universe seems to
be "fine-tuned" to be suitable for life/intelligence, and so it is reasonable to believe the universe was designed.

12. THEIST: One who believes that there is a God.

13. AGNOSTIC: One who isn't sure whether or not there is a God.

14. ATHEIST: One who believes that there is no God.

15. OMNIPOTENT: All powerful.

16. OMNISCIENT: All knowing.

17. THE PROBLEM OF SUFFERING: Does the existence of suffering show
that there could not be a God who is omnipotent (all-powerful), omniscient (all-knowing), and perfectly good?

18. THE FREE WILL DEFENSE: A defense of a perfect God allowing suffering by an appeal to the value of free will and the claim that God
cannot both grant free will and guarantee there is no suffering.

19. THE VIRTUE DEFENSE: A defense of a perfect God allowing suffering
on the grounds that virtues are great goods and require suffering.

20. THE WAGER ARGUMENT: Pascal's argument that given the lack of
evidence for God's existence along with the possibility of heavenly
reward if you believe and you are right, it is more rational to believe in
God than not.

21. FIDEISM: The view that faith is the way to God and that reason is
irrelevant—perhaps even harmful—to acquiring that faith.

Questions

(Please explain your answers, making specific reference to relevant passages in the discussion.)

1. Suppose you began to have some "visions." How would you decide
whether they represented some objective reality or were merely fantasies or hallucinations?

2. a. In ordinary cases of perception, how do we decide whether or not
what we are seeing is "real"?

    b. How would religious experiences be judged in terms of the above criteria?

3. "The Vision," of course, presents an odd sort of "religious experience." Do you feel that the religious experiences connected to whatever religion you are most familiar with have a greater chance of being veridical? Why or why not?

4. Anselm says that to say the "greatest conceivable being" (God) does not exist is contradictory. Explain his argument.

5. Descartes makes a similar argument about a "perfect being." Explain his argument.

6. Kant is considered to have formulated the most powerful objection to the "ontological argument." What is his objection?

7. "Everything must have a beginning so there must be a First Cause, namely, God." What are some problems with this argument?

8. What is the importance of Big Bang cosmology to the cosmological argument?

9. In what ways might the Big Bang theory be in accord with, or be at variance with, the creation account in the Book of Genesis?

10. How might quantum theory relate to the cosmological argument?

11. "The universe is so complex it baffles our greatest scientific minds. Something like that couldn't have just happened by chance. It must have been created by some intelligent being, namely God." Do you agree with this argument? Why or why not?

12. In what ways does the theory of evolution affect the argument from design?

13. What is the "fine-tuning argument" for the existence of God? What are its strengths and possible weaknesses?

14. What is the "problem of suffering"?

15. "Even an omnipotent God could not do contradictory things." Why?

16. "God couldn't create a world that's all happy because human beings aren't capable of being happy all the time." Critique this statement.

17. Present the free will defense and a possible objection to it.

18. Present the virtue defense and a possible objection to it.

19. Try to imagine the following sort of world: A world with more abundance than anyone could use up, including space for living; people with free will but with a tendency toward good (as we are now supposed to have a tendency toward selfishness or evil); people with bodies that

can suffer some painful injuries and diseases but can't be in agony or be maimed or be killed. In this world, people can have adventures and take risks and display moral qualities, though not to the degree that we can (because of the limits on suffering).

    a. Is there anything contradictory about this world? Explain.

    b. Would such a world be better or worse than our own? Explain.

20. Summarize Clifford's ship-owner story. He is using the story to make what point?

21. How does Clifford's approach to belief accord with your own approach to belief—in terms of both your general beliefs and your religious beliefs?

22. Compare and contrast Clifford and James in terms of their views of what would/does legitimate belief in a particular religious view entail?

23. What is Pascal's "wager argument"? What are some possible problems with it? Do you think that overall it's a good argument?

24. Why does Kierkegaard think the Christian faith is "absurd"? How is that connected to a leap of faith?

25. What do you think of the fideist idea that the intellectually difficult aspects of religion are a test of faith? Would that be a fair test?

Notes

Traditional Arguments for the Existence of God

The Ontological/Definitional Argument:

"The first philosopher to propose the ontological argument seems to have been Anselm of Canterbury." Anselm: From *Proslogium*, in *St. Anselm: Basic Writings*, ed. S. N. Deane. LaSalle, IL: Open Court, 1962.

"Another version . . . was used by Descartes." *Meditations on the First Philosophy.* By René Descartes, Translated by Laurence J. LaFleur. New York: Macmillan, 1979.

"One of Anselm's contemporaries, Gaunilo. . . . " See selection from Gaunilo in *Philosophy of Religion: Selected Readings.* Michael Peterson, William Hasker, Bruce Reichenbach, and David Basinger (eds.). New York: Oxford University Press, 1996.

"What seems to be the decisive objection . . . was first formulated by Immanuel Kant." *The Critique of Pure Reason.* By Immanuel Kant. Translated by J.M.D. Meiklejohn. New York: Colonial Press, 1900.

"In the contemporary period, some philosophers of religion have tried to resurrect the ontological argument by arguing that a perfect or a greatest conceivable being would have 'necessary existence.'. . . " See Further Readings for a list of readings on this topic.

The Cosmological/First Cause Argument

"The cosmological argument . . . was given its most famous formulations . . . [by] Saint Thomas Aquinas." Saint Thomas Aquinas, "Whether God Exists" from *Summa Theologica*. New York: Benziger Brothers, 1911.

"Since the general acceptance of the "Big Bang" theory. . . ." See Further Readings for a list of readings on this topic.

"As physicist Paul Davies says. . . ." From "A Naturalistic Account of the Universe" in *Philosophy of Religion*/Peterson.

The Teleological/Design Argument

"Neil A. Manson summarizes this fine-tuning argument. . . ." Neil Manson. "The Fine-Tuning Argument." *Philosophy Compass* 4, no. 1 (2009): 271–286.

"According to Michael Behe. . . ." Michael Behe. *Darwin's Black Box: The Biochemical Challenge to Evolution*. New York: Free Press, 1996. P. 39.

Atheism and the Problem of Suffering

The Free Will Defense
"As John Hick puts it. . . ." John Hick. *Philosophy of Religion*. Englewood Cliffs, NJ: Prentice-Hall, 1963.

The Virtue Defense
"According to John Hick. . . ." Hick. *Philosophy of Religion*. "Well, my dear Pangloss. . . ." Voltaire. Candide See www.esp.org/books/voltaire/candide.pdf. p. 91.

"John Hick . . . admits elsewhere. . . ." John Hick. *Evil and the Love of God*. New York: HarperSanFrancisco, 1977. Pp. 333–334. (Hick goes on to suggest that the mystery itself might also be seen as a test.)

Faith and Reason

"William K. Clifford . . . presents a story about a ship owner. . . ." William K. Clifford. "The Ethics of Belief." In *Philosophy of Religion: An Anthology*, 2nd edition. Louis P. Pojman (ed.). Belmont, CA: Wadsworth, 1994.

"Clifford set forth a stark principle. . . ." Clifford, "The Ethics of Belief."

"William James (1841–1910) attacked Clifford's position in 'The Will to Believe'. . . ." William James, "The Will to Believe." In *Philosophy of Religion*/ Pojman.

"He says that we have the [legitimate] option to believe without sufficient evidence. . . ." James, "The Will to Believe."

"James then brings his principle to bear on religious belief. 'We cannot escape. . . .'" James, "The Will to Believe."

". . . the famous 'wager argument' by . . . Blaise Pascal. . . ." Blaise Pascal, "The Wager." In *Philosophy of Religion*/ Pojman.

"[James] argues that 'if we put ourselves. . . .'" James, "The Will to Believe."

"[James] argues that 'we lose the good. . . .'" James, "The Will to Believe."

"Kierkegaard says that 'subjectivity is truth.'. . ." Søren Kierkegaard, "Subjectivity Is Truth." (*From Concluding Unscientific Postscript to the Philosophical Fragments*, 1844). In *Philosophy of Religion*/ Pojman.

Further Materials

Anthologies

Manson, Neil A. (ed.). *God and Design: The Teleological Argument and Modern Science*. London: Routledge, 2003. Sophisticated essays by philosophers and scientists on various versions of the design argument.

Peterson, Michael, Hasker, William, Reichenbach, Bruch, and Basinger, David (eds.). *Philosophy of Religion: Selected Readings*, 5th edition. Oxford: Oxford University Press, 2004. Includes readings on the following subjects: Religious Experience (including James); Faith and Reason (including Pascal, Clifford, James, and Kierkegaard); and Arguments about God's Existence (including Anselm, Gaunilo, Aquinas, and Paley; also Alvin Plantinga on a Modal Version of the Ontological Argument).

Pojman, Louis P (ed.). *Philosophy of Religion: An Anthology*, 5th edition. Boston: Cengage Learning, 2007. Includes essays on the following: religious experience, including the full reading by William James; the traditional arguments for the existence of God, including selections by Anselm, Aquinas, Descartes, Kant and Paley—as well as articles by Plantinga and Rowe on the modal version of the ontological argument; the problem of evil, including a reading by Hick; and on faith and reason, including selections from Clifford, James, Pascal, and Kierkegaard.

Quinn, Phillip L., and Taliaferro, Charles (eds.). *A Companion to Philosophy of Religion*, 2nd edition. Oxford: Wiley-Blackwell, 1997. Includes essays on the ontological, cosmological, and teleological arguments for the existence of God, on religious experience, and on the problem of evil.

Secondary Sources

Craig, William Lane, and Sinnot-Armstrong, Walter. *God? A Debate between a Christian and an Atheist*. Oxford: Oxford University Press, 2004.

Davies, Brian. *An Introduction to the Philosophy of Religion*, *3rd edition*. Oxford: Oxford University Press, 2004.

Gardiner, Patrick. *Kierkegaard: A Very Short Introduction*. Oxford: Oxford University Press, 1988.

Hick, John. *Evil and the Love of God*. New York: HarperSanFrancisco, 1977.

Van Inwagen, Peter. *The Problem of Evil*. Oxford: Oxford University Press, 2008.

CHAPTER 6

Morality
Fiction

READING 1: The Land of Certus

PREVIEW

In this story, a medieval traveler is thrilled to stumble upon a land where good and bad are clearly marked with strange lights. As you read the story, ask yourself:

* *If you came upon such a land, would you be inclined to accept the lights as indicating the good and the bad? Why or why not?*
* *Is there anything that would convince you that the lights don't really indicate the good and bad? If so, what? And why?*

Of all those lands in which I have traveled, the most wondrous is the land of Certus. The people there are to be envied above all others, for that which is to us the most perplexing mystery of existence is to them no mystery at all.

As I stepped from that treacherous forest through which I had wandered, lost, for five days, the first being I encountered in the land of Certus was Felanx. He was a roughhewn, kindly farmer who greeted me at the edge of his fields and offered me the hospitality of his home. Yet he frightened me at first. For when he smiled, there came from his face a strange green light, and I drew back, thinking him a sorcerer. But after a time, he succeeded in calming me with his gentle manner. He said that the light would not harm me and that he would explain it presently.

Felanx led me to the high stone walls of the town, past the sentry at the gate, through the narrow cobblestone streets to his home. As his family welcomed me, there were more flashes of that green light. But his son, who would not approach me, glowed a faint red. Felanx spoke harshly to the boy and dismissed him.

I was seated by the fire, given warm drink, and promised supper. I was no longer fearful of those strange lights, but my curiosity became too much to bear. I asked Felanx to provide me with the explanation he had promised.

"It is quite simple," he said. "From others who have come to our land, we know that these lights do not exist in other parts of the world. So I understand your confusion. Yet to us the lights seem most natural, and we cannot imagine a land that is otherwise. The green light is the light of the good. The red light, it shames me to say, is the light of the bad. You saw it around my youngest son. Most of the time he is a good boy, but sometimes he does not show the proper hospitality to strangers. He has been disciplined. Please accept my apologies on his behalf."

"The lights of good and bad!" I exclaimed. "This is trickery. Do you take me for a fool?"

As I spoke thus to my host, red light burst before my eyes, and I began to stammer in confusion. But once again, Felanx put me at ease. He said that he understood and forgave my skepticism. He said that once I had had a chance to observe his land further and to reflect on the matter, I would realize that he had spoken the truth.

I marveled at the words of my host. To have all good and bad deeds clearly marked so that everyone should know them for what they were: Could anything be a greater boon to humanity? I hesitated to believe, and yet had I not seen these lights with my own eyes? After some thought I inquired about the origin of the lights. "To that question," said Felanx, "there is no answer that seems to satisfy all. One answer is given in The Book of the Beginning. It says that the Creator made the skies and the earth and then, because He was lonely, He created human beings to be His companions. He put human beings in the most beautiful place on earth, the Valley of Peace, and He dwelt there with them. For a time all was happiness. But after a number of years, some people became restless. They said that they wanted to see what lay beyond the valley. The Creator told them there was nothing beyond the valley so happy and so lovely as it was. Still, many wanted to go. The Creator granted them permission at last, saying that He would constrain no one to stay with Him. But He was very angry. He told those who departed that they would find great sorrow in the lands beyond the valley and that they would never find their way back.

"But then one woman bowed down before the Creator and pleaded in tears for her descendants. Was it right, she asked, that they should all suffer for the folly of her headstrong daughter, who was among those who wished to leave? At her words, the Creator relented. He said that He would give those who departed the lights of good and bad, so that they would know how to make themselves worthy to return to the valley. He said that one day He would walk the earth and lead those who glowed with the goodness of green back to the Valley of Peace.

"That, I say, is just one answer. It is the one that my wife accepts. Others have argued that there is no Creator, that the skies and the earth have always been. They say that the lights of good and bad are simply natural events that require no supernatural explanation. The light of the good, they say, is no more mysterious than the other colors of things whose significance is beauty. I, myself, am of this opinion."

I remarked that in my land there were also doubts about a Creator. But the disputes of the Certans were as nothing compared with ours. For in my land, people interpreted good and bad "according to their own lights," and what each person saw was different. At least in Certus there were no doubts about goodness and badness: The lights were the same for everyone. And if there were doubts about a Creator, at least there could be no doubt about how to please Him, should He exist.

The next day, Felanx showed me around the town and introduced me to many of the townspeople. All those I met showed me the utmost kindness. They were eager to hear stories of my travels and to answer any questions I might have. In fact, I was preoccupied with just one question, and it was answered not by what was said to me but by what I observed for myself. I saw that the green lights did indeed mark acts of goodness and the red lights acts of badness. Not that the Certans are a bad people. On the contrary, they are a fine people. But they are human, and they make mistakes. The red light allows them to see their mistakes at once and to correct them.

At one home, we drank a delicious plum whiskey, and the green light over the gathering answered for me a question that divided those in my land, the question of whether it is evil to drink alcohol. The green light told me that drinking is good, though only in moderation. When one of the group became drunken, he glowed with a red light. He was led from the room, apologizing to us all.

As we emerged from another house, I noticed a ragged fellow stumbling as if inebriated, glowing the brightest of reds. The others with me jeered at him, but the fellow only smiled and made a sign with his hands, which I was given to understand was the vilest of profanities. I was surprised by the existence of this reprobate in Certus, and I asked Felanx about him.

"His name is Georges, and he is a difficult case," said Felanx. "At first, some thought that he might be blind to the lights of good and bad, as some are blind to colors and shapes. But he answers questions about the lights correctly. He just won't be guided by them. He knows the good but doesn't want to do it. His case is now before the town council. My guess is that there will be extreme punishment."

"But how can a man know the good and not want to do it?" I exclaimed.

At once I saw the foolishness of my remark, remembering that in the sacred book of my land it says that many fall not through ignorance but through the wickedness of the heart. I told Felanx of this.

"And so it says in The Book of the Beginning. But Georges is especially dangerous. Not only does he say that he often prefers wickedness to goodness, but he suggests that everyone should do so. He says that people should do what pleases them and should disregard the lights."

"But how can he be dangerous?" I asked. "Surely anyone can see that if all were to do as they pleased, with no thought of the good, with no thought of others, the result must be chaos, disastrous for all."

"Of course," said Felanx. "But Georges is subtle. He says that people should promote the happiness of others as well as their own. It is this that seems to absolve him of selfishness in the eyes of the young, and many are drawn by his words."

I shook my head sadly, reflecting on the perversity of human beings. As we walked on through the streets, my attention was drawn to the cannons placed along the town walls. I asked Felanx about them.

"You have learned today that there are two towns in Certus: ours, which is Rechtsen, and another, which is Linksen. What I have not told you about is the terrible perversity of the Linksens. But now that you know of the wicked Georges, you might as well know all.

"The Linksens are our mortal enemies. They have a religion that denies our own. They say that the lights of good and bad are not the work of the Creator, but the work of the Creator's enemy. They say that the lights of good and bad have been put in this land to confuse and lead astray the Creator's true friends. They say that we should not follow the lights but should instead follow the laws written in their book. These laws, they believe, express the Creator's true wishes."

I could not restrain myself at this absurdity.

"But surely they could be shown the truth. Listen: If at this moment, heaven forbid, I should strike you down for no reason, there would be a ferocious blaze of red. Is it not so?"

"Of course."

"And would it be the same in Linksen?"

"It would. The lights are the same in Linksen."

"There, then. Surely the Linksens cannot believe that such an act could be right or that the Creator would wish it. Were they to believe so, there would now be none of them left. This must prove to them that the lights show the truth."

Felanx lowered his head, and I sensed that he was close to tears.

"Alas, they too have their vicious subtleties. Were you to compare their rules of the good and the bad with the lights of the good and the bad, you would find much agreement. It is this, they say, that shows the cleverness of the Creator's enemy. He makes the lights so that they seem to show the truth in every case. It is this that misleads so many. The Linksens say that women should be equal to men, that animals are not to be eaten, and that the Rechtsens are to be destroyed. That the red light shows on such deeds, they say, is the triumph of deception."

The day that had begun with such joy had turned out sad, and I went to bed that evening with a heavy heart. I had always held the hope that as the nature of goodness became clearer to human beings, they would become better and better. Yet here in Certus, where all had been made clear, wickedness and dissension continued. Was there indeed any hope for humanity?

I awoke the next morning to the sound of a crowd yelling in the courtyard. I moved through the empty house and went outside. A hundred of the townspeople were gathered in the marketplace, viewing some spectacle. Moving into the crowd, I saw what it was. Georges was lying naked on a wooden platform, his body shackled. He was writhing and screaming, as one of the men standing over him slowly snapped the bones in his fingers with some heavy metal instrument. A glance at Georges's body and at the fiendish instruments held by the men around him showed that this was just one moment in a long process of torture. Nearby was a stake and a mound of wood where later they would burn his disfigured body.

I turned away in anger and horror, searching the faces in the crowd. All were watching the brutal spectacle with slight, solemn smiles. I saw Felanx near me and grabbed his arm.

"How can you do this?" I cried. "You who say you love the good."

"Georges is paying the price of his wickedness. The council decided last night. Georges ignores the good and incites others to do the same. He has to be punished. He has to be made an example. It is right that he be punished."

"Punished, yes," I said. "Perhaps even killed. But not like this. This is barbaric! This is horrible!"

Felanx pulled away from me, and his expression became fierce. He moved his hand, and for a moment I thought he was going to strike me. Instead he pointed toward Georges.

"Look again," he commanded.

"No. It is too terrible."

"Look at the men who are carrying out the sentence."

Reluctantly, I glanced toward the terrible scene. Then I saw what had escaped my attention before. The torturers of Georges were all glowing a faint green. This act that I had so readily condemned was, in fact, good. Suddenly my horror turned to shame.

"Forgive me," I said, bowing my head.

There was a moment of silence before Felanx spoke.

"You are forgiven, my friend. But I must concern myself now with your safety. The Linksens know of Georges's punishment. Their leaders have told the people that Georges is their spy and is suffering for their cause. This is not so, and the leaders know it. It is a mere pretext for attack. They will attack our city. You must leave at once."

"Let me stay," I pleaded, ashamed at having wrongly condemned the Rechtsens. "Life is not so much to me that I would not gladly sacrifice it for the sake of the good."

"I believe that," said Felanx. "But this is not your land, and this is not your battle. You must go."

I kept pleading until I noticed that a red glow began to arise from my body. Then I stopped. I had already committed one grievous error that day; I must not commit another. If it was wrong for me to stay there, then I must go.

An hour later, Felanx led me to the town gate, where he bade me goodbye and turned me over to the guide who was to lead me through the woods along a tortuous trail, which I fear I shall never find again.

The land of Certus is often in my thoughts. For it seems to me that if there is any hope for humankind, it must lie with those brave people of Rechtsen who know the good, follow it, and will fight for it to the end. May the Creator help them in their struggle.

Questions

1. In "The Land of Certus," the Rechtsens claim to see what is good and bad via perception of the lights. What, if anything, do you "see" when you see that something is good?

2. In making moral decisions, the Rechtsens are guided by the lights, the Linksens by the commands of their holy book, and Georges (apparently) by some principle to the effect that one ought to increase pleasure and diminish pain. They differ as to what is the correct evidence of good and bad. Can you imagine some way in which this dispute might be resolved?

3. In observing that the green light illuminates the torture of Georges, the narrator of "Certus," who had previously considered torture repulsive, decides that it is, after all, good. Presumably you continued to feel repulsed and pronounced the act of torture bad. Obviously, there is an intimate connection between feelings and value judgments. What is this connection?

READING 2: Those Who Help Themselves

> **PREVIEW**
>
> The table of contents introduces this story as follows: "The planet Omega had the 'only truly moral civilization that ever existed.' What was their secret?" As you read the story, ask yourself:
>
> * In what ways is the Omegan civilization portrayed as better than other societies? (You may not agree with the narrator's assessment in every respect.)
> * To the degree that Omegan civilization is more moral than others, what is their secret?

The war with the planet Omega is won. Its cities have been destroyed, its social institutions overthrown, its people injured and anguished. We have just destroyed what may have been the only truly moral civilization that ever existed.

All the civilizations that remain are morally defective. On Earth, in this twenty-third century after Jesus, in this fourth century after Marx, we certainly have not achieved what anyone would be tempted to call "utopia."

At the moment, of course, the situation is fairly stable. Birth control and the calamitous Far Eastern wars have drastically reduced the Earth's population. The nutrition extracted from the oceans and the wealth "extracted" from other worlds have appeased, momentarily, those who are left alive. But we still have our cruelties, our injustices; we still have our victors and victims.

As for other planets, the pathetic, vegetable-like creatures on Beta, though incapable of doing us harm, are vicious: They kill one another with grotesque frequency. The Alphas, who have more military capability, have friendly relations with us, but they are unspeakably cruel to their slave classes. The Gammas seemed to be the finest people we had encountered, until we discovered that they were merely protoplasmic machines and hence exempt from moral judgments. And so it goes through the whole of the known universe.

Ten years ago, the age-old pessimism about "human nature" had developed into a pessimism about all "living nature." At least such pessimism affords a certain comfort. If moral failure is indeed universal, then it may be inevitable and therefore no one's fault. The discovery of Omega challenged this deterministic view and threatened us with self-contempt.

No doubt we would have liked the moral contrast between us and the Omegans to be blurred by extreme dissimilarities of other sorts. But there were none of any consequence. The Omegans are a tall people, averaging just over 7 feet in height, and their flesh color ranges from dark brown to dark green. They have three eyes in a triangular formation, one mouth, and 15 sound receptors located on various parts of the body. They have two legs and also two appendages at each side of the upper body. Two of these appendages function like our arms and hands. The other two create, by the friction of the "fingers," the complex sounds by which they communicate. Their conceptual structure is analogous to our own and was easily deciphered by the Q-104 Computer Language Translator. The Omegans we confronted were a people fairly similar to us in all but one respect: They were morally good.

Naturally, we tried to explain away the apparent superiority of the Omegans. Could it be that they, like the Gammas, really had no minds? No: They had thoughts and feelings just as we did. Was there an overabundance of material goods on Omega? No: They also had problems of scarcity. Had they been endowed, through an evolutionary fluke, with an innate compulsion to be unselfish—a compulsion for which they, of course, could claim no credit? No: They were a people with that strong self-interest which morality attempts to tame. There seemed to be no way to rationalize the goodness of those people.

We were not, of course, struck at once by the moral superiority of the Omegans; goodness cannot be seen at a glance. We became aware of it only gradually. In fact, our first impression of the Omegans was quite negative. Initially, they were hostile to us, and they remained suspicious throughout our visit. Admittedly, such inhospitality toward strangers could be considered a moral defect. Nonetheless, it is true that, within their civilization, the Omegans' conduct was nearly impeccable.

The distribution of goods on Omega was not equal but was closer to equal than on any other world we had encountered. The Omegans were a highly competitive people who loved their pleasures and enjoyed what wealth they could accumulate, but they were nearly unanimous in supporting a system that assured that those less well off were well taken care of.

The Omegan government was democratic. The Omegans had a lively interest in debate, but they avoided ad hominem arguments, addressing themselves to issues rather than personalities, and their debates had a high moral tone. Campaigning for public office was vigorous but marked by neither excessive ambition nor rancor. All individuals showed a real concern for the ongoing welfare of the whole.

We got a sense of some existing biases relating to sex and skin color, but these seemed mild; in any case, a constitution ensuring strong individual rights ruled out these biases as factors in the public sphere.

The Omegans had a considerable interest in the arts and sciences. None of us was qualified to judge their "music," which, because of the vastly different sounds they made, was incomprehensible to us. Similarly, their literary style was difficult to judge, but the content of their literature seemed intricate and imaginative, entertaining, and sometimes profound. We were particularly impressed by their art, which showed a fine sense of line and color.

For the most part, their scientific achievements were the equal of ours. However they had been slower to develop space technology, presumably because they had little incentive to leave their planet. For obvious reasons, they had not developed sophisticated weaponry—at least until 50 years ago. At that time, they had begun to decode communications between other planets and had discovered, to their shock, the hostile nature of other life forms. Defense development had begun at once, and their crash program yielded remarkable weapons in a relatively short period of time. They had even managed to repel an attack from the planet Alpha some years before we came to Omega. Astonishingly, the Omegans never used such weapons against one another.

If many Earth people felt that the Omegan society was not quite ideal, many Omegans felt the same way. In fact, there were a number of political parties. The biggest opposition party wanted to enlarge the competitive market for goods. Another party, somewhat smaller, wanted no competition and a perfectly equal distribution of goods. There were disagreements about the conditions for redistribution—how much should be based on need and how much on work—but these debates rarely became hostile, and workable compromises were achieved.

As on Earth, there were cultural critics who claimed that the society was too focused on material well-being and too little on the arts and sciences, too little on ideals and the development of character. These critics claimed that society, through its social institutions, should focus less on the skills necessary to individual and social material well-being and more on developing skills and knowledge that would make the Omegans a better, not just happier, people. Different visions were offered as to what an ideal Omegan would be—more industrious or more tranquil and attuned to the natural world, more warrior-like or more gentle, more scientifically analytic or more emotional and intuitive. But the smaller parties and the various critics and visionaries all constituted a loyal opposition. All felt that the Omegan society was close enough to their ideal so that they could live happily enough with the status quo while trying to make their reforms. All recognized the ongoing value of democracy and of relative stability. No party—indeed, no person—had ever advocated a violent revolution. Because of the conspicuous absence of religion on Omega, there was no inclination to disrupt human welfare for the sake of some supernatural ideal.

Perhaps it is not correct to say that there was no religion on Omega. Certainly, there was no belief in a God, and there were no ceremonies of reverence for the universe. But there was one metaphysical belief, shared by all Omegans, that might be considered "religious." It apparently developed in their prehistory, and, if its beginnings were associated with revelations or proofs, there were no existing indications of such, even in the guise of myths. That this belief was so implicit in the Omegans' consciousness—no one had to be persuaded, it was never argued—kept it from our notice for some time. At first, we even misinterpreted the Omegans' expression of this belief. A phrase like "that unfortunate man might be me" sounded so much like the imaginative exhortations of our moralists that we failed to comprehend that the phrase was intended literally. Finally, we did understand, and, in understanding, I suppose, we discovered the "secret" of the Omegans' moral behavior.

The Omegans believed in the perpetual reincarnation of souls, which was not the work of some divinity but simply the natural way of things. Almost as soon as a person died, the soul was reborn in the body of some infant, with all memories of the past life erased. This reincarnation, they believed, was not only natural but random: Merits and demerits in a past life had nothing whatever to do with a soul's placement in the next life, and one's inclinations and abilities were not transferred from one life to another. In the next life, the woman of great intellect might be intellectually disabled, the man of good health might be diseased, the person of great culture might be interested only in popular entertainments—or vice versa. One might be reborn the same or quite different; sex, skin color, and looks could change from one reincarnation to the next. There was no way of knowing in advance.

The moral efficacy of this belief is obvious. It is a consequence of this belief that, in promoting a nondiscriminatory society in which each person helps others, one is quite literally helping oneself. No one was willing to neglect another because soon one might be in the same position.

There were, as has been noted, some differences of opinion on Omega concerning the moral and political status quo. Apparently, those supporting the largest opposition party were gamblers: They were willing to risk the possibility of some misfortune in the next life for the possibility of gaining great wealth in this life. Those on the opposite end of the political spectrum were unwilling to gamble at all with their future lives: They wanted to be guaranteed an equal share of the wealth. Those who supported the majority party wanted some guarantees and some chances to gamble. But none was willing to gamble too much with his or her future life, to risk being diseased, mentally defective, or hungry, and being without help. Thus, each agreed that all should be helped. Guarantees in no way sapped the industriousness of the Omegans, since all would share in the future benefits of their own labors. There were, of course, some moral lapses. Like all people, the Omegans were tempted to emphasize their present rather than their future welfare. But only rarely did they give in to this temptation.

The belief in perpetual reincarnation softened but did not do away with the vigorous debates about ideals. Some argued that, apart from matters of social morality, society should be neutral about what sorts of ideals, if any, individuals chose to guide their lives. Others argued that the values of certain ideals weren't dependent on what people wanted; instead, they were the standards for what people *should* want. They argued that society should push (though not compel) Omegans to be a certain way—for instance, to develop a knowledge of history and the sciences, to develop and use what individual talents they might have. Still, no one was willing to push the debate to the point where it might disrupt the well-being of the Omegans' society. The Omegans were, indeed, an enviable people.

Some Earth critics of the Omegan war say that we came to conquer. Leaving aside our moral qualms (which those critics might deny we have), we simply do not have the power to conquer and control a universe. On these grounds alone, we always prefer a peaceful relationship of mutually profitable cooperation.

The problem was that the Omegans refused to acknowledge the moral rights of creatures other than Omegans. Just as twenty-third-century Christians cannot believe that Jesus died to save Betas and Epsilons, just as Marxists don't know what to think about economic determinism on other worlds, so the Omegans could not believe that their souls might migrate beyond their own race. They had no incentive at all to treat other beings fairly, and, in fact, after a time, they began to treat us very badly.

Perhaps if the crisis had not come so quickly, some say, the Omegans might have adjusted their morality to include other life forms. But this would not have happened as long as those others did not share the beliefs of the Omegans.

Perhaps, then, some add, we would have come to share the religion of the Omegans. This is a lovely fantasy, indeed. If a religion is to be judged by its moral efficacy, the "religion" of the Omegans is the best we have ever encountered. But this is mere speculation. One does not change religions as one changes clothes. Earth has its religions already, and, for good or ill, we seem to be stuck with them.

Then we should have left the Omegans alone, say the critics. But this is naive. No one gets left alone, on Earth or beyond. Either people get along, or they fight. We fought. The conflict was inevitable.

In another place and time, when war meant human beings facing human beings, the Omegans would have been unbeatable. Their firm belief in a perpetual reincarnation would have made them supremely courageous and persistent. But such qualities count for nothing against missiles. The weapons they had been able to develop within 50 years may have been good enough against Alpha but not against Earth. The war, of course, was brief—and, for the Omegans, devastating.

Few faiths survive such catastrophes. The faith of the Omegans has not. Already, for the first time in the recorded history of Omega, questions are being raised, questions for which no one has answers. Whatever the Omegans may be in the future, it is clear that they will never be the same. Their past civilization will become a footnote to the depressing history of the universe, a footnote both beguiling and accusatory: It was the only truly moral civilization that has ever existed.

Questions

1. According to the narrator of "Those Who Help Themselves," the Omegans' belief in reincarnation motivated them to be moral. In what way does this belief relate to morality? What general considerations or principles did the Omegans employ in determining what is good and bad?

2. What moral disagreements were there among the Omegans? How did the belief in perpetual reincarnation temper these?

3. The theme of "Those Who Help Themselves" suggests that frequently a conflict arises between self-interest and the dictates of morality, at least for the people of Earth. Give some everyday examples of this conflict, and try to explain what it is about morality that tends to conflict with one's self-interest.

4. If you believed in a morality like the Omegans, what sort of society and what sorts of moral principles would you endorse? Does your answer differ in any way from the kind of society and the kinds of moral principles you now endorse?

5. Apart from pressuring people to obey just laws, do you think society should pressure people to be a certain way, to develop certain abilities and character, and to achieve certain goals? Explain.

Discussion

PREVIEW

At the end of this discussion you should be familiar with:

* *the distinction between metaethics and normative ethics;*
* *the theories of moral objectivism and moral subjectivism, and the argument given for moral subjectivism;*
* *the problems with the simpler forms of moral subjectivism and how the theory has been modified to take care of those problems;*
* *the theory of cultural relativism;*
* *the idea of the moral point of view and how it relates to the theories of Adam Smith and Immanuel Kant;*
* *the debate between the utilitarian and John Rawls from the moral point of view;*
* *virtue ethics and the ethics of care, and the strengths and weaknesses of both theories;*
* *the difficulties in dealing with racial issues using Rawls's ideal social contract model;*
* *the meaning of terms listed in "Definitions" (which are also marked in bold in the discussion).*

Metaethics Versus Normative Ethics

"The Land of Certus" raises two sorts of moral or ethical questions. First, "Certus" emphatically raises **metaethical questions**: questions concerning whether or not moral/ethical judgments are true and false and, if so, whether or not we can know which ones are true and false. Initially, it seems as if there are no troublesome metaethical issues in Certus. Good things are those that glow green, whereas bad things are those that glow red. If someone says that something is good and that thing glows green, then the statement is true. Knowing good and bad is just a matter of looking at the colors. However, it turns out that there are others in Certus who say that the lights do not correctly mark the good and bad. The Linksens say that knowledge of good and bad is really to be found in their book. Georges disregards both the lights and the religious book and identifies good and bad with pleasure and pain, respectively. Here we confront the issue of how moral questions are to be decided.

"Certus" also brings up—though without much emphasis— **normative ethical questions**: questions about what things are good or bad, right or wrong, about what things should or should not be done. The Rechtsens, the Linksens, Georges, and the people from the narrator's land each have opinions about what is good and bad. It is obvious that there are differences of opinion among them, even if these differences are not elaborated. The following normative questions are noted: "Is torture ever permissible?" "Ought men and women to be treated equally?" "Is it permissible to do whatever pleases you if no one else is harmed?"

Other normative questions are raised by "Those Who Help Themselves." Many of these questions are raised in a social/political context, but they all have moral underpinnings. How much, if anything, does society owe to the less fortunate, and what, if anything, should society demand in return? What rights do people have? Do our larger moral obligations relate only to the material and emotional well-being of others, or are there also moral obligations to develop our characters and capacities beyond our inclinations, to push ourselves to be stronger, more knowledgeable, and more capable people?

We shall begin by considering metaethical questions about the nature of morality and moral judgments. What are we saying when we make a moral judgment? Are we stating beliefs about objective moral properties in the world—properties such as goodness and badness, rightness and wrongness? Is there such a thing as the moral truth? Can moral judgments be justified and, if so, in what way? Or are they all just subjective or relative?

The terms "moral" and "ethical" (as we shall treat them here) are synonymous and similarly ambiguous. Used as normative ethical terms to make moral judgments, their opposites are "immoral" and "unethical." Used as metaethical terms their meaning is "pertaining to moral or ethical questions"; their opposites are "nonmoral" and "nonethical." (For instance, aesthetics would involve evaluations that are nonmoral.) In this metaethical usage, it is uncontroversial to say that both Gandhi and Hitler had moral/ethical theories—that is, theories about what is good or bad, right or wrong.

Moral judgments are a type of value judgment, along with judgments in the domains of aesthetics, etiquette, and personal taste. There's a familiar distinction made between value judgments and **factual judgments**, between fact and value. To claim that this apple tastes better than that apple is a value judgment; to claim that this apple is heavier than that apple is a factual judgment (we can weigh the apples on a scale). The claim that abortion is wrong would be a value judgment; the claim that three million abortions are performed in the United States in a year would be a factual judgment—one that could be shown to be true or false by gathering data.

To call a judgment "factual" is not to imply that it is true; in fact, the claim that three million abortions are performed in the United States every year is false. The latest data from the two leading compilers of abortions statistics in the United States —the Centers for Disease Control and the Guttmacher Institute—show that abortions for the years 2013 and 2014 were under a million in each of those years. To call a judgment "factual" is only to say that it's the sort of judgment that might be resolved through empirical evidence.

Predicting the abortion figure for 2040 would be a factual judgment; we'd have to wait for the figures, but eventually we should have them.

The ultimate contrast here is between value judgments and factual judgments, with moral judgments being a type of value judgment. We would all agree that many value judgments are subjective, being a matter of personal preference. But many people believe that moral judgments (unlike other value judgments) *are* objective; they are analogous to factual judgments in that respect.

Let's ask: Is morality ultimately objective or subjective?

Moral Objectivism and Moral Subjectivism

The **moral objectivist** says that where we have a moral judgment and its negation, one of these judgments must be true and the other false. In this sense, moral judgments are analogous to judgments in the domain of science. We would all agree that where we have two statements like "There is microbial life on Mars" and "There is no microbial life on Mars," one of these statements must be true and the other false (assuming "microbial life" is defined carefully enough). We know this, even if we do not know which of the statements is true and which is false. According to the moral objectivist, the same is the case with moral judgments. Where we have two judgments like "All abortion is wrong" and "Not all abortion is wrong," one of the judgments must be true and the other false.

The moral objectivist says that of the various moral theories, at most one of these theories can be true, and the rest must be false. One and only one moral theory could correctly describe the phenomena relevant to moral questions. In this sense, there is such a thing as *the* moral truth.

Precisely what the phenomena are that moral judgments purport to describe is a matter of debate among objectivists. One theory, **naturalism**, claims that those phenomena are features of the natural world to which scientific theories (including psychology) also refer; for instance, the claim that "right" means "increasing happiness and diminishing unhappiness" would be a naturalist claim. Another theory, **non-naturalism**, says that those phenomena are special properties not reducible to natural properties. A third theory, **supernaturalism**, states that those phenomena are the commands of God. There's overlap here. "The Land of Certus" was written with a cartoonish version of non-naturalism in mind, with special nonphysical lights marking what's good and bad. Yet Felanx finds these lights quite "natural" and his wife believes they have a supernatural origin, having been placed there by God.

In any case, all objectivists agree that moral theories are rival theories about some sort of moral phenomena. Many objectivists would claim to know which moral theory is true. Almost all objectivists would claim to know at least that certain moral theories are false—for instance, those that endorse human slavery or the extermination of some racial group. Other moral objectivists would claim that some moral theory must be true, but that they do not know which one is true.

In the "Land of Certus," the Rechtsens believe that morality is objective. The green lights mark the good and the red lights mark the bad. The Rechtsens do disagree about the origins of the lights, but they all believe the lights mark *the* moral truth—a truth that applies to everyone (i.e., is universal). When Georges rejects the lights in favor of following pleasure, the Rechtsens believe he is accepting a moral view that is false. When the Linksens, following their own religion, reject the lights in favor of rules that overlap but don't perfectly coincide with what the lights indicate, Rechtsens believe the Linksens have false moral views.

In contrast, the **moral subjectivist** claims that where we have a moral judgment and its negation, neither judgment need be false. There is no one correct answer to moral questions; there is no such thing as *the* moral truth. Moral questions are not analogous to scientific questions; rather, they are analogous to questions of taste. We all agree that there are questions of taste, for example: "Is yellow prettier than blue?" "Does apple pie taste better than cherry pie?" Most of us would agree that when one person says, "This apple pie is good" and another says, "This apple pie is not good," neither judgment need be false. In such cases, what is at issue are not conflicting descriptions of the apple pie but differing reactions toward the pie.

Analogously, according to the moral subjectivist, moral judgments express attitudes toward persons, actions, or events, rather than being descriptions of such things. When one person says, "All abortion is wrong" and another says, "Not all abortion is wrong," each is expressing a different attitude toward abortion and neither judgment need be false. Moral goodness or badness, rightness or wrongness—like prettiness, like deliciousness—are "in the eye of the beholder." Moral issues are fundamentally "subjective."

The idea that morality is fundamentally subjective should strike you as a familiar view. It is dramatized in much of the existentialist literature: The universe contains no intrinsic values, so each individual must "invent" his or her own. It is presupposed by much of the current talk about "value-free" scientific theories: True science, it is thought, should deal only with factual matters because matters of values are too subjective.

An Argument for Moral Subjectivism

Having outlined the theories of moral objectivism and moral subjectivism, let us now consider an argument for moral subjectivism.

When we consider a scientific question, we do not always agree on the answer. But we can agree on what evidence would decide the issue. For example, we may not know whether there is microbial life on a particular planet, but we do agree on what evidence would show that such life on that planet exists.

With regard to questions of taste, however, there is no conceivable evidence that would resolve such issues. There is no conceivable evidence that would demonstrate that yellow is prettier than blue or that apple pie is better than cherry pie.

If moral questions are indeed analogous to scientific questions, then we ought to be able to specify what evidence would decide moral questions. According to the moral subjectivist, we cannot do this. There is no evidence that would demonstrate that abortion is right or wrong, that an equal distribution of goods is or is not better than competition for goods. Thus, says the subjectivist, moral questions cannot be analogous to scientific questions. Instead, they are analogous to questions of taste.

Put more formally, the moral subjectivist argument is this:

1. Moral questions are like either scientific questions (objective) or questions of taste (subjective).

2. Being like scientific questions implies that one can always specify what evidence would decide the questions.

3. With moral questions, one can't always specify what evidence would decide the questions.

4. (Therefore) moral questions are not like scientific questions (objective) (from 2 and 3).

5. (Therefore) moral questions are like questions of taste (subjective) (from 1 and 4).

"The Land of Certus" explores the possibility of decisive moral evidence, and the story is slanted in favor of the moral subjectivist. In Certus, apparently, the good is clearly marked with a green light and the bad with a red light. Seemingly, there ought to be no moral disputes in Certus. But there are such disputes. Georges and some of the younger people claim that one ought to ignore the lights whenever they conflict with the principle that one ought to promote the happiness of oneself and others. The Linksens abide by a religious book that sometimes contradicts what is indicated by the lights. The Linksens say that their book, not the lights, shows what is truly good and bad.

Toward the end of the story, the narrator is shocked when the green light illuminates an act of torture, but he decides that if the green light so indicates, then the act of torture must be good. Presumably, many readers formed the opposite conclusion: The act of torture would not be good no matter what the lights indicated.

Here the subjectivist could issue the following challenge: Suppose that an act that you found abhorrent were labeled as good by some law or by public opinion or by some magical light as in Certus. Would you conclude that the act you find abhorrent is good? Or would you conclude that the act cannot be good, since you find it abhorrent? Wouldn't you say the latter? And doesn't this indicate that morality is basically a matter of how you feel about things?

Many readers may have an ethic based on what they believe to be divine commands, and they may feel that the argument for moral subjectivism seems forceful only because it neglects religious considerations. Such a reader might argue that throughout history, our ethical beliefs have been reflections of what we believed to be the wishes of the gods, or God; if an omnipotent, omniscient creator was revealed to all and was to make known what we were to do and not do, that would show everyone what things are good or bad, right or wrong.

Some quasi-subjectivists have claimed that moral disputes are unresolvable only because no God exists to "answer" moral questions. However, full-fledged moral subjectivists would deny that even the clear commands of a God would resolve all moral disputes. This is not to say that such a God could not force everyone to follow these commands. But "might" is not necessarily "right." The issue here is whether the clear commands of a God would result in a rational resolution of moral disputes.

Moral subjectivists might begin an attack on the idea that good is what God commands by bringing up a famous dilemma related to the connection between religion and morality that goes back at least to the ancient Greeks: (a) Is something good because God commands it, or (b) Does God command it because it is good?

Option a implies that the mere act of God's commanding us to do or not do something is enough to make that something right or wrong. What reasons, if any, God may have for the command are irrelevant. The only morally relevant feature is that God did indeed command it. This is often called **the divine command theory** of ethics.

Option b implies that God commands things for certain reasons, and it is these reasons that make things right or wrong—not the mere fact of God's commanding.

Option a provides the closest tie between God and morality. However, the problem many people have with the divine command theory is that it sets no prior limits on what God might have commanded. It commits one to saying that even if God had commanded gratuitous, terrible acts of torture, such acts would necessarily be good or right. To those theists who are willing to accept these consequences, subjectivists could say the following: Even if you would be willing to accept something as good just because God commanded it, many people, including many theists, would not. These other theists would say that even God must have some satisfactory justification for a command if that command is to be good. This shows that the clear commands of God per se would not be the supposed evidence that would resolve all moral disputes—including moral disputes between human beings and God. (If you have trouble imagining a human being having a moral disagreement with God, think back to the argument between Martin and God in "Surprise! It's Judgment Day.")

Those who say that God commands something because it is good avoid having to say that a terrible act of torture would be good by the simple supposition of God's commanding it. They can say that torture is objectively bad, and God wouldn't command something that was bad. But this position undercuts the argument against moral subjectivism given above. That argument supposed that the clear commands of God would be the evidence that would resolve all moral disputes. But to say that God commands something because it is good supposes that God decides what is good or bad on the basis of some evidence. Now the theists must start all over again and specify what, if any, evidence would resolve all moral disputes—including moral disputes between human beings and God.

Some theists are inclined to say: "What God commands must be good because God is omniscient and hence knows what is good." Or: "What God commands must be good because God is Goodness." Note that these arguments, as stated, beg the question, assuming rather than supporting the conclusion they purport to establish. What is at issue here is whether goodness is a matter of knowledge rather than of attitude and whether goodness is an objective property or a subjective matter of attitude. Such arguments simply assume the conclusion they are supposed to support. They simply assume a form of moral objectivism.

The moral subjectivist claims that no evidence, even the revelation of some divine law, would resolve our moral disputes. In the last analysis, what is approved of is pronounced "good" and what is disapproved of is said to be "bad." Moral judgments, then, are basically expressions of one's attitudes and feelings.

LET'S REVIEW

* *What is the difference between metaethics and normative ethics? Is moral subjectivism a metaethical or normative ethical theory? Explain.*
* *What is divine command theory? If true, would it make morality objective? What are the difficulties with divine command theory?*
* *Make sure you understand the basic argument for moral subjectivism.*

Moral Subjectivism Reconsidered

If this argument for moral subjectivism seems forceful, note that this position still has not been stated precisely. If we are to evaluate moral subjectivism properly, we need to describe it in greater detail.

There have been some terribly implausible versions of moral subjectivism. We'll start with a crude version of moral subjectivism and then see how, and why, it has been altered to yield a more sophisticated version.

One crude form of moral subjectivism claims that moral judgments or theories are simple descriptions of the speaker's attitudes. The statement "X is right" means "I approve of X"; the statement "X is wrong" means "I disapprove of X." According to this theory, all sincere moral judgments are true. When one person says, "All abortion is wrong" and another says, "Not all abortion is wrong," neither statement need be false because the second does not really contradict the first. One person is saying, "I (Brenden Weaver) disapprove of all abortion" and the other, "I (Valeria Osorio) do not disapprove of all abortion." (Note that some philosophers reserve the name "moral subjectivism" for this crude "I-approve" version. We are using the label "subjectivism" in a broader sense that contrasts more properly with "objectivism.")

That this version of moral subjectivism is implausible—or, at least, incomplete—can be seen by noting certain features of our moral discourse that are highlighted in the story, "Those Who Help Themselves." The people on Omega debate moral issues and come to considerable agreement. We on Earth may not reach so much agreement, but we certainly do debate moral matters. We attempt to persuade others of our moral views and we occasionally succeed. We have a saying: "There's no disputing matters of taste." Yet we dispute matters of morals. How can this be if moral judgments are nothing more than statements about one's own tastes or preferences?

"Those Who Help Themselves" assumes that there is at least a theoretical distinction between doing what is in one's self-interest and doing what is morally right. In part, at least, this relates to the distinction between what is in one's own interest and what is in the interest of others. On Omega, in practice, there is little real conflict in this matter. The moral efficacy of the Omegan's belief in perpetual, random reincarnation is that it leads them to believe that in promoting a society that helps others, they are helping themselves. On Earth there is considerable conflict between a person's own interests and that which is morally right or between one's own interests and the interests of others. This conflict is not only external but internal: We sometimes feel pulled between what we want to do and what we feel we ought to do. Yet there is no hint of the distinction between one's self-interest and that which is morally right in the subjectivist view that moral judgments are only statements of preference.

These are forceful objections to the simple form of moral subjectivism presented earlier. Moral subjectivists have recognized the force of these criticisms and have attempted to revise subjectivism to meet them.

Moral judgments, say these subjectivists, do not (or do not merely) have the function of stating preferences. They have the function of attempting to influence the preferences and actions of others. The I-approve-of-it analysis of moral judgments is not adequate. The judgment "It is good, or right" would be better analyzed as meaning "I approve of this; you should approve of this as well; you should do this sort of thing." Or "Let's do (not do) this sort of thing."

Furthermore, present-day subjectivists would say that moral preferences are a particular type of preference. One's **moral preferences** express how one would like to see all people treat one another; they express general prescriptions, rules for human behavior. Moral preferences are not the I-prefer-to-do-this type of preference. Rather, they imply the message: Let us all act in this sort of way. Moral preferences are one's preferences from the standpoint of a hypothetical legislator for all human beings. A person's preferred rules count as moral rules only if they are not prejudiced in favor of one's particular circumstances. To propose moral rules is to imply that such rules should apply even if one were in the other person's position. As the eighteenth-century philosopher Immanuel Kant termed it, moral judgments are **universalizable**.

A person who, using imagination, discounts his or her particular circumstances, surveys the human condition, and thinks about what rules all human beings should follow is said to be taking the **moral point of view**. To express a moral preference is to express a preference from the moral point of view.

In addition to "moral preferences," people have **personal preferences**. Our personal preferences have to do with what we each want for ourselves. Our personal desires often conflict, however. Our desire to spend two weeks at the beach, for example, may conflict with our desire to save money for some new clothing. In an analogous way, says the subjectivist, our moral preferences and our personal preferences may conflict. From the moral point of view, we may wish that people would keep their promises. From the personal point of view, we may wish to break a promise we find very inconvenient to keep. Thus it is that there is often a conflict between self-interest and that which is morally right, says the subjectivist. This is not a matter of a clash between personal preferences and the dictates of some objective moral rules. Rather, it is a matter of a clash between personal preferences and moral preferences (preferences from the moral point of view).

We'll talk more about moral subjectivism and the moral point of view. But first: Many of you have heard attacks on the objectivity of ethics put in terms not of subjectivism but of "relativism," especially "cultural relativism." To get you oriented, let's talk about "cultural relativism" and how it fares as a metaethical theory, while also discussing the relationship between relativism and subjectivism.

What About Cultural Relativism?

In evaluating cultural relativism as a rival metaethical theory, it's important to make certain distinctions and guard against certain confusions.

If you asked someone what cultural relativism is, you might get the following answer: Cultural relativism says the beliefs of any culture are as good or as true as the beliefs of any other culture.

However, it's important that we not use the terms "good" and "true" as if they're synonyms. To say a belief is true is to say something about its reflecting the way the world or our common experience is. To say a belief is good or bad (rather than true or false) is to say something very different.

Imagine an aunt in the hospital who has a very serious illness. Her spirits are good because she believes she's going to recover. However, you and the rest of the family have just seen the most recent test results and those results indicate that your aunt will die within days. You and the family debate whether to "tell her the truth" (let's say she would accept the results if she saw them) or let her go on with a false belief that is good in that it spares her immediate suffering. Whether or not a belief is good says nothing about whether or not it's true. If we want to view cultural relativism as a metaethical theory, we need to focus on truth: that the beliefs of different cultures are equally true.

Another definition you might get is the following: Cultural relativism says it is wrong to judge another culture. This is cultural relativism as a normative theory—usually as a demand for tolerance—not as a metaethical theory. It is not a claim about the meanings of ethical terms. It is not a talk about truth and cultural norms. It is a normative moral judgment about how we should view other cultures.

We need to distinguish the following types of moral/ethical relativism:

a. **Metaethical relativism**
   i. **Cultural relativism**
   ii. **Individual relativism**
b. **Normative relativism**

Cultural relativism is the notion that moral judgments make reference to cultural norms; **individual relativism** says that moral judgments make reference to individual norms. **Normative relativism** takes a moral position, affirming that it is wrong to judge other cultures (or perhaps other individuals).

Cultural relativism (CR) makes two claims:

> CR1: The predominant moral beliefs of different cultures are equally true.
>
> CR2: Moral beliefs within a culture are true or false depending on whether or not they agree with the predominant moral beliefs of that culture.

To say that all moral beliefs are equally true would be a form of individual relativism. In order to qualify as cultural relativism, the theory has to tie truth and falsity to the dominant norms of the culture. CR2 isn't always made explicit by cultural relativists, but it has to be included to make cultural relativism a distinct and complete metaethical view.

A number of factors have tended people toward cultural relativism: notably, the discovery of the extreme diversity of cultures; anthropological studies of native cultures that initially made them seem monolithic; and sympathy for native cultures beset by Western prejudice and imperialism.

One can see how the position of cultural relativism arose. Still, moral relativism put in terms of cultures must include CR2. And CR2 is false.

If CR2 were true, we would resolve moral questions by finding out what the majority of people in our society believes. That is not what we do.

Suppose I'm a conservative Catholic who believes that abortion is wrong in almost every case. Reliable opinion polls show that the vast majority of Americans disagree with me. Am I forced to conclude that my views on abortion are false? Of course not. Nobody thinks that right and wrong should be determined by opinion polls. But that's just what cultural relativism implies.

If moral disagreement is to be used as evidence for relativism, it would have to be for individual relativism, not cultural relativism. Note that individual relativism doesn't deny the evidence adduced for cultural relativism in terms of the vast differences between the moral beliefs of different cultures. It acknowledges that many people adopt the beliefs of their cultures. It also acknowledges that many people may think in terms of their cultural mores when deciding ethical questions. What it denies is that the relativity of morals stops at the level of culture. It says that the relativity goes all the way down to the individual.

Individual relativism can be seen as the view that every conflicting moral judgment is equally true. Once you start spelling out this view, you

RUTH BENEDICT (1887–1948), an American anthropologist, was quite explicit about CR2: "Mankind has always preferred to say, 'It is good,' rather than 'It is habitual.'. . . . But historically the two phrases are synonymous. . . . The concept of the normal is properly a variant of the concept of good. It is that which society has approved."

run into the same problems subjectivists ran into with their simple I-approve version. The theory that "X is good" means "I approve of X" makes every sincere moral judgment true but yields an implausible metaethical theory. To get a plausible theory of individual relativism you need to view moral judgments as expressing attitudes and giving prescriptions. As a result you end up with the same metaethical view as sophisticated subjectivism: Moral views are equal in being neither true nor false.

One attraction of cultural or individual relativism is its apparent demand for tolerance. However, this is a mistake. Normative cultural relativism does not follow from metaethical cultural relativism. If metaethical cultural relativism were true and I was in a culture that was intolerant of other cultures, then the judgment "I should not be tolerant of other cultures" would be true. As for individual relativism/subjectivism, "I ought to be tolerant of others" and "I ought not to be tolerant of others" are equal in being neither true nor false. So although there is often a psychological connection between a belief in metaethical relativism and a belief in the rightness of tolerance, there is no logical connection.

One more observation before we return to moral subjectivism and the moral point of view: The current metaethical debate has gotten very complex and technical in recent years. While such sophistication is generally beyond the scope of this text, it might be worth placing our discussion in that more sophisticated context in case you do further reading in metaethics. (If the discussion thus far has been technical enough for you, you could skip the next section, which is not essential for understanding the remainder of the chapter.)

LET'S REVIEW

* What are some problems with the subjectivist view that "X is right" means "I approve of X"?
* Explain the distinction between personal preferences and moral preferences.
* What is metaethical cultural relativism? What is one major problem with it?
* What is normative cultural relativism? Is it implied by metaethical cultural relativism?

A More Technical Take on Metaethics

To get a fix on some of the complexities of current metaethical debates, we'll present an **expanded definition of moral objectivism**. All of these elements were implied by the previous definition, but more details are necessary to see how various positions branch off from objectivism. Let's say that moral objectivists would endorse the following three claims:

1. Moral judgments state beliefs about moral properties in the world.
2. There are such moral properties in the world.
3. At least some of these properties apply to all human beings.

Claim 1, that moral judgments state beliefs about moral properties in the world, is called **cognitivism**. Note that moral judgments do have a form similar to that of descriptive statements about the world. Compare:

FACTUAL	MORAL
"Giving to charity is tax-deductible."	"Giving to charity is praiseworthy."
"Stealing is against the law."	"Stealing is morally wrong."
"Child abuse is on the rise."	"Child abuse is a terrible sin."

Cognitivists say that moral judgments, being claims about properties in the world are "**truth-apt**"—such as to be true or false.

The denial of claim 1 leads to a position called **noncognitivism**: the view that moral judgments, in spite of their form, do not make truth-apt statements about properties of the world. Actually, they don't make any statements at all. Instead they are used to express approvals and disapprovals (**expressivism**) or to prescribe rules for general conduct (**prescriptivism**). Noncognitivism is close to the expanded definition of subjectivism we've been using, which is a combination of expressivism and prescriptivism.

Claim 2, that there in fact exist the kinds of moral properties referred to in a cognitivist account of moral judgments, is called **moral realism**. If you think moral judgments are descriptions about something out there (call them "moral properties") and if you think that some moral judgments are true (e.g., torturing children is wrong), then you must think that the *wrongness* (e.g., of torturing children) is a property out there. Those who deny moral realism are sometimes called **antirealists**.

Naturalists, non-naturalists, and supernaturalists are all cognitivists and moral realists. They claim that moral judgments make truth-apt claims about properties in the world and that there are such properties. Of course, they differ in terms of what they think moral properties are—natural, non-natural, or supernatural.

Noncognitivists (and what we've been calling "subjectivists") are antirealists: Since moral judgments don't make claims about properties and instead are expressions of attitude and/or prescriptions for rules of behavior, there can be no properties that qualify as moral properties.

Claim 3, that at least some of these properties apply to all human beings, we could call **universalism**. The claim that some moral judgments are universally true seems integral to most religious moralities—certainly those connected with monotheistic religions which hold that there is one God for all human beings. It is also implied by claims of (universal) human rights.

The metaethical theory of cultural relativism would be cognitivist/realist but not universalist. It is cognitivist because it claims that moral judgments make claims about moral properties (cultural norms), and it is realist because it claims that such properties/norms exist. It is not universalist because it claims that the norms vary from culture to culture.

The argument for moral subjectivism given earlier was an argument for noncognitivism (against cognitivism) and for moral antirealism (against moral realism). The question of universalism has been left open. In what follows, how one answers the question of universalism will depend on how one interprets the moral point of view.

LET'S REVIEW

* *Give the three-part expanded definition of objectivism.*
* *Such objectivism is "cognitivist," "realist," and "universalist." Explain these three terms.*
* *Here's a tough one: Is the "'It is good' means 'I-approve-it'" version of subjectivism cognitivist or noncognitivist? realist or antirealist? universalist or nonuniversalist? (Hint: It's analogous to cultural relativism in this respect. Try to see why.)*

From the Moral Point of View

Let's now return to our discussion of the sophisticated subjectivist view. If you'll remember, that view says that to make a moral judgment is to express a moral preference as opposed to a personal preference. Moral preferences are one's preferences from the standpoint of a hypothetical legislator for all human beings. A person's preferred rules count as moral rules only if they are not prejudiced in favor of one's particular circumstances. To propose moral rules is to imply that such rules should apply even if one were in the other person's position. Moral judgments are "universalizable." A person who, using imagination, discounts her particular circumstances, surveys the human condition, and decides what rules all human beings should follow is said to be taking the "moral point of view."

Does this complex modification of subjectivism amount to something more than the patching up of a theory that states that morality and moral debate are fundamentally nonrational? To many philosophers it seems so. Many subjectivists feel that the recognition of the special nature of moral preferences, of the moral point of view, has important implications for ethical debate. The idea that morality involves recommending rules that all should follow, rules one is committed to following if one were in the other person's position, seems to make a place for rationality in moral debate. If there is enough similarity in human psychology, it might bring us back—not to objectivity (given the way objectivity has been defined)—but to a large degree of intersubjective agreement. This degree of rationality and possibly intersubjective agreement comes not through the recognition of objective moral properties—there are none, according to the subjectivist—but through the logical constraints on what counts as a moral judgment (in the metaethical sense of "moral").

One cannot deduce a particular morality from the definition of the moral point of view. This is as it should be. The definition, after all, is supposed to represent something implied by all moral judgments. Nonetheless, it is conceivable that many people make judgments which they claim to be moral judgments but which they would not endorse if they seriously took the moral point of view. They may be proposing rules that they say are moral rules, but that they would not be willing to acknowledge if they were in the other person's position. Such people are inconsistent in that they are claiming to take a point of view that they are not really adopting at all.

Some people are fortunate enough to make millions of dollars. They may endorse a survival-of-the-fittest morality and say: Let the poor fend for themselves. Suppose these people were to be deprived of their money and their ability to make more. Would they then say: "I'm not fit, let me perish"? Or would they say: "Let's have a good social welfare program"? If the latter, then their original judgments were not moral preferences but personal preferences.

Would anything be gained by persuading people to admit that certain of their views constituted personal preferences and not moral preferences? In some cases, no. Some people are content to be amoral. But many people care very much about morality. After all, to engage in moral dialogue is to engage in a kind of intellectual arbitration. As in any kind of arbitration, one may sometimes lose, but the arbitration procedure does offer certain protections. To abandon morality would be to agree to let human relations be governed by whim and strength. This prospect bothers many people very much. Also, the psychology of most adults seems to be such that believing they are moral is crucial to their feelings of self-respect. Few adults like to admit that they are amoral or immoral; instead, people tend to adjust their morality to agree with their self-interest. But such adjustments are not really compatible with having a morality.

In any case, the question raised by the consideration of subjectivism and individual relativism is whether or not there can be a rational resolution of moral questions. Whether, and to what degree, people are willing to be moral, willing to act on their moral preferences rather than on their personal ones, is a very serious question, but it is also a quite different question from the one we are considering.

In "Those Who Help Themselves," the metaphysical beliefs of the Omegans motivate them to take the moral point of view constantly. They believe in a perpetual, random reincarnation of souls that will eventually place each of them in different social positions and circumstances. They are motivated continuously to ask: What if I were in the other person's position? Probably this question is one most of us manage to avoid a good deal of the time.

In the story, taking the moral point of view does not resolve all moral questions. There remain disagreements about whether or not there ought to be competition or an equal distribution of goods and whether or not one ought to promote excellence as well as happiness. Nonetheless, the story implies that people who really did take the moral point of view would be in close enough agreement that they would be able to get along quite well.

There are certainly precedents for the moral point of view in religion and philosophy. The Golden Rule is found in many religions, and its injunction to do unto others as you would have them do unto you implies that morality has to do with general practices that involve thinking about yourself in the other person's position.

What has become known as the **ideal observer theory** claims that, in formulating a moral judgment, we are implying that such a judgment would be endorsed by an ideal observer who was sympathetic to all human beings and their concerns, was not biased toward any particular individual or group, and had a general knowledge of the world. The first person to formulate the ideal observer theory seems to have been Adam Smith (1723–1790), the author of the *Wealth of Nations*. In his *Theory of Moral Sentiments*, Smith argued that the basis for morality was sympathy for other human beings.

According to Smith, morality might develop through sympathy, but it also requires impartiality. This impartiality develops through our imaginatively identifying with others and also through recognizing their imaginative identification with us. As a result of being able to see and judge himself as one moral being among others, a person develops within himself an **impartial spectator**. The impartial approvals and disapprovals of human conduct we develop from this perspective will result in moral rules of thumb that we can use to guide our conduct.

Some have criticized the idea of sympathy as a ground for morality, pointing out that sympathy can be episodic: Maybe I'm not feeling very sympathetic the day I have to decide how to vote on a bill to help the poor. However, according to Smith we needn't—in fact, we shouldn't—rely on sympathy in making our day-to-day moral judgments. Instead, the sympathetic impartial spectator in me decides general rules, and it is those rules that I follow in making my decisions.

We have already mentioned Immanuel Kant in connection with the claim that moral judgments—which Kant sees as imperatives—are "universalizable." Kant distinguishes between two kinds of imperative statements that he calls **hypothetical imperatives** and **categorical imperatives**.

Hypothetical imperatives take the following form: If you want X, you ought to do Y. For example, "If you want to impress your socially conscious date (or get a good grade in your class on Hunger in America), you ought to spend an afternoon sorting food items for a hunger-relief organization and then make a point of discussing what you did." This sort of "ought"

IMMANUEL KANT (1724–1804) is possibly the greatest modern philosopher. Provoked by Hume's skepticism, he developed a complex theory of knowledge in which he argued that we could understand the world of experience because our minds structured that world. He wrote works on moral philosophy, political philosophy, religion, and free will that remain enormously influential today.

statement would not be a moral judgment, according to Kant. A moral "ought" is categorical: You ought to help feed the hungry.

Kant wants to find an objective basis for morality. He claims to find it in human rationality and in a general categorical imperative we will call **the Categorical Imperative**: "Act only according to that maxim by which you can at the same time will that it should become a universal law." Specific maxims (rules) are to be derived from the Categorical Imperative. Deriving those rules would go something like this:

A man, jealous that someone else has more money, is tempted to steal some of that money. With an eye to the Categorical Imperative, the man must ask himself this question: "How would it be if there were a universal rule saying that it's all right to steal from anyone who has more than oneself?" If there were such a rule, it would lead to so much stealing that the whole idea of private property would become meaningless, and hence the idea of stealing would become meaningless. Therefore, the only sensible rule is, "One ought not to steal."

Kant seemed to think that it was a matter of logic that only one set of moral rules could pass the test of the Categorical Imperative. Most philosophers disagree. It's difficult to get anywhere formulating universalizable moral judgments without resort to a wider account of what you and others want and would be willing to do. The point here is that Kant was very influential in how others think of the moral point of view.

We said a little earlier that the moral point of view "is supposed to represent something implied by all moral judgments." However, the moral point of view does exclude from consideration any justification of right and wrong purely in terms of divine commands. Given that we're focusing on the justification of moral judgments, this should not be too troubling. We've seen that the divine command theory doesn't capture a common meaning of moral judgments. It implies the ethically questionable premise that might is right and has implications that are morally odious to most of us (i.e., that the torture of children would be right if God commanded it). The fact that divine command theory is excluded does not rule out the possibility that alternate justifications might not be found for those judgments that believers have taken to be divine commands. But such a justification must be found if such judgments are to be rational.

More troubling perhaps is the idea that the moral point of view, especially with the element of sympathy included, rules out the justification of moral judgments in terms of what might be called, with some prejudice, a **misanthropic ethic**. This would be an ethic that sees human beings as a whole as being so defective, impure, and unworthy that their happiness and unhappiness don't matter; what they deserve is punishment or harsh redemption, not happiness. Obviously, the Golden Rule, the sympathetic ideal observer, and the moral approach of the Omegans would be totally irrelevant if one took the misanthropic stance.

This exclusion might not seem a problem until one realizes it includes a familiar type of religious ethic that we might call a **judgmental God ethic**. In such an ethic, God holds out difficult or nearly impossible standards for humans to follow and says that all humans deserve harsh punishments for being the way they are. The emphasis of such an ethic is not human happiness but finding a way to escape punishment. Judgmental God ethics seems to have diminished in the modern world, but it still forms a partial element of many standard religions. How much excluding such an ethic in defining the moral point of view prejudices the following discussion I leave for you to decide. At the very least, the moral point of view does offer a framework for those whose moral judgments are predicated largely on a concern for human well-being.

The moral point of view certainly doesn't eliminate all religious ethics. It accommodates anything we might call a **sympathetic-God ethic**. One can see God as the sympathetic ideal observer endorsing rules that promote human happiness and well-being.

It has been argued that an ideal observer would endorse an ethic that promoted as much human happiness as possible: This suggests an ethic called "utilitarianism." Let's discuss utilitarianism and then take up a critique of utilitarianism by John Rawls (1921–2002). What makes Rawls's critique particularly interesting is how he formulates it quite explicitly from an analogue of the moral point of view.

LET'S REVIEW

* *What is the moral point of view? How does it fit with a modified subjectivist view?*
* *Explain the ideal observer theory.*
* *Explain Kant's Categorical Imperative.*

Utilitarianism and John Rawls

Jeremy Bentham, an early proponent of utilitarianism, defined the doctrine as follows in his 1789 work, *Principles of Moral and Political Philosophy*:

> By the principle of utility is meant that principle which approves or disapproves of every action whatsoever, according to the tendency which it appears to have to augment or diminish the happiness of the party whose interest is in question. . . . I say of every action whatsoever; and therefore not only of every action of a private individual, but of every measure of government.

The word "utility," which literally means "usefulness," is used by philosophers and economists to mean "happiness," "satisfaction," or "well-being."

According to **utilitarianism**, that act or set of policies is right which leads to the greatest happiness of the greatest number. Utilitarianism, as originally formulated, has three different components:

1. *It is a **consequentialist ethic***: An act or policy is right or wrong solely in terms of its consequences. The opposite of consequentialist ethics is "deontological ethics." **Deontological ethics** (*deon* in Greek means "duty") are generally those that lay down rules with do's and don'ts, duties, and obligations. Most ethical systems are deontological.
2. *It sees happiness as the one intrinsic good*. The only consequences we need to consider morally are those that relate to happiness and unhappiness.
3. *Its sole moral focus is the sum total of happiness* created by an act or a set of policies.

There are two major versions of utilitarianism. With **act utilitarianism**, the utilitarian principle is applied to each individual action by the agent performing that action. With **rule utilitarianism**, the utilitarian principle is used to decide a set of rules that would lead to the greatest happiness of the greatest number. Individual agents then follow those rules whether or not acting on the rules leads to the greatest happiness in the particular case.

Act utilitarianism has been subjected to some very convincing criticisms. For example, this principle doesn't seem to give enough moral weight to promises and property. It seems to imply that if stealing your rent money and taking my friends out for dinner would create more happiness than letting you keep the money, then I ought to steal. The same would be the case with money I borrowed and promised to pay back.

JEREMY BENTHAM (1748–1832) was an English philosopher and social reformer. He is considered the founder of utilitarianism. His view that the ultimate moral good is the greatest happiness of the greatest number underlay much of his social theory. He called for the separation of church and state, freedom of expression, equal rights for women, the abolition of the death penalty, and the abolition of slavery.

An act utilitarian can respond by talking about how such actions might influence others and undermine the practices of promising and protecting property that are beneficial to the long-term happiness of society. However, such a response gets us close to rule utilitarianism, where the utilitarian principle is applied to practices, not general acts. With rule utilitarianism, if rules against lying and stealing would produce the greatest overall good in the long run, then one shouldn't lie or steal even if doing so would lead to the greater happiness in a particular case.

Obviously, rule utilitarianism is more appropriate than act utilitarianism for formulating social practices and institutions. However, though rule utilitarianism seems the better form of utilitarianism, it still faces some serious objections. The objection we will focus on is that utilitarianism doesn't put enough emphasis on, or doesn't give enough protections to, the individual. Utilitarianism seems to favor the happiness of the majority even when the cost to the minority might be terrible. If the greatest overall happiness would be gained through a system that involved the serfdom or slavery of a small minority, it seems as if utilitarianism ought to endorse that system.

If you think that morality ought to promote happiness (and the reduction of unhappiness) but you believe that utilitarianism doesn't give individuals enough protections, you might try to supplement utilitarianism with rights: Individuals have rights that afford them certain protections and guarantees; beyond that, social policy is decided according to the utilitarian principle. (Note that historically much free-market philosophy has been given a utilitarian justification.)

It seems that the ideal observer could be used to argue for a rule-utilitarianism-plus-rights view if the ideal observer, like a loving God, were conceived of as a parent rather than a calculating device. An ideal parent would want to make sure that every child received a certain basic level of care, even if that left the better-off children with fewer benefits than they might otherwise have had.

John Rawls formulates his critique of utilitarianism not in terms of an ideal observer but of ideal agents. He asks us to imagine these agents in an idealized social contract situation that forces them, like our Omegans, to choose principles that would be acceptable to them even if they were very different kinds of people in very different situations. Rawls asks us to imagine that we are about to enter life. We do have general information about human wants and abilities, as well as about economics, history, and so on. However, we do not know what our interests and abilities or goals will be; we do not know what our position in society will be. From this "original position of equality," behind this **veil of ignorance**, we must decide what general principles will govern society. Rawls's hypothetical agents are in a position analogous to that of the Omegans trying to determine what principles should govern a society that they will be (re)born into, having no specific information about what sort of looks, abilities, and personality one will have. In fact, "Those Who Help Themselves" was written with Rawls in mind.

Rawls is concerned with **distributive justice**, namely, how the goods of a society ought to be distributed among its members. Should all the goods be distributed on the basis of competition? Or should all the goods be distributed equally? Or should every individual be guaranteed a certain minimum of goods, and the remaining goods be distributed on the basis of competition? If the last, how much should the guaranteed minimum be?

JOHN RAWLS (1921–2002), an American philosopher, is considered by many to be the most important political philosopher of the twentieth century. Certainly, his *A Theory of Justice* (1971) with its critique of utilitarianism and its use of ideal social contract theory revived and altered normative political theory. His *Political Liberalism* (1993) sought to reconcile political agreement with deep disagreement over the nature of the good life.

As we've seen, utilitarianism emphasizes the greatest happiness rather than the greatest number. If the greatest total happiness in society would be achieved by, say, a competitive system that allocated most of the goods to 75 percent of the members, rather than by a less competitive system that distributed goods more equally, then utilitarianism would favor the first system.

This is not to say that utilitarianism per se favors competition and unequal distribution. We would also need factual information about what social system would create the greatest total happiness in a particular society. Nonetheless, it is the case that utilitarianism does not insist upon a guaranteed minimum for all individuals.

A number of philosophers have criticized utilitarianism as "unjust" in this respect: They have said that a more acceptable normative theory would be one that insisted upon substantial guarantees for every individual— along with other protections for the individual against the majority. Rawls is one of these critics. He argues that people in the original position would not choose to live according to the utilitarian principle, a principle that might allow a minority group in society to be sacrificed for the general happiness. He claims people in the original position wouldn't want to bet their one life on a society in which they might be sacrificed for the general welfare.

Instead, Rawls argues that people in the original position would choose the following two principles:

> [T]he first requires equality in the assignment of basic rights and duties, while the second holds that social and economic inequalities, for example inequalities of wealth and authority, are just only if they result in compensating benefits for everyone, and in particular for the least advantaged members of society. These principles rule out justifying institutions on the grounds that the hardships of some are offset by a greater good in the aggregate. . . .

Rawls is arguing that people in the original position would opt for basic rights and duties before any principle regarding the distribution of goods. He further argues that people would select as their principle of distribution what he calls the "difference principle." Rawls's difference principle is extremely egalitarian: It says that society should deviate from an equal distribution of goods only if, and only to the extent that, unequal distribution works to the greatest benefit of the least advantaged member of society.

How Rawls's difference principle would work out in practice requires some speculation, but it's likely it would yield a kind of democratic socialism—this in contrast to a pure utilitarian system that would be more likely to lead to our current system, or perhaps to one more extreme in terms of inequalities of wealth.

Some utilitarians have countered that even granting Rawls's metaethical test, the utilitarian principle would be the most rational one to choose. If you're going to bet your life on a social system, it would make more sense to choose a utilitarian system, since a system promoting the greatest happiness of the greatest number would give you the best odds of being happy.

Rawls counters that people "betting" their one life on a social system would pick a more conservative strategy. The idea of losing out completely would be so awful that people would pick a society where the worst-off still did pretty well.

A third possibility—which would accord with people being cautious risk-takers—is that people would opt for a society with a substantial guaranteed minimum and the rest set up to give the best odds on wealth.

"Those Who Help Themselves" imagines that all would insist on at least some guaranteed minimum but would differ as to the distribution of goods beyond that.

> Apparently, those supporting the largest opposition party were gamblers: They were willing to risk the possibility of some misfortune in the next life for the possibility of gaining great wealth in this life. Those on the opposite end of the political spectrum were unwilling to gamble at all with their future lives: They wanted to be guaranteed an equal share of the wealth. Those who supported the majority party wanted some guarantees and some chances to gamble. But none was willing to gamble too much with his or her future life, to risk being diseased, mentally defective, or hungry, and being without help.

The story also touches on another issue besides that of how goods should be distributed in a society.

> [T]here were cultural critics who claimed that the society was too focused on material well being and too little on the arts and sciences, too little on ideals and the development of character. These critics claimed that society, through its social institutions, should focus less on the skills necessary to individual and social material well being and more on developing skills and knowledge that would make the Omegans a better, not just happier, people.
>
> Different visions were offered as to what an ideal Omegan would be—more industrious or more tranquil and attuned to the natural world, more warrior-like or more gentle, more scientifically analytic or more emotional and intuitive.

Here we are talking not about social principles regarding the distribution of goods or the rights of individuals. We're asking about what role, if any, society should take in promoting certain ideals of what constitutes a good life, as well as worthwhile character traits (often called **virtues**).

LET'S REVIEW

* *What is the difference between consequentialist and deontological ethics?*
* *Define utilitarianism and explain the two forms of the theory.*
* *Explain John Rawls's idealized social contract situation with its "original position of equality" and its "veil of ignorance." Why is it constructed this way, and what is it designed to show?*
* *Why does Rawls think his ideal agents would reject utilitarianism? What principles does he think they would choose instead?*

Morality, Virtue, and Living Well

If we evaluate a person's life—choices, lifestyle, character, achievements—we can do so from a moral or nonmoral perspective. Provisionally, let's say we're evaluating a life from a nonmoral perspective if we're evaluating that life apart from how the person's choices affect the interests of others. Later we'll reassess that definition and ask if the category of the moral should be broader than we're making it here.

Operating within a nonmoral context, let's ask: What makes a life a good life? What constitutes living well? What things are worth having and doing and being?

Since ancient times, philosophers have made the distinction between something being good as an end (an **intrinsic good**) and good as a means (an **instrumental good**). The distinction isn't hard and fast. Having fun might be good in itself, but it could also be good as a means if your work is slipping and you need a break to refresh yourself.

Many thinkers throughout history have claimed that the one intrinsic good (the one thing we value as an end in itself) is happiness—construed as the experience of happiness or what psychologists today call **subjective well-being (SWB)**. The claim that happiness (SWB) is the only intrinsic good—the only thing valued for its own sake—has a certain appeal. If we start asking people questions about what they *really* want, pressing on them questions like "Why do you want *that*?" or "What do you want *that* for?" the answers often end up being phrased in terms of good feelings: that you need a good job or a good marriage or a comfortable lifestyle in order to be happy. It's easy to conclude that the one thing people value intrinsically is happiness. However, this claim becomes less obvious when you examine it more closely—as in the following thought-experiment of mine from another text:

> Imagine you are a space traveler and run across two separate planets with very different civilizations: On the first planet, "Planet Primeval," people live at a very basic level of civilization, comparable, say, to the transition between the hunter-gatherer stage and early agriculture. Thanks to an abundance of vegetation on this planet, people have a fairly easy life, though there are enough diseases to keep the population relatively stable. They have no writing, their music is only basic chants (and perhaps simple notes on a lute), and insofar as their mythological conception of the world attempts to convey the nature of the physical universe (as opposed to the spiritual), you can see that their myths are almost completely false.

On the second planet, "Planet Progresso," people have complex literature, music, and religion; advanced science and technology; architecture that is both functionally and artistically sophisticated; a complex social structure; and a general picture of the universe that is much closer to the one your even more advanced civilization has developed.

Let us suppose that the people on Planet Primeval and those on Planet Progresso live comparably happy lives. If that supposition seems at all problematic to you, we can add additional suppositions that help balance out the happiness: We might imagine that the people on Planet Primeval live peacefully with each other and harmoniously with the physical world. We might suppose that on Planet Progresso competition, stress, and maybe occasional threats of war offset the real benefits for human happiness of greater wealth and more advanced medicine.

Are both planets equally good or worthwhile? Many people would say that Planet Progresso was the better world in that it exemplifies a greater development of human capacities—a higher level of human "flourishing."

The word "**flourishing**" sounds a bit flowery (it does in fact come from the Latin word for flower), but it represents an attempt to come up with a word that doesn't really exist in English—a word that covers the development of certain human capacities we'd consider worthwhile, such as courage, intelligence, sensitivity, inquisitiveness, adventurousness, freedom, loyalty, love, and spirituality.

The two-planets thought experiment is meant to show that a case can be made for viewing human flourishing, as well as happiness, as being intrinsically good. Jonathan Glover says that to evaluate a person's life, we need a kind of "binocular vision" to assess "two strands of the good life."

> One strand is about the fit between what you want and value and what your life is like. Part of having a good life is being happy, in the (limited) sense of being reasonably content with how your life is going. The second strand is about how rich your life is in human goods: what relationships you have with other people, your state of health, how much you are in charge of your own life, how much scope for creativity you have, and so on.

Both of these perspectives are "nonmoral" in our sense of the term, since neither directly involves the interests of other people. One perspective is an interior view in terms of the person's happiness; the other is an exterior view in terms of flourishing. Each of us can use these perspectives to evaluate our own life or the lives of others. You might ask yourself: "Am I as happy as I could be?"; or "Am I really doing enough to develop my abilities?" Or you might think of someone you know: "She's certainly successful, but I wish she were a little happier."

In addition to Glover's two nonmoral perspectives, there is a moral one—evaluating our lives from the moral point of view. So we have three perspectives from which to evaluate our own lives and the lives of others:

MORAL: (From the moral point of view)
NONMORAL: (Setting aside the moral point of view)
             Happiness
             Flourishing

What would constitute a flourishing life? It might involve such things as good health, looks, natural charm, and natural talents—things we would be lucky to have. It might involve certain successes. It would also involve certain worthwhile character traits one has cultivated, such as courage, inquisitiveness, adventurousness, perseverance, and self-control. Such worthwhile character traits are often reflections of ideals, types of persons we aspire to be.

Worthwhile character traits are found in the realm of morality as well. Moral character traits such as fairness, benevolence, conscientiousness, and honesty help make a person morally good.

Worthwhile character traits are often referred to as "virtues"—both moral virtues and nonmoral virtues. As with the word "flourishing," virtue has unfortunate connotations, conjuring up Victorians obsessed with sex. To offset that image, consider that the Latin word from which it comes—*virtus*—designated a wide range of desirable characteristics, including those of the warrior. The point is that we want to divest the word "virtue" of all those associations and think of it primarily as designating worthwhile character traits, whether moral or nonmoral.

Virtues are dispositions to act in certain ways that are good, dispositions that habitually result in action. For instance, being kind means doing kind things, not just thinking kind thoughts; being adventurous means having adventures, not just reading adventure novels. We should think of virtues as to some degree earned. Innate talents aren't virtues; skills developed from those talents are. Natural beauty, natural charm, and inherited wealth aren't virtues, however nice they may be to have. We want to think of virtues as something we would commend a person for possessing.

The mention of moral virtues, however, has introduced another complication into our perspectives of assessing lives. So far we've talked about morality in terms of establishing rules and practices and then acting according to those rules and practices. Once we bring in moral virtues, though, our list of the perspectives of evaluation should look more like this:

MORAL:　　　(From the moral point of view)
　　　　　　　Acting according to moral rules
　　　　　　　Displaying moral virtues
NONMORAL: (Setting aside the moral point of view)
　　　　　　　Being happy
　　　　　　　Flourishing (including displaying nonmoral virtues)

A familiar tendency in modern ethical thinking is to see ethics/morality as concerned primarily with formulating moral principles or rules that would govern social institutions and social interactions. That is certainly what we were looking for from the moral point of view. Thinkers who believe that morality primarily concerns such rules generally acknowledge that it is important to promote moral virtues as well. Someone with a good character is more likely to know the morally right thing to do and to do it. But, say such thinkers, what moral character is and why it's important derive from what the moral rules say we should do.

As for flourishing and exhibiting what we've call the "nonmoral virtues," that is often seen as admirable but, from the standpoint of morality, optional.

Since the mid-twentieth century, this view of virtues has been challenged by thinkers who have revived an ethical tradition prominent in the ancient world. Confucius (551–479 BCE), the most famous Chinese philosopher, taught an ethics that was centered on character rather than action, listing character traits that in today's terminology would be both moral (being humane) and nonmoral (having wisdom). Interestingly, humaneness for Confucius involved following a version of the Golden Rule, though he believed our love for others should be proportional to the benefit we receive from them. (For this perspective, he was criticized by his contemporary, Mozi, who thought the highest virtue was universal love.)

The Greek philosopher Aristotle (4th century BCE) also emphasized virtues in his ethical theory. According to most translations of Aristotle, he said that the good life was one that achieved happiness, but the word he used—**"eudaimonia"**—is better translated as "human flourishing." For Aristotle, what we're calling subjective well-being might be a component of the happy life but only a part of it and certainly not the point of it. The central concern of Aristotle's *Nicomachean Ethics* is what human flourishing is and how you obtain it.

ARISTOTLE (384–322 BCE) is, along with his teacher, Plato, one of the two greatest figures in Greek philosophy. He founded the field of logic, and his writings on the physical sciences were accepted in large part through the Middle Ages and into the Renaissance. His metaphysics strongly influenced Aquinas and thus much of Roman Catholic theology. His writings on ethics continue to be hugely influential.

Aristotle claimed that *eudaimonia* consisted of **arête,** which is translated as "virtue" and should be taken as it has been defined above as consisting of worthwhile character traits.

Some modern philosophers have argued that it would be best if we put aside the predominant ethics of rules (such as utilitarianism and Kantian ethics) and return to an **ethics of virtue**. Such an ethic would focus on good character rather than right action and include a whole spectrum of virtues, including those that an ethics of rules might see as nonmoral. A person would learn how to be moral by observing virtuous people rather than searching for rules as in an **ethics of rules**.

The arguments that have been or can be given for this view include the following:

1. An ethics of rules reflects an age when people believed in a God who set down rules ("laws") for human beings to follow. In this more secular

age, people no longer think we can decide questions of right and wrong by looking in some religious text. Yet those same people understand well what it is to praise someone for being compassionate or loyal or to condemn someone for being unfair or disloyal. It would make more sense, says the virtue ethicist, to stop talking about right and wrong and instead talk about such things as being compassionate or mean.

2. An ethics of rules without a divine rule-giver to enforce those rules through the prospect of divine rewards and punishment leaves ethics without any obvious motivational component beyond the thin desire to do one's duty. Virtue ethics deals in character traits such as compassion or honesty that already incorporate motivation.

3. An ethics of rules imagines people pursuing their own self-interest except when morality says they "have" to do something that goes against those interests. In contrast, virtue ethics combines the

ELIZABETH ANSCOMBE (1919–2001) was an important British philosopher who taught at Cambridge and Oxford. Her 1958 paper, "Modern Moral Philosophy," argued that a law conception of ethics wasn't appropriate for a secular society and called for a return to concepts such as virtue and flourishing.

moral virtues with the so-called nonmoral virtues in an expanded concept of flourishing. Living well and being moral are integrated in the same package.

4. To many people, the good life for humans ought to involve something beyond the lowest-common-denominator life glorified by commercial advertising—something beyond the pleasures of Bud Light, rock and roll, Monday Night Football, and celebrity gossip. It seems as if morality ought to put *some* pressure on us to develop our capabilities and our characters—to flourish. An ethics of virtue, unlike an ethics of rules, does just that.

With so much going for it, one can see why some people might conclude that virtue ethics is superior to the sorts of ethics of rules put forth by the utilitarians or the Kantians. However, a number of objections have been made to the idea of replacing an ethics of rules with an ethics of virtue:

a. Virtue ethics seems to have the point of ethics backwards. What's ultimately wrong with cheating someone is not that you're a cheater but that they got cheated; what's ultimately wrong with being mean to someone is not that you're a mean person but that they got hurt.

b. One of the main purposes of ethics at the deepest levels is to justify the laws and policies of society. Society needs to decide how wealth and other goods are to be distributed and what protections should be given to its members. It seems that we need an ethics of rules to decide on those policies and laws. It is hard to see how studying how a just person behaves would be enough to help us decide what a just economic policy would be.

c. It seems that you need to decide on an ethic of rules before you can decide on which virtues are to be emphasized. Many thinkers throughout history have emphasized the aristocratic or heroic virtues of the "few," often despising the "many." In opposition, many religious thinkers have seen the highest virtues as being almost the diametrical opposite of those aristocratic virtues: humility rather than pride, pacifism rather than warrior virtues, otherworldliness rather than success in this world. Modern commercial societies have often begun by emphasizing "commercial virtues" such as discipline, thrift, and hard work before then making a virtue of conspicuous consumption. It's difficult to see how one could debate which virtues are to be promoted before first deciding on one's ethic.

d. Along the same lines, promoting—even making obligatory—a particular conception of a flourishing life is going to be enormously controversial in a society with different conceptions of flourishing. Does the good life involve a scientific approach to the world or one based on revelation and faith? (If revelation and faith, which revelations, which faith?) Does it involve an acquisitive lifestyle or one devoted to service to others? Does it involve a life devoted to culture and higher learning or to popular enjoyments and technical skills? Because of these complications, the tendency is to leave flourishing to the realm of personal values—to leave in the nonmoral category whatever virtues don't directly support the ethics of rules. This is what Rawls suggested.

None of this is to say, however, that moral virtues shouldn't play a crucial role in any acceptable morality. For people to live moral lives, they need to develop the habits of morality—which is precisely what moral virtues are. And thinking in terms of virtues or good character is a way of integrating morality with your self and self-esteem. You can try to be kind as well as capable, fair as well as successful, and to feel good about both.

Nor is this to say that flourishing isn't an important value, that you shouldn't strive to develop your character and capabilities, that you shouldn't feel pride in yourself for what you accomplish and admire the accomplishments of others. Nor is it to say that you shouldn't share your values with others, help promote what you consider the best of human science and culture through education and various cultural institutions. It is only to say that it is difficult to see how flourishing and nonmoral virtues can be obligatory the way acting morally is.

Before we conclude our discussion of morality, let's take up two topics of particular contemporary importance: Feminist ethics in general, along with one particular feminist ethical theory, called the "ethics of care"; and issues of racial justice as they relate to our discussion of the moral point of view.

LET'S REVIEW

* *Is it reasonable to think that happiness is the only intrinsic non moral good? Explain.*
* *What is flourishing? What are the virtues? What is virtue ethics?*
* *What arguments can be given for and against virtue ethics?*

Feminism and the Ethics of Care

The beginning of the woman's rights movement is often marked as 1848, the year a young housewife and mother, Elizabeth Cady Stanton, along with some friends, held a convention in Seneca Falls, New York, a convention "to discuss the social, civil, and religious condition and rights of woman." According to the National Women's History Project,

> As the women set about preparing for the event, Elizabeth Cady Stanton used the Declaration of Independence as the framework for writing what she titled a "Declaration of Sentiments." In what proved to be a brilliant move, Stanton connected the nascent campaign for women's rights directly to that powerful American symbol of liberty. The same familiar words framed their arguments: "We hold these truths to be self-evident; that all men and women are created equal; that they are endowed by their Creator with certain inalienable rights; that among these are life, liberty, and the pursuit of happiness."

Stanton declared that the "history of mankind is a history of repeated injuries and usurpations on the part of man toward woman, having in direct object the establishment of an absolute tyranny over her" and listed areas of life where women were treated unjustly:

* Women were not allowed to vote.
* Women had to submit to laws when they had no voice in their formation.
* Married women had no property rights.
* Husbands had legal power over and responsibility for their wives to the extent that they could imprison or beat them with impunity.
* Divorce and child custody laws favored men, giving no rights to women.
* Women had to pay property taxes although they had no representation in the levying of these taxes.
* Most occupations were closed to women and when women did work they were paid only a fraction of what men earned.
* Women were not allowed to enter professions such as medicine or law.
* Women had no means to gain an education since no college or university would accept women students.
* With few exceptions, women were not allowed to participate in the affairs of the church.
* Women were robbed of their self-confidence and self-respect, and were made totally dependent on men.

ELIZABETH CADY STANTON (1815–1902). During the Civil War, Stanton was active in the abolitionist movement but after the war resumed her focus on women's rights. With Susan B. Anthony, she founded the National Woman Suffrage Association and wrote the first three volumes of the *History of Women Suffrage*. She advocated for a woman's rights to property, divorce, and birth control.

Looking at Cady's list in the twenty-first century, one can see how far the woman's movement has come and how far it has to go. What's important for purposes of our discussion is to note how Cady's argument is put in terms of rights, freedom, and equality. This is still the mode in which much feminist argument proceeds today. Here's just one example, a comment from Teresa Younger, the CEO and president of the Ms. Foundation, when asked for her definition of "feminism."

> The definition, as I have spent my life believing it to be, is the belief that men and women should have equal social, political, and economic rights and opportunities. I do think that that is the most inclusive definition of what feminism is about. It's about equality for both men and women and a playing field that respects the voices of women. True equality, true feminism is recognition of the dynamics that each person brings to the table. And I say "each person" because

women will have reached truest levels of equality when men also have truest levels of equality. As long as we stay and assign task and duty, responsibility and opportunity to a particular gender, then we are not actually striving for true feminism.

Although the fight for equal social, political, and economic rights for women is ongoing, there has been a move in the last 50 years to turn the focus of ethical theory to what have been thought of as more traditional or typical female perspectives and values. A crucial impetus for this change of focus was Carol Gilligan's 1982 book, *In a Different Voice: Psychological Theory and Women's Development.*

Gilligan's work began as a critique of the work of psychologist Lawrence Kohlberg (1927–1987) who had developed a theory of the stages of moral development based on the responses children gave to moral dilemmas. Kohlberg identified six stages of moral development ascending from (1) obeying authority and avoiding punishment to (3) thinking of right in terms of social roles and relationships to (6) recognizing and following abstract principles that apply to all humanity. In one of Kohlberg's moral dilemmas, the wife of a man named Heinz is dying; the one thing that might save her is a drug discovered by a pharmacist who is selling the drug at the exorbitant price (for the time) of $2000. Heinz can only come up with $1000, which he offers to the pharmacist; the pharmacist turns him down. Would it be right for Heinz to steal the drug?

Jake, an 11-year-old boy in the study, said Heinz should steal the drug because "a human life is worth more than money" and "if the pharmacist only makes $1000, he will still live." Amy, an 11-year-old girl, doesn't want Heinz to steal the drug but find "other ways . . . like if he could borrow the money or make a loan." She says, "If he stole the drug, he might save his wife then, but if he did, he might have to go to jail, and then his wife might get sicker again, and he couldn't get more of the drug, and it might not be good. So they should really just talk it out and find some other way to make the money."

Given Kohlberg's moral development scale, Amy is reasoning at a lower level of moral development than Jake. Amy is operating at level 3, thinking in terms of relationships, while Jake is at a higher level, reasoning according to principle (i.e., "a human life is worth more than money").

Kohlberg's hierarchy of moral reasoning was challenged by Gilligan, who argued that Amy's response was not inferior to Jake's. Gilligan agreed that the girls in the study tended to reason differently than the boys but argued that this wasn't a lower level of moral reasoning.

> The moral imperative that emerges repeatedly in the women's interviews is an injunction to care, a responsibility to discern and alleviate the "real and recognizable trouble" of this world. For the men Kohlberg studied, the moral imperative appeared rather as an injunction to respect the rights of others and thus to protect from interference the right to life and self-fulfillment.

Gilligan claimed that on the one hand male moral thinking tends to be oriented toward the marketplace, the courts, or the legislature, where impartiality and contractual thinking are appropriate. On the other hand, women were more likely to be nurses or teachers, wives, and mothers. These situations involve care-based relationships where a different style of thinking was appropriate. Gilligan argued that this female way of thinking was of equal worth.

Gilligan's work has had an enormous influence on **feminist ethics**, which, as a philosophical discipline, is in part an attempt to identify and correct male biases in traditional ethical theories. For example, Alison Jaggar has argued that traditional ethics has let down women in a number of ways—enumerated by the *Stanford Encyclopedia of Philosophy* as follows:

> First, it shows less concern for women's as opposed to men's issues and interests. Second, traditional ethics views as trivial the moral issues that arise in the so-called private world, the realm in which women do housework and take care of children, the infirm, and the elderly. Third, it implies that, in general, women are not as morally mature or deep as men. Fourth, traditional ethics overrates culturally masculine traits like "independence, autonomy, intellect, will, wariness, hierarchy, domination, culture, transcendence, product, asceticism, war, and death," while it underrates culturally feminine traits like "interdependence, community, connection, sharing, emotion, body, trust, absence of hierarchy, nature, immanence, process, joy, peace, and life." Fifth, and finally, it favors "male" ways of moral reasoning that emphasize rules, rights, universality, and impartiality over "female" ways of moral reasoning that emphasize relationships, responsibilities, particularity, and partiality.

Gilligan thought that male and female ways of thinking were equally valid. Others argued that the care-based ethical thinking of the females was superior. In her 1984 book, *Caring: A Female Approach to Ethics and Moral Education*, Nel Noddings argued that caring "rooted in receptivity, relatedness and responsiveness" is preferable to the more masculine, justice-based approaches to ethics that abstract from the concrete situation to formulate universalizable rules. Noddings claimed that a caring relationship can exist only if the one caring can interact with the one being cared for and that where there was no such relationship, there was no obligation. (Thus, for instance, she said there was no obligation to help "the needy of the earth.")

An ethical approach that sees the care relationship as fundamental to ethical theory has come to be known as **the ethics of care**. It is not *the* feminist ethic: It has a lot of feminist critics. But it is the closest thing to a new ethical theory to emerge from feminism, and it is one well worth considering.

If traditional ethical theory is encapsulated in the sympathetic ideal observer, the ethics of care as formulated by someone like Noddings might be represented as an localized ideal mother. With the ideal observer, sympathy is generated from a universal viewpoint and is spread equally and impartially over all human beings (or, in some specific applications, all members of a society). From this overall viewpoint, rules are generated for all to follow. With the localized ideal mother, the sympathy emerges from the mother/caregiver in a particular family, diminishes as it spreads out to friends and acquaintances, and dissipates altogether as it moves out toward the larger society and world. The ethics of care downplays reason and equality and impartiality. It favors partiality toward family members and friends; it favors the more intuitive, emotional, contextual approaches to problems found in family relationships of dependency and interdependency.

The ethics of care has evolved considerably since its early formulations. For one thing, empirical research hasn't borne out the claim that females think very differently about moral problems than males do. These days ethics of care theorists ground their theory more cautiously on caregiving relationships and perspectives that have been more often, though not exclusively, associated with women. Ethics of care theorists have also enlarged the scope of care, seeing it as the basis for a broader ethic applying to the larger society and the world. They further acknowledge that considerations of justice can't be dispensed with altogether. However, ethics of care theorists insist that the thought processes, practices, and dilemmas faced by caregivers in care relationships should be at the heart of ethics. They insist that the ethics of care provides an alternative model of ethical thinking that is at least as justified, perhaps more justified, than those offered by the rule-governed theories like those of the utilitarians and Kantians.

In her book, *The Ethics of Care*, Virginia Held cited the following common features among the various versions of the ethics of care (in contrast to what she calls the "dominant" moral theories of utilitarianism and Kantian ethics):

1. The ethics of care focuses primarily on the moral importance of "meeting the needs of the particular others for whom we take responsibility." People are dependent beings for much of their lives—as children, as the very old—sometimes even for much of their lives through sickness and disability. The dominant moral theories ignore dependency, treating individuals as if they were all independent and autonomous. Caring should be a prime focus of morality, not something relegated to the edges or seen as outside of it.

2. The ethics of care, unlike the dominant moral theories, doesn't reject emotion in deciding what would be morally right. Emotions such as sympathy and responsiveness should work alongside reason to determine what's the best thing to do and the best way to do it.

3. Dominant moral theories tend to look at moral problems as if they were conflicts between "egoistic individual interests on the one hand, and universal moral principles on the other." The ethics of care focuses on the area between those extremes. Persons who care for others aren't focused primarily on serving their own interests, nor are they acting for the sake of all humanity.

   [They] seek instead to preserve or promote an actual human relation between themselves and particular others. Persons in caring relations are acting for self-and-other together. Their characteristic stance is neither egoistic nor altruistic; these are the options in a conflictual situation, but the well-being of a caring relation involves the cooperative well-being of those in the relation and the well-being of the relation itself.

4. An ethics of care rejects the view "built into the dominant moral theories . . . that the household is a private sphere beyond politics into which government, based on consent, should not intrude."

VIRGINIA HELD (1929–), a leading feminist moral and political philosopher, was named Distinguished Professor at the City University of New York Graduate Center and Hunter College in 1996. In addition to her work on care ethics, she has written on the morality of political violence and on the limits of markets.

Further, the view that morality involves "unrelated, independent, and mutually indifferent individuals assumed to be equal" is not applicable to family life.

In the context of the family, it is typical for relations to be between persons with highly unequal power who did not choose the ties and obligations in which they find themselves enmeshed. For instance, no child can choose her parents yet she may well have obligations to care for them. Relations of this kind are standardly noncontractual, and conceptualizing them as contractual would often undermine or at least obscure the trust on which their worth depends. The ethics of care addresses rather than neglects moral issues arising in relations among the unequal and dependent, relations that are often laden with emotion and involuntary, and then notices how often these attributes apply not only in the household but in the wider society as well. . . .

5. The ethics of care "usually works with a conception of persons as relational, rather than as the self-sufficient independent individuals of the dominant moral theories."

In contrast to Noddings's initial view that a care ethic should be limited to persons close to us, Held envisions care on a global level.

> A globalization of caring relations would help enable people of different states and cultures to live in peace, to respect each others' rights, to care together for their environments, and to improve the lives of their children.

It's incontrovertible that throughout history male philosophers have put forth atrocious views of women; that until recently philosophers woefully ignored the perspectives of women; and that very little work in ethics has focused on moral issues within families. These are serious problems that feminists and others are seeking to correct. (See Further Readings for more material on these issues.)

Within the context of our general discussion of ethics, though, let's focus on the ethics of care as an alternate ethical theory.

1. One attraction of the ethics of care is that, in its earlier formulations, it reflects our normal priorities and problems. We are partial to ourselves and those close to us. We are involved in care relations that involve dependency and interdependency, embed us in relationships too intimate to analyze in terms of self-interest and altruism, involve emotion as much as reason, and involve muddling through with vague guidelines and fuzzy ideals rather than rigid rules. None of this is found in the dominant theories, which have always been uneasy dealing with families, when they've bothered dealing with them at all. At the same time, the early formulations of the ethics of care make it seem at best a family ethic and at worst an anti-ethic, a determination to ignore the larger world beyond the domain of family and friends. However, philosophers like Held who have enlarged the ethics of care insist that it not be looked at as "'family ethics' confined to the 'private' sphere."

> Although some of its early formulations suggested this, and some of its related values are to be seen most clearly in personal contexts, an adequate understanding of the ethics of care should recognize that it elaborates values as fundamental and relevant to political institutions and to how society is organized, as those of

justice. Perhaps its values are even more fundamental and more relevant to life in society than those traditionally relied on.

2. One way to enlarge an ethics of care would be to imagine family-like caring expanding outward toward the larger world—diminishing but not disappearing—so that it could include, for example, concern for the "needy of the earth." Such an expansion would yield what many of us would consider a more moral outlook on the world than was offered by early versions of the ethics of care. However, it's difficult to see how expanding the ethics of care from an individualized viewpoint could give us the kind of general vantage point needed to formulate law and social policies and to assess them in terms of their effects on society-wide justice and social welfare.

3. One would think that care theorists who are after a global ethic would need to embed care in something like the moral point of view. Certainly, that would be congenial to our earlier description of the moral point of view. But this raises some questions: When care is turned into something more universal, can it really retain the qualities it had in close relationships, or will it transform itself into a more generalized sympathy. Further, would this really be so bad?

The viewpoint of the sympathetic ideal observer and the more specific theory of utilitarianism constitute "care" ethics in the most general sense of the term. In fact, utilitarianism was responsible for pushing social reforms that ethics of care theorists would applaud. Jeremy Bentham, as noted earlier, argued for equal rights for women, including the right to divorce. He called for the abolition of slavery and of physical punishment. He argued for prison reform, emphasizing the need to rehabilitate. He called for the abolition of the death penalty. He argued that things could not be considered wrong because they were "unnatural" and said that an "antipathy" toward homosexuality was no justification for making it illegal.

Bentham and other utilitarians were hostile to the idea of human rights as something morally basic. They didn't dismiss rights altogether but made them contingent on whether and to what degree they furthered the greatest happiness of the greatest number. As we've seen, utilitarians have been criticized for their position on human rights. Held seems to agree with this criticism and sees rights as important in the fight for justice and equality. At the same time, she wants to say that care can generate sufficiently strong rights. Can it?

We saw earlier how this might be done from the standpoint of the sympathetic ideal observer:

> It seems the ideal observer could be used to argue for a rule-utilitarianism-plus-rights view if the ideal observer, like a loving God, is conceived of as a parent rather than a calculating device. An ideal parent would want to make sure that every child received a certain basic level of care, even if that left the better-off children with fewer benefits than they might otherwise have had.

4. One could convert something like Rawls's approach to one that is more compatible with the ethics of care. It's true that Rawls insists that his individuals in the original position are all egoists, but the choices those egoists make behind a veil of ignorance are going to promote the welfare of others and thus have a *de facto* sympathy (or care) dimension. The great divergence between Rawls's approach and the concerns of feminists and ethics of care theorists may stem from the nature of the background information Rawls allows his ideal agents to have. Rawls wants to make it impossible for ideal agents to tailor their choice of principles to their real situation in the world and thus restricts the information they have about themselves. But Rawls has to allow the agents information about the world and human beings, or the agents might as well be choosing an ethic for Martians. Yet none of the information Rawls envisions includes such things as what it's like to bear and raise children, to be in intimate relationships, to function in families, to experience the world in traditionally female ways, to be dependent on someone, to be disabled, and so on. Rawls does argue for substantial financial guarantees for those at the bottom, and such guarantees would certainly alleviate any effects of discrimination. But there is nothing in the background information that would provoke the agents to think about policies related to families, policies that would enable people to care and flourish, policies that would help avoid the kind of subtle oppression that feminism is trying to fight.

5. The sympathy implicit in certain ethical views can get diluted as it gets transformed into general rules and regulations governing social policy. However, it's a question of whether this is the fault of the ethics or the unwillingness of people to apply the ethics. Also, there's a minimalist trend in ethics and political theory that goes beyond any male bias and is a response to real problems of agreement within society—problems that pose a challenge to any ethics of sympathy or care.

Consider social contract theory—one of the theories often attacked by ethics of care theorists. So far we've only seen the social contract idea as idealized by Rawls in something like the analogue of the moral point of view. But social contract theory has often existed in an unidealized form that yields a minimalist, rather undemanding, ethic. It arose in the modern period when doctrinal disputes and religious wars led some to fear that there was no such thing as one moral truth that all people would recognize. A different approach was needed to justify political authority if society wasn't to dissolve in violence.

Thomas Hobbes (1588–1679) famously argued that, prior to the foundation of government, humankind had lived in a state of nature in which life was "solitary, poor, nasty, brutish, and short." The state of nature involved constant war because people were selfish and because no one had sufficient strength to impose his will on others. The only way to escape the state of nature was for people to agree to rules by which they were to be governed and to create a government that could enforce those rules. Hobbes called this agreement the "social contract." He thought that the only government that could keep society from falling back into a state of nature was a monarchy.

The idea that historical societies were actually formed by social contracts was discredited by anthropologists long ago. Today the social contract idea is conceived as a hypothetical test: If we had to agree to a set of rules to establish society, what sorts of rules would they be? How do such rules compare to the rules we have now?

With what we'll call "**basic social contract theory**," the contract situation is conceived of as hypothetical but not idealized. Here we are egoists who know our abilities and interests; nothing like sympathy, empathy, or care is forced upon us, only negotiation. Realism is the key. We ask ourselves what would we be willing to agree to that others would agree to as well. It's supposed that we would pick democracy, wanting an ongoing say in society. It's further supposed that we would choose freedom of religion, being afraid that someone else would impose their beliefs on us. As for the economic system, it is supposed that we'd pick a free market for the generation of wealth. If you're doing well, you, being by hypothesis an egoist, would want the minimum social welfare you could get others to agree to.

It's easy to see why ethics of care theorists, among others, would consider basic social contract theory totally inadequate as an ethical theory, especially because such a theory denies primary moral status to those who can't negotiate for themselves—for instance, children and people with mental disabilities.

However, we do need a functioning society, and there are obstacles to finding enough ethical or political agreement to make such a society possible. We face contesting, if not actually warring, religious factions; multicultural differences and sensitivities; a tendency toward relativism or subjectivism among many contemporary thinkers; and a widespread resistance to having to comply with anything more than minimal moral demands, especially demands that might cost us money. Many contemporary ethical theorists feel that they have to work within those constraints and look to basic social contract theory as the only way out.

Given that rights and justice are an integral part of basic social contract theory, feminists are probably on safer ground arguing their cause on the basis of rights and justice rather than the ethics of care. We can certainly applaud the ethics of care, as well as other ethics of sympathy or love, for seeking to push us beyond such minimalist contractual ethics. But it is a tough sell.

Let's move on now to a discussion of race from the moral point of view.

Race from the Moral Point of View

The moral point of view is set up in such a way as to be "color blind." In universalizing moral principles, one must formulate principles that would apply if one were in the other person's position, including having the other person's skin color. Rawls's ideal agents choosing what kind of society they would endorse would have no idea what color their skin would be. Either approach would presumably lead to a society that did not discriminate against people of color.

However, some critics have argued that it is not sufficient to discuss the problems of racism in terms of ideal justice with color blind principles: Even if such ideal justice recommends nondiscriminatory principles, it fails dismally to recognize past racial injustices and the impact they have on people's life prospects. If a discussion of ideal justice could convince people to stop discriminating now, the result still wouldn't be fair if past discrimination made those previously discriminated against unable to compete or qualify or flourish in ways that other people could.

Charles W. Mills presents this argument in works such as *The Racial Contract*. His main theoretical target is Rawls's ideal social contract approach and its perceived failure to deal with issues of race. However, unlike some philosophers dealing with race, Mills doesn't think that Rawls's social contract theory needs to be abandoned; Mills believes it can be reformed so that it can deal with real-world racial injustice and past discrimination.

Mills points out that the social contract idea flourished between 1650 and 1800 in the work of Thomas Hobbes, John Locke, Jean-Jacques Rousseau, and Immanuel Kant, and then died out for a time before being revived in spectacular fashion by John Rawls. Mills says that even though it is literally false as "historical anthropology," the idea of the social contract as an imaginative device seems powerful and long-lasting.

Mills thinks that we should conceptualize societies like ours as being based not on a social contract brought about by equal human beings but on a **domination contract**: a cooperative agreement by one segment of society, which includes the intention to dominate other segments of society. In the case of his concept of the racial contract, it involves the domination of whites over people of color. Mills says he got the idea of the racial contract from a book by Carole Pateman called *The Sexual Contract,* which talked about society's agreed-on systematic discrimination against women. But Mills says the idea of a discriminatory contract was also anticipated by Rousseau in his

Charles W. Mills is Distinguished Professor of Philosophy at The Graduate Center, City University of New York. His research interests are in social/political philosophy, particularly in oppositional political theory centered on class, gender, and race.
Photo courtesy of Jasmine Lorae Hatten.

Discourse on the Origin of Inequality. According to Mills, Rousseau thought of contract theory as a "stratagem by the rich to entrench their power behind a façade of consent and democracy." Pulling together these strands, we can construe the domination contract as involving "gender, class and race."

Presumably, Mills isn't recommending that we think of society as nothing but a domination contract. It is true that the U.S. Constitution countenanced slavery and allowed voting to be restricted to white property-holding males. But both the U.S. Constitution and the Bill of Rights were eloquent in support of the ideas of freedom and equality. These real ideals initially applied only to those doing the dominating, but they also supplied a valuable resource that the dominated could use to fight back. Mills undoubtedly would agree with this. It seems that what he wants to insist on is that domination be seen as central to anything we could construe as past social contracts and not as some unfortunate incidental feature of such contracts.

Rawls distinguished between ideal and nonideal theory. Ideal theory derives principles that govern "a well-ordered society under favorable circumstances." Nonideal theory deals with less favorable circumstances where "injustice already exists." Rawls thought that ideal theory had to come first in order to define what justice was before moving on to dealing with existing injustices. However, says Mills, while Rawls did talk about moving on to nonideal theory, he and his followers never did so, certainly not in a way that took into account issues of compensatory or corrective justice for past wrongs such as racial injustice.

According to Mills, Rawls says that once the two basic principles of justice are chosen,

> we are then supposed to seek to derive other principles, such as principles of corrective justice, by a four-stage sequence in which the veil (i.e., deliberators' ignorance about their own identities and societal interests) is gradually lifted. But Rawls gives no details on what happens if, when the veil lifts, you turn out to be (as you will turn out to be) in an ill-ordered society, for which the dismantling of an oppressive basic structure is the imperative.

Mill suggests that we revise Rawls's thought experiment, giving the agents more and different information that will produce a nonideal theory that takes account of historical injustices. To quote Mills at length:

> We imagine ourselves behind a veil, choosing—again on prudential grounds—among different principles of justice, mindful of the possibility that when the veil lifts, we will be a person of color in a white

supremacist state. Say, a black woman in South Side Chicago, or a Native American on the reservation, or a Latina in the Southwest. An ideal society with no history of racial or any other kind of injustice is not a choice option; the question is what measures of corrective justice we would want to see put in place to correct for this history of white supremacy. . . . I suggest that we would choose principles of corrective justice in three main spheres of "primary goods" that correspond to the ones Rawls demarcates: the ending of second-class citizenship (both in terms of electoral questions—e.g., the problem of white majoritarianism—and other areas like police brutality and the general biases of the criminal justice system); the ending of racial exploitation (not just ongoing practices of discrimination but also the legacy of past practices in the form of the huge wealth gap between white and black and Latino households); and the ending of racial disrespect in its multiple dimensions (e.g., routine pejorative media representations of blacks, the Confederate Flag issue, the symbolism of Civil War monuments, the use of mascots, Eurocentric school textbooks, and so forth). Obviously all kinds of political and judicial complexities will be involved here, for example existing white property rights, and what they supposedly rule out, and First Amendment guarantees. But the point is that we would then be able to discuss these matters in a nonideal theory contract framework that made while racial domination central rather than marginal.

We have covered an enormous amount of material in this chapter. We distinguished metaethics versus normative ethics and then discussed the opposing metaethical theories of moral objectivism and moral subjectivism. We went over a rather powerful argument for moral subjectivism, including a rejection of a specific form of religious metaethics called divine command theory. However we then noted that moral subjectivism in its simpler forms—such as the claim that "x is right" means "I approve of x"—was clearly inadequate. It needed to be modified to view ethical judgments as prescriptions for rules of action, prescriptions that expressed moral as opposed to personal preferences. Moral preferences were preferences from the moral point of view, universalizable prescriptions for how all people should treat each other.

We broke from the main line of discussion to examine cultural relativism and saw that as a metaethical theory it was either incorrect or another version of subjectivism. We also (for those who chose to read that particular discussion) gave a more technical take on the various metaethical theories.

We then returned to our modified subjectivism as expressing preferences from the moral point of view. We compared the moral point of view to various moral theories such as the Golden Rule, the ideal observer theory, and Kant's Categorical Imperative.

We examined the normative ethical theory of utilitarianism, which some thinkers have claimed is implied by the sympathetic ideal observer theory. We discussed the differences between act utilitarianism and rule utilitarianism; we found the latter superior but suggested it might have to be supplemented by rights. We saw how John Rawls critiqued utilitarianism in terms of an idealized social contract framework, arguing that the result would not only be the institution of rights but of more equal distribution of goods.

We talked about views of the good life from a nonmoral perspective and saw the case for considering flourishing as well as happiness as things good-in-themselves. We saw how flourishing included within it certain worthwhile character traits—called "virtues." We talked about moral as well as nonmoral virtues and discussed how and why a number of contemporary philosophers thought that an ethics of virtues was superior to an ethics of rules. We acknowledged the importance of virtues while doubting that an ethics of virtue could take precedence over an ethics of rules.

We discussed one feminist approach to ethics which emphasizes rights and another which emphasizes care, the latter taking its cue from caring relations within families traditionally practiced by females. We examined the ethics of care, seeing it as too limited in its original reformulations to serve as a general ethic; we then compared it to sympathy ethics as the ethics of care broadened its scope. We also talked about how the ethics of care or sympathy has to contend with basic social contract theory which, seeing ethical/political agreement as being hard to reach, settles for an ethic that demands and gives the minimum.

The chapter also described Charles W. Mills's critique of Rawlsian ideal contract theory as failing to deal with societies that have been systematically unfair to people of color, as well as to women and the poor. Mills claims that as hypothetical ideal agents, we should select principles "mindful of the possibility that when the veil lifts, we will be a person of color in a white supremacist state."

You should now have a general theoretical structure that should help you frame your thoughts about both metaethical and normative issues—including normative issues involving some of today's most prominent moral controversies.

Definitions

(Terms are defined in the order in which they appeared in the text.)

1. METAETHICS: The branch of ethics that deals with questions concerning whether or not normative ethical judgments are true/false and if so, whether or how we can know which ones are true/false.
2. NORMATIVE ETHICS: A branch of ethics that deals with questions about what things are good or bad, right or wrong.
3. FACTUAL JUDGMENT: A judgment that might be resolved through empirical evidence.
4. MORAL OBJECTIVISM/MORAL OBJECTIVIST (partial definition): A theory that claims that where we have a moral judgment and its negation, one of these judgments must be true and the other false.
5. NATURALISM: An objectivist theory that claims moral judgments describe natural phenomena.
6. NON-NATURALISM: An objectivist theory that claims moral judgments describe non-natural phenomena.
7. SUPERNATURALISM: An objectivist theory that claims moral judgments describe the commands of God.
8. MORAL SUBJECTIVISM/MORAL SUBJECTIVIST: A theory thatclaims that where we have a moral judgment and its negation, neither judgment need be false.
9. THE DIVINE COMMAND THEORY OF ETHICS: A theory that holds that the mere act of God's commanding us to do (not do) something is enough to make that something right (wrong).
10. MORAL PREFERENCES: Preferences related to how one would like people to treat one another.
11. UNIVERSALIZABLE: To say that moral judgments are "universalizable" is to say that such rules should apply even if one were in the other person's position.
12. MORAL POINT OF VIEW: The viewpoint of someone who, using imagination, discounts his or her particular circumstances, surveys the human condition, and decides what rules all human beings should follow.
13. PERSONAL PREFERENCES: Preferences related to what we each want for ourselves.
14. METAETHICAL RELATIVISM: Moral judgments refer to cultural or individual norms.

15. CULTURAL RELATIVISM: Moral judgments refer to cultural norms.
16. INDIVIDUAL RELATIVISM: Moral judgments refer to individual norms.
17. NORMATIVE RELATIVISM: It is wrong to judge other cultures (or perhaps other individuals).

Terms from "Technical Interlude"

    a. MORAL OBJECTIVISM (expanded definition): (1) Moral judgments state beliefs about moral properties in the world; (2) there are such moral properties in the world; and (3) at least some of these properties apply to all human beings.

    b. COGNITIVISM: The view that moral judgments state beliefs about moral properties in the world.

    c. TRUTH-APT: Judgments that are such as to be true or false.

    d. NONCOGNITIVISM: The view that moral judgments, in spite of their form, do not make truth-apt statements about properties of the world. In fact, they don't make any statements at all.

    e. EXPRESSIVISM: The view that moral judgments are fundamentally used to express approval and disapproval.

    f. PRESCRIPTIVISM: The view that moral judgments are fundamentally used to prescribe rules for general conduct.

    g. MORAL REALISM: The view that there in fact exist the kinds of moral properties referred to in our moral judgments.

    h. MORAL ANTIREALISM: The view that moral properties do not exist.

    i. UNIVERSALISM: The view that at least some moral properties apply to all human beings.

18. IDEAL OBSERVER THEORY: The theory that in formulating a moral judgment we are implying that such a judgment would be endorsed by an ideal observer who was sympathetic to all human beings and their concerns; was not biased toward any particular individual or group; and had general knowledge of the world.
19. IMPARTIAL SPECTATOR (Adam Smith): Being able to see ourselves as just one moral being among others.
20. A HYPOTHETICAL IMPERATIVE: An imperative of the form, If you want X, you ought to do Y.
21. A CATEGORICAL IMPERATIVE: An imperative of the form, You ought to do X.

22. THE CATEGORICAL IMPERATIVE (Kant): "Act only according to that maxim by which you can at the same time will that it should become a universal law."

23. A MISANTHROPIC ETHIC: Any ethic that sees human beings as a whole as being so awful that what they deserve is punishment, not happiness.

24. A JUDGMENTAL GOD ETHIC: A misanthropic ethic with God as the harsh judge.

25. A SYMPATHETIC GOD ETHIC: An ethic that sees God as the sympathetic ideal observer endorsing rules that promote human happiness and well-being.

26. UTILITARIANISM: The view that the only thing valuable in itself is happiness and that a society ought to promote the greatest happiness of the greatest number.

27. CONSEQUENTIALIST ETHICS: An ethics that claims an act or policy is right or wrong solely in terms of its consequences.

28. DEONTOLOGICAL ETHICS: Generally, those ethics that lay down rules with do's and don'ts, duties and obligations.

29. ACT UTILITARIANISM: The utilitarian principle is applied to each individual action by the agent performing that action.

30. RULE UTILITARIANISM: The utilitarian principle is used to decide a set of rules that would lead to the greatest happiness of the greatest number. Individual agents then follow those rules whether or not acting on the rules leads to the greatest happiness in the particular case.

31. VEIL OF IGNORANCE: Rawls's ideal agents in their original position of equality don't know what their interests and abilities or goals will be, or what their position in society will be.

32. DISTRIBUTIVE JUSTICE: How the goods of a society ought to be distributed among its members.

33. VIRTUE: A worthwhile character trait.

34. INTRINSIC GOOD: Good as an end.

35. INSTRUMENTAL GOOD: Good as a means.

36. SUBJECTIVE WELL-BEING (SWB): The experience of happiness.

37. FLOURISHING: Developing certain human capacities considered worthwhile.

38. EUDAIMONIA: Greek word sometimes translated as "happiness" but is better translated as "human flourishing."

39. ARÊTE: Greek word for virtue.

40. ETHICS OF VIRTUE. An ethic that would focus on good character rather than right action and would include a whole spectrum of virtues, including those that an ethics of rules might see as nonmoral.
41. ETHICS OF RULES: An ethic that would focus on rules rather than virtues.
42. FEMINIST ETHICS: A philosophical discipline that, in part, attempts to identify and correct the male biases in traditional ethics.
43. THE ETHICS OF CARE: An ethical approach that sees the care relationship found within families as being fundamental to ethical theory.
44. BASIC SOCIAL CONTRACT THEORY: A hypothetical but unidealized test in which egoists who know their interests and abilities try to negotiate the most advantageous social structure others would agree to.
45. DOMINATION CONTRACT: A version of a social contract in which one segment of society—white or male or those with property—contracts to dominate other segments of society. Other versions would be the "racial contract" or "sexual contract." Mills, Pateman, and others argue that insofar as there is anything that could be considered a social contract, it is closer to a domination contract than to a more ideal contract.

Questions

(Please explain your answers, making specific reference to relevant passages in the discussion.)

1. What is the difference between normative ethical questions and meta-ethical questions?
2. Distinguish moral subjectivism from moral objectivism.
3. Present an argument for moral subjectivism.
4. Consider the following moral judgments:
   a. It's wrong to abort a fetus.
   b. A person who murders another person ought to be executed
      Can you imagine any kind of evidence that would prove or disprove either of these statements?
5. "Moral judgments are simply statements of preference." In what ways, and for what reasons, has this version of moral subjectivism been modified?
6. What does it mean to take the "moral point of view"?
7. Define utilitarianism. What are the differences between act utilitarianism and rule utilitarianism?

8. In what way does Rawls consider utilitarianism "unjust"? What principles does he argue for in place of the utilitarianism principle?

9. Why does Rawls think his principles would be chosen behind the veil of ignorance? Why do others think the utilitarian principle would be chosen instead?

10. *Four coworkers entered a contest together and have won the right to race through a grocery store/pharmacy and keep whatever they can manage to get outside the store in half an hour. (They must use grocery carts but each can make more than one trip.) The store is huge, and it would be impossible for any one of the four to get around to the different departments in the time allotted. The four people are going to rely heavily on what they collect for their sustenance in the next couple of weeks, since they've all been laid off and are broke. Some other facts:*

– No one is allowed to collect anything until all four have agreed on a procedure for collecting goods and dividing them up. (Each can simply collect and keep his own if they agree to that.)

– Since the person running the contest loves X-treme sports, a few spots on the floor of the store have been waxed to a dangerous sheen; in the past, several contestants have suffered bad sprains and were unable to complete their collecting.

– All four contestants are competitive and perform at top efficiency when there's a reward for doing better than others.

Considering the hypothetical situation described above, answer the following questions:

a. What kind of procedure would you suggest if you were one of the four?

b. How would the four reason if they were utilitarians?

c. How would they reason if they followed Rawls?

11. What is the difference between an intrinsic good and an instrumental good?

12. What is flourishing? What's an argument for the claim that flourishing, as well as happiness, is an intrinsic good?

13. What does the word "virtue" mean? Give some examples of moral and nonmoral virtues.

14. What did Aristotle consider to be the good life?

15. What is virtue ethics (or an ethics of virtue)?

16. What are some arguments for the claim that virtue ethics should replace an ethics of rules? What are some problems with this claim?

17. Compare/contrast the views of Lawrence Kohlberg and Carol Gilligan on the differences in reasoning between males and females.

18. What is the ethics of care? Indicate some ways it has evolved from its earlier formulations (e.g., the view of Nel Noddings) to its later formulations (e.g., the views of Virginia Held).

19. According to Held, what are some of the male biases in the "dominant moral theories" that ethics of care theorists seek to correct?

20. What is "basic social contract theory"? What problems is it designed to solve?

21. How does basic social contract theory contrast with ethics of care or sympathy?

22. According to Mills, what is wrong with an ideal ethical theory that yields color blind ethical principles?

23. What does Mills mean by the "domination contract"? How does this relate to his critique of Rawls?

24. According to Mills, what other factors or possibilities should the agents in Rawls's original position take account of in choosing the most desirable ethical/social principles?

Notes

Moral Subjectivism Reconsidered

"Kant . . . moral judgments are "universalizable." Immanuel Kant. *Fundamental Principles of the Metaphysics of Morals*. Trans. T. K. Abbot. Amherst, NY: Prometheus Books, 1988.

Cultural Relativism

"Ruth Benedict . . . 'Mankind has always preferred to say. . . .'" Ruth Benedict. "Anthropology and the Abnormal." *Journal of General Psychology* 10 (1934).

From the Moral Point of View

"The first person to formulate the ideal observer theory seems to have been Adam Smith. . . ." Adam Smith. *Theory of Moral Sentiments* (1759).

"Kant distinguishes. . . ." Kant. *Fundamental Principles of the Metaphysics of Morals*.

Utilitarianism and John Rawls

"Jeremy Bentham, an early proponent of utilitarianism. . . ." Jeremy Bentham. *Principles of Moral and Political Philosophy* (1789).

"By the principle of utility. . . ." Bentham, ch. 1.

"John Rawls formulates his critique of utilitarianism. . . ." John Rawls. *A Theory of Justice*. Cambridge, MA: Belknap Press of Harvard University Press, 1971.

. . . The first requires equality in. . ." Rawls, pp. 14–15.

Morality, Virtue, and Living Well

"the following thought-experiment of mine from another text. . . ." Thomas D. Davis. *Contemporary Moral and Social Issues: An Introduction Through Original Fiction, Discussion and Readings.* Malden, MA: Wiley Blackwell, 2014, pp. 15–16.

Jonathan Glover says. . . ." Jonathan Glover. *Choosing Children: Genes, Disability and Design.* Oxford: Clarendon Press, 2006, p. 93.

"Confucius . . . taught. . . ." Confucius, *The Analects.* Trans Raymond Dawson. Oxford: Oxford University Press: 2008.

The Greek philosopher Aristotle. . . ." Aristotle. *The Nicomachean Ethics.*

"ELIZABETH ANSCOMBE. . . ." "Modern Moral Philosophy," in G. E. M. Anscombe, *Ethics, Religion and Politics: Collected Philosophical Papers Volume III.* Oxford: Basil Blackwell, 1981.

Feminism and the Ethics of Care

"According to the National Women's History Project. . . ." www.nwhp.org/resources/womens-rights-movement.

"Teresa Younger . . . definition of 'feminism.'" *Forbes*, interview by Bonnie Marcus, March 31, 2015.

"Carol Gilligan's 1982 book. . . ." Carol Gilligan. *In a Different Voice: Psychological Theory and Women's Development.* Cambridge, MA: Harvard University Press, 1982.

"Alison Jaggar has argued. . . ." From "Feminist Ethics" by Rosemary Tong and Nancy Williams in the *Stanford Encyclopedia of Philosophy.*

"In her 1984 book, *Caring.* . . ." Nel Noddings. *Caring: A Female Approach to Ethics and Moral Education.* Berkeley: University of California Press.

"In her book, *The Ethics of Care.* . . ." Virginia Held. *The Ethics of Care: Personal, Political and Global.* Oxford: Oxford University Press, 2006.

"meeting the needs of the particular others. . . ." Held, p. 10.

"egoistic individual interests on the one hand. . . ." Held, p. 12.

"seek instead to preserve or promote. . . ." Held, p. 12.

"built into the dominant moral theories. . . ." Held, p. 12.

"In the context of the family. . ." Held, p. 12.

"A globalization of caring relations. . ." Held, p. 168.

"Although some of its early formulations suggested this. . . ." Held, p. 18.

Thomas Hobbes . . . famously argued. . . ." Thomas Hobbes. *Leviathan.* 1651.

"Charles W. Mills presents such an argument. . . ." Charles W. Mills. "Philosophy and the Racial Contract." In *The Oxford Handbook of Philosophy and Race.* Naomi Zack (ed.). Oxford: Oxford University Press, 2017.

"Rousseau thought of. . . ." Mills, p. 67.

"Rawls distinguished. . . ."Rawls, *A Theory of Justice*, p. 244f.

". . . we are then supposed to seek to derive other principles. . . ." Mills, p. 72.

"We imagine ourselves behind a veil. . . ." Mills, pp. 72–73.

Further Materials

General Sources

Principles of Moral Philosophy: Classic and Contemporary Approaches. Eds. Steven
  M. Cahn and Andrew T. Forcehimes. Oxford: Oxford University Press: 2016.
  (Referenced as "Cahn.")
*Contemporary Moral and Social Issues: An Introduction Through Original Fiction,
  Discussion and Readings.* Malden, MA: Wiley-Blackwell, 2014. (Referenced as
  "Davis.")

Cultural Relativism

Ruth Benedict, "Moral Relativism: A Defense" in Cahn, Part 2.
Mary Midgley, "Moral Isolationism" in Cahn, Part 2.
James Rachels "discusses 'the challenge of cultural relativism.'" Davis, Part II,
  Readings.

A More Technical Take on Metaethics

Andrew Fisher. *Metaethics: An Introduction.* Durham, UK: Acumen, 2013.
From the Moral Point of View
Immanuel Kant, Groundwork for the Metaphysics of Morals. Cahn, Part 6, or
  Immanuel Kant "argues that ethics is based on the 'categorical imperative.'"
  Davis, Part II, Readings.

Utilitarianism and John Rawls

Jeremy Bentham, "An Introduction to the Principles of Morals and Legislation."
  Cahn, Part 6, or
Jeremy Bentham "presents a classic statement of the principle of utility." Davis,
  Part II, Readings.
Brad Hooker. "Rule-consequentialism versus Act-consequentialism." Cahn, Part 7.
John Rawls. "A Theory of Justice." Cahn, Part 9, or, John Rawls "argues that
  from an original position of equality we would reject utilitarianism in favor of
  his two principles of justice." Davis, Part II, Readings.

Morality, Virtue, and Living Well

Julia Annas. "Virtue Ethics." Cahn, Part 10.
Elizabeth Anscombe. "Modern Moral Philosophy," in G. E. M. Anscombe. *Ethics,
  Religion and Politics: Collected Philosophical Papers Volume III.* Oxford: Basil
  Blackwell, 1981.
Aristotle. " Nicomachean Ethics." Cahn, Part 10, or, Aristotle "analyzes happiness
  as a life lived according to virtue." Davis, Part I, Readings.
Confucius. *The Analects.* Trans Raymond Dawson. Oxford: Oxford University
  Press, 2008.
Jonathan Glover "discusses the dual values of happiness and flourishing." Davis,
  Part I, Readings.

Feminism and the Ethics of Care

Carol Gilligan. "Moral Orientation and Moral Development." Cahn, Part 10.

Jean Grimshaw "discusses the idea of a female ethic." Davis, Part II, Readings. Nel Noddings. *Caring: A Female Approach to Ethics and Moral Education*. Berkeley: University of California Press.

Virginia Held. *The Ethics of Care: Personal, Political and Global*. Oxford: Oxford University Press, 2006.

Thomas Hobbes. "Leviathan. " Cahn, Part 9.

Rosemary Tong and Nancy Williams. "Feminist Ethics" in the *Stanford Encyclopedia of Philosophy*.

Race from the Moral Point of View

Mills, Charles W. *The Racial Contract*. Ithaca, NY: Cornell University Press, 1997.

Pateman, Carol. *The Sexual Contract*. Stanford, CA: Stanford University Press, 1988.

Taylor, Paul C. *Race: A Philosophical Introduction* (2nd ed). Cambridge, UK: Polity Press, 2013.

Zack, Naomi (ed.). *The Oxford Handbook of Philosophy and Race*. Oxford: Oxford University Press, 2017.

PHOTO CREDITS

INDEX